Study Guide

for use with

Prepared by RICHARD B. STALLING
BRADLEY UNIVERSITY

RONALD E. WASDEN
BRADLEY UNIVERSITY

and ANDREW J. HOWELL
GRANT MACEWAN COLLEGE

NELSON EDUCATION

Study Guide for use with Psychology: Themes and Variations, Second Canadian Edition

by Wayne Weiten and Doug McCann

Prepared by Richard B. Stalling, Ronald E. Wasden, and Andrew J. Howell

Associate Vice President, Editorial Director:
Evelyn Veitch

Editor-in-Chief, Higher Education:
Anne Williams

Senior Acquisitions Editor:
Lenore Taylor-Atkins

Marketing Manager:
Ann Byford

Developmental Editor:
Sandy Matos

Content Production Manager:
Christine Gilbert

Proofreader:
Cathy Witlox

Manufacturing Manager—Higher Education:
Joanne McNeil

Design Director:
Ken Phipps

Managing Designer:
Franca Amore

Printer:
Webcom

Printed and bound in Canada
1 2 3 4 12 11 10 09

For more information contact Nelson Education Ltd., 1120 Birchmount Road, Toronto, Ontario, M1K 5G4. Or you can visit our Internet site at http://www.nelson.com

ISBN-13: 978-0-17-647402-7
ISBN-10: 0-17-647402-1

To the Student

In Weiten and McCann's *Psychology: Themes and Variations, Second Canadian Edition*, you will encounter a truly remarkable book. The authors have an extraordinary ability to create vivid, self-relevant examples that weave the diverse fields of psychology into a fabric. We are amazed at the breadth and the beauty of this text.

So, what is there left for us to do? It turns out that the concepts in an introductory course are complex. It is also the case that understanding and memory are not automatic. How does one process information and put things into memory? We remember more easily if we can relate concepts to our selves, the self-reference effect. And we also remember through the process of elaboration, thinking of examples and links to information already in memory (described in Chapter 7: Human Memory). So that is what we've tried to do in this study guide: provide examples and practice, with the goal in mind of helping the student remember, both for practical reasons now (e.g., tests) and for use in the future after the course is over.

What's the best way to work with this study guide? There are four parts of each chapter: the *Review of Key Ideas* (comprising most of each Study Guide chapter), the *Review of Key Terms* (a matching exercise involving important concepts), the *Review of Key People* (matching confined to major researchers in each area), and a *Self-Quiz*. We suggest that you try this: Work on each learning objective one at a time. Read each objective, read the part of the textbook that relates to it, and then complete the exercises and check your answers. Finally, do the matching exercises and take the Self-Quiz.

You may find it more useful to select only certain parts of the study guide that provide practice with particular concepts. (For example, if you are having difficulty understanding the Freudian defence mechanisms or the difference between operant and classical conditioning, do the practice exercises relating to these specific topics.) Whatever method you use, the learning objectives will serve as an excellent review. At the end of your study of a particular chapter, you can quiz yourself by reading over the learning objectives, reciting answers aloud, and checking your answers. This procedure roughly parallels the SQ3R study technique introduced in the Personal Application section of Chapter 1.

We hope you will find this study guide to be a useful tool for mastering the textbook material, and we hope that you become as enthralled about psychology as each of us is.

Rick Stalling
Ron Wasden
Andrew Howell

Table of Contents

Chapter One
THE EVOLUTION OF PSYCHOLOGY

Review of Key Ideas

FROM SPECULATION TO SCIENCE: HOW PSYCHOLOGY DEVELOPED

1. Summarize Wundt's accomplishments and contributions to psychology.

1-1. If you ask most college graduates to name the founder of psychology, they might mention the name of a famous psychologist (for example, maybe Sigmund Freud), but they almost certainly would *not* say Wilhelm Wundt. Yet, among psychologists, Wundt is generally acknowledged to be the "founder" of our field.

1-2. Wundt established the first experimental psychology laboratory, in Leipzig, Germany, in 1879. He also established the first journal devoted to publishing psychological research.

1-3. The subject matter of Wundt's psychology was (consciousness/behaviour).

1-4. Wundt's major contributions to the evolution of psychology may be summarized as follows: He is the founder of psychology as an independent academic field, and he insisted that psychology can and must use the ____________ method.

Answers: 1-1. founder **1-2.** laboratory, journal **1-3.** consciousness **1-4.** founder, scientific (experimental). (Personal note from RS: I visited Leipzig in the former East Germany recently and looked for the famous founding laboratory. It wasn't there! I found Wundt Street, but no lab. An English–U.S. bombing raid destroyed the laboratory in 1943.)

2. Summarize Hall's accomplishments and contributions to psychology.

2-1. Wundt had many important students. Among them was G. Stanley Hall, an American. In 1883, just four years after Wundt created his laboratory in Leipzig, Hall established the first American psychological laboratory at Johns Hopkins. Hall also founded America's first ____________ devoted to publishing material in the field of psychology.

2-2. In 1892, with 26 of his colleagues, Hall began the American Psychological Association, known by the initials ______. Hall also became the first __________________ of the Association. The APA now includes more than 155,000 members.

Answers: 2-1. laboratory, journal **2-2.** APA, president.

3. Describe structuralism and its impact on the subsequent development of psychology.

3-1. Another of Wundt's students, Edward Titchener, developed the school of psychology known as __________________. The major tenet of this viewpoint was that psychology should study the structure of __________________ by breaking it down into its basic components or __________________.

3-2. These basic elements of consciousness were thought to be the sensations (or images or feelings) that people reported when they observed some object. Subjects were first trained to observe (or listen to) something and then, after careful introspection, to report on their conscious experience. Thus, the subject matter of structuralism was __________________, and its method involved training observers in the technique of __________________.

Answers: 3-1. structuralism, consciousness, elements **3-2.** consciousness, introspection.

4. Describe functionalism and its impact on the subsequent development of psychology.

4-1. Rather than breaking down consciousness into basic elements, the __________________ school emphasized determining the __________________ or purpose of consciousness.

4-2. The origins of functionalism are associated with William James. Influenced by Darwin's concept of natural selection, James concluded that psychology should study the basic (elements/purpose) of consciousness.

4-3. Which "school" is characterized by each of the following descriptions? Place an "S" for structuralism or "F" for functionalism in the appropriate blanks.

____ Concerned with the purpose (or function) of consciousness.

____ Trained observers to introspect about consciousness.

____ Assumed that consciousness could be broken down into basic elements (in the same way that physical matter is composed of atoms).

____ Interested in the flow of consciousness.

____ Focused on the adaptive (evolutionary) value of consciousness.

____ Emphasized sensation and perception in vision, hearing, and touch.

4-4. The focus of functionalism may have attracted women into the field of psychology, including Mary Washburn, whose book *The Animal Mind* served as a precursor to _____________; Leta Hollingworth, who did work on children's intelligence; and Mary Whiton Calkins, who served as the first female president of the ____________

____________ ____________.

4-5. While neither structuralism nor functionalism survived as viable theories of psychology, functionalism had a more lasting impact. The emphasis of functionalism on the practical (or the adaptive or purposeful) led to the development of these two areas of modern psychology: __________________ and __________________ psychology.

Answers: 4-1. functionalist, function **4-2.** purpose **4-3.** F, S, S, F, F, S **4-4.** behaviourism, American Psychological Association **4-5.** behaviourism, applied.

5. Summarize Watson's views on the appropriate subject matter of psychology, nature versus nurture, and animal research.

5-1. A literal translation of the root words of psychology (*psyche* and *logos*) suggests that psychology is the study of the __________________. For both Wundt and James, this was the case: They studied human __________________. For Watson, however, the subject matter of psychology was __________________.

5-2. Watson believed that psychology could not be a science unless it, like the other sciences, concentrated on __________________ rather than unobservable events.

5-3. Which of the following are observable behaviours? Place an "O" in the blank if the event is observable and an "N" if it is not.

____ writing a letter

____ feeling angry

____ saying "Please pass the salt"

____ passing the salt

____ perceiving a round object

____ experiencing hunger

____ walking rapidly

5-4. Watson largely discounted the importance of genetic inheritance. For Watson, behaviour was governed by the __________________.

5-5. Watson also made a shift away from human introspection by using __________________ as the subjects for research. Why the change in orientation? First, animal behaviour is observable; human consciousness is not. Second, the environment of laboratory animals, in contrast to that of humans, is subject to much more __________________.

5-6. Let's briefly review structuralism and behaviourism:

(a) As defined by the structuralists, what was the subject matter of psychology?

(b) For behaviourists, what was the subject matter of psychology?

(c) While structuralists and behaviourists differed in their views of the subject matter of psychology, their approach to the new field was similar in one major respect. In what way were the two systems similar?

Answers: 5-1. soul (or mind), consciousness, behaviour **5-2.** observable (behaviour) **5-3.** O, N (you can't see or hear your own or another person's feelings of anger; you may see the results of anger), O, O, N (you can't see or hear perception), N (you can't see or hear hunger), O **5-4.** environment **5-5.** animals, control (manipulation) **5-6.** (a) conscious experience (consciousness), (b) animal or human behaviour, (c) They studied "parts" rather than "wholes." Both systems believed that the task of psychology was to break down psychological phenomena into their smallest elements. (For the structuralists, the smaller elements were the sensations or images that made up consciousness; for the behaviourists, the elements were the stimulus–response bonds thought to make up behaviour.)

6. Summarize Freud's principal ideas and why they inspired controversy.

6-1. For Wundt, the subject matter of psychology was human consciousness. For Freud, a major subject of study was what he termed the ___________________. With this concept, Freud asserted that human beings are (aware/unaware) of most of the factors that influence their thoughts and behaviour.

6-2. There is a word beginning with *s* that means the same thing as feces. This word, however, may be more likely to cause laughter, embarrassment, or anger than the word *feces*. Why do two words that mean the same thing produce such differing reactions? Freud would assert that our more emotional response to one of the words would be caused by the

___________________.

6-3. Although generally not accessible to us, the unconscious is revealed in several ways, according to Freud. Freud thought, for example, that the unconscious is revealed in mistakes, such as "___________________ of the tongue," or the symbolism in nighttime

___________________.

6-4. Freud's ideas were (and still are) considered quite controversial. The general public tended to find Freud's ideas unacceptable because of his emphasis on ___________________. And scientific psychologists, with their increasing emphasis on observable behaviour, rejected Freud's notion that we are controlled by ___________________ forces. Nonetheless, Freud's theory gradually gained prominence and survives today as an influential theoretical perspective.

Answers: 6-1. unconscious, unaware **6-2.** unconscious **6-3.** slips, dreams **6-4.** sex (sexuality, sexual instincts), unconscious.

7. Summarize Skinner's work, views, and influence.

7-1. While he did not deny their existence, Skinner said that (mental/environmental) events are not observable and cannot be studied scientifically.

7-2. The fundamental principle of behaviour, according to Skinner, is that organisms will tend to ____________________ behaviours that lead to positive outcomes (and tend not to repeat responses that lead to neutral or negative outcomes).

7-3. Skinner asserted that because behaviour is under the lawful control of the environment, our feeling of ____________________ is an illusion.

7-4. According to Skinner, to adequately account for and predict behaviour, psychologists must understand:

a. the relationship between thinking and behaviour
b. the physiological basis of action
c. the way environmental factors affect behaviour
d. all of the above

7-5. Skinner's influence went beyond academia due in part to his 1948 book, ____________ ______, in which he presented a fictional account of a utopian society based on behavioural principles, and his 1971 book, *Beyond Freedom and Dignity*. Within the discipline of psychology, Skinner's influence was reflected in a 1990 survey of psychologists' opinions concerning the field's most important contributors, in which he ranked number ____.

Answers: 7-1. mental **7-2.** repeat **7-3.** free will **7-4.** c (not d: Although Skinner acknowledged that thinking exists and that physiology is the basis of behaviour, he thought that explanations in terms of these factors did not contribute to a science of behaviour.) **7-5.** *Walden Two*, one.

8. Summarize Rogers' and Maslow's ideas and the contributions of humanistic psychology.

8-1. Both Rogers and Maslow, like other ____________________ psychologists, emphasized the (similarities/differences) between human beings and other animals.

8-2. While Freud and Skinner stressed the way in which behaviour is *controlled* (by unconscious forces or by the environment), Rogers and Maslow emphasized human beings' ____________________ to determine their own actions.

8-3. Rogers and Maslow also asserted that human beings have a drive to express their inner potential, a drive toward personal ____________________.

8-4. Perhaps the greatest contribution of the humanistic movement has been in producing (scientific findings/new approaches) in psychotherapy.

Answers: 8-1. humanistic, differences **8-2.** freedom **8-3.** growth (expression) **8-4.** new approaches.

9. Describe important contributions to the emergence of experimental psychology in Canada.

9-1. The first experimental psychology laboratory in Canada was established in the year __________ by ________ ________ ___________ at the University of ___________.

9-2. Early psychology courses were often taught through Departments of Philosophy. But the first Department of Psychology was established in the year ______ at ________ University, followed by departments established at the universities of ____________, __________ __________, and _______________.

9-3. The Canadian Psychological Association was formed in the year ______ to advance psychology as a science, and currently has over _____ thousand members.

9-4. Women currently make up about _______% of Canadian full-time psychology professors, and women outnumber men in psychology graduate programs. Women who have made particularly significant contributions to Canadian psychology include Brenda Milner, one of the founders of ___________ in Canada. Mary Salter Ainsworth made important contributions to __________ theory and developmental psychology. Mary Wright has the distinction of being the first female president of the Canadian Psychological Association. Doreen Kimura has contributed importantly to our understanding of the neuromotor mechanisms in human communication and ______ ____________ in cognition.

Answers: 9-1. 1891, James Mark Baldwin, Toronto **9-2.** 1924, McGill, Toronto, Western Ontario, Manitoba **9-3.** 1939, five **9-4.** 30, neuropsychology, attachment, sex differences.

10. Use the Featured Study to discuss the strengths and weaknesses of some research methods.

10-1. Prior to this study by Craig and Pepler of York University, research on bullying made use of _____________ methodologies rather than directly observing bullying behaviour.

10-2. In this research, observers rated the behaviour of both ___________ and socially competent children as reflected in videotaped recordings of lunch and recess activities.

10-3. Results showed that about ____% of bullying episodes involved verbal aggression, ____% involved physical aggression, and 21% involved a mixed of both types of aggression. Boys engaged in about __________ as much bullying as girls. Aggressive children (did/did not) engage in more bullying than socially competent children.

10-4. Naturalistic observation research such as the Featured Study has the advantage of documenting behaviour outside of the ____________ but does not allow clear statements concerning the ________ of behaviour. Naturalistic observation research also raises the possibility that the process of being observed alters participants' behaviour.

Answers: 10-1. questionnaire **10-2.** aggressive **10-3.** 50, 29, twice, did not **10-4.** laboratory, causes.

11. Describe the typical areas of expertise of various types of applied or professional psychologists.

11-1. Applied psychology is the part of psychology that is concerned with (research issues/ practical problems). Prominent among the applied areas of psychology is the field of ________________ psychology, which deals with the treatment of psychological disorders.

11-2. Other applied areas followed later, including the fields of industrial and ___________ psychology, counselling psychology, and school psychology.

Answers: 11-1. practical problems, clinical **11-2.** organizational.

12. Explain how historical events have contributed to the emergence of psychology as a profession.

12-1. Clinical psychologists were relatively rare in a field devoted primarily to research. One of the historical events that changed this picture was the advent of ______________. With the increased need for screening recruits and treating emotional casualties, the Veterans Administration in the United States began funding many new training programs in the field of ___________________ psychology.

12-2. In the U.S., some psychologists became concerned with an increasing emphasis on applied psychology within the American Psychological Association. They formed their own association, the _____________ ______________ ____________. Similarly, the Canadian Society for _________, __________, and __________ __________ was established.

12-3. In contrast to its founding in the 19th century as a research or academic endeavour, psychology in the 20th century has developed a prominent ___________________ branch directed toward solving practical problems.

Answers: 12-1. World War II, clinical. **12-2.** American Psychological Society, Brain, Behaviour, Cognitive Science **12-3.** applied or professional.

13. Describe two recent trends in research in psychology that reflect a return to psychology's intellectual roots.

13-1. Two recent trends in research in psychology involve the reemergence of areas largely discarded or ignored by the behaviourists. What are these two areas?

13-2. Think about sucking on a lemon. When you do, the amount of saliva in your mouth will increase measurably. While it would be enough to describe your observable response as a function of my observable instruction, it is also obvious that thinking, or cognition, is involved: My instruction changed your ___________________ image, which was accompanied by a change in salivation.

13-3. The study of mental imagery, problem solving, and decision making involves ___________________ processes. The second, more recent trend also concerns "internal" processes: Research on electrical stimulation of the brain, brain specialization, and visual signals involves ___________________ processes.

13-4. A Canadian psychologist who was an early pioneer in studying physiological processes was ___________ ___________. Hebb completed his Ph.D. at Harvard with Lashley and joined the faculty of __________ University in Montreal. Hebb argued that the basis of behaviour could be found in the ________. He introduced the concept of the _____-________, which provided an early model for how neural networks might operate. The Canadian Psychological Association named one of its most prestigious awards after Hebb.

Answers: 13-1. cognition (consciousness or thinking) and physiological (or biological) processes **13-2.** mental **13-3.** cognitive, physiological (biological) **13-4.** Donald Hebb, McGill, brain, cell assembly.

14. Explain why Western psychology traditionally had scant interest in other cultures and why this situation has begun to change.

14-1. Several factors contributed to the narrow focus of Western, and especially North American, psychology:

(a) First, studying other cultures is expensive and time-consuming. It's much __________________ for researchers to study people in their own country (and especially middle-class students at their own schools).

(b) Second, some psychologists worry that study of diverse groups may inadvertently foster __________________, especially with regard to groups that have historically been an object of prejudice.

(c) Third, there may be a tendency among Western psychologists to view their own group as superior, the group tendency referred to as __________________.

14-2. The situation has begun to change in recent years for two primary reasons: (1) increased communication and trade worldwide, the so-called __________________ economy or global interdependence; and (2) increased diversity of ethnic groups within the countries of the Western world, including the __________________ mosaic characteristic of the Western world.

Answers: 14-1. (a) cheaper (easier), (b) stereotypes, (c) ethnocentrism **14-2.** global; multicultural.

15. Summarize the basic tenets of evolutionary psychology.

15-1. According to evolutionary psychologists, all aspects of human behaviour—including not only aggression and mate selection but perception, language, personality, and cognition—are strongly influenced by the __________________ value that these factors have had for the human species.

15-2. While Darwin's influence is clear in other psychological theories (e.g., those of James, Freud, and Skinner), the new emphasis on natural selection is (less/more) comprehensive and widely researched than the earlier versions.

15-3. The viewpoint has its critics. Some charge that evolutionary conceptions are simply post hoc accounts rather than explanations and that the theory is not subject to scientific ________________. Nonetheless, the viewpoint has gained a high degree of acceptance and is clearly a major new perspective in contemporary psychology.

Answers: 15-1. survival (adaptive) **15-2.** more **15-3.** test (evaluation, disconfirmation, proof).

16. Summarize the focus taken within the movement called positive psychology.

16-1. Martin Seligman is a major contributor to a new movement in psychology called ________ psychology. Positive psychology uses theory and research to better understand the positive, adaptive, creative, and fulfilling aspects of human existence.

16-2. The first area of interest within positive psychology is positive _________ _________ (positive emotions), the second is positive _________ __________ (strengths and virtues), and the third is positive ____________ and _____________.

Answers: 16-1. positive **16-2.** subjective experiences, individual traits, institutions, communities.

PSYCHOLOGY TODAY: VIGOROUS AND DIVERSIFIED

17. Discuss the growth of psychology and the most common work settings for contemporary psychologists.

17-1. Psychology can be defined as the _________ that studies behaviour and the __________ and _________ processes that underlie it, and it is the __________ that applies the accumulated knowledge of this science to practical problems.

17-2. Psychology was founded in a university, and earlier in this century almost all psychologists were employed as academics. Today, however, more than two-thirds of psychologists are employed in (university/nonacademic) settings that include hospitals, business and industry, schools, and government agencies.

Answers: 17-1. science, physiological, cognitive, profession **17-2.** nonacademic.

18. List and describe seven major research areas in psychology.

18-1. Read over the descriptions of the research areas in Figure 1.6. Then match the names of the areas with the sample research topics by placing the appropriate letters in the blanks. (Note that the separation between these areas is not always perfect. For example, a personality theorist might also be a psychometrician who has a physiological focus in explaining behaviour. Nonetheless, the following topics have been chosen so that one answer is correct for each.)

A. Experimental ____ attitude change, group behaviour

B. Physiological ____ personality and intelligence assessment, test design, new statistical procedures

C. Cognitive ____ personality assessment, personality description

D. Developmental ____ "core" topics (e.g., perception, conditioning, motivation)

E. Psychometrics ____ influence of the brain, bodily chemicals, genetics

F. Personality ____ child, adolescent, and adult development

G. Social ____ memory, decision making, thinking

18-2. In case you want to remember the list of seven research areas, here's a mnemonic device: Peter Piper Picked Some Exceptionally Costly Dills. List the seven research areas by matching them with the first letter of each word.

Answers: 18-1. G, E, F, A, B, D, C **18-2.** physiological, psychometrics, personality, social, experimental, cognitive, developmental.

19. List and describe the four professional specialties in psychology.

19-1. Review Figure 1.7. Then match the following specialties with the descriptions by placing the appropriate letter in the blanks.

A. Clinical	____	Treatment of less severe problems and problems involving family, marital, and career difficulties.
B. Counselling	____	Treatment of psychological disorders, behavioural and emotional problems.
C. Educational and school	____	Involves work on curriculum design and achievement testing in school settings.
D. Industrial and organizational	____	Psychology applied to business settings; deals with personnel, job satisfaction, etc.

19-2. What is the difference between psychology and psychiatry? The major difference is a matter of degree (this is a pun, folks). Psychiatrists have __________________ degrees. Clinical psychologists generally have __________________ degrees (although some clinical psychologists have Ed.D. or Psy.D. degrees).

19-3. The major portion of psychiatrists' training occurs in __________________ schools and in the residency programs in psychiatry that follow medical school. Clinical psychologists' training occurs in __________________ schools.

19-4. While clinical psychologists and psychiatrists frequently use the same psychotherapeutic treatment procedures, only __________________, as physicians, are licensed to prescribe drugs and engage in other medical treatment.

Answers: 19-1. B, A, C, D **19-2.** medical (M.D.), Ph.D. **19-3.** medical, graduate **19-4.** psychiatrists.

PUTTING IT IN PERSPECTIVE: SEVEN KEY THEMES

20. Summarize the text's three unifying themes relating to psychology as a field of study.

20-1. When my (R.S.'s) older daughter, Samantha, was about three years old, she pulled a sugar bowl off of a shelf and broke it while I was not present. Later, when I surveyed the damage, I said, "I see you've broken something." She said, "How do yer know? Did yer see me do it?" I was amused, because while it was obvious who had broken it, her comment reflected psychology's foundation in direct observation. **Theme 1** is that psychology is __________________. Empiricism is the point of view that knowledge should be acquired through __________________.

20-2. My daughter's comment caused me to think about one other aspect of empiricism: She expressed *doubt* (albeit somewhat self-serving with regard to the sugar bowl). One can describe belief systems along a continuum from *credulity*, which means ready to believe, to *skepticism*, which means disposed toward doubt. Psychology, and the empirical approach, is more disposed toward the __________________ end of the continuum.

20-3. We would ordinarily think that if one theory is correct, any other theory used to explain the same data must be wrong. While scientists do pit theories against each other, it is also the case that apparently contradictory theories may both be correct—as with the explanation of light in terms of both wave and particle theories. Thus, **Theme 2** indicates that psychology is theoretically ____________________.

20-4. Psychology tolerates (and in fact encourages) different theoretical explanations because:

20-5. As is the case with science in general, psychology does not evolve in a vacuum. It is influenced by and influences our society. For example, the current interest in cultural diversity has prompted increased interest in cross-cultural research, which in turn affects the viewpoints in our society. As stated in **Theme 3**, psychology evolves in a ____________________ context.

Answers: 20-1. empirical, observation **20-2.** skepticism **20-3.** diverse **20-4.** more than one theory may be correct; or one theory may not adequately explain all of the observations **20-5.** sociohistorical.

21. Summarize the text's four unifying themes relating to psychology's subject matter.

21-1. When looking for an explanation of a particular behaviour, someone might ask: "Well, why did he do it? Was it greed or ignorance?" The question implies the very human tendency to reason in terms of (one cause/multiple causes) for each event.

21-2. What influences the course of a ball rolled down an inclined plane? Gravity. And also friction. And the presence of other objects, and a number of other factors. That is the point of **Theme 4**: even more than is the case for physical events, behaviour is determined by ____________________ ____________________.

21-3. Among the multiple causes of human behaviour is the category of causes referred to as *culture*. Cultural factors include the customs, beliefs, and values that we transmit across generations—what we eat, how we walk, what we wear, what we say, what we think, and so on. **Theme 5** indicates that our behaviour is shaped by our ____________________ heritage.

21-4. For example, North Americans may believe that "the squeaky wheel gets the grease," whereas Asians may believe that "the nail that stands out gets pounded down." While we are shaped by our ____________________ ____________________, we are often (aware/unaware) of the precise rules and customs that affect us.

21-5. **Theme 6** relates to the influence of heredity and environment. What is the consensus among psychologists about the effect of heredity and environment on behaviour?

21-6. The scientific method relies on observation, but observation by itself isn't sufficient. Why isn't it?

21-7. **Theme 7** indicates that our experience is subjective. What does this mean?

Answers: 21-1. one cause **21-2.** multiple causes **21-3.** cultural **21-4.** cultural heritage, aware **21-5.** Theme 6 states that heredity and environment *jointly* affect behaviour. While the relative influence of each is still debated, theorists no longer assert that behaviour is entirely a function of one or the other. **21-6.** Because (Theme 7) people's experience of the world is highly subjective. **21-7.** Different people experience different things; even if we observe the same event at the same time, we do not "see" the same things; we selectively focus on some events and ignore others.

PERSONAL APPLICATION * IMPROVING ACADEMIC PERFORMANCE

22. Discuss three important considerations in designing a program to promote adequate studying.

22-1. Three features of successful studying are listed below. Elaborate on them by providing some of the details asked for.

(a) A schedule: When should you plan your study schedule? Should you write it down? Should you do the simpler tasks first or begin the major assignments? What is a major difference between successful and unsuccessful students regarding time management?

(b) A place: What are the major characteristics of a good study place?

(c) A reward: When should you reward yourself? What kinds of rewards are suggested?

Answers: 22-1. (a) Set up a general schedule for a particular semester, and then, at the beginning of each week, plan the specific assignments for each study session. Put your plans in writing. It may be best to tackle the major assignments first, breaking them into smaller components. Successful students regulate their time more effectively than unsuccessful students. (b) Find one or two places to study with minimal distractions: little noise, few interruptions. (c) Reward yourself shortly after you finish a particular amount of studying; snacking, watching TV, or calling a friend is suggested. **Suggestion:** You are studying now. Is this a good time for you? If it is, why not write out your weekly schedule now. Include schedule preparation as part of your study time.

23. Describe the SQ3R method and explain what makes it effective.

23-1. Below are descriptions of an individual applying the five steps of the SQ3R method to Chapter 1 of your text. The steps are not in the correct order. Label each of the steps and place a number in the parentheses to indicate the correct order.

(   ) ___________________ Vanessa looks at the title of the first subsection of the chapter. After wondering briefly what it means for psychology to have "parents," she formulates this question: How was the field of psychology influenced by philosophy and physiology?

(   ) ___________________ Vanessa turns to the back of Chapter 1 and notes that there is a chapter review. She turns back to the first page of the chapter, sees that the outline on that page matches the review at the end, and browses through some of the other parts of the chapter. She has a rough idea that the chapter is going to define the field and discuss its history.

( ) ____________________ Keeping in mind the question she has posed, Vanessa reads the section about the meeting of psychology's "parents" and formulates a tentative answer to her question. (She also formulates some additional questions: "Who was Descartes?" and "What method did philosophers use?")

( ) ____________________ Vanessa answers her first question as follows: "Philosophy (one of the parents) posed questions about the mind that made the study of human thinking and actions acceptable; physiology (the other parent) contributed the scientific method." She decides to note down her answer for later review.

( ) ____________________ When she has finished step 4 for all sections, Vanessa looks over the entire chapter, section by section. She repeats the questions for each section and attempts to answer each one.

23-2. What makes the SQ3R technique so effective?

Answers: 23-1. (2) Question (1) Survey (3) Read (4) Recite (5) Review **23-2.** It requires active processing and identifying key ideas.

24. Summarize advice provided on how to get more out of lectures.

24-1. Indicate true (T) or false (F) for the following statements:

____ Poor class attendance is associated with poor grades.

____ Research has shown that the average student records less than 40% of the crucial ideas in lectures.

24-2. Using a few words for each point, summarize the four points on getting more out of lectures.

Answers: 24-1. T, T **24-2.** Listen actively; focus full attention on the speaker, and try to anticipate what's coming. For complex material, read ahead. Take notes in your own words, and attend to clues about what is most important. Consider asking questions during lectures (to keep involved and to clarify points presented).

25. Summarize advice provided on improving test-taking strategies.

25-1. Is it better to change answers on multiple-choice tests or to go with one's first hunch?

25-2. Following are situations you might encounter while taking a test. Reread the section on general test-taking tips and then indicate what you would do in each situation.

(a) You run into a particularly difficult item:

(b) The answer seems to be simple, but you think you may be missing something:

(c) The test is a timed test:

(d) You have some time left at the end of the test:

25-3. Following are samples of the situations mentioned under the discussion of tips for multiple-choice and essay exam questions. Based on the suggestions, what would you do?

(a) In a multiple-choice test, item *c* seems to be correct, but you have not yet read items *d* and *e*: What would you do next?

(b) You know that items *a* and *b* are correct, are unsure of items *c* and *d*, and item *e* is an "all of the above" option. Which alternative (a, b, c, d, or e) would you choose?

(c) You have no idea which multiple-choice alternative is correct. You note that option *a* has the word "always" in it, items *b* and *c* use the word "never," and item *d* says "frequently."

(d) You have read the stem of a multiple-choice item but you have not yet looked at the options.

(e) Faced with an essay, you wonder whether to simply begin writing and let the ideas flow or to spend a few minutes in organization.

Answers: 25-1. In general, changing answers seems to be better. Available research indicates that people are more than twice as likely to go from a wrong answer to a right one as from a right answer to a wrong one. **25-2.** (a) Skip it and come back to it, if time permits. (b) Maybe the answer is simple! Don't make the question more complex than it was intended to be. (c) Budget your time, checking the proportion of the test completed against the time available. (d) Review, reconsider, check over your answers. **25-3.** (a) Read all options. (b) Answer *e*. (c) Answer *d*. (Still good advice and generally the best procedure to follow. But note that some professors, aware of the strategy, may throw in an item in which "always" is part of a correct answer! It's sort of like radar detectors: Someone builds a better detector and someone else tries to build radar that can't be detected.) (d) Try to anticipate the correct answer *before* reading the options. (e) Spend a few minutes looking over the questions and allocating time, planning, organizing, and possibly even outlining. Many examiners will appreciate your use of headings or numbers to identify points made.

CRITICAL THINKING APPLICATION * DEVELOPING CRITICAL THINKING SKILLS: AN INTRODUCTION

26. Explain the nature of critical thinking skills and why they need to be taught.

26-1. The previous section on test-taking strategies asked whether it is better to change answers or go with one's first hunch. Actually, that is a critical thinking question. While our hunches are often pretty good, sometimes they don't lead to the desired outcome. When we use critical thinking, we use the same principles that we would use in a ___________________ investigation. We also use formal and informal rules of ___________________ and carefully evaluate the quality of ___________________.

26-2. Critical thinking is not something that we come by naturally. And critical thinking (is also/is not) a normal part of instruction in most subject areas. So, for people to develop the skill of critical thinking, it has to be deliberately and consciously ___________________ to them.

Answers: 26-1. scientific, logic, information **26-2.** is not, taught.

27. Discuss some weaknesses in evolutionary explanations for gender differences in spatial abilities.

27-1. Some evidence suggests that males tend to have slightly better visual–spatial perception than females and that females have better memories for locations. The reason for these gender differences, according to evolutionary psychologists, is that in our evolutionary past natural selection favoured a division of labour in which men were ___________________ and women were ___________________. Hunting (aiming a spear, travelling long distances) required ___________________ perception, while gathering required ___________________ of locations of food.

27-2. As previously discussed, evolutionary psychology is a major new theoretical perspective in psychology. While the interpretation of the evolutionary psychologists is certainly plausible, critical thinking urges us to consider the following two questions when assessing a truth claim: (1) Are there _________________ explanations for these results? And (2) are data available that _________________ the evidence provided?

27-3. It turns out that the answer to both of these questions is a qualified "yes." For example, it may be that most cultures encourage male children to engage in visual–spatial activities (e.g., playing with blocks) that would provide an ___________________ interpretation to one based on evolutionary principles. In addition, some scholars have suggested that women in early hunter–gatherer societies often did, in fact, travel long distances to obtain food and were also involved in hunting. While certainly not "disproving" evolutionary theory, this type of evidence would ___________________ some of the data presented by evolutionary psychologists.

Answers: 27-1. hunters, gatherers, visual–spatial, memory **27-2.** alternative, contradict **27-3.** alternative, contradict (challenge, dispute, weaken).

Review of Key Terms

Applied psychology
Behaviour
Behaviourism
Clinical psychology
Cognition
Critical thinking
Culture
Empiricism
Ethnocentrism
Evolutionary psychology
Functionalism
Humanism
Introspection
Natural selection
Positive psychology
Psychiatry
Psychoanalytic theory
Psychology
SQ3R
Stimulus
Structuralism
Testwiseness
Theory
Unconscious

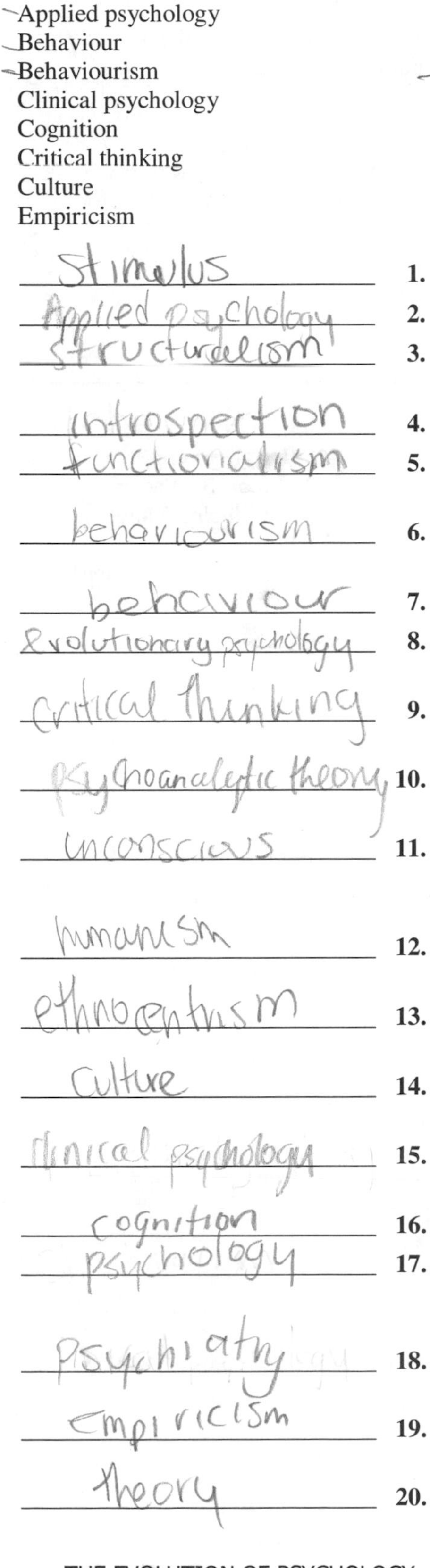

1. Any detectable input from the environment.
2. The branch of psychology concerned with practical problems.
3. School of thought based on notion that the task of psychology is to analyze consciousness into its basic elements.
4. Observation of one's own conscious experience.
5. School of thought asserting that psychology's major purpose was to investigate the function or purpose of consciousness.
6. The theoretical orientation asserting that scientific psychology should study only observable behaviour.
7. An observable activity or response by an organism.
8. Examines behavioural processes in terms of their adaptive or survival value for a species.
9. The use of cognitive skills and strategies to increase the probability of a desirable outcome.
10. Freudian theory that explains personality and abnormal behaviour in terms of unconscious processes.
11. According to psychoanalytic theory, that portion of the mind containing thoughts, memories, and wishes not in awareness but nonetheless exerting a strong effect on human behaviour.
12. The psychological theory asserting that human beings are unique and fundamentally different from other animals.
13. The tendency to view one's own group as superior to other groups.
14. Widely shared customs, beliefs, values, norms, and institutions that are transmitted socially across generations.
15. The branch of psychology concerned with the diagnosis and treatment of psychological disorders.
16. Mental processes or thinking.
17. The science that studies behaviour and the physiological and cognitive processes that underlie it, and the profession that applies this knowledge to solving various practical problems.
18. The branch of medicine concerned with the diagnosis and treatment of psychological problems and disorders.
19. The point of view that knowledge should be based on observation.
20. A system of ideas used to link together or explain a set of observations.

SQ3R **21.** A five-step procedure designed to improve study skills.

testwizeness **22.** Ability to use the characteristics and formats of a test to maximize one's score.

natural selection **23.** The Darwinian principle that characteristics that have a survival advantage for a species are more likely to be passed on to subsequent generations.

positive psychology **24.** Uses theory and research to better understand adaptive, creative, and fulfilling aspects of human existence.

Answers: 1. stimulus **2.** applied psychology **3.** structuralism **4.** introspection **5.** functionalism **6.** behaviourism **7.** behaviour **8.** evolutionary psychology **9.** critical thinking **10.** psychoanalytic theory **11.** unconscious **12.** humanism **13.** ethnocentrism **14.** culture **15.** clinical psychology **16.** cognition **17.** psychology **18.** psychiatry **19.** empiricism **20.** theory **21.** SQ3R **22.** testwiseness **23.** natural selection **24.** positive psychology.

Review of Key People

Sigmund Freud	William James	Martin Seligman
G. Stanley Hall	Brenda Milner	B. F. Skinner
Donald Hebb	Carl Rogers	John B. Watson
		Wilhelm Wundt

Wilhelm Wundt **1.** Founded experimental psychology and the first experimental psychology laboratory.

G. Stanley Hall **2.** Established the first American research laboratory, launched America's first psychological journal, and was the first president of the APA.

William James **3.** Chief architect of functionalism; described a "stream of consciousness."

John B. Watson **4.** Founded behaviourism.

Sigmund Freud **5.** Devised the theory and technique known as psychoanalysis.

Skinner **6.** Identified operant conditioning.

Rogers **7.** A major proponent of "humanistic" psychology.

Hebb **8.** A Canadian psychologist who described the concept of the cell assembly.

Seligman **9.** A founder of positive psychology.

Milner **10.** A founder of neuropsychology in Canada.

Answers: 1. Wundt **2.** Hall **3.** James **4.** Watson **5.** Freud **6.** Skinner **7.** Rogers **8.** Hebb **9.** Seligman **10.** Milner.

Self-Quiz

1. Structuralism is the historical school of psychology that asserted that the purpose of psychology was to:
a. study behaviour
b. discover the smaller elements that comprise consciousness
c. explore the unconscious
d. examine the purposes of conscious processes

2. Of the two parents of psychology, physiology and philosophy, which provided the method? What is the method?
   a. philosophy; logic, reasoning
   b. philosophy; intuition, introspection
   c. physiology; observation, science
   d. physiology; anatomy, surgery

3. Who is Wilhelm Wundt?
   a. He founded the first experimental laboratory.
   b. He founded the American Psychological Association.
   c. He discovered the classically conditioned salivary reflex.
   d. He founded behaviourism.

4. For John B. Watson, the appropriate subject matter of psychology was:
   a. animal behaviour
   b. the unconscious
   c. consciousness
   d. human physiology

5. Which of the following represents a major breakthrough in the development of applied psychology?
   a. the use of the method of introspection
   b. the functionalist school of thought
   c. establishment of the first animal laboratory
   d. Wundt's founding of experimental psychology

6. Within the field of psychology, Freud's ideas encountered resistance because he emphasized:
   a. human consciousness
   b. human behaviour
   c. introspection
   d. the unconscious

7. Which of the following would be considered the major principle of operant conditioning?
   a. Human behaviour derives in part from free will; animal behaviour is determined by the environment.
   b. Humans and other animals tend to repeat responses followed by positive outcomes.
   c. The majority of human behaviour is based on thoughts, feelings, and wishes of which we are unaware.
   d. Human beings are fundamentally different from other animals.

8. Which of the following theorists would tend to emphasize explanations in terms of freedom and potential for personal growth?
   a. Carl Rogers
   b. Sigmund Freud
   c. B. F. Skinner
   d. all of the above

9. Recent research trends in psychology involve two areas largely ignored by early behaviourists. These two areas are:
   a. observable and measurable responses
   b. cognition (thinking) and physiological processes
   c. classical and operant conditioning
   d. the effect of environmental events and the behaviour of lower animals

10. Which core psychological research area is primarily devoted to the study of such topics as memory, problem solving, and thinking?
a. physiological
b. social
c. cognitive
d. personality

11. Critical thinking refers to:
a. analysis of problems in terms of scientific principles
b. making decisions based on formal and informal logic
c. thinking that includes consideration of probabilities
d. all of the above

12. The assertion that "psychology is empirical" means that psychology is based on:
a. introspection
b. logic
c. observation
d. mathematics

13. In looking for the causes of a particular behaviour, psychologists assume:
a. one cause or factor
b. multifactorial causation
c. free will
d. infinite causation

14. Contemporary psychologists generally assume that human behaviour is determined by:
a. heredity
b. environment
c. heredity and environment acting jointly
d. heredity, environment, and free will

15. What does SQ3R stand for?
a. search, question, research, recommend, reconstitute
b. silence, quietude, reading, writing, arithmetic
c. summarize, quickly, read, research, reread
d. survey, question, read, recite, review

16. What type of research methodology was used in the Featured Study on bullying?
a. questionnaires
b. case study
c. review of archival records
d. naturalistic observation

17. Which of the following is a founder of positive psychology?
a. Watson
b. Skinner
c. Freud
d. Seligman

Answers: 1. b **2.** c **3.** a **4.** a **5.** b **6.** d **7.** b **8.** a **9.** b **10.** c **11.** d **12.** c **13.** b **14.** c **15.** d **16.** d **17.** d.

InfoTrac Keywords

Applied Psychology
Clinical Psychology
Humanism
Natural Selection
Psychoanalytic Theory

Chapter Two
THE RESEARCH ENTERPRISE IN PSYCHOLOGY

Review of Key Ideas

LOOKING FOR LAWS: THE SCIENTIFIC APPROACH TO BEHAVIOUR

1. Describe the goals of the scientific enterprise in psychology.

1-1. The three interrelated goals of psychology and the other sciences are: (a) measurement and description, (b) understanding and prediction, and (c) application and control. Match each of the following descriptions with the goal it represents by placing the appropriate letters in the blanks. (There is considerable overlap among these goals; pick the closest match.)

____ Muscle relaxation techniques are found to be useful in reducing anxiety and improving concentration and memory.

____ A psychologist develops a test or procedure that measures anxiety.

____ Researchers find that participants in an experiment conform more to the judgments of someone similar to themselves than to someone who is dissimilar.

Answers: 1-1. c, a, b.

2. Explain the relations between theory, hypothesis, and research.

2-1. What's a theory? Your text defines a theory as a system of ideas that is used to explain a set of observations. So, a theory is a *system*, which means that it integrates (or organizes or classifies) a series of observations; and it helps ___explain___ those observations. And it does one thing more: It suggests ideas, or predictions, or ___hypothesis___ to be tested in research.

2-2. Researchers can't test a theory all at once, but they can test one or two hypotheses derived from the theory. This is the relationship between theory, hypothesis, and research: Theories suggest ____________________ (questions or predictions), which are then tested in ____________________. If the hypotheses are supported, confidence in the concepts of the ____________________ is strengthened.

Answers: 2-1. explain, hypotheses (questions) **2-2.** hypotheses, research, theory.

3. Outline the steps in a scientific investigation.

3-1. Following are the five steps generally used in performing a scientific investigation. Fill in the missing key words.

a. Formulate a testable ____________________.

b. Select the research ____________________ and design the study.

c. ____________________ the data.

d. ____________________ the data and draw conclusions.

e. ____________________ the findings.

3-2. Following are descriptions of various phases in the study by Dutton and Aron (1974). Indicate which step of this study is being described by placing a letter from the previous question (a, b, c, d, or e) in the appropriate blank.

____ The authors prepared a report of their findings that was accepted for publication in *Journal of Personality and Social Psychology*.

____ The researchers used statistics to determine whether their hypotheses were supported.

____ Dutton and Aron thought that arousal would heighten sexual attraction. Before they began, they made precise operational definitions of both arousal and sexual attraction.

____ The researchers decided to compare males crossing a high bridge with those crossing a low bridge in terms of their sexual attraction toward an experimental confederate they met after crossing the bridge.

____ The researchers recorded the number of calls to the experimental confederate after participants crossed one of the bridges.

Answers: 3-1. (a) hypothesis (b) method (c) collect (d) analyze (e) report (publish, write up) **3-2.** e, d, a, b, c.

4. Discuss the advantages of the scientific approach.

4-1. We may agree with the commonsense adage "haste makes waste." Although we agree, it's not absolutely clear what the proverb means. What are the two major advantages of the scientific approach over the commonsense approach?

Answers: 4-1. First, scientific descriptions generally have a clarity and precision lacking in commonsense proverbs. (While we have a general idea about the meaning of haste, for example, we don't know precisely when, in what way, or how much haste we should avoid.) Second, science is relatively intolerant of error (before accepting a conclusion, scientists will demand objective evidence from empirical studies that support the idea).

LOOKING FOR CAUSES: EXPERIMENTAL RESEARCH

5. Describe the experimental method, explaining independent and dependent variables, experimental and control groups, and extraneous variables.

5-1. Dutton and Aron proposed that *sexual attraction* is caused (in part) by level of *arousal.* What was their independent variable? ________________ Dependent variable? ________________

5-2. The variable that is manipulated or varied by the experimenter is termed the ________________ variable. The variable that is affected by, or is dependent on, the manipulation is termed the ________________ variable.

5-3. What is the name of the variable that *results from* the manipulation? ________________ What is the name of the variable that *produces* the effect? ________________

5-4. The group of subjects that receives the experimental treatment is known as the ________________ group; the group that does not is known as the ________________ group.

5-5. Control and experimental groups are quite similar in most respects. They differ in that the experimental group receives the experimental ________________, and the control group does not. Thus, any differences found in the measure of the ________________ variable are assumed to be due to differences in manipulation of the ________________ variable.

5-6. In Dutton and Aron's study, the experimental group experienced a high level of ________________. Results were that the experimental group, the high arousal group, had a greater tendency to __________ __________ __________ __________ an opposite-sex other than did the control group.

5-7 In the research described by Wolfe and colleagues (2003), the type of treatment that teens received is the ____________ variable, and the experience of abuse in relationships is the ____________ variable.

5-8. An extraneous variable is any variable other than the ________________ variable that seems likely to cause a difference between groups as measured by the ________________ variable. In the Dutton and Aron study, a possible confounding variable was differences in ____________.

5-9. To review the parts of an experiment: Suppose a researcher is interested in the effect of a drug on the running speed of rats. The ________________ group is injected with the drug, and the ________________ group is not. Whether or not the rats received the drug would be the __________________ variable, and running speed would be the __________________ variable.

5-10. Suppose also that the average age of the experimental rats is two years while the average age of the control rats is 3 months. What is the extraneous variable in this experiment? __________________ Why does this variable present a problem?

5-11. Researchers generally control for extraneous variables through random __________________ of subjects to groups. Write a definition of this procedure.

Answers: 5-1. arousal, attraction (note that a second independent variable in the study was sex of the experimental confederate) **5-2.** independent, dependent **5-3.** dependent, independent **5-4.** experimental, control **5-5.** treatment, dependent, independent **5-6.** arousal, become sexually attracted toward **5-7.** independent, dependent **5-8** independent, dependent, personality **5-9.** experimental, control, independent, dependent **5-10.** age. Any difference between groups could be due to age rather than the independent variable. **5-11.** assignment. All subjects have an equal chance of being assigned to any group or condition.

6. Describe the Featured Study on the effects of fear on sexual attraction.

6-1. The purpose of the study was to examine whether strong emotional arousal experienced by men would enhance their ______________ toward an attractive female.

6-2. This question arose from Schacter's (1964) theory of emotion, which suggests that ____________ cues may at times be used to re-label emotional experiences.

6-3. Participants were men who crossed either a high, unstable bridge or a low, solid bridge. They were then met by a male or female experimental confederate. They then completed the __________ ____________ ___________ (TAT) to measure their sexual imagery and were given the confederate's phone number.

6-4. Thus, the study manipulated two _________________ variables. One was the type of bridge crossed by the participant, which generated either __________ or __________ fear/arousal. The second was the sex of the experimental confederate.

6-5. The __________________ variables included amount of _________ __________ on responses to the TAT and the number of __________ ___________ made to the experimental confederate.

6-6. Results were as follows: Compared to men who crossed the low, stable bridge, men who crossed the high, unstable bridge revealed _________ sexual imagery in their TAT stories and were _______ likely to call the female experimental confederate.

Answers: 6-1. attraction **6-2.** environmental **6-3.** Thematic Apperception Test **6-4.** independent, high, low **6-5.** dependent, sexual imagery, telephone calls **6-6.** more, more.

7. Explain the major advantages and disadvantages of the experimental method.

7-1. What is the major advantage of the experimental method?

7-2. What are the two major disadvantages of the experimental method?

7-3. Suppose a researcher is interested in the effect of drinking large amounts of coffee on health (e.g., 30 cups per day over an extended period of time). What would be a major *disadvantage* of using the experimental method to examine this particular question?

Answers: 7-1. The major advantage is that it permits researchers to make cause–effect conclusions. **7-2.** The major disadvantages are that (a) precise experimental control may make the situation so artificial that it does not apply to the real world, and (b) ethical or practical considerations may prevent one from manipulating independent variables of interest. **7-3.** To the extent that excessive coffee drinking is a suspected factor in health problems, it would be unethical, and perhaps impossible, to require an experimental group to drink that much per day.

LOOKING FOR LINKS: DESCRIPTIVE RESEARCH

8. Discuss three descriptive/correlational methods: naturalistic observation, case studies, and surveys.

8-1. Naturalistic observation involves study of human beings or animals in their natural environments conducted (with/without) direct intervention from the observer.

8-2. A case study is an in-depth and generally highly subjective or impressionistic report on (a group of people/a single individual) that may be based on interviews, psychological testing, and so on.

8-3. The third descriptive procedure is the survey technique. Surveys use ___________________ to find out about specific aspects of human attitudes or opinions.

8-4. List the three descriptive/correlational methods in the space below.

Answers: 8-1. without **8-2.** a single individual **8-3.** questionnaires (or interviews) **8-4.** naturalistic observation, case studies, surveys.

9. Explain the major advantages and disadvantages of descriptive/correlational research.

9-1. While descriptive/correlational methods extend the scope of psychological research, they do not permit scientists to ___________________ variables. Nor do they permit one to demonstrate ___________________ relationships among variables.

9-2. For example, suppose you have data indicating that people who happen to drink a lot of coffee tend to have cardiovascular problems. Is this experimental or descriptive/correlational research? ___________________ Would it be correct to conclude (from these data) that coffee drinking causes cardiovascular problems?

____

9-3. An advantage of the descriptive/correlational methods is that they allow researchers to study phenomena that they could not study with experimental methods. Thus, the descriptive/correlational methods (narrow/broaden) the scope of phenomena studied.

Answers: 9-1. manipulate (control), cause–effect (causal) **9-2.** descriptive/correlational (because the variables are not manipulated by the experimenter), no **9-3.** broaden.

LOOKING FOR CONCLUSIONS: STATISTICS AND RESEARCH

10. Describe three measures of central tendency and one measure of variability.

10-1. To review the meaning of the three measures of central tendency, determine the mean, median, and mode of the following scores: 3, 5, 5, 5, 6, 6, 7, 9, 80.

Mean: _____

Median: _____

Mode: _____

10-2. One can describe a group of data with a single number by using one of the measures of central tendency. In the blanks below, indicate which measure of central tendency is being described.

_____________ The score that occurs most frequently.

_____________ The sum of all scores divided by the total number of scores.

_____________ Half the scores fall above this measure and half below.

_____________ Very sensitive to extreme scores.

_____________ Usually the most useful, because it may be used in further statistical manipulations.

_____________ The middle score.

10-3. What is the median of data set A below? _________ Of set B? _________ Which of these sets is more variable, A or B? _________

A. 30, 40, 50, 60, 70 B. 10, 30, 50, 70, 90

10-4. What is the name of the statistic used as a measure of variability?

____________________ ____________________.

Answers: 10-1. 14, 6, 5 **10-2.** mode, mean, median, mean, mean, median **10-3.** 50, 50, B **10-4.** standard deviation.

11. Distinguish between positive and negative correlations.

11-1. Which of the following relationships are positive and which are negative? (Indicate with a + or - sign.)

____ The better students' grades are in high school, the better their grades tend to be in college.

____ The more alcohol one has drunk, the slower his or her reaction time.

____ The higher the anxiety, the poorer the test performance.

____ The greater the arousal, the greater the sexual attraction.

11-2. Which of the following indicates the *strongest correlational relationship*?

a. 1.12

b. -.92

c. .58

d. .87

Answers: 11-1. +, -, -, + **11-2.** b (not *a*, because correlations cannot exceed +1.00 or -1.00).

12. Discuss correlation in relation to prediction and causation.

12-1. Suppose you have data indicating that the more money people make, the less depressed they report being on a mood survey. Thus, if you know the incomes of people in a comparable group, you should be able to ________________, with some degree of accuracy, their self-reported depressed mood.

12-2. The accuracy of your prediction will depend on the size of the correlation coefficient. Which of the following correlation coefficients would allow you to predict with the greatest accuracy?

a. +.41

b. +.54

c. -.65

12-3. What kind of conclusion is justified on the basis of the previous relationship: a conclusion involving prediction or one involving a statement about causation? ________________

12-4. Consider the relationship described in an earlier question: You discover that the more money people make, the greater their happiness. Which of the following conclusions is justified? Explain why.

a. Money makes people happy.

b. Happiness causes people to earn more money.

c. Both happiness and money result from some unknown third factor.

d. Any of the above.

12-5. Again, consider the relationship between money and happiness. Assume that money does not cause happiness, and happiness does not cause money. What possible *third factor* can you think of that could cause both? (I'm asking you to make a wild speculation here just to get the idea of how third variables may operate.)

12-6. We aren't justified in making causal conclusions from a correlation, but we can predict. Let's examine what prediction means in the case of our hypothetical example. If the relationship really exists, what prediction would you make about people who are rich? What prediction would you make concerning people who are unhappy?

Answers: 12-1. predict **12-2.** c **12-3.** prediction (Generally, one can't make causal conclusions from a correlation.) **12-4.** d. Any of the statements is a possible *causal* explanation of the relationship, but we don't know which one(s) may be correct because the data are correlational. Therefore, no *causal conclusions* are justified. **12-5.** For example, poor health might cause one to be both unhappy *and* poverty stricken (while good health would cause one to be both happy and wealthy). Intelligence, aggressiveness, stubbornness, or a number of other physiological or behavioural factors could be causally related *both* to income and to happiness without those two factors being causes of one another. **12-6.** You would predict that a group that was rich would also be happy and that a group that was unhappy would be poor. No causation is implied in these statements.

13. Explain the meaning of statistical significance.

13-1. In the hypothetical experiment described in your text, there are two groups, largely equivalent except that the ______________________ group receives the computerized tutoring sessions and the __________________ group does not. What is the hypothesis of this experiment?

13-2. Researchers statistically evaluate the hypothesis by comparing means and determining the likelihood or probability that a difference between means of the size obtained (or larger) would occur by __________________. If the probability that such a difference would occur by chance is very low, say less than five times in 100, the researchers would conclude that the difference (is/is not) due to chance. They would declare the difference statistically __________________ at the __________ level of significance.

13-3. *Statistically significant* does not mean important or significant in the usual sense of that word. What does *statistically significant* mean?

13-4. How do we reach a conclusion when the results of different studies often produce contradictory results? One method for doing so is the relatively new technique known as __________________, a (statistical/journalistic) technique for combining results from many different studies.

Answers: 13-1. experimental, control. The hypothesis is that special tutoring would increase reading scores. **13-2.** chance, is not, significant, .05 **13-3.** It means that a difference that large would be rare on a chance basis, so it is assumed *not* to be due to chance, or, more simply, it is assumed that the difference between means is due to treatment. **13-4.** meta-analysis, statistical.

LOOKING FOR FLAWS: EVALUATING RESEARCH

14. Explain what makes a sample representative, and discuss the problem of sampling bias.

14-1. Sampling bias exists when the sample is not representative of the __________________ from which it was drawn.

14-2. Suppose that Professor Brutalbaum distributes a questionnaire in an attempt to find out how the students react to his teaching. The day that he chooses for the evaluation, the day before a scheduled vacation, about half of the students are absent. Is the sample that attended class that day a representative sample of the class? _____ What is a representative sample?

Answers: 14-1. population **14-2.** No. A representative sample is one that is similar in composition to the population from which it is drawn. In this case, it seems likely that students who attend are different from those who do not (e.g., perhaps more enthusiastic, harder working, more fearful, etc.). Since the sample is not representative, the flaw illustrated is *sampling bias.*

15. Explain when placebo effects are likely to be a problem.

15-1. A student in Professor Brutalbaum's class orders some audiotapes that promise to produce sleep learning. (Brutalbaum is dubious, because from his observations students sleep a lot in class but still don't seem to learn very much.) The student runs the experiment in Brutalbaum's class. She describes the anticipated sleep-learning benefits to the class and then *gives the sleep tapes to a random half of the students and nothing to the other half.* After the next test, she analyzes the results. The mean test score of the experimental group is statistically significantly higher than that of the control group. What is the flaw in this experiment?

a. sampling bias

b. possible placebo effects

c. time of day

d. none of the above

15-2. What are placebo effects?

Answers: 15-1. b **15-2.** The tendency for people's behaviour to change because of their expectation that the treatment will have an effect.

16. Describe the typical kinds of distortions that occur in self-report data.

16-1. Professor Brutalbaum is now concerned about class attendance and decides to find out what proportion of students miss class regularly. He distributes a questionnaire asking students to indicate how many classes they have missed. Which of the four common flaws is he likely to encounter? ____________________

16-2. For a number of reasons, people may not answer questions correctly, including the fact that they may not understand the question or may not remember accurately. Respondents also frequently want to create a favourable impression, the response tendency known as the social ____________________ bias. Some measures are less susceptible to socially desirable responding, including _________ measures, such as the Implicit Association Test. People may also be predisposed to respond in particular ways regardless of the question, for example, to agree or disagree regardless of content. This type of response tendency is known as a response _________.

Answers: 16-1. distortions in self-report **16-2.** desirability, implicit, set.

17. Describe Rosenthal's research on experimenter bias.

17-1. When we ask a question, we frequently expect a particular answer. When scientists form a hypothesis, they also may expect a particular answer, and in some cases the scientist's hypotheses or expectations may influence the answers that they obtain. When a researcher's expectations about the outcome of a study influence the results, then the flaw in procedure known as __________________ has occurred.

17-2. Experimenter bias or influence may occur in subtle ways. Rosenthal has repeatedly demonstrated that when the experimenter merely knows which treatment condition a subject is in, the fact of that knowledge or expectation alone may influence the subject's behaviour. For this reason, it is extremely important in research to maintain the __________________ procedure, in which neither participants nor experimenters know which treatment condition the subject is in.

Answers: 17-1. experimenter bias **17-2.** double-blind.

LOOKING INTO THE FUTURE: THE INTERNET AND PSYCHOLOGICAL RESEARCH

18. Discuss the pros and cons of Internet-mediated research.

18-1. In the space below, identity advantages of Internet-based research.

18-2. In the space below, identity disadvantages of Internet-based research.

Answers: 18-1. Advantages include larger and more diverse samples, and more efficient collection of data **18-2.** Disadvantages include sample bias due to self-selection, higher dropout rates, and less control over data collection.

LOOKING AT ETHICS: DO THE ENDS JUSTIFY THE MEANS?

19. Discuss the pros and cons of deception in research with human subjects.

19-1. In the space below, present arguments against the use of deception in research. What is the major argument in defence of the use of deception in research?

Answers: 19-1. Deception is, after all, lying; it may undermine people's trust in others; it may cause distress. Many research issues could not be investigated without deception.

20. Identify the four key principles of psychological research as set forth by the Canadian Psychological Association.

20-1. Fill in the spaces below to describe each of the four Key Principles:

Principle I: Respect for the _____________ of Persons.

Principle II: Responsible _____________.

Principle III: Integrity in _____________.

Principle IV: Responsibility to _____________.

20-2. Treating all individuals respectfully and fairly (for example, regardless of their culture or nationality) would fall under principle number _____.

20-3. The ethical conduct of research with animals is also governed by guidelines developed by the Canadian Council on the ________ ____ __________.

Answers: 20-1. Dignity, Caring, Relationships, Society **20-2.** I **20-3.** Care of Animals.

PUTTING IT IN PERSPECTIVE

21. Explain how this chapter highlighted two of the text's unifying themes.

21-1. One of the text's unifying themes is that psychology is _______________, which means that its conclusions are based on systematic _______________, and that it tends to be (skeptical/credulous).

21-2. In what way did the discussion of methodology suggest that psychology tends to be skeptical of its results?

21-3. People's experience of the world is highly subjective. Which of the methodological problems discussed point out psychology's awareness of the subjective nature of our experience?

Answers: 21-1. empirical, observation (research), skeptical **21-2.** Researchers constantly look for methodological flaws and subject their results to critical scrutiny by other scientists. **21-3.** Behavioural scientists try to guard against subjective reactions by building in appropriate experimental controls for *placebo effects* and *experimenter bias*.

PERSONAL APPLICATION * FINDING AND READING JOURNAL ARTICLES

22. Describe the nature of technical journals.

22-1. A journal publishes technical material in a field, generally the results of research or other scholarly activity. Since journal articles are written primarily for (the layman/other professionals), they frequently contain technical language that makes it difficult for people outside the field to understand.

22-2. In psychology, most journal articles are reports of research or other empirical studies. Some journals also publish articles that summarize findings from a large number of studies; these articles are known as __________________ articles. Some review articles employ the statistical technique of __________________, a procedure that combines the results of many different studies.

Answers: 22-1. other professionals **22-2.** review, meta-analysis.

23. Explain how to use PsycINFO, and discuss the advantages of computerized literature searches.

23-1. PsycINFO is a computerized database that contains abstracts or concise __________________ of articles published in psychological journals.

23-2. To find information about a particular journal article referred to in the popular press, for example, you could begin your search by entering the name of the __________________. If you have an idea of when the article was published, you could further narrow your search by entering the approximate __________________ in which the article might have been published.

23-3. You can also search under topic. To further reduce your search, enter ________ topics (e.g., insomnia and mood). By pairing two topics, you are more likely to find articles relevant to your particular question.

23-4. The advantages of computerized over manual searches (in the print journal *Psychological Abstracts*) include:

a. speed or power

b. decreased likelihood of missing relevant articles

c. the option of pairing topics in a search

d. all of the above

Answers: 23-1. summaries **23-2.** author, years (dates, time period) **23-3.** two **23-4.** d.

24. Describe the standard organization of journal articles reporting on empirical research.

24-1. In the blanks below, list the six parts of the standard journal article in the order in which they occur. (The initial letters of each section are listed on the left.)

A__________________

I__________________

M__________________

R__________________

D___________________

R___________________

(Hint: A way to remember the first letter of these parts of a journal, in order, is with the acrostic "Andrew Is Most Relaxed During a Run").

24-2. In the blanks below, match the name of the sections of the standard journal article with the descriptions.

___________________ States the hypothesis and reviews the literature relevant to the hypothesis.

___________________ A list of all the sources referred to in the paper.

___________________ A summary.

___________________ Presents the data; may include statistical analyses, graphs, and tables.

___________________ Describes what the researchers did in the study; includes participants, procedures, and data collection techniques.

___________________ Interprets or evaluates the data and presents conclusions.

Answers: 24-1. abstract, introduction, method, results, discussion, references **24-2.** introduction, references, abstract, results, method, discussion.

CRITICAL THINKING APPLICATION * THE PERILS OF ANECDOTAL EVIDENCE: "I HAVE A FRIEND WHO . . ."

25. Explain why anecdotal evidence is flawed and unreliable.

25-1. Anecdotal evidence consists of personal stories that support a particular point of view. Anecdotes are frequently persuasive because they are concrete and vivid and, therefore, easy to ___________________.

25-2. What's wrong with anecdotal evidence? First, one cannot generalize from a single case. Although a political candidate's story about a coal miner named Bob (or a physician named Alice, etc.) may be memorable, Bob's experiences cannot be ___________________ to other people or situations.

25-3. Second, people tend to represent themselves in the most favourable light. To the extent that Bob is the source of the anecdote, Bob's self-report data may reflect the social ___________________ bias.

25-4. In addition, stories change with the telling, so that later versions may bear little resemblance to the original event. Stories one has heard second- or third-hand, so-called _____________ evidence, are likely to be particularly unreliable.

25-5. Nor is it likely that Bob, or the story about Bob, was picked randomly. The candidate selects an anecdote to make a particular point, a process similar to ___________________ bias in a research setting. The clear alternative to anecdotal evidence is to solve problems based on solid evidence, the so-called _______________-based decision-making process.

Answers: 25-1. remember **25-2.** generalized **25-3.** desirability **25-4.** hearsay **25-5.** sampling, evidence.

Review of Key Terms

Anecdotal evidence
Case study
Confounding of variables
Control group
Correlation
Correlation coefficient
Data collection techniques
Dependent variable
Descriptive statistics
Double-blind procedure
Experiment
Experimental group
Experimenter bias
Extraneous variables
Hypothesis
Independent variable
Inferential statistics
Internet-mediated research
Journal
Mean
Median
Mode
Naturalistic observation
Operational definition
Participants
Placebo effects
Population
Random assignment
Replication
Research methods
Response set
Sample
Sampling bias
Social desirability bias
Standard deviation
Statistical significance
Statistics
Subjects
Survey
Theory
Variability
Variables

_______________ 1. Any of the factors in an experiment that are controlled or observed by an experimenter or that in some other way affect the outcome.

_______________ 2. A tentative statement about the expected relationship between two or more variables.

_______________ 3. Precisely defines each variable in a study in terms of the operations needed to produce or measure that variable.

_______________ 4. Persons or animals whose behaviour is being studied; means the same thing as *participants*.

_______________ 5. Differing ways of conducting research, which include experiments, case studies, surveys, and naturalistic observation.

_______________ 6. A research method in which independent variables are manipulated and which permits causal interpretations.

_______________ 7. A condition or event that an experimenter varies in order to observe its impact.

_______________ 8. The variable that results from the manipulation in an experiment.

_______________ 9. The group in an experiment that receives a treatment as part of the independent variable manipulation.

_______________ 10. The group in an experiment that does not receive the treatment.

_______________ 11. Any variables other than the independent variables that seem likely to influence the dependent measure in an experiment.

_______________ 12. Distribution of subjects in an experiment in which each subject has an equal chance of being assigned to any group or condition.

_______________ 13. A link or association between variables such that one can be predicted from the other.

_______________ 14. The statistic that indicates the degree of relationship between variables.

_______________ 15. A research method in which the researcher observes behaviour in the natural environment without directly intervening.

_______________ 16. An in-depth, generally subjective, investigation of an individual subject.

_______________ 17. A questionnaire or interview used to gather information about specific aspects of subjects' behaviour.

_______________ 18. Procedures for making empirical observations, including questionnaires, interviews, psychological tests, and physiological recordings.

_______________ 19. Statistics helpful in organizing and summarizing (but not interpreting) data.

_______________ 20. Statistical procedures used to interpret data in an experiment and draw conclusions.

_______________ 21. The use of mathematics to organize, summarize, and interpret numerical data.

_______________ 22. A descriptive statistic and measure of central tendency that always falls in the exact halfway point of a distribution of data.

_______________ 23. The arithmetic average.

_______________ 24. The score that occurs most frequently.

_______________ 25. The spread or dispersion of data, including the extent to which scores vary from the mean.

_______________ 26. A measure of variability in data.

_______________ 27. A judgment inferred from statistics that the probability of the observed findings occurring by chance is very low.

_______________ 28. A repetition of a study to determine whether the previously obtained results can be duplicated.

_______________ 29. A group of subjects taken from a population.

_______________ 30. A larger group from which a sample is drawn and to which the researcher wishes to generalize.

_______________ 31. Exists when a sample is not representative of the population from which it was drawn.

_______________ 32. Also known as subjects, the individuals whose behaviour is systematically observed in a study.

_______________ 33. Occurs when a researcher's expectations influence the results of the study.

_______________ 34. Effects that occur when subjects experience a change due to their expectations (or to a "fake" treatment).

_______________ 35. The tendency to respond in a particular way (e.g., agreeing) that is unrelated to the content of questions asked.

_______________ 36. Occurs when an extraneous variable makes it difficult to sort out the effects of the independent variable.

_______________ 37. The tendency to answer questions about oneself in a socially approved manner.

_______________ 38. A research strategy in which neither the subjects nor experimenters know which condition or treatment the subjects are in.

_______________ 39. A periodical that publishes technical and scholarly material within a discipline.

_______________ **40.** A system of interrelated ideas used to explain a set of observations.

_______________ **41.** Support for a particular point of view through the use of personal (and frequently vivid) stories.

_______________ **42.** Studies in which data collection is done using the Web.

Answers: 1. variables **2.** hypothesis **3.** operational definition **4.** subjects **5.** research methods **6.** experiment **7.** independent variable **8.** dependent variable **9.** experimental group **10.** control group **11.** extraneous variables **12.** random assignment **13.** correlation **14.** correlation coefficient **15.** naturalistic observation **16.** case study **17.** survey **18.** data collection techniques **19.** descriptive statistics **20.** inferential statistics **21.** statistics **22.** median **23.** mean **24.** mode **25.** variability **26.** standard deviation **27.** statistical significance **28.** replication **29.** sample **30.** population **31.** sampling bias **32.** participants **33.** experimenter bias **34.** placebo effects **35.** response set **36.** confounding of variables **37.** social desirability bias **38.** double-blind procedure **39.** journal **40.** theory **41.** anecdotal evidence **42.** Internet-mediated research.

Review of Key People

Arthur Aron
Donald Dutton
Neal Miller
Robert Rosenthal
Stanley Schachter
David Wolfe

_______________ **1.** Along with Dutton, studied the effects of arousal on sexual attraction.

_______________ **2.** Co-investigator with Aron.

_______________ **3.** Asserted that the benefits of animal research (e.g., the resulting treatments for mental and physical disorders) far outweigh the harm done.

_______________ **4.** Argued that emotions can be re-labelled according to environmental cues.

_______________ **5.** Studied experimenter bias, a researcher's unintended influence on the behaviour of subjects.

_______________ **6.** Studies a psychological intervention for at-risk teens.

Answers: 1. Aron **2.** Dutton **3.** Miller. **4.** Schachter **5.** Rosenthal **6.** Wolfe.

Self-Quiz

1. The work of a clinical psychologist to reduce suffering of an individual reflects the goal of:
a. measurement and description
b. understanding and prediction
c. application and control
d. all of the above

2. An experimenter tests the hypothesis that physical exercise helps people's mood (makes them happier). Subjects in the experimental group participate on Monday and Tuesday and those in the control group on Wednesday and Thursday. What is the *independent* variable?
a. the hypothesis
b. the day of the week
c. the exercise
d. the mood (degree of happiness)

3. Regarding the experiment described in the previous question: What is the *dependent* variable?
   a. the hypothesis
   b. the day of the week
   c. the exercise
   d. the mood (degree of happiness)

4. Regarding the experiment described above: What is an *extraneous* (confounding) variable?
   a. the hypothesis
   b. the day of the week
   c. the exercise
   d. the mood (degree of happiness)

5. The major advantage of the experimental method over the correlational approach is that the experimental method:
   a. permits one to make causal conclusions
   b. allows for prediction
   c. is generally less artificial than correlational procedures
   d. permits the study of people in groups

6. In looking through some medical records, you find that there is a strong relationship between depression and chronic pain: The stronger the physical pain that people report, the higher their scores on an inventory that measures depression. Which of the following conclusions are justified?
   a. Depression tends to produce chronic pain.
   b. Chronic pain tends to produce depression.
   c. Both chronic pain and depression result from some unknown third factor.
   d. None of the above.

7. What is the mode of the following data: 2, 3, 3, 3, 5, 5, 7, 12?
   a. 3
   b. 4
   c. 5
   d. 6

8. What is the median of the following data: 1, 3, 4, 4, 5, 6, 9?
   a. 3
   b. 4
   c. 4.57
   d. 6

9. Researchers find a negative relationship between alcohol consumption and speed of response: The more alcohol consumed, the slower the response speed. Which of the following fictitious statistics could possibly represent that correlation?
   a. -4.57
   b. -.87
   c. .91
   d. .05

10. The term *statistical significance* refers to:
   a. how important the data are for future research on the topic
   b. the conclusion that there are no reasonable alternative explanations
   c. the inference that the observed effects are unlikely to be due to chance
   d. the representativeness of the sample

11. An instructor wishes to find out whether a new teaching method is superior to his usual procedures, so he conducts an experiment. Everyone in his classes is quite excited about the prospect of learning under the new procedure, but of course he cannot administer the new teaching method to everyone. A random half of the students receive the new method, and the remaining half receive the old. What is the most obvious flaw in this experiment?
a. Subjects should have been systematically assigned to groups.
b. The sample is not representative of the population.
c. Placebo effects or experimenter bias are likely to affect results.
d. Distortions in self-report will affect results.

12. What procedure helps correct for experimenter bias?
a. extraneous or confounding variables
b. sleep learning or hypnosis
c. a higher standard for statistical significance
d. use of the double-blind procedure

13. With regard to the topic of deception in research with human subjects, which of the following is true?
a. Researchers are careful to avoid deceiving subjects.
b. Some topics could not be investigated unless deception was used.
c. Deception does not resemble lying.
d. All psychological research must involve some deception.

14. Which of the following is NOT one of the four Key Principles of Psychological Research, according to the Canadian Psychological Association's ethical guidelines?
a. Respect for the Dignity of Persons
b. Responsible Caring
c. Integrity in Relationships
d. Responsibility to Oneself

15. In the Featured Study by Dutton and Aron (1974), one of the independent variables was:
a. sexual imagery in TAT responses
b. the sex of participants
c. making a telephone call to the experimental confederate
d. the sex of the experimental confederates

16. Which of the following is one of the six standard parts of a psychological journal article?
a. conclusions
b. bibliography
c. data summary
d. discussion

17. PsycINFO is a computerized database containing:
a. standard diagnostic information for classifying behaviour disorders
b. abstracts of and bibliographic references for journal articles
c. psychological profiles of known felons
d. names of authors who specialize in abstractions

Answers: 1. c **2.** c **3.** d **4.** b **5.** a **6.** d **7.** a **8.** b **9.** b **10.** c **11.** c **12.** d **13.** b **14.** d **15.** d **16.** d **17.** b.

InfoTrac Keywords

Anecdotal Evidence

Correlation

Placebo Effects

Chapter Three
THE BIOLOGICAL BASES OF BEHAVIOUR

Review of Key Ideas

COMMUNICATION IN THE NERVOUS SYSTEM

1. Describe the various parts of the neuron and their functions.

1-1. The neuron has three basic parts: the dendrites, the cell body or soma, and the axon. The major mission of the average neuron is to receive information from one neuron and pass it on to the next neuron. The receiving part is the job of the branchlike parts called ________________. They then pass the message along to the nucleus of the cell, called the cell body, or ______________. From there, the message is sent down the ____________ to be passed along to other neurons.

1-2. Many axons are wrapped in a fatty jacket called the __________ __________, which permits faster transmission of information and prevents messages from getting on the wrong track. Like the covering on an electrical cord, myelin acts as an ____________ material.

1-3. When the neural message reaches the end of the axon, it excites projections called terminal ____________, which then release a chemical substance into the junction that separates them from other neurons. This junction between neurons is called the ____________.

1-4. Identify the major parts of a neuron in the figure below. Note that the arrow indicates the direction of the flow of information.

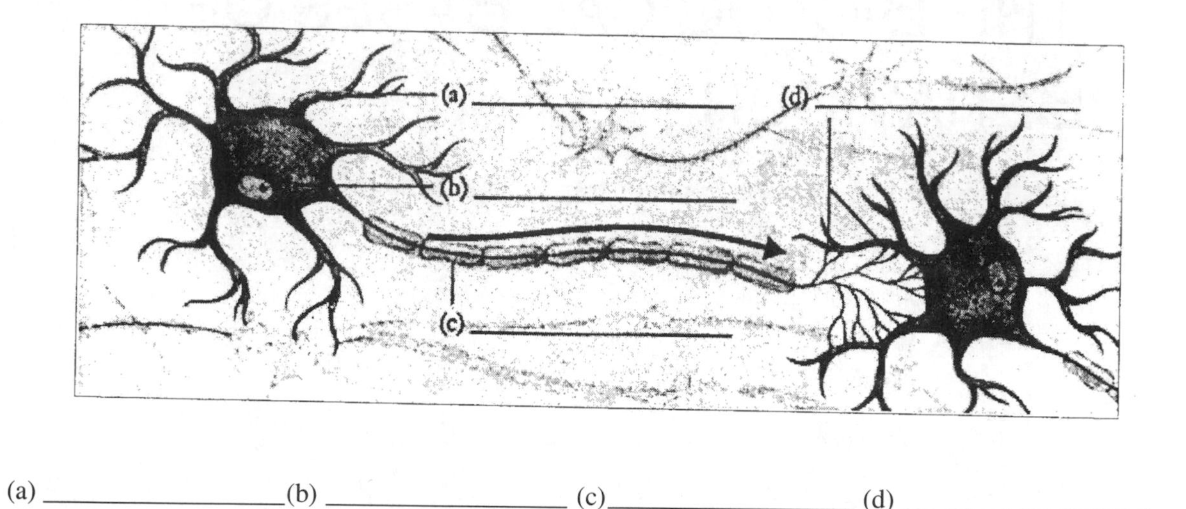

(a) ________________ (b) ________________ (c) ________________ (d) ________________

Answers: 1-1. dendrites, soma, axon **1-2.** myelin sheath, insulating **1-3.** buttons, synapse **1-4.** (a) dendrites, (b) cell body or soma, (c) axon, (d) terminal buttons.

2. Describe the main functions of glia.

2-1. Glia are a second category of nervous system cells. Glia are much ________ than neurons, and they outnumber neurons by a ratio of about ____ to 1.

2-2. Glia supply ____________ to neurons, help remove neurons' ____________ products, and provide ____________ around the axon of neurons.

2-3. More recently, glia cells have been shown to ________ and ________ chemical signals. They have also been implicated in such diseases as Alzheimer's disease, chronic pain, schizophrenia, and mood disorders.

Answers: 2-1. smaller, 10 **2-2.** nourishment, waste, insulation **2-3.** send, receive.

3. Describe the neural impulse.

3-1. When it is at rest, the neuron is like a tiny battery in that it contains a weak (negative/positive) charge. When the neuron is stimulated, the cell membrane becomes more permeable. This allows positively charged ____________ ions to flow into the cell, thus lessening the cell's negative charge.

3-2. The change in the charge of the cell caused by the inflow of positively charged sodium ions, called an ____________ potential, travels down the ________________ of the neuron. After the firing of an action potential, there is a brief period in which no further action potentials can be generated. This brief period is called the absolute ____________ period.

3-3. The text likens the neuron to a gun in that it either fires or does not fire. This property of the neuron is called the ________________ law. Neurons transmit information about the strength of a stimulus by variations in the number of action potentials generated. For example, in comparison to a weak stimulus, a strong stimulus will generate a (higher/lower) rate of action potentials.

Answers: 3-1. negative, sodium **3-2.** action, axon, refractory **3-3.** all or none, higher.

4. Describe how neurons communicate at chemical synapses.

4-1. A neuron passes its message on to another neuron by releasing a chemical messenger into the gap or ____________ that separates it from other neurons. The sending neuron, called the ______________, releases a chemical messenger into the synaptic cleft, which then excites the _____________neuron.

4-2. The chemical messenger that provides this transmitting service is called a _____________. The chemical binds with specifically tuned receptor sites on the postsynaptic neurons. In other words, the receptor sites accept some neurotransmitters and reject __________.

Answers: 4-1. synaptic cleft, presynaptic, postsynaptic **4-2.** neurotransmitter, others.

5. Describe the two types of postsynaptic potentials and how neurons integrate and form neural circuits.

5-1. When the neurotransmitter combines with a molecule at the receptor site, it causes a voltage change at the receptor site called a _____________ potential (PSP). One type of PSP is excitatory and (increases/decreases) the probability of producing an action potential in the receiving neuron. The other type is inhibitory and _____________the probability of producing an action potential.

5-2. Whether or not a neuron fires depends on the number of excitatory PSPs it is receiving and the number of ___________ PSPs it is receiving. PSPs (do/do not) follow the all or none law.

5-3. Put the five steps of communication at the synapse in their correct order (by using the numbers 1 through 5):

_____ The reuptake of transmitters by the presynaptic neuron.

_____ The enzyme inactivation or drifting away of transmitters in the synapse.

_____ The synthesis and storage of transmitters.

_____ The binding of transmitters at receptor sites on the postsynaptic membrane.

_____ The release of transmitters into the synaptic cleft.

5-4. Whether or not a neuron fires depends upon the balance between excitatory PSPs and ___________ PSPs.

5-5. Most neurons are interlocked in complex networks that are constantly changing, eliminating old networks and adding new ones. Which process, adding networks or pruning, plays the larger role in moulding the neural networks?

5-6. Hebb described learning as involving changes that take place at the _____________. Specifically, he postulated that "When an axon of Cell A is near enough to excite a cell B and repeatedly or persistently takes part in firing it, some growth process or metabolic change takes place in one or both cells such that A's efficiency, as one of the cells firing B, is ______________."

Answers: 5-1. postsynaptic, increases, decreases **5-2.** inhibitory, do not **5-3.** (a) 5, (b) 4, (c) 1, (d) 3, (e) 2 **5-4.** inhibitory **5-5.** pruning **5-6.** synapse, increased.

6. Discuss some of the functions of acetylcholine and the monoamine neurotransmitters.

6-1. Our moods, thoughts, and actions all depend on the action of neurotransmitters. For example, the movement of all muscles depends on ________________ (ACh). Like other neurotransmitters, ACh can bind to only specific sites, much like a lock and ____________. However, other chemical substances can fool the receptor sites. For example, an agonist like nicotine can (block/mimic) the action of ACh, while an antagonist like curare can (block/mimic) the action of ACh.

6-2. Three neurotransmitters, dopamine, norepinephrine, and serotonin, are collectively known as ______________. Both Parkinson's and schizophrenia have been linked with alterations in ___________ activity, while the mood changes found in depression have been linked to receptor sites for norepinephrine and ______________. Serotonin also plays a key role in the regulation of ___________ and wakefulness and perhaps ______________ behaviour in animals.

Answers: 6-1. Acetylcholine, key, mimic, block **6-2.** monoamines, dopamine, serotonin, sleep, aggressive.

7. Discuss how GABA, glycine, glutamate, and endorphins are related to behaviour.

7-1. GABA and its partner glycine are peculiar in that they appear to produce only (excitatory/inhibitory) PSPs.

7-2. Glutamate is a major _________ neurotransmitter and contributes to learning and memory, including playing a key role in long-term _________.

7-3. Endorphins are chemicals internally produced by the body that have effects similar to those produced by the drug _____________ and its derivatives. That is, they are able to reduce pain and also induce _____________, such as the "runner's high" sometimes experienced by joggers.

Answers: 7-1. inhibitory **7-2.** excitatory, potentiation **7-3.** opium, pleasure (or euphoria).

ORGANIZATION OF THE NERVOUS SYSTEM

8. Provide an overview of the peripheral nervous system, including its subdivisions.

With approximately 100 billion individual neurons to control, it is important that the central nervous system has some kind of organizational structure. This organizational structure is depicted in Figure 3.6 of the text (page 91), and it will prove helpful if you have this figure in front of you while answering the following questions.

8-1. Answer the following questions regarding the organization of the peripheral nervous system:

(a) What constitutes the peripheral nervous system?

(b) What two subdivisions make up the peripheral nervous system?

(c) What is the role of the afferent and efferent nerve fibres?

(d) What two subdivisions make up the autonomic nervous system?

(e) Describe the opposing roles of the sympathetic and parasympathetic nervous systems.

Answers: 8-1. (a) All of the nerves that lie outside of the brain and spinal cord. (b) The somatic nervous system and the autonomic nervous system. (c) Afferent fibres carry information inward from the periphery, while efferent fibres carry information outward to the periphery. (d) The sympathetic nervous system and the parasympathetic nervous system. (e) The sympathetic system prepares the body for fight or flight, and the parasympathetic system conserves the body's resources.

9. Distinguish between the central nervous system and the peripheral nervous system.

9-1. What are the two parts of the central nervous system?

9-2. What is the name given to all of the nerves that lie outside of the central nervous system?

Answers: 9-1. The brain and the spinal cord. **9-2.** The peripheral nervous system.

LOOKING INSIDE THE BRAIN: RESEARCH METHODS

10. Describe how the EEG, lesioning, ESB, and transcranial magnetic stimulation are used to investigate brain function.

10-1. The electroencephalograph, or ___________, is a device that can measure the brain's ___________ activity. Electrodes are placed on the scalp, and the brain's electrical activity is then monitored by the EEG machine and transformed into line tracings called ___________ waves.

10-2. Answer the following questions regarding the use of lesioning and ESB to investigate brain function:

(a) What are some limitations of studying people such as H.M. who have suffered naturally occurring brain damage?

(b) What technique involves the actual destruction of brain tissue in order to examine the resulting effect on behaviour?

(c) What technique would most likely be employed by a neurosurgeon to map the brain of a patient?

(d) Which techniques employ the use of electrodes and electrical currents?

(e) In what fundamental way does lesioning differ from ESB?

(f) Who is the well-known Canadian neurosurgeon who mapped functions of the brain with mild electrical probes?

10-3. ______________ ______________ ______________ is a technique that allows scientists to temporarily increase or decrease activity in a specific area of the brain. This allows, for example, the creation of "_____________ _____________" using a painless, noninvasive method, which in turns allows investigators to examine the function of various brain areas.

Answers: 10-1. EEG, electrical, brain **10-2.** (a) Few subjects are available, the location and severity of the damage can't be controlled, and numerous extraneous variables are present. (b) lesioning, (c) ESB, (d) lesioning and ESB, (e) Lesioning is used to actually destroy tissue, whereas ESB is used to merely elicit behaviour. (f) Penfield **10.3** transcranial magnetic stimulation, virtual lesions.

11. Describe the new brain-imaging methods that are used to study brain structure and function.

11-1. There are three new kinds of brain-imaging procedures that have come into recent use. One of these procedures consists of a computer enhanced X-ray machine that compiles multiple X-rays of the brain into a single vivid picture. The resulting images are called ___________ scans. An even newer device that produces clearer three-dimensional images of the brain goes by the name of magnetic resonance imaging scanner, and the images it produces are known as ___________ scans.

11-2. Unlike CT and MRI scans, which can show only the structure of the brain, the positron emission tomography scanner can portray the brain's actual ___________ over time. The images produced by this procedure are called ___________ scans. Newer variations of MRI scans can also monitor brain activity, such as blood and oxygen flow, and thus provide both functional and structural information. These scans are called ______________ magnetic resonance images (fMRI).

Answers: 11-1. CT, MRI **11-2.** activity, PET, functional.

THE BRAIN AND BEHAVIOUR

12. Summarize the key functions of the medulla, pons, cerebellum, and midbrain.

12-1. Three separate structures make up the hindbrain: the cerebellum, the pons, and the medulla. Identify these structures from the descriptions given below.

(a) This structure is essential for executing and coordinating physical movement.

(b) This structure attaches to the top of the spinal cord and controls many essential functions such as breathing and circulation.

(c) This structure forms a bridge of fibres between the brainstem and cerebellum and plays an important role in both sleep and arousal.

12.2 Helping to locate objects in space is one of the major roles of the ______________. In addition, dopamine-releasing neurons originate here and help to regulate the performance of ______________ movements carried out by higher brain centres. It also shares a structure with the hindbrain that is essential for the regulation of sleep and wakefulness as well as modulation of muscular reflexes, breathing, and pain perception. This structure is called the ______________ formation.

Answers: 12-1. (a) cerebellum, (b) medulla, (c) pons **12-2.** midbrain, voluntary, reticular.

13. Summarize the key functions of the thalamus and hypothalamus.

13-1. The structure that serves as a way station for all sensory information headed for the brain is called the ___________. The thalamus also appears to play an active role in ___________ sensory information.

13-2. In addition to its role in controlling the autonomic nervous system and linking the brain to the endocrine system, the hypothalamus also plays a major role in regulating basic biological drives such as fighting, ___________, feeding, and ___________.

Answers: 13-1. thalamus, integrating **13-2**. fleeing, mating.

14. Describe the nature and location of the limbic system, and summarize some of its key functions.

14-1. An interconnected network of structures involved in the control of emotion, motivation, and memory is known as the ___________ system. The hippocampus, for example, appears to play a key role in the formation of ___________. However, the limbic system is best known for its role as the seat of ___________. Electrical stimulation of particular areas of the limbic system in rats (particularly in the medial forebrain bundle) appears to produce intense ___________. These "pleasure centres" actually appear to be neural circuits that release the neurotransmitter ___________.

Answers: 14-1. limbic, memories, emotion, pleasure, dopamine.

15. Name the four lobes in the cerebral cortex, and identify some of their key functions.

15-1. The cerebrum is the brain structure that is responsible for our most complex ___________ activities. Its folded outer surface is called the ___________ cortex. The cerebrum is divided into two halves, known as the right and ___________ cerebral hemispheres. The two hemispheres communicate with each other by means of a wide band of fibres called the ___________ ___________.

15-2. Each cerebral hemisphere is divided into four parts called lobes. Match these four lobes (frontal, parietal, occipital, temporal) with their key function. (Hint: You can remember these, in order starting from the front of the hemisphere and going around clockwise, with the acronym "FPOT").

_____ (a) Contains the primary motor cortex that controls the movement of muscles.

_____ (b) Contains the primary visual cortex, which initiates the processing of visual information.

_____ (c) Contains the primary auditory cortex, which initiates the processing of auditory information.

_____ (d) Contains the primary somatosensory cortex that registers the sense of touch.

15-3. The prefrontal cortex seems to play an active role in higher-order functions involving working memory and relational reasoning, suggesting to some that it houses an "executive ____________ system."

Answers: 15-1. mental, cerebral, left, corpus callosum **15-2.** (a) frontal, (b) occipital, (c) temporal, (d) parietal **15-3.** control.

16. Summarize evidence on the brain's plasticity.

16-1. The brain's ability to change structure and function is known as plasticity. One line of evidence supporting plasticity is that ____________ can sculpt the brain, as when string musicians show an enlarged representation of left-hand fingers in the somatosensory cortex.

16.2. A second line of evidence for plasticity is that neural reorganization often follows ____________ of brain tissue.

16.3 A third line of evidence is ____________, or the formation of new neurons. Adults have been shown to form new neurons in the olfactory bulb and the ____________. Some believe that neurogenesis helps contribute to the natural repair processes that occur after brain damage.

Answers: 16-1. experience **16.2** destruction **16.3** neurogenesis, hippocampus.

RIGHT BRAIN/LEFT BRAIN: CEREBRAL LATERALITY

17. Explain why scientists viewed the left hemisphere as the dominant hemisphere, and describe how split-brain research changed this view.

17-1. Until recent years, it was believed that the left hemisphere dominated a submissive right hemisphere. Evidence for this belief came from several sources, which all seemed to indicate that the left hemisphere played the dominant role with respect to the use of ___________. For example, damage to an area in the frontal lobe known as ___________ area was associated with speech deficits. Also, damage to another area located in the temporal lobe was found to be associated with difficulty in speech comprehension. This area is called ___________ area. Both of these areas are located in the ___________ cerebral hemisphere.

17-2. Answer the following questions regarding split-brain research:

(a) What was the result of severing the corpus callosum in these patients?

(b) Which hemisphere was found to be primarily responsible for verbal and language tasks in general?

(c) Which hemisphere was found to be primarily responsible for visual and spatial tasks?

17-3. What can be concluded with respect to hemispheric domination from split-brain studies?

Answers: 17-1. language, Broca's, Wernicke's, left **17-2.** (a) The two cerebral hemispheres could no longer communicate with each other. (b) the left cerebral hemisphere, (c) the right cerebral hemisphere **17-3.** Neither hemisphere dominates; rather, each has its own specialized tasks.

18. Describe how neuroscientists conduct research on cerebral specialization in normal subjects and what this research has revealed.

18-1. Canadian researchers have compared younger and older children on their ability to perform a task involving integration across the two hemispheres. They showed that ___________ children, who have a less mature ___________ ___________, performed less well on such a task, suggesting that a mature corpus callosum is necessary for integration of information across the two hemispheres.

18-2. Researchers have looked at left–right imbalances in the speed of visual or auditory processing in the two hemispheres and (have/have not) observed perceptual asymmetries in normal subjects.

18-3. Answer the following questions regarding the conclusions that can be drawn from the research on hemispheric asymmetry:

(a) Are you more likely to identify verbal stimuli quickly and accurately when presented to the right visual field (left hemisphere) or when presented to the left visual field (right hemisphere)?

(b) Are you more likely to identify visual–spatial information quickly and accurately, such as recognizing a face, when the stimuli are presented to the right visual field (left hemisphere) or when presented to the left visual field (right hemisphere)?

(c) What conclusions can be drawn from the research on normal subjects regarding hemispheric specialization with respect to cognitive tasks?

Answers: 18-1. younger, corpus callosum **18-2.** have **18-3.** (a) when presented to the right visual field (left hemisphere), (b) when presented to the left visual field (right hemisphere), (c) The two hemispheres are specialized to handle different cognitive tasks.

THE ENDOCRINE SYSTEM: ANOTHER WAY TO COMMUNICATE

19. Describe some of the ways in which hormones regulate behaviour.

19-1. Answer the following questions regarding the workings of the endocrine system:

(a) What is the role played by the hormones in the endocrine system?

(b) While many glands comprise the endocrine system, which one functions as a master gland to control the others?

(c) What structure is the real power behind the throne here?

19-2. Fill in the boxes in the diagram below to show the role of the pituitary gland in the "fight or flight" response to stress.

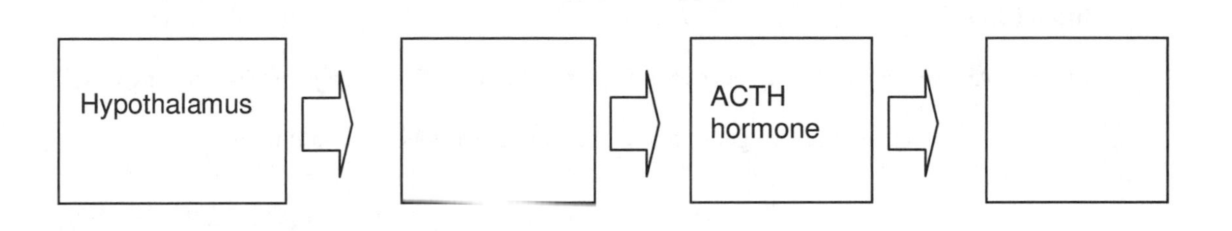

19-3. What is the role of sexual hormones:

(a) Prior to birth?

(b) At puberty?

19-4. Research has examined whether circulating hormones are associated with behaviour. For example, there is evidence that levels of ____________ correlate positively with aggression in both males and females.

Answers: 19-1. (a) They serve as chemical messengers. (b) the pituitary gland, (c) the hypothalamus **19-2.** pituitary, adrenal gland **19-3.** (a) They direct the formation of the external sexual organs. (b) They are responsible for the emergence of the secondary sexual characteristics. **19-4.** testosterone.

HEREDITY AND BEHAVIOUR: IS IT ALL IN THE GENES?

20. Describe the structures and processes involved in genetic transmission.

20-1. When a human sperm and egg unite at conception, they form a one-celled organism called a ___________. This cell contains 46 chromosomes, half of which are contributed by each ___________, thus making 23 pairs. Each member of a pair operates in conjunction with its ___________ member. The zygote then evolves to form all of the cells in the body, each of which has ___________ pairs of chromosomes.

20-2. Each chromosome is actually a threadlike strand of a ___________ molecule, and along this threadlike structure are found the individual units of information, called ___________, that determine our biological makeup. Like chromosomes, genes operate in ___________. For example, type of ear lobe is determined by a pair of genes. If both parents contribute a gene for the same type, the child will inherit this type, and the two genes are said to be ____________. If the parents contribute genes for two different types of ear lobe, the genes are said to be ____________, and the child will inherit the type carried by the dominant gene. When heterozygous genes are paired, the dominant gene masks the ____________ gene.

Answers: 20-1. zygote, parent, opposite, 23 **20-2.** DNA, genes, pairs, homozygous, heterozygous, recessive.

21. Explain the difference between genotype and phenotype and the meaning of polygenic inheritance.

21-1. Answer the following questions about the difference between genotype and phenotype:

(a) What are the two genes that make up your ear lobe type said to be?

(b) What is your resulting ear lobe type said to be?

(c) Can your genotype or phenotype change over time?

21-2. What is meant when it is said that most human traits are polygenic?

Answers: 21-1. (a) your genotype, (b) your phenotype, (c) Only your phenotype can change. **21-2.** They are determined by two or more pairs of genes.

22. Explain the special methods used to investigate the influence of heredity on behaviour.

22-1. If a trait is due to heredity, then more closely related members of a family should show (lesser/greater) resemblance on this trait than less closely related family members. Studies using this method are called ____________ studies. Data gathered from family studies (can/cannot) furnish conclusive proof as to the heritability of a specific trait. Even when it is demonstrated that a particular trait is highly related to the degree of family relationship, the cause for this relationship could be either heredity or ____________.

22-2. A second method in this line of investigation is to compare specific traits across identical twins and fraternal twins. This method, called ____________ studies, assumes that inherited traits are much more likely to be found among (identical/fraternal) twins. These studies do in fact show that for many characteristics, such as intelligence and extraversion, the resemblance is closest for ____________ twins. However, since identical twins are far from identical on these characteristics, ____________ factors must also play a role here.

22-3. A third method in this line of investigation is to study children who have been separated from their biological parents at a very early age and raised by adoptive parents. The idea behind these __________ studies is that if the adoptive children more closely resemble their biological parents with respect to a specific trait, then it can be assumed that __________ plays a major role. On the other hand, if the adoptive children more closely resemble their adoptive parents with respect to a specific trait, it would indicate that __________ plays a major role. Studies using this method to study the heritability of intelligence have found that adoptive children ___________ resemble their biological and adoptive parents on this particular trait. This would indicate that a trait such as intelligence is influenced by both heredity and _____________.

22-4. The process of determining the location and chemical sequence of genes on specific chromosomes is called __________ __________. While single genes responsible for certain medical conditions have been identified, behavioural traits such as intelligence likely involve multiple genes. Such traits are said to be ___________.

Answers: 22-1. greater, family, cannot, environment **22-2.** twin, identical, identical, environmental **22-3.** adoption, heredity, environment, equally, environment **22-4.** genetic mapping, polygenic.

THE EVOLUTIONARY BASES OF BEHAVIOUR

23. Explain the four key insights that represent the essence of Darwin's theory.

23-1. Darwin's four key insights are listed below. Match each one with the statement that best reflects the essence of the insight.

1. Organisms vary in endless ways.
2. Some of these characteristics are heritable.
3. Organisms tend to reproduce faster than the available resources necessary for their survival.
4. If a specific heritable trait contributes to survival or reproductive fitness, its prevalence will increase over generations.

______ (a) The gazelle that runs the fastest is most likely to leave offspring behind.

______ (b) The members of most species die from starvation or other side effects of overcrowding.

______ (c) Birds fly, fish swim, and lions roar.

______ (d) We all have some traits that are very similar to our grandparents'.

Answers: 23-1. 1 (c), 2 (d), 3 (b), 4 (a).

24. Describe some subsequent refinements to evolutionary theory.

24-1. Although contemporary theorists accept Darwin's basic theory of natural selection, they have found that natural selection operates on a gene pool that is also influenced by genetic drift, mutations, and gene flow. Match these terms with the definitions given below.

(a) Spontaneous, heritable changes in a piece of DNA can occur in an individual organism. ______________

(b) Gene frequencies in a population can shift because of emigration (outflow) and immigration (inflow). ______________

(c) There can be random fluctuations in a gene pool. ______________

Answers: 24-1. (a) mutation, (b) gene flow, (c) genetic drift.

25. Provide some examples of animal behaviour that represent adaptations.

25-1. Answer the following questions about behavioural adaptations:

(a) What advantage do grasshoppers gain by being camouflaged?

(b) What advantage do gazelles that stot gain when spotting a cheetah?

Answers: 25-1. (a) It makes detection by a predator more difficult. (b) It increases their chances of escaping.

PUTTING IT IN PERSPECTIVE

26. Explain how this chapter highlighted three of the texts unifying themes.

26-1. Indicate which of the three unifying themes (heredity and environment jointly influence behaviour; behaviour is determined by multiple causes; and psychology is empirical) is particularly illustrated in each of the following situations:

(a) The discovery of the numerous factors that lead to the development of schizophrenia disorders.

(b) The development of many new techniques and instruments that led to the discovery of cerebral specialization.

(c) A new look at the two major factors that influence the development of personal characteristics such as intelligence and temperament.

Answers: 26-1. (a) Behaviour is determined by multiple causes. (b) Psychology is empirical. (c) Heredity and environment jointly influence behaviour.

PERSONAL APPLICATION * EVALUATING THE CONCEPT OF "TWO MINDS IN ONE"

27. Critically evaluate each of the five ideas on cerebral specialization and cognitive processes discussed in the chapter.

27-1. Your text lists five popular ideas that have found support among some neuroscientists and psychologists. These ideas are:

(a) The two hemispheres are _____________ to process different cognitive tasks.

(b) Each hemisphere has its own independent stream of _______________.

(c) The two hemispheres have _____________ modes of thinking.

(d) People vary in their ______________ on one hemisphere as opposed to the other.

(e) Schools should place more emphasis on teaching the ______________ side of the brain.

27-2. We will now proceed through each of these five assumptions to show how each has to be qualified in light of currently available evidence.

(a) The idea that the left and right brains are specialized to handle different kinds of information (is/is not) supported by research. However, there is evidence that this specialization hardly occurs in some persons, while in other persons the specialization is reversed, particularly among ____________handed persons. Moreover, most tasks require the ongoing cooperation of _____________ hemispheres.

(b) The evidence that each hemisphere has its own mind, or stream of consciousness, is actually very weak, except in persons who have undergone __________-__________surgery. The resulting "two minds" in these patients appear to be a byproduct of the surgery.

(c) The assertion that each hemisphere has its own mode of thinking is (plausible/confirmed). A big problem here, however, is that mode of thinking, or cognitive style, has proven difficult to both define and _____________.

(d) The assertion that some people are left-brained while others are right-brained (is/is not) conclusive at this time. Abilities and personality characteristics (do/do not) appear to be influenced by brainedness.

(e) The notion that most schooling overlooks the education of the right brain (does/does not) really make sense. Since both hemispheres are almost always sharing in accomplishing an ongoing task, it would be _________ to teach only one hemisphere at a time.

Answers: 27-1. (a) specialized, (b) consciousness, (c) different, (d) reliance (dependence), (e) right **27-2.** (a) is, left-, both, (b) split-brain, (c) plausible, measure, (d) is not, do not, (e) does not, impossible.

CRITICAL THINKING APPLICATION * BUILDING BETTER BRAINS: THE PERILS OF EXTRAPOLATION

28. Explain how neuroscience research has been overextrapolated by some education and child care advocates who have campaigned for infant schooling.

28-1. Answer the following questions regarding neuroscience research:

(a) What happened to kittens deprived of light to one eye for the first four to six weeks of life?

(b) What happened to kittens deprived of light to one eye for the same amount of time after four months of age?

(c) What is the name given to that early period in the kitten's life when light is essential for the normal development of vision?

(d) What difference was found in synapses in rats that were raised in "enriched" environments when compared to rats raised in "impoverished" environments?

28-2. Answer the following questions regarding the overextrapolation of neuroscience findings:

(a) What findings argue against the notion that brain development is more malleable during the first three years of life?

(b) There are findings that argue against the notion that greater synaptic density is associated with greater intelligence. Which of the following is/are correct?

1. Infant animals and human beings begin life with an overabundance of synaptic connections.
2. Infant animals and human beings begin life with an insufficient number of synaptic connections.
3. Learning involves the pruning of inactive synapses and reinforcing heavily used neural pathways.

Answers: 28-1. (a) They became blind in the light-deprived eye. (b) They did not suffer blindness in that eye. (c) critical period, (d) They had more synapses. **28-2.** (a) It has been found that the brain remains malleable throughout life. (b) 1 and 3 are correct.

Review of Key Terms

Absolute refractory period
Action potential
Adaptation
Adoption studies
Afferent nerve fibres
Agonist
Antagonist
Autonomic nervous system (ANS)
Axon
Behavioural genetics
Central nervous system (CNS)
Cerebral cortex
Cerebral hemispheres
Cerebrospinal fluid (CSF)
Chromosomes
Corpus callosum
Critical period
Dendrites
Dominant gene
Efferent nerve fibres
Electrical stimulation of the brain (ESB)
Electroencephalograph (EEG)
Endocrine system
Endorphins
Excitatory PSP
Family studies
Fitness
Forebrain
Fraternal (dizygotic) twins
Genes
Genetic mapping
Genotype
Glia
Heterozygous condition
Hindbrain
Homozygous condition
Hormones
Hypothalamus
Identical (monozygotic) twins
Inclusive fitness
Inhibitory PSP
Lesioning
Limbic system
Midbrain
Mutation
Myelin sheath
Natural selection
Nerves
Neurogenesis
Neurons
Neurotransmitters
Parasympathetic division
Perceptual asymmetries
Peripheral nervous system
Phenotype
Pituitary gland
Polygenic traits
Postsynaptic potential (PSP)
Recessive gene
Resting potential
Reuptake
Soma
Somatic nervous system
Split-brain surgery
Sympathetic division
Synapse
Synaptic cleft
Terminal buttons
Testosterone
Thalamus
Transcranial magnetic stimulation
Twin studies
Zygote

______________________ 1. An inherited characteristic that increased in a population (through natural selection) because it helped solve a problem of survival or reproduction during the time it emerged.

______________________ 2. A limited time span for the development of an organism that is optimal for certain capacities to emerge because the organism is especially responsive to certain experiences.

______________________ 3. Refers to the reproductive success of an individual organism relative to the average reproductive success in the population.

______________________ 4. Individual cells in the nervous system that receive, integrate, and transmit information.

______________________ 5. Neuron part that contains the cell nucleus and much of the chemical machinery common to most cells.

______________________ 6. Branchlike parts of a neuron that are specialized to receive information.

______________________ 7. A long, thin fibre that transmits signals away from the soma to other neurons, or to muscles or glands.

______________________ 8. An insulating jacket, derived from glia cells that encases some axons.

______________________ 9. Small knobs at the end of the axon that secrete chemicals called neurotransmitters.

______________________ 10. A junction where information is transmitted between neurons.

______________________ 11. The stable, negative charge of an inactive neuron.

________________ **12.** A brief change in a neuron's electrical charge.

________________ **13.** The minimum length of time after an action potential during which another action potential cannot begin.

________________ **14.** A microscopic gap between the terminal buttons of the sending neuron and the cell membrane of another neuron.

________________ **15.** Chemicals that transmit information from one neuron to another.

________________ **16.** A voltage change at the receptor site of a neuron.

________________ **17.** An electric potential that increases the likelihood that a postsynaptic neuron will fire action potentials.

________________ **18.** An electric potential that decreases the likelihood that a postsynaptic neuron will fire action potentials.

________________ **19.** A technique for assessing hereditary influence by examining blood relatives to see how much they resemble each other on a specific trait.

________________ **20.** A chemical that mimics the action of a neurotransmitter.

________________ **21.** A chemical that opposes the action of a neurotransmitter.

________________ **22.** An entire family of internally produced chemicals that resemble opiates in structure and effects.

________________ **23.** System that includes all those nerves that lie outside the brain and spinal cord.

________________ **24.** Bundles of neuron fibres (axons) that travel together in the peripheral nervous system.

________________ **25.** System made up of the nerves that connect to voluntary skeletal muscles and sensory receptors.

________________ **26.** Axons that carry information inward to the central nervous system from the periphery of the body.

________________ **27.** Axons that carry information outward from the central nervous system to the periphery of the body.

________________ **28.** System made up of the nerves that connect to the heart, blood vessels, smooth muscles, and glands.

________________ **29.** The branch of the autonomic nervous system that mobilizes the body's resources for emergencies.

________________ **30.** The branch of the autonomic nervous system that generally conserves bodily resources.

________________ **31.** System that consists of the brain and spinal cord.

________________ **32.** A solution that fills the hollow cavities (ventricles) of the brain and circulates around the brain and spinal cord.

________________ **33.** A device that monitors the electrical activity of the brain over time by means of recording electrodes attached to the surface of the scalp.

________________ **34.** Assessing hereditary influence by comparing the resemblance of identical twins and fraternal twins on a trait.

________________ **35.** Method that involves destroying a piece of the brain by means of a strong electric current delivered through an electrode.

________________ **36.** Method that involves sending a weak electric current into a brain structure to stimulate (activate) it.

_______________ **37.** Part of the brain that includes the cerebellum and two structures found in the lower part of the brainstem, the medulla and the pons.

_______________ **38.** The segment of the brainstem that lies between the hindbrain and the forebrain.

_______________ **39.** Part of the brain encompassing the thalamus, hypothalamus, limbic system, and cerebrum.

_______________ **40.** A structure in the forebrain through which all sensory information (except smell) must pass to get to the cerebral cortex.

_______________ **41.** A structure found near the base of the forebrain that is involved in the regulation of basic biological needs.

_______________ **42.** A densely connected network of structures located beneath the cerebral cortex, involved in the control of emotion, motivation, and memory.

_______________ **43.** The convoluted outer layer of the cerebrum.

_______________ **44.** The right and left halves of the cerebrum.

_______________ **45.** The structure that connects the two cerebral hemispheres.

_______________ **46.** Assessing hereditary influence by examining the resemblance between adopted children and both their adoptive and biological parents.

_______________ **47.** Surgery in which the corpus callosum is severed to reduce the severity of epileptic seizures.

_______________ **48.** System of glands that secrete chemicals into the bloodstream that help control bodily functioning.

_______________ **49.** The chemical substances released by the endocrine glands.

_______________ **50.** The "master gland" of the endocrine system.

_______________ **51.** Threadlike strands of DNA molecules that carry genetic information.

_______________ **52.** A one-celled organism formed by the union of a sperm and an egg.

_______________ **53.** DNA segments that serve as the key functional units in hereditary transmission.

_______________ **54.** A gene that is expressed when the paired genes are different (heterozygous).

_______________ **55.** A gene that is masked when paired genes are heterozygous.

_______________ **56.** A person's genetic makeup.

_______________ **57.** The ways in which a person's genotype is manifested in observable characteristics.

_______________ **58.** Characteristics that are influenced by more than one pair of genes.

_______________ **59.** The sum of an individual's own reproductive success, plus the effects the organism has on the reproductive success of related others.

_______________ **60.** Left–right imbalances between the cerebral hemispheres in the speed of visual or auditory processing.

_______________ **61.** A spontaneous, inheritable change in a piece of DNA that occurs in an individual organism.

_______________ **62.** An interdisciplinary field that studies the influence of genetic factors on behavioural traits.

_______________ **63.** The two genes in a specific pair are the same.

_______________ **64.** The two genes in a specific pair are different.

_______________ **65.** Twins that emerge from one zygote that splits.

_______________ **66.** Twins that result when two eggs are fertilized simultaneously by different sperm cells, forming two separate zygotes.

_______________ **67.** The process of determining the location and chemical sequence of specific genes on specific chromosomes.

_______________ **68.** Posits that heritable characteristics that provide a survival or reproductive advantage are more likely than alternative characteristics to be passed on to subsequent generations and thus come to be selected over time.

_______________ **69.** A process in which neurotransmitters are sponged up from the synaptic cleft by the presynaptic neuron.

_______________ **70.** Cells that provide various types of support for neurons.

_______________ **71.** The formation of new neurons.

_______________ **72.** A male sex hormone produced by the testes.

_______________ **73.** A technique that allows scientists to temporarily increase or decrease activity in an area of the brain.

Answers: 1. adaptation **2.** critical period **3.** fitness **4.** neurons **5.** soma **6.** dendrites **7.** axon **8.** myelin sheath **9.** terminal buttons **10.** synapse **11.** resting potential **12.** action potential **13.** absolute refractory period **14.** synaptic cleft **15.** neurotransmitters **16.** postsynaptic potential (PSP) **17.** excitatory PSP **18.** inhibitory PSP **19.** family studies **20.** agonist **21.** antagonist **22.** endorphins **23.** peripheral nervous system **24.** nerves **25.** somatic nervous system **26.** afferent nerve fibres **27.** efferent fibres **28.** autonomic nervous system (ANS) **29.** sympathetic division **30.** parasympathetic division **31.** central nervous system (CNS) **32.** cerebrospinal fluid (CSF) **33.** electroencephalograph (EEG) **34.** twin studies **35.** lesioning **36.** electrical stimulation of the brain (ESB) **37.** hindbrain **38.** midbrain **39.** forebrain **40.** thalamus **41.** hypothalamus **42.** limbic system **43.** cerebral cortex **44.** cerebral hemispheres **45.** corpus callosum **46.** adoption studies **47.** split-brain surgery **48.** endocrine system **49.** hormones **50.** pituitary gland **51.** chromosomes **52.** zygote **53.** genes **54.** dominant gene **55.** recessive gene **56.** genotype **57.** phenotype **58.** polygenic traits **59.** inclusive fitness **60.** perceptual asymmetries **61.** mutation **62.** behavioural genetics **63.** homozygous condition **64.** heterozygous condition **65.** identical (monozygotic) twins **66.** fraternal (dizygotic) twins **67.** genetic mapping **68.** natural selection **69.** reuptake **70.** glia **71.** neurogenesis **72.** testosterone **73.** transcranial magnetic stimulation.

Review of Key People

John Connelly	Doreen Kimura	Wilder Penfield
Doug Crawford	Bryan Kolb	Candice Pert & Solomon Snyder
Charles Darwin	Maryse Lassonde	Robert Plomin
Donald Hebb	Brenda Milner	Roger Sperry & Michael Gazzaniga
Alan Hodgkin & Andrew Huxley	James Olds	Sandra Witelson

_______________ **1.** Unlocked the mystery of the neural impulse.

_______________ **2.** Known for their work with the split-brain.

_______________ **3.** Showed that morphine works by binding to specific receptors.

____________________ **4.** Discovered “pleasure centres” in the limbic system.

____________________ **5.** One of the leading behaviour genetics researchers in the last decade.

____________________ **6.** Identified natural selection as the mechanism that orchestrates the process of evolution.

____________________ **7.** Studied H.M., who experienced anterograde amnesia.

____________________ **8.** Described the “cell-assembly.”

____________________ **9.** Studied the effects of sex hormones on brain organization.

____________________ **10.** Mapped the brain of epilepsy patients during neurosurgery.

____________________ **11.** Compared the functioning of the corpus callosum in younger and older children.

____________________ **12.** Studied the role of the parietal cortex in visual control of reaching.

____________________ **13.** Has contributed significantly to the study of brain plasticity.

____________________ **14.** Known for his work on “locked-in” syndrome using EEG.

____________________ **15.** Studied the brain of Einstein.

Answers: 1. Hodgkin & Huxley **2.** Sperry & Gazzaniga **3.** Pert & Snyder **4.** Olds & Milner **5.** Plomin **6.** Darwin **7.** Milner **8.** Hebb **9.** Kimura **10.** Penfield **11.** Lassonde **12.** Crawford **13.** Kolb **14.** Connelly **15.** Witelson.

Self-Quiz

1. Most neurons are involved in transmitting information:
a. from one neuron to another
b. from the outside world to the brain
c. from the brain to the muscles
d. from the brain to the glands

2. Which part of the neuron has the responsibility for receiving information from other neurons?
a. the cell body
b. the soma
c. the axon
d. the dendrites

3. The myelin sheath serves to:
a. permit faster transmission of the neural impulse
b. release the neurotransmitter substance
c. add structural strength
d. all of the above

4. The change in the polarity of a neuron that results from the inflow of positively charged ions and the outflow of negatively charged ions is called the:
a. presynaptic potential
b. postsynaptic potential
c. synaptic potential
d. action potential

5. The task of passing a message from one neuron to another is actually carried out by:
a. the myelin sheath
b. the glia cells
c. the action potential
d. neurotransmitters

6. Which of the following techniques is often used by neurosurgeons to map the brain when performing brain surgery?
a. EEG recordings
b. ESB
c. lesioning
d. transcranial magnetic stimulation

7. The seat of emotion is to be found in the:
a. reticular formation
b. hindbrain
c. limbic system
d. forebrain

8. Persons having difficulty with language and speech following an accident that resulted in injury to the brain are most likely to have sustained damage in the:
a. right cerebral hemisphere
b. left cerebral hemisphere
c. right cerebral hemisphere if they are a male and left cerebral hemisphere if they are a female
d. I have no idea what you are talking about

9. In carrying out the "fight or flight" response, the role of supervisor is assigned to the:
a. adrenal gland
b. pituitary gland
c. hypothalamus
d. parasympathetic nervous system

10. A person's current weight and height could be said to exemplify his or her:
a. genotype
b. phenotype
c. both of the above
d. none of the above

11. Which of the following kinds of studies can reveal the specific genes that influence a particular trait?
a. family studies
b. twin studies
c. adoption studies
d. none of the above

12. The Featured Study using PET scan technology to examine memory processing suggested that self-related tasks:
a. uniquely involved left prefrontal brain activity
b. had no unique brain activity associated with it
c. uniquely involved right prefrontal brain activity
d. uniquely involved left and right parietal brain activity

13. Psychology as a science can be said to be:
a. empirical
b. rational
c. analytic
d. both b and c

14. Which of the following statements is/are correct?
a. The right side of the brain is the creative side.
b. The right and left brains are specialized to handle different kinds of information.
c. Language tasks are always handled by the left side of the brain.
d. Most schooling overlooks the education of the right brain.

15. Which of the following is not one of Darwin's four key insights?
a. Some characteristics are heritable.
b. Organisms vary in endless ways.
c. Genetic drift is a major factor in the evolution of species.
d. Organisms tend to reproduce faster than available resources.

16. The ability of the brain to alter its structure and function is called:
a. elasticity
b. plasticity
c. flexibility
d. alterability

17. The evolution of species is:
a. a fact
b. a theory with a few flaws
c. a theory with many flaws
d. a speculation not open to empirical verification

18. Evolutionary analyses assume that:
a. organisms are controlled by genetic determinism
b. organisms have a motive to maximize reproductive fitness
c. only the physically strongest organisms will survive
d. organisms have a motive to copulate

19. Which of the following is correct?
a. Human beings begin life with an insufficient number of synapses.
b. Human beings begin life with an overabundance of synapses.
c. Synaptic density is associated with intelligence.
d. Brain development is only malleable during the first three years of life.

20. The growth of new neurons is called:
a. neurogenesis
b. neurogrowth
c. rejuvenation
d. neural reinstatement

Answers: **1.** a **2.** d **3.** a **4.** d **5.** d **6.** b **7.** c **8.** b **9.** c **10.** b **11.** d **12.** c **13.** a **14.** b **15.** c **16.** b **17.** a **18.** d **19. b**
20. a.

InfoTrac Keywords

Critical Period
Endorphins
Family Studies
Twin Studies

Chapter Four
SENSATION AND PERCEPTION

Review of Key Ideas

PSYCHOPHYSICS: BASIC CONCEPTS AND ISSUES

1. **Explain how stimulus intensity is related to absolute thresholds.**

1-1. You are sitting on a secluded beach at sundown with a good friend. You make a bet as to who can detect the first evening star. Since you have just recently covered this chapter in your text, you explain to your friend that doing so involves the detection of a stimulus threshold. In this case, the first star that provides the minimal amount of stimulation that can be detected is said to have crossed the ____________. All of our senses have thresholds, but research clearly shows that the minimal amount of stimulation necessary to be detected by any one of our senses (is/is not) always the same. Therefore, the absolute threshold is defined as the stimulus intensity that can be detected _____% of the time.

Answers: 1-1. threshold, is not, 50.

2. **Explain Weber's law and Fechner's law.**

2-1. Weber's law states that the size of a just noticeable difference (JND) is a constant proportion of the intensity (size) of the initial stimulus. This means that as a stimulus increases in intensity, the JND increases proportionally as well. Therefore, it would be more difficult to detect a slight increase in the length of a (1-inch/20-inch) line, a slight decrease in a (quiet/loud) tone, or a slight increase in the weight of a (30-ounce/90-ounce) object.

2-2. Fechner's law states that larger and larger increases in stimulus intensity are required to produce perceptible increments, or ________________, in the magnitude of sensation. What this means is that as the intensity of a stimulus increases, the size of the JND we are able to detect (decreases/increases).

Answers: 2-1. 20-inch, loud, 90-ounce **2-2.** JNDs, increases.

3. Explain the basic thrust of signal-detection theory.

3-1. The major idea behind signal detection theory is that our ability to detect signals depends not only on the initial intensity of a stimulus but on other sensory and decision processes as well. One factor that is particularly important here is the criterion you set for how certain you must feel before you react (what are the gains from being correct and what are the losses from being incorrect). What other factor is particularly important here?

3-2. Define each of the four possible outcomes in signal-detection theory:

(a) Hit: ______________________________

(b) Miss: ______________________________

(c) False alarm: ______________________________

(d) Correct rejection: ______________________________

Answers: 3-1. background noise **3-2.** (a) detecting a signal when it is present, (b) failing to detect a signal when it is present, (c) detecting a signal when it is absent, (d) not detecting a signal when it is absent.

4. Describe some evidence on perception without awareness, and discuss the practical implications of subliminal perception.

4-1. Answer the following questions about the study conducted by Karremans, Stroebe, and Claus (2006):

(a) How did the researchers manipulate subliminal perception?

(b) What was their major finding?

4-2. What general conclusions can be drawn from the research on subliminal perception with respect to its potential persuasive effects?

Answers: 4-1. (a) During a task requiring visual detection, they subliminally presented the words "LIPTON ICE" to half of the participants, whereas others were subliminally presented with neutral words. (b) The group exposed to the "LIPTON ICE" stimulus later rated Lipton iced tea more favourably than did the other group. **4-2.** The effects are weak.

5. Discuss the meaning and significance of sensory adaptation.

5-1. Which of the following examples best illustrates what is meant by sensory adaptation?

(a) You are unable to clearly hear the conversation at the next table even though it sounds intriguing, and you are straining to listen.

(b) The strawberries you eat at grandma's farm at the age of 20 seem not to taste as good as when you ate them at the age of 6.

(c) The wonderful smell you encounter upon first entering the bakery seems to have declined considerably by the time you make your purchase and leave.

5-2. If you answered *c* to the above question, you are right on track and understand that sensory adaptation involves a gradual _____________ in sensitivity to prolonged stimulation. This automatic process means that we are not as likely to be as sensitive to the constants in our sensory environments as we are to the _______________.

Answers: 5-1. c **5-2.** decrease, changes.

OUR SENSE OF SIGHT: THE VISUAL SYSTEM

6. List the three properties of light and the aspects of visual perception that they influence.

6-1. Before we can see anything, ___________ must be present. There are three characteristics of light waves that directly affect how we perceive visual objects; match each of these characteristics with its psychological effect:

_____ wavelength	1. colour
_____ amplitude	2. saturation (or richness)
_____ purity	3. brightness

Answers: 6-1. light waves (light), 1, 3, 2.

7. Describe the role of the lens and pupil in the functioning of the eye.

7-1. Getting light rays entering the eye to properly focus on the retina is the job of the _______________. It accomplishes this task by either thickening or flattening its curvature, a process called _______________. Controlling the amount of light entering the eye is the job of the _______________. It accomplishes this task by opening or closing the opening in the centre of the eye, called the _______________.

7-2. Eye movements, or _________________, are considered necessary for optimal visual experience. For example, sensory adaptation would occur without such movements, causing objects to disappear.

Answers: 7-1. lens, accommodation, iris, pupil **7-2.** saccades.

8. Describe the role of the retina in light sensitivity and in visual information processing.

8-1. The structure that transforms the information contained in light rays into neural impulses that are then sent to the brain is called the _______________. All of the axons carrying these neural impulses exit the eye at a single opening in the retina called the optic _______________. Since the optic disk is actually a hole in the retina, this part of the retina cannot sense incoming visual information, and for this reason, it is called the _______________ spot.

8-2. The specialized receptor cells that are primarily responsible for visual acuity and colour vision are called the _______________. The cones are mainly located in the centre of the retina in a tiny spot called the _______________. The specialized receptor cells that lie outside of the fovea and toward the periphery of the retina are called the _______________. The rods are primarily responsible for peripheral vision and for _______________ vision.

8-3. Both dark and light adaptation are primarily accomplished through _______________ reactions in the rods and cones. The chemical reaction occurs more quickly in the _______________, so they are quicker to show both dark adaptation and light adaptation.

8-4. Light rays striking the rods and cones initiate neural impulses that are then transmitted to _______________ cells and then to _______________ cells. From here, the visual information is transmitted to the brain via the axons running from the retina to the brain, collectively known as the _______________ nerve.

8-5. The processing of visual information begins within the receiving area of a retinal cell called the _______________ field. Stimulation of the receptive field of a cell causes signals to be sent inward toward the brain and sideways, or _______________, to nearby cells, thus allowing them to interact with one another. The most basic of these interactive effects, lateral antagonism, allows the retina to compare light falling in a specific area against the general lighting. This allows the visual system to compute the (relative/absolute) levels of light.

Answers: 8-1. retina, disk, blind **8-2.** cones, fovea, rods, night **8-3.** chemical, cones **8-4.** bipolar, ganglion, optic **8-5.** receptive, laterally, relative.

9. Describe the routing of signals from the eye to the brain and the brain's role in visual information processing.

9-1. Visual information from the right side of the visual field (Figure 4-14 in the text) exits from the retinas of both eyes via the optic nerves and meet at the _______________ chiasm, where it is combined and sent to the _______________ side of the brain. Visual information from the left side of the visual field follows a similar pattern, meeting at the optic chiasm, and then moving on to the _______________ side of the brain.

9-2. After leaving the optic chiasm on their way to the visual cortex, the optic nerve fibres diverge along two pathways. Fill in the missing parts of the pathways below.

Main pathway

(a) Optic chiasm>>>________ ________ ________ (part of the thalamus)>>>Visual cortex

Secondary pathway

(b) Optic chiasm>>>_________ _________ >>> ____________>>>Visual cortex

9-3. The main pathway is subdivided into the magnocellular and parvocellular pathways that simultaneously extract ____________ kinds of information from the same input.

(a) Which channel handles the perception of colour?

(b) Which channel handles the perception of brightness?

9-4. Because the cells in the visual cortex respond very selectively to specific features of complex stimuli, they have been described as _______________detectors. There are two major types of cells in the visual cortex: simple cells and complex cells. Identify them from their descriptions below.

(a) These cells are particular about the width and orientation of a line but respond to any position in their receptive field.

(b) These cells are very particular about the width, orientation, and position of a line.

9-5. There is evidence that cats raised in an environment in which they are never exposed to horizontal lines experience a perceptual deficit on discrimination tasks involving horizontal lines, presumably because development of the __________ is responsive to visual input.

9-6. As signals move further along in the visual processing system, the neurons become (less/more) specialized as to what turns them on, and the stimuli that will activate them become (less/more) complex. For example, cells in the temporal lobe along the "what" pathway best respond to pictures of human ___________, as shown in research by Quiroga and colleagues (2005) demonstrating that specific cells respond differently to different familiar faces or even to the names of the people depicted.

Answers: 9-1. optic, left, right **9-2.** (a) lateral geniculate nucleus, (b) superior colliculus, thalamus **9-3.** different, (a) parvocellular, (b) magnocellular **9-4.** feature, (a) complex cells, (b) simple cells **9-5.** cortex **9-6.** more, more, faces.

10. Identify different methods used in vision research, and describe the McCollough Effect.

10-1. Research methods used by vision researchers include scanning techniques such as ________, microelectrodes, and the study of ____________-_____________ individuals.

10-2. The McCollough Effect is an afterimage phenomenon that reflects both ___________ and ____________ (i.e., line orientation). The fact that some individuals with agnosia (who lacked awareness of line orientation) still experienced the McCollough Effect suggests that the effect (does/does not) depend on conscious form perception.

Answers: 10-1. fMRI, brain-damaged **10-2.** colour, pattern/form, does not.

11. Discuss the trichromatic and opponent process theories of colour vision and the modern reconciliation of these theories.

11-1. The trichromatic theory of colour vision, as its name suggests, proposes three different kinds of receptors (channels) for the three primary colours: red, _______________, and _______________. The opponent process theory of colour vision also proposes three channels for colour vision, but these channels are red versus _______________, yellow versus _______________, and black versus _______________.

11-2. These two theories of colour vision can be used to explain different phenomena. Use T (trichromatic) or O (opponent process) to indicate which theory best explains the following phenomena.

____ (a) The colour of an afterimage is the complement of the original colour.

____ (b) The different kinds of colour blindness suggest three different kinds of receptors.

____ (c) People describing colours often require at least four different names.

11-3. The evidence is now clear that both theories are (incorrect/correct). Each is needed to explain all of the phenomena associated with colour vision. Three different kinds of cones, which are sensitive to each of the three primary colours, have been found in the retina; this supports the _____________ theory. It has also been found that visual cells in the retina, the LGN, and the visual cortex respond in opposite (antagonistic) ways to complementary colours, thus supporting the _____________ _____________ theory.

Answers: 11-1. green, blue, green, blue, white **11-2.** (a) O, (b) T, (c) O **11-3.** correct, trichromatic, opponent process.

12. Distinguish between top-down processing and bottom-up processing.

12-1. The same visual stimulus can result in radically different perceptions, and thus our perceptions of the world are (subjective/objective). We perceive what we expect to perceive (perceptual set), and we may not perceive the unexpected, a phenomenon called _______________ blindness.

12-2. Answer the following questions regarding top-down and bottom-up processing:

(a) Which process appears to assume feature analysis, the process of detecting specific elements in visual input and assembling them into a more complex whole?

(b) Which process appears to account for our ability to rapidly recognize and read long strings of words?

(c) What does the text conclude about which theory is correct?

Answers: 12-1. subjective, inattentional **12-2.** (a) bottom-up processing, (b) top-down processing, (c) Both theories have a place in form perception.

13. Explain the basic premise of Gestalt psychology, and describe Gestalt principles of visual perception.

13-1. The Gestalt view of form perception assumes that form perception is not constructed out of individual elements; rather the form, or whole, is said to be ________________ than the sum of its individual elements. The illusion of movement, called the ________________ phenomenon, is used to support the Gestalt view of form perception because the illusion of movement (is/is not) completely contained in the individual chunks of stimuli that give rise to it. In other words, the illusion, or whole, appears to be ________________ than the sum of its parts.

13-2. Five Gestalt principles of visual perception are illustrated below. Match each illustration with its correct name.

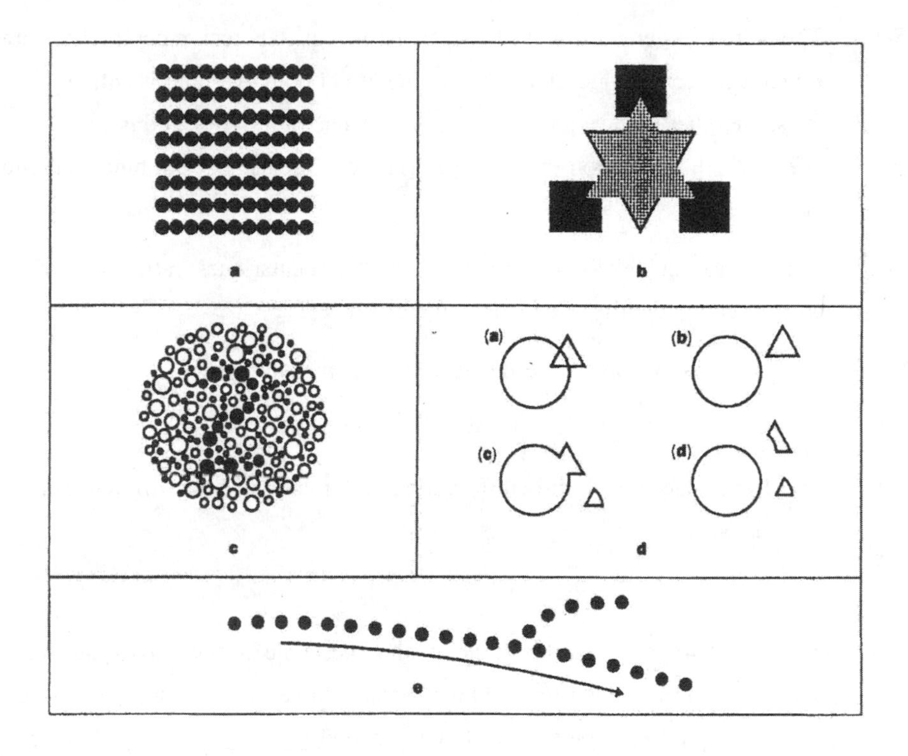

Proximity (a) ________________________________

Similarity (b) ________________________________

Continuity (c) ________________________________

Closure (d) ________________________________

Simplicity (e) ________________________________

13-3. What Gestalt principle is illustrated by the following:

(a) The words printed on this page appear to stand out from the white paper they are printed on.

(b) Things moving in the same direction together get grouped together.

Answers: 13-1. greater (more), phi, is not, greater (more) **13-2.** (a) proximity, (b) closure, (c) similarity, (d) simplicity, (e) continuity **13-3.** (a) figure and ground, (b) common fate.

14. Explain how form perception can be a matter of formulating perceptual hypotheses.

14-1. The objects that surround us in the world outside of our bodies are called ____________ stimuli; the images the objects project on our retinas are called ____________ stimuli. When perceived from different angles or distances, the same distal stimulus projects (similar/different) proximal images on the retina. This forces us to make perceptual ________________ about the distal stimulus.

Answers: 14-1. distal, proximal, different, hypotheses (guesses).

15. Describe the monocular and binocular cues employed in depth perception.

15-1. There are two general kinds of cues that allow us to perceive depth. They are easy to remember because one kind involves the use of both eyes and is called ______________ cues; the other kind requires the use of only one of the eyes and is called ______________ cues. Depth perception (does/does not) require the use of both binocular and monocular cues.

15-2. Here are examples of two different kinds of binocular cues: retinal disparity and convergence. Identify each from these examples:

(a) As a person walks toward you, your eyes turn inward.

(b) The images are slightly different on each retina, and the differences change with distance.

15-3. There are two general kinds of monocular cues. One kind involves the active use of the eye, such as the accommodation used for focusing the eye. The other general kind is used to indicate depth in flat pictures and thus is called ______________ depth cues.

15-4. Identify the following pictorial cues:

(a) Parallel lines grow closer as they recede into the distance.

(b) More distant objects are higher in the field than nearer objects.

(c) When objects appear to be of the same size, closer ones appear larger than more distant ones.

(d) Near objects block or overlap more distant ones.

(e) Texture appears to grow finer as viewing distance increases.

(f) Patterns of light and dark suggest shadows that can create an impression of three-dimensional space.

Answers: 15-1. binocular, monocular, does not **15-2.** (a) convergence, (b) retinal disparity **15-3.** pictorial **15-4.** (a) linear perspective, (b) height in plane, (c) relative size, (d) interposition, (e) texture gradients, (f) light and shadow.

16. Describe perceptual constancies and illusions in vision, and discuss cultural variations in susceptibility to certain illusions.

16-1. The tendency to experience stable perceptions in spite of constantly changing sensory input is called perceptual _______________. For example, even though the retinal image shrinks as a friend walks away, she continues to appear her usual height. This is an example of _______________ constancy.

16-2. Being fooled by the discrepancy between the appearance of a visual stimulus and its physical reality is what is meant by an optical _______________. Both perceptual constancies and optical illusions illustrate the point that we are continually formulating _______________ about what we perceive and also that these perceptions can be quite (subjective/objective).

16-3. What do the variations in cultural susceptibility to certain illusions tell us about our perceptual inferences?

Answers: 16-1. constancy, size **16-2.** illusion, hypotheses, subjective **16-3.** They can be shaped by our experience.

17. Describe the concepts of and the neuroanatomical correlates of vision for perception and vision for action.

17-1. What are the two functions that vision serves?

17-2. The research of Goodale identified two visual pathways in the brain: The _______________ pathway is for perception of the external world, whereas the _______________ pathway is for the visual control of action.

Answers: 17-1. Vision creates an internal representation of the external world (vision for perception), and it is involved in controlling actions toward objects (vision for action) **17-2.** ventral, dorsal.

OUR SENSE OF HEARING: THE AUDITORY SYSTEM

18. List the three properties of sound and the aspects of auditory perception that they influence.

18-1. Name the perceived qualities that are associated with the following properties of sound waves.

Physical property	Description	Perceived quality
(a) purity	kind of mixture	____________
(b) amplitude	wave height	____________
(c) wavelength	wave frequency	____________

Answers: 18-1. (a) timbre, (b) loudness, (c) pitch.

19. Summarize the information on human hearing capacities, and describe how sensory processing occurs in the ear.

19-1. Below are questions concerning human hearing capacities. Match the questions with their correct answers.

Answers	Questions
1. 90 to 120 decibels (dB).	____ (a) What is the frequency range of human hearing?
2. 1,000 to 5,000 Hz.	____ (b) How loud do sounds have to be to cause damage to human hearing?
3. 20 to 20,000 Hz.	____ (c) To what frequency range is human hearing the most sensitive?

19-2. Below is a scrambled sequence of events that occurs when a sound wave strikes the ear. Put these events in their correct order using the numbers 1 through 4.

____ Fluid waves travel down the cochlea, causing the hair cells on the basilar membrane to vibrate.

____ The pinna directs air to the eardrum.

____ The hair cells convert fluid motion into neural impulses and send them to the brain.

____ The motion of the vibrating eardrum is converted to fluid motion by the ossicles.

Answers: 19-1. (a) 3, (b) 1, (c) 2 **19-2.** 3, 1, 4, 2.

20. Compare and contrast the place and frequency theories of pitch perception, and discuss the resolution of the debate.

20-1. One theory of pitch perception assumes that the hair cells respond differentially to pitch depending on their location along the basilar membrane. This is the main idea of the ________________ theory of pitch perception. A second theory assumes a one-to-one correspondence between the actual frequency of the sound wave and the frequency at which the entire basilar membrane vibrates. This is the main idea of the _______________ theory of pitch perception.

20-2. Below are several facts uncovered by research. Tell which theory of pitch is supported by each of these facts.

(a) The hair cells vibrate in unison and not independently.

(b) Even when they fire in volleys, auditory nerves can handle only up to 5000 Hz.

(c) A wave pattern caused by the vibrating basilar membrane peaks at a particular place along the membrane.

20-3. The above facts mean that the perception of pitch depends on both _________________ and _________________ coding.

Answers: 20-1. place, frequency **20-2.** (a) frequency theory, (b) place theory, (c) place theory **20-3.** place, frequency.

21. Discuss the cues employed in auditory localization.

21-1. The sound shadow cast by the head is in a large part responsible for enhancing two important cues used for auditory localization. What are these two cues?

Answers: 21-1. The differences in the intensity and time of arrival of sound waves reaching each ear.

22. Describe the role of music experience in decoding speech prosody.

22-1. Musical aspects of speech, such as its intonation (melody) and stress and timing (rhythm) are referred to as _____________ _____________.

22-2. In the Featured Study, Thompson and his colleagues examined whether _____________ _____________ would enhance the ability to decode emotions from speech prosody. Overall, results of a series of studies suggested that musical training _____________ participants' ability to decode emotions in speech.

Answers: 22-1. speech prosody **22-2.** musical training (note: other forms of training were also included), enhanced.

OUR CHEMICAL SENSES: TASTE AND SMELL

23. Describe the stimuli and receptors for taste, and discuss individual differences in taste perception.

23-1. The stimuli for taste perception are _____________ absorbed in the saliva that stimulate taste cells located in the tongue's ___________ ____________. It is generally thought that there are four fundamental tastes; these are: ____________, ____________, ____________, and ____________.

23-2. What accounts for much of the wide variations in taste preferences among people?

23-3. What are some findings concerning supertasters?

Answers: 23-1. chemicals, taste buds, sweet, sour, salty, bitter (in any order). **23-2.** What they have been exposed to. **23-3.** Supertasters are less fond of sweet and high-fat foods; they react more negatively to alcohol and tobacco; and they respond more negatively to many vegetables.

24. Describe the stimuli and receptors for smell, discuss how well people perform in odour identification tasks, and discuss the role of pheromones.

24-1. The stimuli for the sense of smell are ______________ molecules floating in the air. The receptors for smell are hairlike structures located in the nasal passages, called ______________ ______________. If there are any primary odours, they must be (large/small) in number. Human sensitivity to smell (does/does not) compare favourably with that of many other animals, although some animals surpass us in this respect.

24-2. ______________ are imperceptible chemical messages sent by one organism to another member of the same species. Evidence of pheromones in humans includes the findings of McClintock, who showed that the menstrual cycles of women living together tend to ______________.

Answers: 24-1. chemical, olfactory cilia, large, does. **24-2.** pheromones, converge.

OUR SENSE OF TOUCH: SENSORY SYSTEMS IN THE SKIN

25. Describe processes involved in the perception of pressure and temperature.

25-1. The statements below pertain to either the sense of pressure (P) or the sense of temperature (T). Indicate the correct answers below using the letter P or T.

_____ (a) The somatosensory area of the cortex is the primary receiving area for this sense.

_____ (b) Has receptors specific for either warmth or cold.

_____ (c) The free nerve endings in the skin are in patches that act like receptive fields in vision.

_____ (d) The free nerve endings in the skin fire spontaneously when no stimulus change is being experienced.

Answers: 25-1. (a) P, (b) T, (c) P, (d) T.

26. Describe the two pathways along which pain signals travel, and discuss evidence that the perception of pain is subjective.

26-1. Pain signals travel to the brain by two slightly different pathways. One pathway sends signals directly and immediately through myelinated neurons to the cortex and is called the ______________ pathway. The other sends signals to the cortex through unmyelinated neurons and is called the ______________ pathway. The ______________ pathway mediates lingering, less localized pain.

26-2. Many studies have demonstrated that the perception of pain can be affected by factors such as mood, ethnicity, and culture. Thus, the perception of pain is ________________.

Answers: 26-1. fast, slow, slow **26-2.** subjective.

27. Explain the gate-control theory of pain perception and recent findings related to it.

27-1. Answer the following questions regarding the perception of pain:

(a) What phenomenon did the gate-control theory of pain perception attempt to explain?

(b) What effect do endorphins have with respect to pain?

(c) What seems to be the role of the descending neural pathway that appears to originate in the periaqueductal gray (PAG) area in the midbrain?

27-2. Recent evidence has implicated ______________ cells, such as astrocytes and microglia, in pain modulation.

Answers: 27-1. (a) Why the perception of pain is so subjective. (b) An analgesic, or pain-relieving, effect. (c) It mediates the suppression of pain. **27-2.** glial.

OUR OTHER SENSES

28. Describe the perceptual experiences mediated by the kinesthetic and vestibular senses.

28-1. The system that monitors the positions of various parts of the body is called the ________________ system. This system sends information to the brain about body position and movement obtained from receptors located in the joints and ___muscles___.

28-2. The system that monitors the body's location in space is called the ___vestibular___ system. The receptors for the vestibular system are primarily hair cells contained within the ________________ canals in the inner ear.

28-3. What point does the text make about the kinesthetic and vestibular systems, and indeed all sensory systems, in carrying out their tasks?

Answers: 28-1. kinesthetic, muscles **28-2.** vestibular, semicircular **28-3.** They integrate information from other senses (in carrying out their tasks).

PUTTING IT IN PERSPECTIVE

29. Explain how this chapter highlighted three of the text's unifying themes.

29-1. The fact that competing theories of both colour vision and pitch were eventually reconciled attests to the value of theoretical diversity. Why is this?

29-2. Why must our experience of the world always be highly subjective?

29-3. What do cultural variations in depth perception, taste preferences, and pain tolerance tell us about the physiological basis of perception?

Answers: 29-1. They drove and guided the research that resolved the conflicts. **29-2.** The perceptual processes themselves are inherently subjective. **29-3.** That it is subject to cultural influences.

PERSONAL APPLICATION * APPRECIATING ART AND ILLUSION

30. Discuss how the Impressionists, Cubists, and Surrealists used various principles of visual perception.

30-1. After reading the Personal Application section in your text (pages 179–184), try to answer the following questions by only looking at the paintings:

______ (a) Which Cubist painting depends particularly on the Gestalt principles of continuity and common fate for its effect?

______ (b) Which Surrealist painting makes use of a reversible figure to enhance a feeling of fantasy?

______ (c) Which two Impressionist paintings make use of colour mixing to illustrate how different spots of colours can be blended into a picture that is more than the sum of its parts?

______ (d) Which Cubist painting uses proximity, similarity, and closure to allow you to see its abstract subject (feature analysis applied to canvas)?

Answers: 30-1. (a) Figure 4.61, (b) Figure 4.62, (c) Figures 4.58 and 4.59, (d) Figure 4.60.

31. Discuss how Escher, Vasarely, and Magritte used various principles of visual perception.

31-1. After reading the Personal Application section in your text, try to answer the following questions by only looking at the paintings.

______ (a) Which painting uses variations in context to make identical triangles appear very different?

______ (b) Which two paintings incorporate impossible figures to achieve their effect?

______ (c) Which painting makes particular use of texture gradient and light and dark shadow to convey the impression of depth?

Answers: 31-1. (a) Figure 4.66, (b) Figures 4.63 and 4.64, (c) Figure 4.65.

***CRITICAL THINKING APPLICATION* * RECOGNIZING CONTRAST EFFECTS: IT'S ALL RELATIVE**

32. Explain how contrast effects can be manipulated to influence or distort judgments.

32-1. Which of these contrast strategies is being illustrated in the following situations: the door-in-the-face technique or employing comparitors?

(a) You want to hit the Florida beaches for spring break, but you need extra money from home. Realizing this is going to be a hard sell, you first ask for a week in Paris and then try to settle for the beaches.

(b) When your lover catches you in an indiscretion, you quickly point out many more serious infractions by friends and acquaintances.

32-2. Both of these strategies illustrate the point that our perceptions and judgments are ______________.

Answers: 32-1. (a) the door-in-the-face technique (b) employing comparitors **32-2.** subjective.

Review of Key Terms

Absolute threshold
Additive colour mixing
Afterimage
Auditory localization
Basilar membrane
Binocular depth cues
Bottom-up processing
Cochlea
Colour blindness
Comparitors
Complementary colours
Cones
Convergence
Dark adaptation
Depth perception
Distal stimuli
Door-in-the-face technique
Farsightedness
Feature analysis
Feature detectors
Fechner's law
Fovea
Frequency theory
Gate-control theory
Gustatory system
Impossible figures
Just noticeable difference (JND)
Kinesthetic system
Lateral antagonism
Lens
Light adaptation
Monocular depth cues
Motion parallax
Nearsightedness
Olfactory system
Opponent process theory
Optic chiasm
Optic disk
Optical illusion
Parallel processing
Perception
Perceptual constancy
Perceptual hypothesis
Perceptual set
Pheromones
Phi phenomenon
Pictorial depth cues
Place theory
Proximal stimuli
Psychophysics
Pupil
Receptive field of a visual cell

Retina
Retinal disparity
Reversible figure
Rods
Saccades
Sensation

Sensory adaptation
Signal-detection theory
Subjective contours
Subliminal perception
Subtractive colour mixing
Threshold

Top-down processing
Trichromatic theory
Vestibular system
Visual agnosia
Volley principle
Weber's law

______________ **1.** The stimulation of sense organs.

______________ **2.** The selection, organization, and interpretation of sensory input.

______________ **3.** The study of how physical stimuli are translated into psychological (sensory) experience.

______________ **4.** A dividing point between energy levels that do and do not have a detectable effect.

______________ **5.** The minimum amount of stimulation that can be detected by an organism for a specific type of sensory input

______________ **5.** The minimum amount of stimulation that can be detected by an organism for a specific type of sensory input.

______________ **6.** The smallest amount of difference in the amount of stimulation that can be detected in a sense.

______________ **7.** States that the size of a just noticeable difference is a constant proportion of the size of the initial stimulus.

______________ **8.** Proposes that sensory sensitivity depends on a variety of factors besides the physical intensity of the stimulus.

______________ **9.** Involves a gradual decline in sensitivity to prolonged stimulation.

______________ **10.** States that larger and larger increases in stimulus intensity are required to produce perceptible increments in the magnitude of sensation.

______________ **11.** The transparent eye structure that focuses the light rays falling on the retina.

______________ **12.** The opening in the centre of the iris that helps regulate the amount of light passing into the rear chamber of the eye.

______________ **13.** The neural tissue lining the inside back surface of the eye that absorbs light, processes images, and sends visual information to the brain.

______________ **14.** Specialized receptors that play a key role in daylight vision and colour vision.

______________ **15.** Specialized receptors that play a key role in night vision and peripheral vision.

______________ **16.** A tiny spot in the centre of the retina that contains only cones, where visual acuity is greatest.

______________ **17.** The process in which the eyes become more sensitive to light in low illumination.

______________ **18.** The process in which the eyes become less sensitive to light in high illumination.

______________ **19.** A variety of deficiencies in the ability to distinguish among colours.

______________ **20.** The retinal area that, when stimulated, affects the firing of a particular cell.

_______________ 21. A hole in the retina where the optic nerve fibres exit the eye (the blind spot).

_______________ 22. Neurons that respond selectively to very specific features of more complex stimuli.

_______________ 23. Works by removing some wavelengths of light, leaving less light than was originally there.

_______________ 24. Works by superimposing lights, leaving more light in the mixture than in any one light by itself.

_______________ 25. Proposes that the human eye has three types of receptors with differing sensitivities to different wavelengths.

_______________ 26. Pairs of colours that can be added together to produce grey tones.

_______________ 27. A visual image that persists after a stimulus is removed.

_______________ 28. Proposes that colour is perceived in three channels, where an either-or response is made to pairs of antagonistic colours.

_______________ 29. A drawing compatible with two different interpretations that can shift back and forth.

_______________ 30. A readiness to perceive a stimulus in a particular way.

_______________ 31. A process in which we detect specific elements in visual input and assemble these elements into a more complex form.

_______________ 32. A progression from individual elements to the whole.

_______________ 33. A progression from the whole to the individual elements.

_______________ 34. An apparently inexplicable discrepancy between the appearance of a visual stimulus and its physical reality.

_______________ 35. The illusion of movement created by presenting visual stimuli in rapid succession.

_______________ 36. Stimuli that lie in the distance (in the world outside us).

_______________ 37. The stimulus energies that impinge directly on our sensory receptors.

_______________ 38. An inference about what distal stimuli could be responsible for the proximal stimuli sensed.

_______________ 39. Involves our interpretation of visual cues that tell us how near or far away objects are.

_______________ 40. Clues about distance that are obtained by comparing the differing views of two eyes.

_______________ 41. Clues about distance that are obtained from the image in either eye alone.

_______________ 42. A tendency to experience a stable perception in the face of constantly changing sensory input.

_______________ 43. Locating the source of a sound in space.

_______________ 44. A fluid-filled, coiled tunnel that makes up the largest part of the inner ear.

_______________ 45. A membrane running the length of the cochlea that holds the actual auditory receptors, called hair cells.

_______________ 46. Holds that our perception of pitch corresponds to the vibration of different portions, or places, along the basilar membrane.

_______________ 47. Holds that our perception of pitch corresponds to the rate, or frequency, at which the entire basilar membrane vibrates.

____________________ **48.** Holds that groups of auditory nerve fibres fire neural impulses in rapid succession, creating volleys of impulses.

____________________ **49.** Our sense of taste.

____________________ **50.** Occurs when neural activity in a cell opposes activity in surrounding cells.

____________________ **51.** Objects that can be represented in two-dimensional figures but cannot exist in three-dimensional space.

____________________ **52.** Holds that incoming pain sensations pass through a "gate" in the spinal cord that can be opened or closed.

____________________ **53.** The sense that monitors the positions of the various parts of the body.

____________________ **54.** The system that provides the sense of balance.

____________________ **55.** The point at which the optic nerves from the inside half of each eye cross over and then project to the opposite half of the brain.

____________________ **56.** Clues about distance that can be given in a flat picture.

____________________ **57.** The registration of sensory input without conscious awareness.

____________________ **58.** Involves simultaneously extracting different kinds of information from the same input.

____________________ **59.** A case in which close objects are seen clearly but distant objects appear blurry.

____________________ **60.** A case in which distant objects are seen clearly but close objects are blurry.

____________________ **61.** A depth cue which refers to the fact that objects within 25 feet project images to slightly different locations on your right and left retinas, so the right and left eyes see slightly different images.

____________________ **62.** A binocular cue which involves sensing the eyes converging toward each other as they focus on closer objects.

____________________ **63.** A monocular depth cue which involves images of objects at different distances moving across the retina at different rates.

____________________ **64.** The perception of contours where none actually exist.

____________________ **65.** An inability to recognize familiar objects.

____________________ **66.** Occurs when neural activity in a cell opposes activity in surrounding cells.

____________________ **67.** People, objects, events, and other standards that are used as a baseline for comparison in judgments.

____________________ **68.** Involves making a very large request that is likely to be turned down to increase the chances that people will agree to a smaller request.

____________________ **69.** Chemical messages sent by one organism to another member of the same species.

____________________ **70.** Brief fixations by the eyes as we scan the visual environment.

Answers: 1. sensation **2.** perception **3.** psychophysics **4.** threshold **5.** absolute threshold **6.** just noticeable difference (JND) **7.** Weber's law **8.** signal-detection theory **9.** sensory adaptation **10.** Fechner's law **11.** lens **12.** pupil **13.** retina **14.** cones **15.** rods **16.** fovea **17.** dark adaptation **18.** light adaptation **19.** colour blindness **20.** receptive field of a visual cell **21.** optic disk **22.** feature detectors **23.** subtractive colour mixing **24.** additive colour mixing **25.** trichromatic theory **26.** complementary colours **27.** afterimage **28.** opponent process theory **29.** reversible figure **30.** perceptual set **31.** feature analysis **32.** bottom-up processing **33.** top-down processing **34.** optical illusion **35.** phi phenomenon

36. distal stimuli **37.** proximal stimuli **38.** perceptual hypothesis **39.** depth perception **40.** binocular depth cues **41.** monocular depth cues **42.** perceptual constancy **43.** auditory localization **44.** cochlea **45.** basilar membrane **46.** place theory **47.** frequency theory **48.** volley principle **49.** gustatory system **50.** olfactory system **51.** impossible figures **52.** gate-control theory **53.** kinesthetic system **54.** vestibular system **55.** optic chiasm **56.** pictorial depth cues **57.** subliminal perception **58.** parallel processing **59.** nearsightedness **60.** farsightedness **61.** retinal disparity **62.** convergence **63.** motion parallax **64.** subjective contours **65.** visual agnosia **66.** lateral antagonism **67.** comparitors **68.** door-in-the-face technique **69.** pheromones. **70.** saccades.

Review of Key People

Linda Bartoshuk
Gustav Fechner
Mel Goodale
David Hubel & Torston Wiesel
Ronald Melzack & Patrick Wall
Herman von Helmholtz
Max Wertheimer

_______________ 1. Pioneered the early work in the detection of thresholds.

_______________ 2. These two men won the Nobel Prize for their discovery of feature detector cells in the retina.

_______________ 3. One of the originators of the trichromatic theory of colour vision.

_______________ 4. Made use of the phi phenomenon to illustrate some of the basic principles of Gestalt psychology.

_______________ 5. A leading authority on taste research.

_______________ 6. Proposed a gate-control theory of pain.

_______________ 7. Studied vision for perception and vision for action.

Answers: 1. Fechner **2.** Hubel & Wiesel **3.** Helmholtz **4.** Wertheimer **5.** Bartoshuk **6.** Melzack & Wall **7.** Goodale.

Self-Quiz

1. We have gathered 50 people together to determine the absolute threshold on a particular tone. The absolute threshold will have been reached when:
   a. the first person reports hearing the tone
   b. all persons report hearing the tone
   c. 25 persons report hearing the tone
   d. no persons are able to hear the tone

2. Research shows that subliminal perception:
   a. cannot be reliably demonstrated
   b. produces only weak effects
   c. can exert powerful effects
   d. does not show adaptation effects

3. Which of the following places a major emphasis on subjective factors in the perception of thresholds?
   a. Weber's law
   b. Fechner's law
   c. Steven's power factor
   d. signal detection theory

4. The receiving area of a retinal cell is called the:
   a. cone
   b. foveal field
   c. rod
   d. receptive field

5. The fact that we are generally much more aware of the changes in our sensory environments than we are the constants is the general idea behind:
   a. signal-detection theory
   b. sensory adaptation
   c. the method of constant stimuli
   d. sensory equalization

6. The major difference between a green light and a blue light is the:
   a. wave frequency
   b. wave purity
   c. wavelength
   d. wave saturation

7. Which theory of colour vision best explains why the colour of an afterimage is the complement of the original colour?
   a. the trichromatic theory
   b. the opponent process theory
   c. both theories explain this phenomenon equally well
   d. neither theory adequately explains this phenomenon

8. When watching a wild car chase scene in a movie, we can be thankful for:
   a. chunking
   b. lateral processing
   c. bottom-up processing
   d. the phi phenomenon

9. Which of the following is not one of the pictorial depth cues?
   a. convergence
   b. linear perspective
   c. relative height
   d. texture gradients

10. Which of the following is an example of what is meant by perceptual constancy?
    a. Moths are always attracted to light.
    b. A round pie tin always appears to us as round.
    c. Proximal and distal stimuli are always identical.
    d. Absolute thresholds always remain the same.

11. Gate-control theory is an attempt to explain:
    a. why the perception of pain is so subjective
    b. how subliminal perception works
    c. how receptive fields influence one another
    d. how the optic chiasm directs visual information

12. Research has shown that the perception of pitch depends on:
    a. the area stimulated on the basilar membrane
    b. the frequency at which the basilar membrane vibrates
    c. both the area stimulated and the frequency at which the basilar membrane vibrates
    d. the frequency at which the ossicles vibrate

13. Which of the following is not considered to be one of the four fundamental tastes?
a. sour
b. sweet
c. burnt
d. bitter

14. Our sense of balance depends upon:
a. the semicircular canals
b. the kinesthetic senses
c. visual cues
d. all of the above are involved in our sense of balance

15. Which of the following terms perhaps best describes human perception?
a. accurate
b. objective
c. subjective
d. unknowable

16. Musical experience may affect one's ability to:
a. detect emotion conveyed in the speech of another person
b. perceive certain objects
c. smell certain odours
d. experience certain visual illusions, such as the Muller-Lyer illusion

17. Match the correct visual pathway with the correct visual function.
a. ventral stream; vision for perception
b. rostral stream; vision for action
c. dorsal stream; vision for perception
d. none of the above

18. When politicians point out that their misdeeds are only miniscule when judged against those of their competitors, they are making use of:
a. the door-in-the-face technique
b. comparitors
c. bottom-up processing
d. top-down processing

19. The convergence of the menstrual cycle among women who live together is evidence of:
a. pheromones
b. hormones
c. social learning
d. sensory adaptation

Answers: **1.** c **2.** b **3.** d **4.** d **5.** b **6.** c **7.** b **8.** d **9.** a **10.** b **11.** a **12.** c **13.** c **14.** d **15.** c **16.** a **17.** a **18.** b **19.** a.

InfoTrac Keywords

Dark Adaptation
Depth Perception
Optical Illusions
Reversible Figure

Chapter Five

VARIATIONS IN CONSCIOUSNESS

Review of Key Ideas

ON THE NATURE OF CONSCIOUSNESS

1. **Discuss the nature of consciousness.**

1-1. The personal awareness of internal and external events is how psychologists define ________________. Consciousness is like a moving stream in that it is constantly ________________.

1-2. ___________ ___________ describes people's experience of task-unrelated thoughts, which may take up 15–50% of people's time. Features of mind wandering are that it is less likely to occur during tasks that require significant cognitive ________________, it is associated with (more/less) accurate awareness of external information, and it may be associated with ________________.

1-3. We control some mental processes, but others just seem to happen. ________________ processes refer to thoughts or judgments that we exert some control over, whereas ________________ processes occur without intentional control or effort.

1-4. In the Featured Study on wandering thoughts, the cognitive ability that was thought to affect wandering thoughts was _________ _________ _________ (WMC). It was hypothesized that those with low WMC would engage in (more/less) wandering. The frequency of mind wandering was assessed with _________ _________ methodology, and mind wandering was found to occur about ____% of the time. Those with low WMC did experience more mind wandering relative to those with high WMC, but only during tasks requiring effort and concentration.

Answers: 1-1. consciousness, changing **1-2.** Mind-wandering, resources, less, creativity **1-3.** controlled, automatic **1-4.** working memory capacity, more, event sampling, 33.

2. **Discuss the relationship between consciousness and EEG activity.**

2-1. EEG recordings reveal that there (is/is not) some relationship between brain waves and levels of consciousness. There are four principal bands of brain wave activity, based on the frequency of the wave patterns. These are alpha, beta, delta, and theta. Identify these wave patterns from their descriptions given below.

_____ (a) alert (13–24 cps) _____ (c) asleep (4–7 cps)

_____ (b) relaxed (8–12 cps) _____ (d) deepest sleep (1–4 cps)

2-2. While variations in consciousness are correlated with variations in brain activity, the causal basis of this relationship remains ______________.

Answers: 2-1. is, (a) beta, (b) alpha, (c) theta, (d) delta **2-2.** unknown.

BIOLOGICAL RHYTHMS AND SLEEP

3. **Summarize what is known about our biological clocks and their relationship to sleep.**

3-1. One of the biological rhythms, the daily or 24-hour circadian rhythm, is influential in the regulation of sleep and wakefulness. This is accomplished through the regulation of several bodily processes, including body temperature. Describe below what happens to body temperature when we:

(a) begin to fall asleep

(b) continue into deeper sleep

(c) begin to awaken

3-2. There is evidence that exposure to ________________ is responsible for regulating the 24-hour circadian clock. Sunlight affects the suprachiasmatic nucleus in the hypothalamus, which in turn signals the ________________ gland. The pineal gland then secretes the hormone melatonin, which is a major player in adjusting biological clocks. Getting out of sync with the circadian rhythm is more likely to occur when the days are (shortened/ lengthened). Shift work may also disrupt the circadian rhythm, as evidenced by increased ________________ rates and poorer mental and physical health.

Answers: 3-1. (a) temperature decreases, (b) temperature continues to decrease, (c) temperature begins to increase **3-2.** light (or sunlight), pineal, shortened, accident.

4. Summarize the evidence on the value of melatonin and bright light for resetting biological clocks.

4-1. Research has shown that low doses of melatonin can (circle those that apply):

a. sometimes alleviate the effects of jet lag

b. serve as an effective sedative for some people

c. slow the aging process

d. enhance sex

4-2. Exposure to ___________ ___________ can also improve the sleep quality and alertness in shift workers, although the effects are modest.

Answers: 4-1. Only a and b are correct **4-2.** bright light.

THE SLEEP AND WAKING CYCLE

5. Describe how sleep research is conducted.

5-1. Sleep research is conducted by electronically monitoring various bodily activities such as brain waves, muscular activity, eye movements, and so on, while persons actually ______________ in a specially prepared laboratory setting. Through the use of a television camera or a window, researchers also ______________ the subjects during sleep.

Answers: 5-1. sleep, observe (watch).

6. Describe how the sleep cycle evolves through the night.

6-1. Answer the following questions regarding the sleep cycle.

(a) How many stages are there in one sleep cycle?

(b) Which two stages make up slow-wave sleep?

(c) Which brain waves are prominent during slow-wave sleep?

Answers: 6-1. (a) four (or five if you've included REM sleep) (b) 3 and 4 (c) delta.

7. Compare and contrast REM and NREM sleep.

7-1. What particularly differentiates NREM sleep from rapid eye movement sleep, or ______________ sleep, is that during REM sleep, the brain wave pattern resembles that of a person who is wide ______________. However, REM sleep is actually a fifth stage of sleep in which the muscle tone is extremely relaxed, and the sleeper is virtually ______________. It is also during REM sleep that vivid ______________ is most likely to occur.

7-2. Research suggests that sleep may be important for consolidation of information acquired during the day. In addition, different sleep stages may be related to different types of ____________.

7-3. The sleep cycle is repeated approximately ____________ times during an average night of sleep. NREM sleep dominates the early part of the sleep period, but ____________ sleep and dreaming dominate the later stages of sleep. As one progresses through the night, the depth of NREM sleep tends to progressively (increase/decrease).

Answers: 7-1. REM, awake, paralyzed, dreaming **7-2.** learning **7-3.** four, REM, decrease.

8. Summarize age trends in patterns of sleep.

8-1. Not only do newborns sleep more frequently and for more total hours during a day than do adults, they also spend a greater proportion of time in ____________ sleep. As they grow older, children move toward longer but (more/less) frequent sleep periods, and the total proportion of REM sleep declines from about 50% to the adult level of about _____%. During adulthood there is a gradual shift toward the (lighter/deeper) stages of sleep.

Answers: 8-1. REM, less, 20, lighter.

9. Summarize how culture influences sleep patterns.

9-1. Answer the following questions regarding sleeping patterns across cultures.

(a) Which pattern, children sleeping with their parents (co-sleeping) or children sleeping alone, is the most widely practised?

(b) Where are the "siesta" cultures generally located?

Answers: 9-1. (a) co-sleeping (b) tropical regions.

10. Discuss the neural basis of sleep.

10-1. Sleep and wakefulness is apparently under the control of several neural structures, but one that appears to be particularly essential for both sleep and wakefulness is the reticular ____________. When a part of this system, called the ascending ____________ ____________ system (ARAS), is severed in cats, the cats remain in continuous ____________. When the ARAS is stimulated in normal cats, they act ____________.

10-2. However, many other brain structures and at least five neurotransmitters are also involved in the regulation of sleep. There (is/is not) a "sleep centre" in the brain, nor is there any one neurotransmitter that serves as a ____________ chemical.

Answers: 10-1. formation, reticular activating, sleep, alert or awake **10-2.** is not, sleep.

11. Summarize evidence on the effects of complete and partial sleep deprivation.

11-1. Answer the following questions regarding the effects of different kinds of sleep deprivation.

(a) While both complete and partial sleep deprivation have a negative effect on mood and on performance of both cognitive and perceptual-motor tasks, what is rather surprising about the degree of these negative effects?

(b) In what way might increased sleepiness be a major problem with respect to the workplace?

11-2. Pilcher and Walters showed that sleep-deprived students performed substantially worse on a cognitive task than non-deprived students. How did the sleep-deprived students rate their own effort, concentration, and performance?

Answers: 11-1. (a) The effects tend to be modest. (b) It can lead to increased accidents. **11-2.** They were unaware of these deficits.

12. Discuss the effects of selective deprivation of REM sleep and slow-wave sleep.

12-1. Evidence suggests that REM sleep and slow-wave sleep (SWS) are necessary for memory consolidation of recent experiences. For example, there is a correlation between length of time spent in REM and SWS, on the one hand, and increments in _______________. Reactivation of memories during sleep may also enhance memories in the brain, and sleep may foster _______________ in relation to learning that took place the previous day.

Answers: 12-1. learning, creativity.

13. Discuss the prevalence, causes, and treatments of insomnia.

13-1. While practically everybody will suffer from occasional bouts of insomnia, it is estimated that about _______________ of adults will suffer from insomnia, and of these about _______________ will suffer from chronic problems with insomnia. There are three basic types of insomnia, which are easily remembered because one type occurs at the beginning of sleep, one type during sleep, and the third type at the end of sleep. Thus, one type involves difficulty in initially _______________ asleep; one type involves difficulty in _______________ asleep; and one type involves persistent _______________ awakening.

13-2. While there are a number of different causes of insomnia, most of them appear to revolve around the anxiety and emotional reactions that result from the _______________ of everyday living. Also, health problems or taking certain _______________ can be a factor.

13-3. As there are many different causes of insomnia, it seems reasonable that there (<u>is/is not</u>) a single form of treatment. However, researchers agree that the most commonly used form of treatment, using sedatives, or _____________ pills, is not the treatment of choice. Evidence shows that while sleeping pills do promote sleep, they also interfere with both the slow-wave and ___________ parts of the sleep cycle.

13-4. Longer-lasting benefits may occur with behavioural or ___________-behavioural therapy (CBT). A recent meta-analysis suggests that between _____ and _____% of people with insomnia may benefit from CBT.

Answers: 13-1. 34–35%, 15–17%, falling, remaining, early **13-2.** stress (or problems), drugs **13-3.** is not, sleeping, REM **13-4.** cognitive, 70, 80.

14. Describe the symptoms of narcolepsy, sleep apnea, night terrors, nightmares, and somnambulism.

14-1. Described below are five different case histories of persons suffering from five different sleep disorders. Make the appropriate diagnosis for each one.

(a) Throckmorton is a young child who frequently wakes up during the night with a loud piercing cry, but he cannot describe what happened to him; he usually returns quickly to sleep. A night spent at the sleep clinic discloses that the episodes generally occur during NREM sleep. Throckmorton is most likely suffering from _____________ _____________.

(b) Gazelda reports that occasionally, even when typing a term paper or driving a car, she will quickly drop into a deep sleep. The sleep is often accompanied by dreams, which indicates REM sleep. Gazelda is most likely suffering from _____________.

(c) Ajax is a young child who frequently wakes up terrified and relates vivid dreams to his parents who rush to comfort him. The family physician tells the parents there is probably nothing to worry about, unless these episodes persist, and that the child will most likely outgrow this problem. The diagnosis here is probably _____________.

(d) Mr. Whistletoe will occasionally get up late at night and walk around the house. Unfortunately, Mr. Whistletoe is completely unaware of this behaviour and usually returns to bed without awakening. Upon awakening one morning, he is surprised by a new bruise on his leg, and he wonders how the chair in the living room got tipped over. Mr. Whistletoe would be diagnosed as suffering from _____________, or sleepwalking.

(e) Henrietta complains that during a night's sleep, she frequently wakes up gasping for breath. A visit to the sleep clinic discloses that, indeed, she does stop breathing for brief periods all through the night. Henrietta undoubtedly suffers from _____________ _____________.

Answers: 14-1. (a) night terrors, (b) narcolepsy, (c) nightmares, (d) somnambulism, (e) sleep apnea.

THE WORLD OF DREAMS

15. Discuss the nature of dreams.

15-1. The conventional view of dreams is that they are mental experiences during REM sleep and often have a bizarre storylike quality and vivid imagery. What do many theorists now think of this view?

15-2. In what way do non-REM dreams appear to differ from REM dreams?

Answers: 15-1. They question many aspects of this view. **15-2.** They are less vivid and less storylike.

16. Summarize findings on dream content.

16-1. Calvin Hall, who analyzed the contents of more than 10,000 dreams, concluded that the content of most dreams is (exotic/mundane). They tend to involve __________ settings and people.

16-2. A survey of first-year Canadian university students revealed that the most frequent types of dreams related to being ____________ and to ____________ experiences. Dreams distinctive to women tended to have (negative, positive) themes, including dreams related to phobias and anxiety. Nightmare frequency was about once every _________ _________.

16-3. What did Freud mean when he stated that our dreams reflect day residue?

16-4. What other factor has an inconsistent effect on our dreams?

Answers: 16-1. mundane, familiar **16-2.** chased (or pursued), sexual, negative, two weeks **16-3.** They are influenced by what happens to us in our daily lives. **16-4.** external stimuli (dripping water, ringing phones, etc.).

17. Describe some cultural variations in beliefs about the nature and importance of dreams.

17-1. Identify whether the following statements about dreams are more characteristic of Western cultures (W) or non-Western cultures (NW).

_____________ (a) Little significance paid to the meaning of dreams.

_____________ (b) Remembering dreams is important.

_____________ (c) Dreams can be the focal point of existence.

_____________ (d) These people are likely to report frequent dreams involving food.

Answers: 17-1. (a) W, (b) NW, (c) NW, (d) Persons from any culture who are chronically hungry.

18. Describe the three theories of dreaming covered in the chapter.

18-1. The text mentions three theories about why we need to dream. Tell what cognitive purpose dreaming has, if any, according to each of these theories.

(a) This was Sigmund Freud's theory about the need to dream.

(b) This theory proposed by Rosalind Cartwright is cognizant of the fact that dreams are not restricted by logic or reality.

(c) The activation-synthesis theory of Hobson and McCarley proposes that dreams occur as side effects of neural activation of the cortex by lower brain centres.

Answers: 18-1. (a) Dreams serve the purpose of wish fulfillment. (b) Dreams allow for creative problem-solving. (c) Dreams serve no cognitive purpose.

HYPNOSIS: ALTERED CONSCIOUSNESS OR ROLE PLAYING?

19. Discuss hypnotic susceptibility, and list some prominent effects of hypnosis.

19-1. While there are many different hypnotic induction techniques, they all lead to a heightened state of ____________. Research shows that individuals (do/do not) vary in their susceptibility to hypnotic induction. In fact, approximately ____–____% of the population does not respond at all, and approximately ____–____% are highly susceptible to hypnotic induction. High hypnotizability comprises three components: ____________, which is the capacity to reduce peripheral awareness and narrow the focus of one's attention; ____________, which is the capacity to separate aspects of conscious experience; and ____________, which is the tendency to uncritically accept directions and information.

19-2. The text lists several of the more prominent effects that can be produced by hypnosis. Identify these effects from their descriptions given below.

(a) Reducing awareness of pain. ____________

(b) Engaging in acts one would not ordinarily do. ____________

(c) Perceiving things that do not exist or failing to perceive things that do exist. ____________

(d) Claiming that sour foods taste sweet. ____________ ____________

(e) Carrying out suggestions following the hypnotic induction session. ____________ ____________

(f) Claiming to forget what occurred during the induction session. ____________

Answers: 19-1. suggestibility, do, 10–20, 10–15, absorption, **19-2.** (a) anesthetic, (b) disinhibition, (c) hallucinations, (d) sensory distortions, (e) posthypnotic suggestions, (f) amnesia. dissociation, suggestibility

20. Explain the role-playing and altered-states theories of hypnosis.

20-1. A theory of hypnosis proposed by Barber and Spanos is that hypnosis is really a form of acting or role playing in which the subjects are simply acting as if they are hypnotized. What two lines of evidence support this theory?

20-2. A theory of hypnosis proposed by Hilgard is that hypnosis does in fact result in an altered state of consciousness. This theory holds that hypnosis results in a dissociation or ____________ of consciousness into two parts. One-half of the divided consciousness communicates with the hypnotist while the other half remains ____________, even from the hypnotized subject. In this case, pain perceived by the "hidden" part of the consciousness (is/is not) reported to the "aware" part of the consciousness. The divided state of consciousness proposed by Hilgard (is/is not) a common experience in everyday life. One such example of this commonly experienced state is appropriately called highway ____________.

20-3. Kihlstrom has suggested that these competing perspectives (are/are not) incompatible. Hypnotic phenomena may involve both alterations in consciousness and social interactions shaped by role expectations.

Answers: 20-1. Nonhypnotized subjects can duplicate the feats of hypnotized subjects, and it has been shown that hypnotized subjects are often merely acting out their expectations of how hypnotized subjects should act. **20-2.** splitting or dividing, hidden, is not, is, hypnosis **20-3.** are not.

MEDITATION: PURE CONSCIOUSNESS OR RELAXATION?

21. Summarize the evidence on the physiological correlates and long-term benefits of meditation.

21-1. Certain short-term physiological changes may occur during meditation. One of the most prominent of these changes is that EEG brain waves change from the rapid beta waves to the slower ____________ and theta waves. This change to slower waves is accompanied by (an increase/a decrease) in metabolic activity such as heart rate, oxygen consumption, etc. It is not clear whether these changes are unique to meditation, however.

21-2. The claims made for the long-term effects of meditation may have some merit in that some studies have shown that subjects had lower levels of some stress hormones, improved mental health, and reduced anxiety and drug abuse. These changes can (also/not) be induced by other commonly used methods for inducing relaxation. The claim that meditation can produce a unique state of pure consciousness (has/has not) been conclusively proven.

Answers: 21-1. alpha, a decrease **21-2.** also, has not.

ALTERING CONSCIOUSNESS WITH DRUGS

22. List and describe the major types of abused drugs and their effects.

22-1. The 2004 Canadian Addiction Survey reported that drug use has (increased/decreased) over the past decade. The rate of cannabis use by those aged 18–19 was reported to be _____ %. Somewhat over _____% of those surveyed reported that their use of alcohol or that of others created problems for them.

22-2. The text lists six different categories of psychoactive drugs; identify these drugs from the descriptions given below.

(a) This drug is the most widely used, and abused, of all psychoactive drugs and produces a relaxed euphoria that temporarily boosts self-esteem. Wine and beer are both examples of the drug ________________.

(b) While this class of drugs derived from opium is effective at relieving pain, it can also produce a state of euphoria, which is the principal reason that opiates, or ________________, are attractive to recreational users.

(c) The drugs in this class, such as LSD, mescaline and psilocybin, are known for their ability to distort sensory and perceptual experiences, which is why they are given the collective name of ________________.

(d) The drugs in this class include marijuana, hashish, and THC. Although they vary in potency, each of them can produce a mild and easygoing state of euphoria along with enhanced sensory awareness and a distorted sense of time. This class of drugs gets its name from the hemp plant ________________ from which they are all derived.

(e) This class of drugs is known for its sleep-inducing (sedation) and behavioural depression effects, resulting in tension reduction and a relaxed state of intoxication. While there are several different drugs in this class, the barbiturates are the most widely abused. Commonly known as "downers," they are more properly called ________________.

(f) This class of drugs produces arousal in the central nervous system and ranges from mildly arousing drugs like caffeine and nicotine, to strongly arousing drugs like cocaine and the amphetamines. Known for their ability to produce an energetic euphoria, the drugs in this class go by the name of ________________.

(g) This drug, also known as ecstasy, is a compound related to both amphetamines and mescaline and other hallucinogens. ________________ produces a short-lived high.

Answers: 22-1. increased, 47, 30 **22-2.** (a) alcohol, (b) narcotics, (c) hallucinogens, (d) cannabis, (e) sedatives, (f) stimulants, (g) MDMA.

23. Explain why drug effects vary and how psychoactive drugs exert their effects in the brain.

23-1. Taking a specific drug (will/will not) always have the same effect on the same person. This is because drug effects have ______________ causation; individual, environmental, and drug factors can combine in many ways to produce the final effect. For example, one's expectations can strongly affect reactions to a drug. This is known as the ______________ effect. Moreover, as one continues to take a specific drug, it requires a greater amount of the drug to achieve the same effect. This phenomenon is called drug ______________.

23-2. Psychoactive drugs affect the CNS by selectively influencing ______________ systems in a variety of ways. The action takes place at the juncture between neurons, called the ______________. Amphetamines affect the neurotransmitters ____________ (NE) and ______________ (DA). Opiates bind to ______________ receptors, which elevate the dopamine pathways that modulate ______________. Receptors in the brain for THC, the active ingredient in marijuana, are called ______________ receptors, which are normally activated by endocannabinoids.

23-3. It is now believed that virtually all abused drugs gain their reward effect by (increasing/decreasing) activity in the mesolimbic dopamine pathway, which has been characterized as the "______________ pathway."

Answers: 23-1. will not, multifactorial, placebo, tolerance **23-2.** neurotransmitter, synapse, norepinephrine, dopamine, endorphin, reward, cannabinoid **23-3.** increasing, reward.

24. Summarize which drugs carry the greatest risk of tolerance, physical dependence, and psychological dependence.

24-1. When a person must continue taking a drug to avoid withdrawal illness, addiction, or ______________ dependence, is said to occur. Withdrawal symptoms may be seen as ______________ responses triggered by stimuli paired with drug use in the past. When a person must continue taking a drug to satisfy intense emotional craving for the drug, then ______________ dependence is said to occur.

24-2. The three riskiest drugs in terms of tolerance and physical and psychological dependence are ______________, ______________, and ______________.

24-3. What physiological change in the brain appears to facilitate both physical and psychological dependence?

Answers: 24-1. physical, conditioned, psychological **24-2.** narcotics/opiates, sedatives, stimulants **24-3.** Alterations in synaptic transmission.

25. Summarize evidence on the major physical health risks associated with drug abuse.

25-1. What two physical effects were found in the study in which rats were allowed unlimited access to heroin or cocaine, and which drug was the most deadly?

25-2. There are three major ways in which drugs may affect physical health. The most dramatic way is when a person takes too much of a drug, or drugs, and dies of an ____________. Another way is when drug usage directly damages bodily tissue; this is referred to as a ____________ effect. The third way is when drug usage results in accidents, improper eating and sleeping habits, infections, etc. These effects are collectively called ____________ effects. For example, alcohol can increase students' likelihood of engaging in ____________ sexual behaviour.

Answers: 25-1. loss of body weight and death, cocaine **25-2.** overdose, direct, indirect, risky.

26. Discuss controversies about marijuana's health risks and preliminary evidence on the risks associated with MDMA use.

26-1. Indicate whether the following statements concerning marijuana are true (T) or false (F).

____ (a) Marijuana produces only a slight and insignificant decrease in the immune response.

____ (b) Marijuana can have lasting effects on a male smoker's sexual functioning.

____ (c) Heavy use of marijuana can produce measurable impairments in attention and memory.

26-2. Indicate whether the following statements regarding the long-term use of MDMA are true (T) or false (F).

____ (a) There is evidence linking heavy MDMA use with sleep disorders, depression, anxiety, or hostility.

____ (b) There is no evidence linking MDMA use with subtle effects on cognitive function and memory deficits.

Answers: 26-1. (a) T, (b) F, (c) T **26-2.** (a) T, (b) F.

PUTTING IT IN PERSPECTIVE

27. Explain how the chapter highlighted four of the text's unifying themes.

27-1. Identify which of the underlying themes (psychology evolves in a sociohistorical context; experience is subjective; culture moulds some aspects of behaviour; and psychology is theoretically diverse) is illustrated by the following statements.

(a) Psychologists have followed many different approaches and developed many different theories in their attempt to understand consciousness.

(b) The study of consciousness by psychologists followed rather than preceded renewed public interest in this topic.

(c) There are striking individual differences in the way people respond to hypnosis, meditation, and drugs.

(d) The significance given to dreams and sleep patterns can be influenced by this factor.

Answers: 27-1. (a) Psychology is theoretically diverse. (b) Psychology evolves in a sociohistorical context. (c) Experience is subjective. (d) Culture moulds some aspects of behaviour.

PERSONAL APPLICATION * ADDRESSING PRACTICAL QUESTIONS ABOUT SLEEP AND DREAMS

28. Summarize evidence on common questions about sleep discussed in the Personal Application.

28-1. Answer the following questions about sleep and napping.

(a) How much sleep do we require?

(b) While napping can be refreshing for most people, in what way can it prove inefficient?

(c) Why are drugs such as sedatives and alcohol likely to interfere with refreshing sleep?

(d) What does evidence show about the effectiveness of attempting to learn complex material, such as a foreign language, during deep sleep?

28-2. In addition to developing sensible daytime habits to combat insomnia, there are numerous methods for facilitating actually going to sleep. A common feature in all of them is that they generate a feeling of _____________. Some methods generate a feeling of boredom, which is akin to relaxation. The important point here is that one (does/does not) ruminate on the heavy events in life when attempting to go to sleep.

Answers: 28-1. (a) It varies among individuals. (b) Insufficient time is spent in deeper sleep. (c) They interfere with REM and slow-wave sleep. (d) It is very ineffective. **28-2.** relaxation or calmness, does not.

29. Summarize evidence on the common questions about dreams discussed in the Personal Application.

29-1. While there are some persons who claim they never dream, what is really happening is that they cannot _____________ their dreams. Dreams are best recalled when waking occurs during or immediately following (REM/NREM) sleep. Determination and practice (can/cannot) improve one's ability to recall dreams. A dream whose action takes place over a 20-minute period will actually last for approximately _____________ minutes.

29-2. Freud believed that dreams (do/do not) require interpretation because their true meaning is symbolically encoded in the obvious plot of the dream. Freud's theory that dreams carry hidden symbolic meaning would mean that dream interpretation (is/is not) a very complicated affair. More recent researchers now believe that dreams are (more/less) complicated than Freud believed. Calvin Hall makes the point that dreams require some interpretation simply because they are mostly (visual/verbal).

29-3. In what way does lucid dreaming differ from regular dreaming?

29-4. Indicate whether the following statements are true (T) or false (F).

_____ (a) Evidence shows that some control over one's dreams is possible, but it is not easy and results are not always consistent.

_____ (b) There have been several reported cases of persons reporting their own deaths as the result of fatal dreams.

_____ (c) It has been shown that subjccts can communicate with researchers using prearranged eye signals during lucid dreaming.

Answers: 29-1. remember (or recall), REM, can, 20 **29-2.** do, is, less, visual **29-3.** In lucid dreaming, one is aware that one is dreaming. **29-4.** (a) T, (b) F, (c) T.

***CRITICAL THINKING APPLICATION* * IS ALCOHOLISM A DISEASE: THE POWER OF DEFINITIONS**

30. Discuss the influence of definitions and how they are sometimes misused as explanations for the phenomena they describe.

30-1. Whether alcoholism is a disease or a result of personal failure depends on ____________ gets to make up the definition. In fact, there is (only one/no) conclusive way to determine if alcoholism is a disease.

30-2. To say that someone drinks too much because she is an alcoholic is an example of ______________ reasoning. Definitions can never serve as ______________ of the thing they are defining.

Answers: 30-1. who, no **30-2.** circular, explanations.

Review of Key Terms

Alcohol
Ascending reticular activating system (ARAS)
Biological rhythms
Cannabis
Circadian rhythms
Dissociation
Electroencephalograph (EEG)
Electromyograph (EMG)
Electrooculograph (EOG)
Hallucinogens
Hypnosis
Insomnia
Lucid dreams
MDMA (ecstasy)
Meditation
Mind wandering
Narcolepsy
Narcotics
Nightmares
Night terrors
Non-REM (NREM) sleep
Opiates
Physical dependence
Psychoactive drugs
Psychological dependence
REM sleep
Sedatives
Sleep apnea
Slow-wave sleep (SWS)
Somnambulism
Stimulants
Tolerance

______ 1. A device that monitors the electrical activity of the brain.

______ 2. A device that records muscle activity and tension.

______ 3. A device that records eye movements.

______ 4. Periodic fluctuations in physiological functioning.

______ 5. The 24-hour biological cycles found in humans and many other species.

______ 6. Sleep involving rapid eye movements.

______ 7. Sleep stages 1 through 4, which are marked by an absence of rapid eye movements.

______ 8. Consists of the afferent fibres running through the reticular formation that influence physiological arousal.

______ 9. Drugs that are derived from opium that are capable of relieving pain. These drugs are also called narcotics.

______ 10. Involves chronic problems in getting adequate sleep.

______ 11. A disease marked by sudden and irresistible onsets of sleep during normal waking hours.

______ 12. Reflexive grasping for air that awakens a person and disrupts sleep.

______ 13. Abrupt awakenings from NREM sleep accompanied by intense autonomic arousal and feelings of panic.

______ 14. Anxiety-arousing dreams that lead to awakening, usually from REM sleep.

______ 15. Occurs when a sleeping person arises and wanders about in deep NREM sleep.

______ 16. A systematic procedure that typically produces a heightened state of suggestibility.

______ 17. Involves a splitting off of mental processes into two separate, simultaneous streams of awareness.

______ 18. A family of medical exercises in which a conscious attempt is made to focus attention in a nonanalytical way.

______ 19. Chemical substances that modify mental, emotional, or behavioural functioning.

______ 20. Sleep stages 3 and 4, in which low-frequency delta waves become prominent in EEG recordings.

______ 21. Drugs that have sleep-inducing and behavioural depression effects.

______ 22. Drugs that tend to increase central nervous system activation and behavioural activity.

______ 23. A diverse group of drugs that have powerful effects on mental and emotional functioning, marked most prominently by distortions in sensory and perceptual experience.

______ 24. The hemp plant from which marijuana, hashish, and THC are derived.

______ 25. A variety of beverages containing ethyl alcohol.

______ 26. A progressive decrease in a person's responsiveness to a drug.

______ 27. A condition that exists when a person must continue to take a drug to avoid withdrawal illness.

______ 28. A condition that exists when a person must continue to take a drug to satisfy mental and emotional craving for the drug.

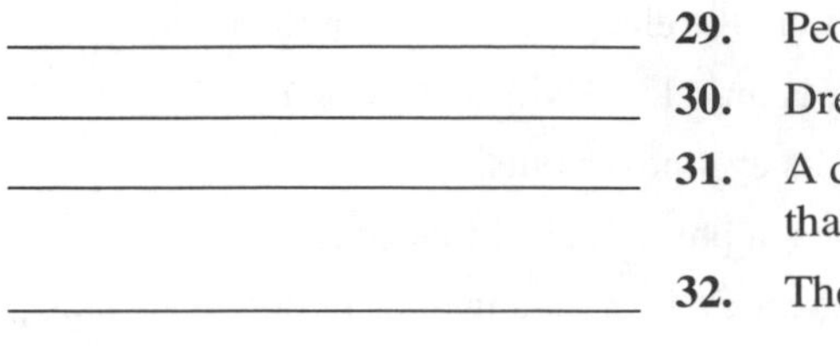

______________________ **29.** People's experience of task-unrelated thoughts.

______________________ **30.** Dreams in which persons are aware that they are dreaming.

______________________ **31.** A drug compounded from both amphetamine and hallucinogens that produces a short-lived high.

______________________ **32.** These drugs are also referred to as opiates.

Answers: 1. electroencephalograph (EEG) **2.** electromyograph (EMG) **3.** electrooculograph (EOG) **4.** biological rhythms **5.** circadian rhythms **6.** REM sleep **7.** non-REM sleep **8**. ascending reticular activating system (ARAS) **9.** opiates **10.** insomnia **11.** narcolepsy **12.** sleep apnea **13.** night terrors **14.** nightmares **15.** somnambulism **16.** hypnosis **17.** dissociation **18.** meditation **19.** psychoactive drugs **20.** slow-wave sleep (SWS) **21.** sedatives **22.** stimulants **23.** hallucinogens **24.** cannabis **25.** alcohol **26**. tolerance **27.** physical dependence **28.** psychological dependence **29.** mind wandering **30.** lucid dreams. **31.** MDMA (ecstasy) **32.** narcotics.

Review of Key People

Theodore Barber	Sigmund Freud	J. Alan Hobson
Rosalind Cartwright	Calvin Hall	William James
William Dement	Ernest Hilgard	Shepard Siegel
		Nicholas Spanos

______________________ **1.** Originated the term "the stream of consciousness."

______________________ **2.** Argued for the existence of the unconscious and the hidden meaning of dreams.

______________________ **3.** As one of the pioneers in early sleep research, he coined the term "REM sleep."

______________________ **4.** After analyzing thousands of dreams, he concluded that their contents are generally quite mundane.

______________________ **5.** Argued that withdrawal effects can be seen as conditioned responses triggered by stimuli associated with drug use.

______________________ **6.** Argued (along with Barber) that hypnotized individuals act out the role of a hypnotic subject.

______________________ **7.** Proposes a problem-solving view as a reason for dreaming.

______________________ **8.** Along with Spanos, one of the authors of the role-playing theory of hypnosis.

______________________ **9.** A proponent of the altered-state (divided consciousness) theory of hypnosis.

______________________ **10.** His activation-synthesis model proposes that dreams are only side effects of neural activation.

Answers: 1. James **2.** Freud **3.** Dement **4.** Hall **5.** Siegel **6.** Spanos **7.** Cartwright **8.** Barber **9.** Hilgard **10.** Hobson.

Self-Quiz

1. Which brain wave is probably operating while you are taking this quiz?
a. alpha
b. beta
c. theta
d. delta

2. What did William James mean by his term “the stream of consciousness”?
a. consciousness always remains at the same level
b. consciousness never stops
c. consciousness is constantly changing
d. consciousness is beyond personal control

3. The circadian rhythm operates around a:
a. 1-year cycle
b. 28-day cycle
c. 24-hour cycle
d. 90-minute cycle

4. The most vivid dreams generally occur during:
a. REM sleep
b. NREM sleep
c. the early hours of sleep
d. when alpha brain waves are present

5. What appears to be responsible for regulating the circadian rhythm?
a. amount of time spent sleeping
b. amount of time spent awake
c. cultural practices
d. exposure to light

6. Severing the ascending reticular activating system in cats caused them to:
a. become very aggressive
b. become very fearful
c. remain in continuous wakefulness
d. remain in continuous sleep

7. The content of most dreams is usually:
a. mundane
b. exotic
c. exciting
d. erotic

8. Which of the following sleep disorders involves frequent stoppages of breathing?
a. nightmares
b. narcolepsy
c. sleep apnea
d. somnambulism

9. Persons can be made to act as if they are hypnotized even without the use of hypnotic induction. This statement is:
a. true
b. false

10. Which of the following physiological changes is unique to meditation?
a. increased alpha rhythms
b. decreased heart rate
c. decreased oxygen consumption
d. all of these thing are common to many forms of relaxation

11. Psychoactive drugs exert their effect on the brain by:
a. decreasing blood supply to the brain
b. altering neurotransmitter activity
c. breaking down essential brain amino acids
d. penetrating the nucleus of the neurons

12. What percentage of Canadians report problematic alcohol use?
a. 10%–20%
b. 5%–10%
c. over 30%
d. over 40%

13. Which of the following is likely to produce highly subjective events?
a. hypnosis
b. meditation
c. psychoactive drugs
d. all of the above can produce highly subjective events

14. Which of the following statements is correct?
a. Most people do not dream in colour.
b. Practice will not improve the ability to recall dreams.
c. From birth until death, everyone dreams.
d. Dreams generally last only 1 or 2 minutes.

15. What was found in the study regarding the effects of sleep deprivation in college students?
a. Sleep deprivation had little effect on their ability to perform cognitive tasks.
b. Sleep deprivation had a substantial negative effect on their mood.
c. Sleep deprivation had a substantial positive effect on their ability to perform cognitive tasks because the students compensated by increasing their effort.
d. The students were unaware of the actual negative effect of the deprivation.

16. What psychological treatment provides long-term, lasting improvement for those with insomnia?
a. dream analysis
b. client-centred therapy
c. psychoanalytic therapy
d. cognitive-behavioural therapy

17. In the Featured Study on wandering thoughts, the cognitive ability that affected frequency of mind wandering was:
a. long-term memory capacity
b. problem-solving ability
c. language capacity
d. working memory capacity

Answers: 1. b **2.** c **3.** c **4.** a **5.** d **6.** d **7.** a **8.** c **9.** a **10.** d **11.** b **12.** c **13.** d **14.** c **15.** d **16.** d **17.** d.

InfoTrac Keywords

Biological Rhythms
Hallucinogens
Meditation
REM Sleep

Chapter Six

LEARNING

Review of Key Ideas

1. Define learning and conditioning, and explain their relevance for understanding the behaviour of humans and other animals.

1-1. Learning is a ___________ ___________ change in behaviour or ____________ that is due to experience. Conditioning is a type of learning in which an organism learns associations between events that occur in its environment.

1-2. These types of learning are relevant to our understanding of behaviour, because they reflect how we acquire knowledge and Skills (such as shooting a puck), and also how we develop habits, personality traits, emotional responses, and personal preferences. Much of our behaviour and the behaviour of other animals reflect learning, and by studying simple forms of learning such as conditioning, we develop the foundation for understanding more complex types of learning.

Answers 1-1. relatively durable, knowledge, associations **1-2.** skills, learning.

CLASSICAL CONDITIONING

2. Describe Pavlov's demonstration of classical conditioning and the key elements in this form of learning.

2-1. Classical conditioning is a type of learning that occurs when two stimuli are paired or associated closely in time. In Pavlov's initial demonstration, the two stimuli were a bell and food.

2-2. The response to one of the two stimuli occurs naturally and does not have to be learned or acquired through conditioning. This "unlearned" stimulus, in this case the food, is technically known as the Unconditioned stimulus.

2-3. The other stimulus is said to be neutral in the sense that it does not initially produce a response. When a response to this neutral stimulus is *acquired* or *learned*, the technical name for it is the Conditioned stimulus. In Pavlov's initial study, the conditioned stimulus was the sound of a bell.

2-4. The unconditioned stimulus in Pavlov's original study was the Food, and the conditioned stimulus was the bell. Salivation to the meat powder is known as the Unconditioned response; salivation to the bell is termed the Condition response.

2-5. Label the parts of the classical conditioning sequence. Place the commonly used abbreviations for these terms in the parentheses.

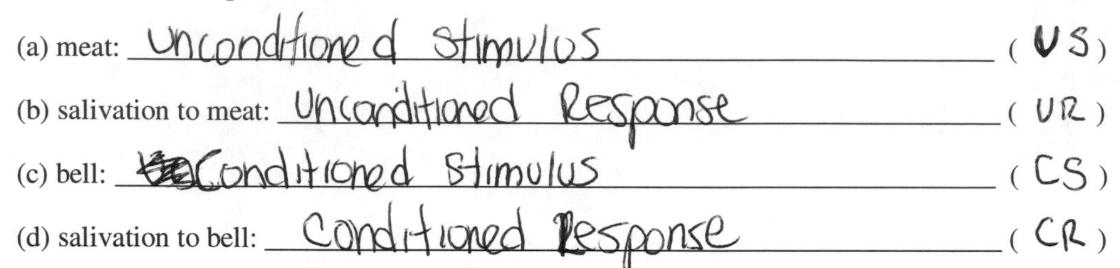

(a) meat: Unconditioned stimulus (US)

(b) salivation to meat: Unconditioned Response (UR)

(c) bell: Conditioned Stimulus (CS)

(d) salivation to bell: Conditioned Response (CR)

Answers: 2-1. meat powder (food) **2-2.** unconditioned **2-3.** conditioned, bell **2-4.** meat powder, bell, unconditioned, conditioned **2-5.** (a) unconditioned stimulus (UCS), (b) unconditioned response (UCR), (c) conditioned stimulus (CS), (d) conditioned response (CR).

3. Discuss how classical conditioning may shape phobias and physiological processes, including drug effects.

3-1. The kids in the neighbourhood where one of us (R.S.) grew up used to dig tunnels in a neighbour's backyard. One day, someone got stuck in the tunnel and couldn't get out. Eventually he got out, but after that, he didn't want to play in tunnels again. To this day, that person still has an intense fear not only of tunnels but of closed-in spaces in general. Label the parts of the classical conditioning process involved in the acquisition of the phobia of closed-in spaces. Use the abbreviations CS, CR, UCS, and UCR. (Hint: Even though "getting stuck" certainly involves a behaviour or response, it also has stimulus components.)

US getting stuck

UR fear produced by getting stuck

CS tunnels and closed-in spaces

CR fear of tunnels and closed-in spaces

3-2. The individual described above had developed an intense fear or phobia, acquired in part through the process of Classical conditioning. Other emotions can be conditioned as well. For example, the playing of a particular song you haven't heard in a while could produce a pleasant emotional response. The song would be considered a Conditioned stimulus.

3-3. Similarly, certain physiological responses can be conditioned. Label the parts of the conditioning process in the study on immunosuppression in rats described in the text. (Use the abbreviations CS, CR, UCS, and UCR.)

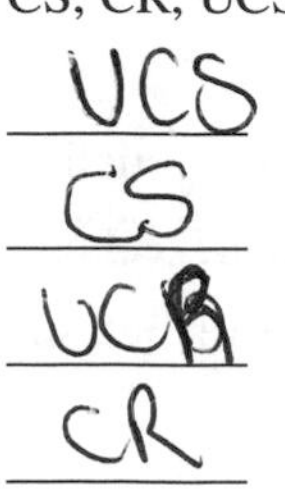

UCS the immunosuppressive drug

CS unusual taste

UCR decreased antibody production produced by the drug

CR decreased antibody production produced by the taste

3-4. Evidently sexual arousal can be classically conditioned as well. For example, quail can be conditioned to become sexually aroused by a neutral stimulus such as a red light if the light has been paired with opportunities to copulate. The red light would be a Conditioned Stimulus. Conditioned arousal produces more sperm, which enhances the likelihood of fertilization and the passing on of one's genes.

3-5. Probably in humans, as in quail, stimuli routinely paired with sex (e.g., lingerie, dim lighting) become Conditioned stimuli for sexual arousal.

3-6. According to Siegel, a drug and its effects can be considered an Unconditioned stimulus, and the body's compensatory response to the drug can be considered an Unconditioned response. Any contextual cue that the drug user is frequently exposed to prior to taking the drug (e.g., nighttime) can come to be a conditioned stimulus, such that over time such stimuli can trigger their own Conditioned response. Because this conditioned compensatory response will grow in strength with repeated drug use under the same conditions, tolerance to the drug may develop. An overdose may occur if drugs are taken in new settings, because of a weaker Conditioned response. Also, exposure to cues that have come to be associated with drug use on occasions when the drug is not used may promote withdrawal symptoms.

Answers: 3-1. UCS, UCR, CS, CR **3-2.** classical, conditioned **3-3.** UCS, CS, UCR, CR. **3-4.** conditioned stimulus **3-5.** conditioned **3-6.** unconditioned, unconditioned, conditioned, conditioned, conditioned, withdrawal.

4. Describe the classical conditioning phenomena of acquisition, extinction, and spontaneous recovery.

4-1. Acquisition of a conditioned response occurs when the CS and UCS are contiguous, or paired. Not all pairings result in conditioning, however. What characteristics of a CS are more likely to produce acquisition of a CR?

4-2. *Acquisition* refers to the formation of a conditioned response. What is the term that refers to the weakening or disappearance of a CR?

4-3. Extinction in classical conditioning occurs when the _______________ stimulus is presented *alone*, without the _______________ stimulus.

4-4. After CRs are extinguished, they may reappear, even without further conditioning.

(a) For example, after extinction of a response, a dog may again show the conditioned response (e.g., salivation to a bell) when returned to the apparatus in which it was originally conditioned. What is the name of this type of "reappearance" of the CR?

(b) When, or under what circumstance, is spontaneous recovery likely to occur?

(b) If an animal is extinguished in a different environment from the one in which conditioning took place, it is likely to again show a CR when returned to the original environment. What is the name of this effect?

Answers: 4-1. A novel or particularly intense CS is more likely to produce conditioning. **4-2.** extinction **4-3.** conditioned, unconditioned **4-4.** (a) spontaneous recovery, (b) after extinction, following a period of nonexposure to the CS, (c) renewal effect.

5. Describe the processes of generalization and discrimination.

5-1. The more similar the stimuli are to the CS, the more likely the organism will _______________ from the CS to the other stimuli. The less similar the stimuli are to the CS, the more likely the organism is to _______________ them from the CS.

5-2. Casey (R.S.'s cat, now deceased) salivated when she heard the sound of food being dumped into her bowl. The process by which this salivary response was learned is _______________ conditioning. The food is a (CS/UCS/CR/UCR). The sound of the food is a (CS/UCS/CR/UCR). Salivation to the sound is a (CS/UCS/CR/UCR).

5-3. Pets are also likely to salivate when they hear other, similar sounds, like bags rustling in the kitchen or dishes being pulled from the cupboard. Salivation to these other sounds represents stimulus _______________.

5-4. With continued training, in which food is paired only with the sound of food entering the bowl and not with the other sounds, the animal will learn to salivate only to the rattling bowl. The process of learning to respond only to one particular stimulus, and not to a range of similar stimuli, is termed _______________.

Answers: 5-1. generalize, discriminate **5-2.** classical, UCS, CS, CR **5-3.** generalization **5-4.** discrimination.

6. Explain what happens in higher-order conditioning.

6-1. Suppose that a bell and meat powder are paired, as in the original Pavlovian study. At some point, a conditioned salivary response to the bell will occur. Suppose that in a new series of trials, a clicking sound (a new, neutral stimulus) is paired with the bell. Assuming that the stimuli are potent enough, that the timing is right, and so on, a conditioned response to the clicking sound will occur.

6-2. The process described above, in which a stimulus that previously functioned as a *conditioned* stimulus was used as an *unconditioned* stimulus, is known as higher-order conditioning.

6-3. In our example, in which the clicking sound and bell were paired, which stimulus acted as the UCS? bell

Answers: 6-1. conditioned **6-2.** higher-order **6-3.** the bell.

OPERANT CONDITIONING

7. Discuss the nature of operant responding in comparison to the types of responding typically governed by classical conditioning.

7-1. A major feature of Pavlovian or classical conditioning is that conditioned responses occur when two stimuli are paired or associated. For example, when a sound and food are paired, a conditioned salivary response occurs to the ________________.

7-2. In contrast, in operant conditioning, learning or conditioning occurs from stimuli that (precede/follow) the response, the stimuli that are the "payoff" or ________________ of that particular behaviour.

7-3. Learning theorists originally supposed that the two types of conditioning controlled different types of responses: that classical conditioning controlled reflexive or (voluntary/involuntary) responses (such as salivation or leg flexion), while operant conditioning controlled voluntary responses. While this distinction holds up (all of the time/much of the time), it is now clear that the only absolute distinction is in terms of procedure.

Answers: 7-1. sound **7-2.** follow, reinforcer (consequence) **7-3.** involuntary, much of the time.

8. Describe Thorndike's work, and explain his law of effect.

8-1. E. L. Thorndike's pioneering work on what he referred to as ________________ learning provided the foundation for Skinner's ________________ conditioning.

8-2. According to Thorndike's law of ________________, if a response leads to a *satisfying effect* in the presence of a stimulus, the association between the stimulus and response is strengthened. Thorndike's law of effect is similar to Skinner's concept of reinforcement: both emphasize the ________________ of behaviour.

Answers: 8-1. instrumental, operant **8-2.** effect, consequences.

9. Describe Skinner's principle of reinforcement and the prototype experimental procedures used in studies of operant conditioning.

9-1. A reinforcer is a stimulus or event that (1) is presented *after* a response and that (2) increases the tendency for the response to be repeated. Apply that definition to this example: Grundoon, a captive monkey, occasionally swings on a bar in his cage. Suppose that at some point Grundoon's trainers decide to give him a spoonful of applesauce whenever he swings. Is the applesauce a reinforcer? In terms of the definition above, how do you know that applesauce is a reinforcer?

9-2. The trainers switch to vinegar. Grundoon, an unusual primate, swings quite frequently when this behaviour is followed by vinegar. Is vinegar a reinforcer here? How do you know?

9-3. The trainers try another approach. They present Grundoon with fresh fruit *just before* they think he is likely to jump. It so happens that Grundoon's rate of jumping does increase. Is the fruit a reinforcer here? Why or why not?

9-4. The prototypical apparatus used in operant conditioning studies is the operant chamber, better known as the ______________ ______________. On one wall of the chamber is mounted a manipulandum, a device that makes for an easily discernible response. For rats, the manipulandum is usually a small ______________; for pigeons, the device is a ______________ that the bird learns to peck.

9-5. A press of the lever or peck at the disk may produce a reinforcer, generally a small bit of food dispensed into the food cup mounted to one side or below the manipulandum. Each of these responses is recorded on a ______________ ______________, a device that creates a graphic record of the number of responses per unit of time.

9-6. The cumulative recorder records the *rate* of the behaviour, that is, the number of ______________ made per unit of ______________.

9-7. Below is a highly stylized version of a cumulative record. About how many responses were made during the first 40 seconds? _______ Which section of the graph (a, b, c, d, or e) has the steepest slope? _______ Which section of the graph illustrates the fastest rate of responding? _______ About how many responses were made between the 40th and 70th seconds? _______

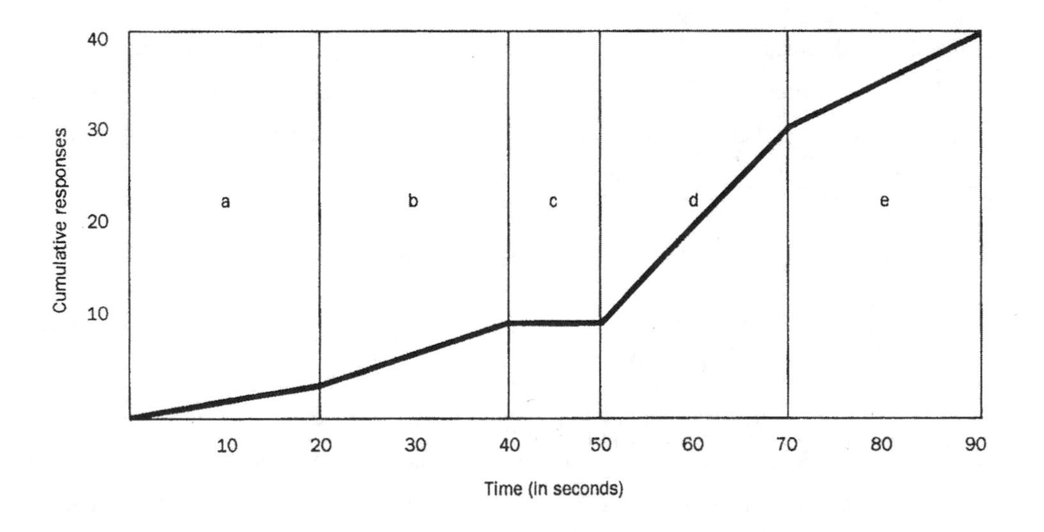

Answers: 9-1. Yes. If the animal's rate of swinging increases when followed by applesauce, then applesauce is a reinforcer. **9-2.** Yes. Because the vinegar is presented *after* the response, and because the response rate *increases*. (Note that this is an imaginary example to illustrate the point that *reinforcement is defined in terms of consequences*, not by subjective judgments about pleasantness and unpleasantness. I don't know of any monkeys that will respond for vinegar.) **9-3.** No. Reinforcing stimuli, by definition, *follow* the response. (Again, this is a contrived example just to illustrate the definition.) **9-4.** Skinner box, lever (or bar), disk **9-5.** cumulative recorder **9-6.** responses, time **9-7.** 10, d, d, 20.

10. Describe the operant conditioning phenomena of acquisition, shaping, and extinction.

10-1. Acquisition refers to the formation of new responses. In classical conditioning, acquisition occurs through a simple pairing of the CS and UCS. In operant conditioning, acquisition usually involves the procedure known as _______________.

10-2. What is shaping? When is it used?

10-3. Extinction in classical conditioning involves removing the UCS while still presenting the CS.

(a) What is the extinction procedure in operant conditioning?

(b) What is the effect of extinction on behaviour (response rate)?

(c) What does the term *resistance to extinction* mean?

Answers 10-1. shaping **10-2.** Shaping is the process of reinforcing closer and closer approximations to the desired behaviour. It is used in the formation of a new response. **10-3.** (a) No longer presenting the reinforcers after a response. (b) Response rate decreases and may eventually stop. (c) Animals may continue to respond, for a period of time, even when reinforcers are no longer presented. The extent to which they will continue to respond during extinction is referred to as *resistance to extinction.*

11. Explain how stimuli govern operant behaviour and how generalization and discrimination occur in operant conditioning.

11-1. Suppose that a rat has been shaped so that when it presses a lever, it receives a food pellet. With further training, the rat may respond only when a light (or sound, etc.) in the chamber is on and not when it is off. The food pellet (which follows the response) is a _______________. The light (which precedes the response) is a _______________ stimulus.

11-2. Reinforcers occur (after/before) the response. Discriminative stimuli occur _______________ the response occurs.

11-3. To create a discriminative stimulus, one reinforces a response only in the presence of a particular stimulus and not in its absence. In time, that stimulus will gain control of the response: animals will tend to emit the response only if the discriminative stimulus is (present/absent) and not if it is _______________.

11-4. For example, rats can be trained to press a lever when a light comes on and not to press when the light is off. Lever presses that occur when the light is on are followed by a food pellet; those that occur in the dark are not. Label each component of this operant-conditioning process by placing the appropriate letters in the blanks below.

______ light (a) discriminative stimulus

______ lever press (b) response

______ food (c) reinforcer

11-5. "Heel, Fido!" says Ralph. Fido runs to Ralph's side. Fido gets a pat on the head. Label the parts of the operant conditioning sequence by placing the appropriate letters in the blanks. (To avoid confusion, the behaviour or response of interest in this example is already labelled.)

______ "Heel, Fido!" (a) discriminative stimulus

______ Fido gets a pat on the head. (b) response

___b___ Fido runs to Ralph's side. (c) reinforcer

11-6. Phyllis will lend money to Ralph, but only after Ralph promises to pay her back. Ralph is also careful to thank Phyllis for her help. The behaviour we are looking at here is Phyllis's lending behaviour.

______ "Thank you very much, Phyllis." (a) discriminative stimulus

___b___ Phyllis lends. (b) response

______ "I promise I'll pay you back." (c) reinforcer

11-7. Generalization occurs in operant as well as classical conditioning. For example, when I put dishes in the sink, our cat would *run to her bowl* looking for food. In technical terms, our cat ________________ between the sound of food dropping in her bowl and the *similar* sound of dishes going into the sink. Despite the fact that food does not follow the sound of clattering dishes, our cat did not learn to ________________ between the sounds in our kitchen.

Answers: 11-1. reinforcer, discriminative **11-2.** after, before **11-3.** present, absent **11-4.** a, b, c **11-5.** a, c, (b) **11-6.** c, (b), a **11-7.** generalizes, discriminate.

12. Discuss primary and secondary (conditioned) reinforcement in operant conditioning.

12-1. Define the following:

(a) Primary reinforcer: biological

(b) Secondary or conditioned reinforcer: external / environment

Answers: 12-1. (a) A primary reinforcer satisfies biological needs, such as needs for food, water, warmth, and sex. (b) A secondary, or conditioned, reinforcer is one that is learned or acquired through association with a primary reinforcer. For humans, secondary reinforcers include praise, attention, and money.

13. Identify various types of schedules of reinforcement, and discuss their typical effects on responding.

13-1. Schedules of reinforcement are either continuous or intermittent. If reinforcers follow each response, the schedule is referred to as a ________________-reinforcement schedule, abbreviated

CRF. If reinforcers follow only some responses and not others (e.g., FR, VR), or occur as a function of the passage of time (e.g., FI, VI), the schedule is referred to as a/an ________________ schedule.

13-2. Identify the following schedules of reinforcement by placing the appropriate abbreviations in the blanks: continuous reinforcement (CRF), fixed ratio (FR), variable ratio (VR), fixed interval (FI), variable interval (VI).

____ A pigeon is reinforced whenever it has pecked a disk exactly 20 times.

____ A pigeon is reinforced for pecking a disk, on the average, 20 times.

____ A rat is always reinforced for the first response that follows a two-minute interval.

____ A slot machine delivers a payoff, on the average, after every 10th pull of the lever.

____ Every time the pigeon pecks a disk, it receives a pellet of food.

____ A rat is reinforced, on the average, for the first response following a two-minute interval.

____ A pig is reinforced for the first response after 30 seconds, then for the first response after 42 seconds, then for the first response after 5 seconds, and so on.

____ Every two weeks Ralph picks up his paycheque at the office.

____ A rat is reinforced after the 73rd response, then after the 22nd response, then after the 51st response, and so on.

13-3. Resistance to extinction refers to the extent to which responses occur during a period of extinction. What is the general effect of the intermittent schedules of reinforcement on resistance to extinction?

13-4. In terms of the effect on *rate* of responding, what is the general difference between the *ratio* schedules (FR and VR) and the *interval* schedules (FI and VI)?

13-5. In terms of the effect on *pattern* of responding, what is the general difference between *fixed* schedules and *variable* schedules?

Answers: 13-1. continuous, intermittent (or partial) **13-2.** FR, VR, FI, VR, CRF, VI, VI, FI, VR **13-3.** The intermittent schedules increase resistance to extinction. **13-4.** Ratio schedules tend to produce more rapid responding than the interval schedules. **13-5.** Variable schedules tend to produce more regular patterns of responding, without pauses or scalloping, than do their fixed counterparts. They also result in more resistance to extinction.

14. Explain the distinction between positive and negative reinforcement.

14-1. Some Skinner boxes may be set up so that a moderate electric shock can be delivered to the feet of the animal through the floor of the box. Suppose that whenever the animal presses the bar, the shock is turned off for a period of time. Will the lever-pressing behaviour be *strengthened* or *weakened*?

14-2. By definition, what effect does reinforcement have on behaviour? What is the effect of positive reinforcement on behaviour? Negative reinforcement?

14-3. With positive reinforcement, a stimulus is *presented* after the response. What is the procedure with negative reinforcement?

Answers: 14-1. strengthened **14-2.** Reinforcement strengthens (increases the frequency of) behaviour. Both positive and negative reinforcement strengthen behaviour. **14-3.** The stimulus (an aversive stimulus) is *removed* after the response.

15. Describe and distinguish between escape learning and avoidance learning.

15-1. Review the section on escape and avoidance learning. In escape learning, the animal first experiences the aversive stimulus and then makes a response that escapes it. In avoidance learning, the animal responds to a cue that permits it to respond *before* the aversive stimulus is delivered, thereby avoiding it altogether. Label the following examples E for escape and A for avoidance.

____ (a) The weather has changed, and Fred is getting cold. He goes inside.

____ (b) Little Sandra rapidly removes her hand from the hot stove.

____ (c) A cue light comes on in a shuttle box. The rat rapidly runs to the other chamber.

____(d) Randolph has been told that he will be mugged if he goes outside, so he stays inside.

____(e) Sue has learned some new verbal behaviour. If she simply says, "No, I don't want that" shortly after a salesman starts his pitch, the salesman will stop bothering her.

____ (f) Alice sees Ruppert in the distance. If Ruppert sees her, he will ask for her course notes, which she doesn't want to lend him. She heads in the other direction.

15-2. What is the major difference between escape learning and avoidance learning?

Answers: 15-1. (a) E, (b) E, (c) A, (d) A, (e) E, (f) A **15-2.** The major difference is that with escape learning there is no cue stimulus, so the animal must first experience the aversive stimulus and then *escape* it. In the case of avoidance learning, a cue preceding the aversive stimulus permits the animal to *avoid* the aversive event altogether.

16. Explain the role of classical conditioning and the role of negative reinforcement in avoidance behaviour.

16-1. Fear of the cue stimulus in avoidance learning is acquired through (classical/operant) conditioning, the association of the stimulus and shock. The running behaviour, on the other hand, is maintained by (classical/operant) conditioning, escape from the conditioned fear.

16-2. Escape increases the strength of a response through (negative/positive) reinforcement. The reason that phobic responses are particularly resistant to extinction is because each time an avoidance response is made, the internal ________________ stimulus is reduced. For example, when people avoid contact with things that they are afraid of (e.g., spiders, elevators, airplanes), they are _______________ reinforced by the removal of conditioned fear. Also, avoidance responses prevent the opportunity to _______________ the conditioned response because these people are never exposed to the conditioned stimulus.

Answers: 16-1. classical, operant **16-2.** negative, fear, negatively, extinguish.

17. Describe punishment and its effects.

17-1. Punishment involves *weakening* a response by presenting an aversive stimulus after the response has occurred or by removing a rewarding stimulus. Review the concepts of reinforcement and punishment by labelling each of the following with one of these terms: *positive reinforcement, negative reinforcement, punishment.*

(a) A stimulus is *presented* after the response; response rate *increases*: _______________

(b) A stimulus is *presented* after the response; response rate *decreases*: _______________

(c) A stimulus is *removed* after the response; response rate *increases*: _______________

(d) A stimulus is *removed* after the response; response rate *decreases*: _______________

17-2. Response rate *increases*. Which of the following procedures may have been used?
a. positive reinforcement
b. negative reinforcement
c. punishment
d. either *a* or *b* above

17-3. Response rate *decreases*. Which of the following procedures may have been used?
a. negative reinforcement
b. positive reinforcement
c. punishment
d. either *b* or *c* above

17-4. When a rat presses a bar in an operant chamber, the electric shock stops. Bar pressing increases. What procedure has been used?
a. positive reinforcement
b. negative reinforcement
c. punishment
d. extinction

17-5. Whenever the dog ran after a car, his master immediately threw a bucket of water on him. The dog stopped running after cars. What procedure was used?
a. positive reinforcement
b. negative reinforcement
c. punishment
d. extinction punishment

17-6. When Randolph spoke back to his parents, they took away his favourite toy. If Randolph stops talking back to his parents, what has occurred?

a. positive reinforcement

b. negative reinforcement

c. punishment

d. bribery

17-7. The use of punishment as a disciplinary procedure for children has drawbacks. For example, punishment is associated with poor parent–child relationships, elevated ________________, delinquency, and an increased likelihood of child ________________. Some of these difficulties will persist into adulthood. Critics of this research have pointed out that the findings should be interpreted as ________________, not ________________.

17-8. When punishment is used, the text suggests the following guidelines: (1) Apply punishment (immediately/after a delay). (2) Use a level of punishment that is (severe/least severe) to be effective. (3) Punish the behaviour consistently (each time/only occasionally) when it occurs. (4) When administering punishment, (explain/do not explain) why it is being given. (5) In general, when employing punishment, try to use (physical punishment/withdrawal of privileges).

Answers: 17-1. (a) positive reinforcement, (b) punishment, (c) negative reinforcement, (d) punishment **17-2.** d **17-3.** c **17-4.** b **17-5.** c **17-6.** c **17-7.** aggression, abuse, correlational, causal **17-8.** immediately, least severe, each time, explain, withdrawal of privileges.

CHANGING DIRECTIONS IN THE STUDY OF CONDITIONING

18. Discuss the phenomena of instinctive drift, conditioned taste aversion, preparedness, and ecological conditioned stimuli.

18-1. What is instinctive drift?

18-2. Why was the occurrence of instinctive drift surprising to operant psychologists? Discuss this question in terms of the supposed *generality* of the laws of learning.

18-3. What is conditioned taste aversion?

18-4. Why is the occurrence of conditioned taste aversion surprising? Discuss this question in terms of classical conditioning relating to (1) CS–UCS delays and (2) the sense of taste compared with other senses.

18-5. Preparedness is Seligman's idea that there are *species-specific* tendencies to be conditioned in some ways and not in others. Both of the findings discussed above, the phenomena of ________________ ________________ and ________________ ________________ ________________ involve the concept of ________________.

18-6. People are much more likely to die in a car than in an airplane, but phobias related to flying are much more common than phobias about driving. Why is this the case? Try to account for this oddity using Seligman's notion of preparedness.

18-7. Domjan argues that, in the real world, conditioned stimuli (are/are not) arbitrary cues unrelated to the unconditioned stimulus. Rather, conditioned stimuli tend to have natural relationships with unconditioned stimuli, such as when specific tastes precede exposure to toxic food. Different patterns of learning may emerge if researchers more frequently studied ________________ ________________ conditioned stimuli. Finally, Domjan argues that conditioning is an ________________ process that occurs in service of reproductive fitness.

Answers: 18-1. It is the tendency for instinctive or innate behaviour to interfere with the process of conditioning. **18-2.** Before the 1960s, operant psychologists assumed that any response that animals could emit could readily be conditioned. This turned out not to be true. Animals may exhibit instinctive drift, the tendency to respond with certain innate behaviours that actually interfere with the process of conditioning. **18-3.** It refers to the somewhat unusual conditioning involving taste and nausea. If the distinctive taste of a particular food is followed some hours later by sickness (nausea, vomiting, etc.), that taste will become aversive and will itself come to elicit the response of nausea. **18-4.** It is surprising because (1) classical conditioning generally does not occur if there are long CS–UCS delays, and (2) taste is only one of several senses stimulated in this situation. Garcia concluded that animals have an innate tendency to associate taste (rather than sight, sound, etc.) with sickness, even though the sickness may occur much later. **18-5.** instinctive drift, conditioned taste aversion, preparedness **18-6.** Seligman's notion of preparedness includes the idea that we are genetically predisposed to develop phobic responses to some stimuli more than to others—to spiders, rodents, and heights more readily than baseballs, lamps, and backyards. Probably because of the heights that are part of flying, flying seems to be more conditionable than driving. **18-7.** are not, ecologically relevant, adaptive.

19. Explain the evolutionary perspective on learning.

19-1. Psychologists used to believe that there were highly general "laws" of learning. More recently, studies like those just referred to, and the developing field of evolutionary psychology, indicate that there probably (are/are not) principles of learning that apply to all species.

19-2. Instead, the new viewpoint emerging among psychologists is that ways of learning have evolved along different paths in different species, so that classical and operant conditioning, for example, are to some extent (universal/species-specific). Finding food, avoiding predators, and reproducing allow a species to survive, but the ways of learning that accomplish these outcomes depend on the ________________ value of these processes.

Answers: 19-1. are not **19-2.** species-specific, adaptive (survival, evolutionary).

20. Describe research on signal relations and response–outcome relations, and explain their theoretical importance.

20-1. In the example of the signal relations study described, the number of conditioning trials in which CS and UCS were paired was the same for two groups, 20 trials. The difference between the two treatment groups was that for one group, the (CS/UCS) was presented *alone* for an additional series of 20 trials.

20-2. Theorists originally assumed that classical conditioning is an automatic, reflexive phenomenon that does not depend at all on higher mental processes. If that actually were true, then what should have been the effect of presenting the UCS alone for additional trials? Remember that both groups received exactly the same number of conditioning trials (CS–UCS pairings).

a. Extinction would occur.

b. The UCS-alone trials would weaken conditioning.

c. The UCS-alone trials would have no effect on conditioning.

20-3. In fact, what did occur in the signal relations studies?

a. Extinction.

b. The UCS-alone trials weakened conditioning.

c. The UCS-alone trials had no effect on conditioning.

20-4. These results suggest that the CS *signals* the occurrence of the UCS and that additional trials with the UCS alone weaken the ________________ value of the CS. What is surprising about these results? Rather than being an automatic, mechanical process, these studies suggest that classical conditioning involves ________________ processes.

20-5. *Response–outcome relations* refers to the connection between an operant response and its consequences. For example, for a rat in a Skinner box, the relationship between the lever press (the response) and the food pellet (the outcome) is this: the rat gets the food *only if* it presses the lever. In other words, the reinforcer is (contingent/not contingent) on the response.

20-6. But does the animal "know" the connection between the response and reinforcer, or is the connection stamped in automatically? That is the crux of the response–outcome relations issue. Evidence suggests that (choose one of the following):

a. reinforcement and punishment are relatively automatic, mindless processes

b. cognition is not involved in an organism's responding in an operant chamber

c. humans and other animals actively try to figure out the contingencies, the relationship between response and outcome

20-7. Thus, research on signal relations and response–outcome relations has forced the development of new theories that emphasize a much more ________________ explanation of conditioning, an explanation in which organisms actively attempt to detect the *relationship* between their behaviours and environmental events.

20-8. Why are the signal relations studies in classical conditioning and response–outcome relations studies in operant conditioning surprising and of theoretical importance?

Answers: 20-1. UCS (If the CS were presented alone, it would be extinction!) **20-2.** c **20-3.** b **20-4.** signalling, cognitive (higher mental) **20-5.** contingent **20-6.** c **20-7.** cognitive **20-8.** These studies indicate that conditioning is not, as assumed earlier, an automatic process but, instead, depends to a considerable degree on higher mental (cognitive) processes.

OBSERVATIONAL LEARNING

21. Discuss the nature and importance of observational learning.

21-1. Observational learning occurs when an organism learns by observing others, who are called ________________. This type of learning occurs in (humans/animals/both).

21-2. Why is the concept of observational learning so important? For one thing, the idea was surprising to theorists who assumed that all learning could be accounted for by operant and classical conditioning. For another, it extends classical and operant conditioning to include not only *direct* experience but ________________ or vicarious experience. We learn not only when we behave but when we ________________ the behaviour of others.

21-3. Bandura's theory has helped explain some puzzling aspects of conditioning in human behaviour. For example, what happens when parents physically punish aggressive behaviour in their children? While punishment by definition (increases/decreases) the behaviour it follows, a parent using physical punishment also serves as a ________________ for aggressiveness. In this way, events intended to decrease aggression may, in the longer run, ________________ aggression through the process of ________________ learning.

Answers: 21-1. models, both **21-2.** indirect, observe **21-3.** decreases, model, increase, observational.

22. List the basic processes in observational learning and discuss Bandura's view on whether reinforcement affects learning or performance.

22-1. In the space below, list and define the four processes that Bandura has identified as crucial components of observational learning. The first letter of each concept is listed at the left.

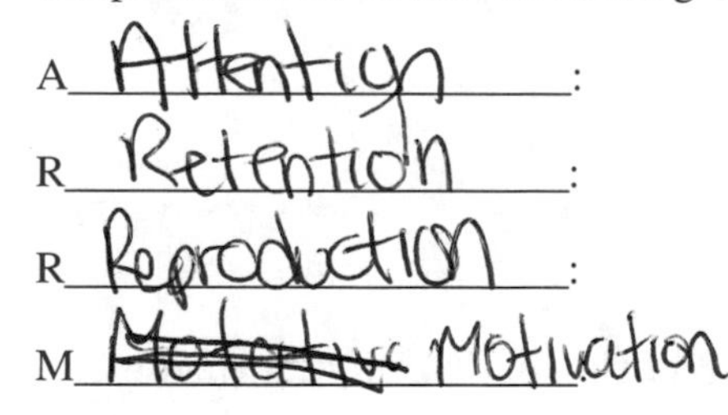

A________________:

R________________:

R________________:

M________________

22-2. Is reinforcement essential for learning? Many learning theorists used to think so, but in Bandura's view, reinforcement is essential only for (learning/performance). Bandura asserts that we may learn, without being reinforced, simply by ________________ the behaviour of a model, but we are unlikely to perform the response unless we are ________________ for doing so.

Answers: 22-1. Attention: Paying attention to a model's behaviour and consequences. Retention: Retaining in memory a mental representation of what one has observed. Reproduction: Having the ability to reproduce what one sees, to convert the image to behaviour. Motivation: Having the inclination, based on one's assessment of the likely payoff, to reproduce the observed behaviour **22-2.** performance, observing, reinforced.

23. Describe research on observational learning and the media violence controversy, including the Featured Study.

23-1. In the Featured Study, Huesmann and colleagues examined whether early exposure to ________________ on television predicted later ________________. Television viewing habits were assessed during childhood, and many years later, the amount of aggression and antisocial behaviour of participants was assessed through various measures, including self-report and report by significant others. Results showed that childhood viewing of violent TV correlated significantly with adult aggressive behaviour for both male and female participants. These findings were upheld even when the researchers controlled for participants' level of _______________ during childhood.

23-2. In the "Bobo Doll" experiment, children who saw a model get rewarded for being aggressive were more likely to be aggressive themselves than were children who saw a model get punished for being aggressive. This demonstrated the effect of observational learning on _______________ of a behaviour. However, all the children behaved aggressively if they were offered a reward for imitating the model's behaviour (i.e., all children revealed evidence of the _______________ of the behaviour).

23-3. Overall, research shows that media violence does foster aggression in both _____________ and _____________. Exposure to video game violence produces (similar/different) results.

Answers: 23-1. violence, aggression, aggression **23-2.** performance, acquisition **23-3.** children, adults, similar.

24. Describe research on mirror neurons and their role in observational learning.

24-1. Mirror neurons are neurons that are activated by performing an _____________ or by seeing another person perform the same action. Therefore, mirror neurons are believed to _____________ _____________ actions. They are found in the frontal and parietal lobes within humans, and may be relevant to our understanding of facial expressions, emotion recognition, empathy, autism, and language learning.

Answers: 24-1. action, internally represent.

PUTTING IT IN PERSPECTIVE

25. Explain how the chapter highlighted two of the text's unifying themes.

25-1. Skinner emphasized the importance of *environmental* events (reinforcers, punishers, discriminative stimuli, schedules of reinforcement) as the determinants of behaviour. One of our unifying themes, however, is that heredity and environment interact. In support of this theme, list the names of three phenomena that show that *biology* has a powerful effect on *conditioning*.

(1) ______________________________

(2) ______________________________

(3) ______________________________

25-2. The second theme well illustrated in this chapter is that psychology evolves in a sociohistorical context. Discuss one concept from operant psychology that appears to have influenced our everyday lives.

Answers: 25-1. instinctive drift, conditioned taste aversion, preparedness **25-2.** Operant psychology has probably influenced the trend in our society toward relying more on the use of positive reinforcement than punishment in child-rearing, in educational settings (e.g., the use of programmed learning), and as a management technique in business.

PERSONAL APPLICATION * ACHIEVING SELF-CONTROL THROUGH BEHAVIOUR MODIFICATION

26. Describe how to specify your target behaviour and gather baseline data for a self-modification program.

26-1. What behaviour do you want to change? The question sounds simple, but the task of defining a ________________ behaviour is often quite tricky.

26-2. The behaviour that you select must be defined in terms of observable events, so that you will know if and when it changes. For example, for the problem of anger control, which of the following would be the most *directly observable* definition of *anger*?

a. inner turmoil

b. intense hostility

c. loud voice and clenched fists

26-3. Once you specify the target behaviour, you must gather ________________ data on your behaviour prior to the intervention. At this time, you should also keep track of events that precede the target behaviour, the ________________ events, and also the positive and negative reinforcers that follow it, the ________________ of your behaviour.

Answers: 26-1. target (specific) **26-2.** c, although even those behaviours would have to be further described in a behaviour modification program. Alternative a is not really observable. Alternative b could be behaviourally defined, but as it stands, it is hard to know precisely which behaviours "intense hostility" refers to.
26-3. baseline, antecedent, consequences.

27. Discuss your options for increasing or decreasing a response in designing a self-modification program.

27-1. To increase a target behaviour, you would use ____________________. The reinforcer (can/cannot) be something that you already are receiving. For example, you probably already watch TV, go to movies, or buy things for yourself, so you could make one of these events ________________ on an increased frequency of the target behaviour.

27-2. You would specify exactly what behavioural goals must be met before you receive the reinforcer; that is, you would arrange the ________________. If your goal is to increase studying, you might specify that TV watching for one hour is ________________ on having studied for two hours.

27-3. Or you might specify that for each hour you studied, you would earn points that could be "spent" for watching TV, going to movies, talking with friends, and so on. This type of arrangement is referred to as a ________________ economy.

27-4. A fairly obvious way to decrease a target behaviour is to use ________________. The problem with this approach is that it is difficult to follow through with self-punishment. So, there are two guidelines to keep in mind when using punishment in a self-control program: (1) Use punishment only in conjunction with ________________ reinforcement; and (2) use a relatively ________________ punishment that you, or perhaps a third party, will be able to administer.

27-5. It is also possible to use reinforcement to alter a problematic behaviour. For example, if you want to gradually reduce the amount that you smoke, you could reinforce yourself whenever you smoke fewer than a particular number of cigarettes per day. In this case, the behaviour being reinforced is "________________ ________________."

27-6. In some cases, you may be able to identify events that reliably precede the behaviours you are trying to stop. For example, for some people, smoking is at least partially affected by certain types of social events. So, one strategy for decreasing a behaviour is to identify, and then avoid, the (antecedent/consequent) events that may control the behaviour.

Answers: 27-1. reinforcement, can, contingent **27-2.** contingency, contingent **27-3.** token **27-4.** punishment, positive, mild **27-5.** smoking less **27-6.** antecedent.

28. Discuss how to execute, evaluate, and end a self-modification program.

28-1. Successful execution of the program depends on several factors. To avoid cheating, try creating a formal, written, behavioural ________________. Or make an arrangement so that (only you/someone else) delivers the reinforcers and punishments.

28-2. If your program isn't working, some small revision may turn it around. Try increasing the strength of the reinforcer or try ________________ the delay between the behaviour and delivery of the reinforcer.

28-3. It is generally a good idea to specify in advance the conditions under which you would end the program. You may wish to phase it out by having a/an (gradual/immediate) reduction in the frequency or potency of reinforcers, although for some successful programs, the new behaviours become self-maintaining on their own.

Answers: 28-1. contract (agreement), someone else **28-2.** decreasing **28-3.** gradual.

CRITICAL THINKING APPLICATION * MANIPULATING EMOTIONS: PAVLOV AND PERSUASION

29. Describe how classical conditioning is used to manipulate emotions.

29-1. It is easy to forget that Pavlovian conditioning involves more than salivating dogs. It involves emotion, and in that respect, it is important for a range of reactions—from phobias to sexual arousal to the effects of advertising. For practice with conditioning concepts, label each of the following:

(a) A glamorous woman is shown entering an automobile. Label each of the following with CS, UCS, CR, and UCR. (Assume, for the sake of this example, that the target audience is initially more attracted to the woman than the car. It could work the other way, too.)

____ the woman

____ the car

____ attraction to the car

____ attraction to the woman

(b) A politician stands in front of a Stanley Cup–winning hockey team.

What is the CS? __________________

The UCS? __________________

(c) A salesman takes you to lunch.

What is the CS? __________________

The UCS? __________________

The CR? __________________

29-2. Of course, there's more going on in these examples than just classical conditioning. When we receive a favour, not only are we being conditioned, but we may feel obliged to pay back or ______________ the person's favour.

29-3. While the examples we've used involve liking or attraction, other emotions may be conditioned as well—such as feelings of masculinity and femininity. Want to be more masculine? Smoke these cigarettes, ads may suggest. Not that we must be conscious of manipulation attempts, for conditioning (does/does not) seem to require our awareness.

29-4. How do we protect ourselves against attempts to manipulate our emotions? One suggestion from research on persuasion is that merely being ______________ of the pervasiveness of conditioning will by itself provide some protections against manipulation strategies.

Answers: 29-1. (a) UCS, CS, CR, UCR, (b) the politician, the winning team, (c) the salesman (or his product), the lunch, liking of the salesman (or his product) **29-2.** reciprocate **29-3.** does not **29-4.** forewarned (aware).

Review of Key Terms

Acquisition
Antecedents
Avoidance learning
Behavioural contract
Behaviour modification
Classical conditioning
Conditioned reinforcers
Conditioned response (CR)
Conditioned stimulus (CS)
Conditioning
Continuous reinforcement
Cumulative recorder
Discriminative stimuli
Elicit
Emit
Escape learning
Extinction
Fixed-interval (FI) schedule
Fixed-ratio (FR) schedule
Higher-order conditioning
Instinctive drift
Instrumental learning
Intermittent reinforcement
Law of effect
Learning
Mirror neurons
Negative reinforcement
Observational learning
Operant chamber
Operant conditioning
Partial reinforcement
Pavlovian conditioning
Phobias
Positive reinforcement
Preparedness
Primary reinforcers
Punishment
Reinforcement
Reinforcement contingencies
Resistance to extinction
Schedule of reinforcement
Secondary reinforcers
Shaping
Skinner box
Spontaneous recovery
Stimulus discrimination
Stimulus generalization
Token economy
Trial
Unconditioned response (UCR)
Unconditioned stimulus (UCS)
Variable-interval (VI) schedule
Variable-ratio (VR) schedule

learning **1.** A relatively durable change in behaviour or knowledge that is due to experience.

phobia **2.** Irrational fears of specific objects or situations.

Classical conditioning **3.** The most common name for a type of learning in which a neutral stimulus acquires the ability to evoke a response that was originally evoked by another stimulus.

pavlovian conditioning **4.** Another name for classical conditioning, derived from the name of the person who originally discovered the conditioning phenomenon.

______________ **5.** Reducing the rate of a behaviour by following occurrence of the behaviour with presentation of an aversive stimulus or by removal of a positive stimulus.

______________ **6.** A stimulus that evokes an unconditioned response.

______________ **7.** The response to an unconditioned stimulus.

______________ **8.** A previously neutral stimulus that has acquired the capacity to evoke a conditioned response.

______________ **9.** A learned reaction to a conditioned stimulus that occurs because of previous conditioning.

______________ **10.** To draw out or bring forth, as in classical conditioning.

______________ **11.** Any presentation of a stimulus or pair of stimuli in classical conditioning.

______________ **12.** The formation of a new response tendency.

______________ **13.** Neurons that are activated by performing an action or seeing another person performing an action.

______________ **14.** The gradual weakening and disappearance of a conditioned response tendency.

______________ **15.** The reappearance of an extinguished response after a period of nonexposure to the conditioned stimulus.

______________ **16.** Occurs when an organism responds to new stimuli that are similar to the stimulus used in conditioning.

______________ **17.** Occurs when an organism learns not to respond to stimuli that are similar to the stimulus used in conditioning.

______________ **18.** Occurs when a conditioned stimulus functions as if it were an unconditioned stimulus.

______________ **19.** This term, introduced by Skinner, refers to learning in which voluntary responses come to be controlled by their consequences.

______________ **20.** Another name for operant conditioning, this term was introduced earlier by Edward L. Thorndike.

______________ **21.** Law stating that if a response in the presence of a stimulus leads to satisfying effects, the association between the stimulus and the response is strengthened.

______________ **22.** Occurs when an event following a response strengthens the tendency to make that response.

______________ **23.** A standard operant chamber in which an animal's responses are controlled and recorded.

______________ **24.** Production of voluntary responses in responding in operant conditioning.

______________ **25.** The circumstances or rules that determine whether responses lead to presentation of reinforcers, or the relationship between a response and positive consequences.

________________ **26.** Device that creates a graphic record of operant responding as a function of time.

________________ **27.** The reinforcement of closer and closer approximations of the desired response.

________________ **28.** Occurs when an organism continues to make a response after delivery of the reinforcer for it has been terminated.

________________ **29.** Cues that influence operant behaviour by indicating the probable consequences (reinforcement or nonreinforcement) of a response.

________________ **30.** Stimulus events that are inherently reinforcing because they satisfy biological needs.

________________ **31.** Stimulus events that acquire reinforcing qualities by being associated with primary reinforcers.

________________ **32.** A specific pattern of presentation of reinforcers over time.

________________ **33.** Occurs when every instance of a designated response is reinforced.

________________ **34.** The name for all schedules of reinforcement in which a designated response is reinforced only some of the time.

________________ **35.** The schedule in which the reinforcer is given after a fixed number of nonreinforced responses.

________________ **36.** The schedule in which the reinforcer is given after a variable number of nonreinforced responses.

________________ **37.** The schedule in which the reinforcer is given for the first response that occurs after a fixed time interval has elapsed.

________________ **38.** The schedule in which the reinforcer is given for the first response that occurs after a variable time interval has elapsed.

________________ **39.** Occurs when a response is strengthened because it is followed by the arrival of a rewarding (presumably pleasant) stimulus.

________________ **40.** Occurs when a response is strengthened because it is followed by the removal of an aversive (unpleasant) stimulus.

________________ **41.** Occurs when an organism engages in a response that brings aversive stimulation to an end.

________________ **42.** Occurs when an organism engages in a response that prevents aversive stimulation from occurring.

________________ **43.** Learning associations between events that occur in an organism's environment.

________________ **44.** Occurs when an animal's innate response tendencies interfere with conditioning processes.

________________ **45.** Occurs when an organism's responding is influenced by the observation of others, who are called models.

________________ **46.** A systematic approach to changing behaviour through the application of the principles of conditioning.

________________ **47.** Events that typically precede your target behaviour and may play a major role in governing your target response; also, another term for discriminative stimuli.

________________ **48.** A system for distributing symbolic reinforcers that are exchanged later for a variety of genuine reinforcers.

________________ **49.** A written agreement outlining a promise to adhere to the contingencies of a behaviour-modification program.

________________ **50.** When a designated response is reinforced only some of the time; another name for intermittent reinforcement.

________________ **51.** Another name for secondary reinforcers.

______________ **52.** A species-specific predisposition to be conditioned in certain ways and not in others.

______________ **53.** A small enclosure in which an animal's responses are recorded and followed by specified consequences; a Skinner box.

Answers: 1. learning **2.** phobias **3.** classical conditioning **4.** Pavlovian conditioning **5.** punishment **6.** unconditioned stimulus (UCS) **7.** unconditioned response (UCR) **8.** conditioned stimulus (CS) **9.** conditioned response (CR) **10.** elicit **11.** trial **12.** acquisition **13.** mirror neurons **14.** extinction **15.** spontaneous recovery **16.** stimulus generalization **17.** stimulus discrimination **18.** higher-order conditioning **19.** operant conditioning **20.** instrumental learning **21.** law of effect **22.** reinforcement **23.** Skinner box **24.** emit **25.** reinforcement contingencies **26.** cumulative recorder **27.** shaping **28.** resistance to extinction **29.** discriminative stimuli **30.** primary reinforcers **31.** secondary reinforcers **32.** schedule of reinforcement **33.** continuous reinforcement **34.** intermittent reinforcement **35.** Fixed-ratio (FR) schedule **36.** variable-ratio (VR) schedule **37.** Fixed-interval (FI) schedule **38.** variable-interval (VI) schedule **39.** positive reinforcement **40.** negative reinforcement **41.** escape learning **42.** avoidance learning **43.** conditioning **44.** instinctive drift **45.** observational learning **46.** behaviour modification **47.** antecedents **48.** token economy **49.** behavioural contract **50.** partial reinforcement **51.** conditioned reinforcers **52.** preparedness **53.** operant chamber.

Review of Key People

Albert Bandura
John Garcia
Ivan Pavlov
Robert Rescorla
Martin Seligman
B. F. Skinner
E. L. Thorndike

______________ **1.** The first to describe the process of classical conditioning.

______________ **2.** Developed a principle known as the law of effect; coined the term *instrumental learning*.

______________ **3.** Elaborated upon the learning process known as operant conditioning; investigated schedules of reinforcement; developed programmed learning.

______________ **4.** Asserted that environmental stimuli serve as signals and that some stimuli in classical conditioning are better signals than others.

______________ **5.** Described and extensively investigated the process of observational learning.

______________ **6.** Discovered that taste aversion was conditioned only through taste and nausea pairings and not through other stimulus pairings, such as taste and shock.

______________ **7.** Proposed the theory of preparedness, the notion that there are species-specific predispositions to condition to certain stimuli and not to others.

Answers: 1. Pavlov **2.** Thorndike **3.** Skinner **4.** Rescorla **5.** Bandura **6.** Garcia **7.** Seligman.

Self-Quiz

1. In Pavlov's original demonstration of classical conditioning, salivation to the bell was the:
   a. conditioned stimulus
   b. conditioned response
   c. unconditioned stimulus
   d. unconditioned response

2. Sally developed a fear of balconies after almost falling from a balcony on a couple of occasions. What was the conditioned response?
a. the balcony
b. fear of the balcony
c. almost falling
d. fear resulting from almost falling

3. When the UCS is removed and the CS is presented alone for a period of time, what will occur?
a. classical conditioning
b. generalization
c. acquisition
d. extinction

4. Sally developed a fear of balconies from almost falling. Although she has had no dangerous experiences on bridges, cliffs, or tall buildings, she now fears these stimuli as well. Which of the following is likely to have produced a fear of these other stimuli?
a. instinctive drift
b. spontaneous recovery
c. generalization
d. discrimination

5. A researcher reinforces closer and closer approximations to a target behaviour. What is the name of the procedure she is using?
a. shaping
b. classical conditioning
c. discrimination training
d. extinction

6. John says, "Please pass the salt." Ralph passes the salt. "Thank you," says John. John's request precedes a behaviour (salt passing) that is reinforced ("Thank you"). Thus, the request "Please pass the salt" is a _____________ for passing the salt.
a. discriminative stimulus
b. response
c. positive reinforcer
d. conditioned stimulus (CS)

7. A rat is reinforced for the first lever-pressing response that occurs, *on the average*, after 60 seconds. Which schedule is the rat on?
a. FR
b. VR
c. FI
d. VI

8. When the rat presses a lever, the mild electric shock on the cage floor is turned off. What procedure is being used?
a. punishment
b. escape
c. discrimination training
d. avoidance

9. A cue light comes on in the dog's shuttle box. It jumps the hurdle to the other side. What procedure is being used?
a. punishment
b. escape
c. discrimination training
d. avoidance

10. In avoidance learning, the cue stimulus acquires the capacity to elicit fear through the process of:
a. operant conditioning
b. classical conditioning
c. generalization
d. discrimination

11. The contingencies are as follows: If the response occurs, a stimulus is *presented*; if the response does not occur, the stimulus is not presented. Under this procedure, the strength of the response *increases*. What procedure is being used?
a. positive reinforcement
b. negative reinforcement
c. punishment
d. avoidance training

12. In terms of the traditional view of conditioning, research on conditioned taste aversion was surprising for two major reasons:
a. There was a long delay between CS and UCS, and cues other than taste did not condition.
b. The dislike of a particular taste was operantly conditioned, and non-taste cues were classically conditioned.
c. Conditioning did not occur to taste cues, but conditioning did occur to all other stimuli present when the food was consumed.
d. The senses of taste and smell seem to be relatively weak.

13. Animal trainers (the Brelands) trained pigs to put coins in a piggy bank for a food reward. The animals learned the response, but instead of depositing the coins immediately in the bank, the pigs began to toss them in the air, drop them, push them on the ground, and so on. What had occurred that interfered with conditioning?
a. conditioned taste aversion
b. blocking
c. instinctive drift
d. signal relations

14. Which of the following produces strong resistance to extinction?
a. a continuous reinforcement schedule
b. an intermittent reinforcement schedule
c. optimal foraging behaviour
d. discrimination and differentiation

15. Earlier learning viewpoints considered classical and operant conditioning to be automatic processes that did not depend at all on biological or cognitive factors. Research involving which of the following topics cast doubt on this point of view?
a. signal relations
b. ecologically relevant conditioned stimuli and conditioned taste aversion
c. response–outcome relations
d. all of the above

16. According to Siegel, cues in the environment that are repeatedly associated with the taking of a drug may come to be:
a. conditioned responses
b. unconditioned stimuli
c. conditioned stimuli
d. conditioned responses

Answers: 1. b **2.** b **3.** d **4.** c **5.** a **6.** a **7.** d **8.** b **9.** d **10.** b **11.** a **12.** a **13.** c **14.** b **15.** d **16.** c.

InfoTrac Keywords

Behaviour Modification

Classical Conditioning

Operant Conditioning

Chapter Seven
HUMAN MEMORY

Review of Key Ideas

ENCODING: GETTING INFORMATION INTO MEMORY

1. **Describe the three basic human memory processes.**

1-1. The three basic human memory processes are:

(a) Putting the information in, a process called _______________.

(b) Holding onto the information, a process called _______________.

(c) Getting the information back out, a process called _______________.

Answers: 1-1. (a) encoding, (b) storage, (c) retrieval.

2. **Discuss the role of attention in memory.**

2-1. If you are being introduced to a new person and you want to remember his or her name, it is first necessary to give selective ______________ to this information. This requires ______________ out irrelevant sensory input. The debate between early and late selection theories of attention is an argument over when this filtering takes place: before or after ______________ is given to the arriving material.

2-2. Although there is ample evidence to support both early- and late-selection theories of attention, what conclusion have some been led to?

2-3. What effect does divided attention have on memory and many other tasks, such as using a cellular telephone while driving?

2-4. Canadian psychologists Hasher and Zacks distinguished between ______________ (intentional) processing of information and _____________ (nonintentional) processing of information. This distinction means that, at times, people can know information but not remember how they acquired the knowledge.

Answers: **2-1.** attention, filtering, meaning **2-2.** The location of the attention filter may be flexible rather than fixed. **2-3.** It decreases performance. **2-4.** effortful, automatic.

3. Describe the three levels of information processing proposed by Craik and Lockhart and how processing relates to memory.

3-1. Craik and Lockhart proposed three levels for encoding incoming information, with ever-increasing retention as the depth of processing increases. In their order of depth, these three levels are:

(a) ____________________ (b) ____________________ (c) ____________________

3-2. Below are three-word sequences. Tell which level of processing each sequence illustrates and why.

(a) cat IN tree ____________________

(b) car BAR czar ____________________

(c) CAN CAP CAR ____________________

3-3. If this theory is correct, then we would expect most persons to best remember the sequence in ____________________. This is because the words in this sequence have greater____________________ than do the other two sequences. It has been found that processing time (<u>is/is not</u>) a reliable index of depth of processing, and thus what constitutes "levels" remains vague.

Answers: **3-1.** (a) structural, (b) phonemic, (c) semantic **3-2.** (a) Semantic because we immediately give meaning to the words. (b) Phonemic because the words sound alike. (c) Structural because the words look alike. **3-3.** (a) cat in tree, meaning, is not.

4. Describe three techniques for enriching encoding and research on each.

4-1. Elaboration helps us to better remember the words RUN FAST CAT than the words WORK SLOW TREE. Why is this?

4-2. According to Paivio's dual-coding theory, why is it easier to remember the word APPLE than the word PREVAIL?

4-3. What is the general idea behind self-referent encoding?

Answers: **4-1.** Because the words RUN FAST CAT allow us to make richer and more elaborate associations among them than do the other three words (e.g., you can imagine a cat running fast). **4-2.** Because it is easier to form a visual image of the word APPLE, thus allowing for storage of both the word and image. **4-3.** We are more likely to remember information when it is relevant to ourselves.

STORAGE: MAINTAINING INFORMATION IN MEMORY

5. Describe the role of the sensory store in memory.

5-1. Sensory memory allows for retention of information for a very (brief/long) period of time. The retention time for sensory memory for both vision and audition is about _______________. During this brief period, the information (remains in/is changed from) its original sensory form.

Answers: 5-1. brief, 1/4 second, remains in.

6. Discuss the characteristics of short-term memory (STM).

6-1. Indicate whether the following statements regarding short-term memory are true (T) or false (F).

_______(a) Has a virtually unlimited storage capacity.

______ (b) Has a storage capacity of seven, plus or minus two, items.

_______(c) Requires continuous rehearsal to maintain information in storage for more than 20 or 30 seconds.

______ (d) Stores information more or less permanently.

_______(e) Chunking can help to increase the capacity of this system.

_______ (f) Experts chunk information differently and more efficiently than nonexperts.

Answers: 6-1. (a) F, (b) T, (c) T, (d) F, (e) T, (f) T.

7. Discuss Baddeley's model of working memory.

7-1. Indicate which component of Baddeley's working memory (phonological rehearsal loop, visuospatial sketchpad, executive control system, or episodic buffer) is operating in the following situations.

(a) You successfully divide your attention between the TV and a friend's conversation.

(b) You continue to recite a phone number as you walk toward the phone.

(c) You are describing the location of a restaurant to a friend.

(d) You are able to compare your memory of what an old friend looked like with his or her current appearance.

7-2. Research has supported Baddeley's model of working memory. For example, tasks that involve the visuospatial _____________ do not interfere with tasks that engage in the phonological _____________.

Answers: 7-1. (a) executive control system, (b) phonological rehearsal loop, (c) visuospatial sketchpad, (d) episodic buffer **7-2.** sketchpad, loop.

8. Evaluate the hypothesis that all memories are stored permanently in long-term memory (LTM).

8-1. There are two views regarding the durability of information in LTM. One is that no information is ever lost, and the other is that _____________ information is lost. Those who favour the permanent view explain forgetting as a failure of _____________. The information is still there; we just cannot get it out.

8-2. How do those who doubt the permanency of long-term memory counter the following two lines of evidence cited by the permanent proponents?

(a) Flashbulb memories of previous events?

(b) Penfield's electrically triggered memories?

Answers: 8-1. some, retrieval **8-2.** (a) They often tend to be inaccurate and less detailed with the passage of time. (b) The memories were often incorrect and resembled dreams or hallucinations more than real events.

9. Evaluate the issues in the debate about whether short-term and long-term memory are really separate.

9-1. The traditional view is that short-term memory differs from long-term memory in that it depends on phonemic (sound) encoding while long-term memory depends on _____________ (meaning) encoding. These two systems are also said to differ in the manner in which forgetting occurs. The loss of memory in STM is thought to result from time-related decay, while LTM forgetting is attributed to _____________.

9-2. What research findings undermine the traditional view?

9-3. Which view, multiple stores or a single system, dominates at the present time?

Answers: 9-1. semantic, interference **9-2.** Semantic encoding and interference have also been found in short-term memory. **9-3.** multiple stores.

10. Describe conceptual hierarchies, schemas, and semantic networks, and their role in long-term memory.

10-1. Group the following words into two groups or categories:

rose dog grass cat tree rat

You probably grouped the words into plants and animals, which is the general idea behind ______________. Thus, clustering leads to forming categories (concepts), and in turn the categories are organized into ______________ hierarchies. For example, the categories of plants and animals can be placed under the higher category (hierarchy) of ______________ things.

10-2. It also appears that LTM stores information in clusters of knowledge about particular objects or events, called ______________. For example, in the study cited by the text, the subjects who falsely recalled seeing books did so because of their schema of what a professor's ______________ looks like. Although people are (more/less) likely to remember things consistent with their schemas, this is not always true, particularly with objects that contrast (dramatically/casually) with their schema-based expectations. It has also been suggested that people can possess ______________ schemas, which are representations of events that surround interpersonal interactions. These are thought to affect how we process information about others and ourselves.

10-3. In addition to conceptual categories, it appears that LTM also stores information in terms of semantic networks. If you understand the idea behind semantic networks and its related idea of spreading activation, you should be able to answer the questions below.

Person A attends an urban university and frequently studies while riding a bus to and from school. Person B attends a university located in a rural area and frequently studies outside in one of the many parklike areas surrounding the school.

(a) When asked to think of words associated with the word STUDY, which of the students is most likely to think of the word GRASS? ______________

(b) Which person is most likely to think of the word TRAFFIC? ______________

(c) Which person is most likely to think of the word PEACEFUL? ______________

Answers: 10-1. clustering, conceptual, living **10-2.** schemas, office, more, dramatically, relational **10-3.** (a) person B (b) person A (c) person B.

11. Explain how parallel distributed processing (PDP) models view the representation of information in memory.

11-1. Parallel distributed processing (PDP) models assume that a piece of knowledge is represented by a particular ______________ of activation across an entire system of interconnected neural networks. This approach is called "connectionism" because the information lies in the strengths of the ______________.

Answers: 11-1. pattern, connections.

RETRIEVAL: GETTING INFORMATION OUT OF MEMORY

12. Explain how retrieval cues and context cues influence retrieval.

12-1. Tulving distinguished between poor retrieval that is due to a lack of ______________ of the information (the information is no longer in the memory system) versus poor retrieval that reflects lack of ______________ of the information (available but not accessible at the moment).

12-2. In the following examples, indicate whether retrieval cues or context cues are being used to retrieve information from long-term memory.

(a) In trying to recall the name of a high school classmate, you get the feeling that his first name began with an *L* and begin saying names like Larry, Leroy, Lionel, etc.

(b) Or you may attempt to recall the high school classmate by imagining the history class in which he sat in the row next to you.

12-3. The term "the ______________ ______________ principle" is used to refer to situations in which memory is improved because the conditions during encoding and retrieval are similar. Even matching a person's ______________ state, such as a state of intoxication or a particular mood state, at encoding and retrieval may facilitate memory.

Answers: 12-1. availability, accessibility **12-2.** (a) retrieval cues (b) context cues **12-3.** encoding specificity, internal.

13. Discuss Bartlett's work and research on the misinformation effect.

13-1. Bartlett's work with the "War of the Ghosts," found that the subjects reconstructed the original tale to fit with their already established ______________. Since we use schemas to move information in and out of long-term memory, it is not too surprising that retrieved information may be altered by these schemas.

13-2. For example, Elizabeth Loftus found that subjects who were originally asked, "How fast were the cars going when they (hit/smashed) into each other?" were much more likely to falsely recall having seen broken glass in a videotaped scene when tested at a later date. In this case, the word *smashed* resulted in a different ______________ than did the word *hit*. The distortion of memory by the word *smashed* is an example of how post-event information can result in the ______________ of an original memory. This phenomenon has been called the ______________ effect.

Answers: 13-1. schemas **13-2.** smashed, schema, reconstruction, misinformation.

14. Discuss the implications of evidence on source monitoring and reality monitoring.

14-1. A third explanation for distorted memory retrieval involves source monitoring. Both source monitoring and its subtype, reality monitoring, require us to make attributions about the _______________ of memories. Errors in memory from both kinds of monitoring are (rare/common).

14-2. Say whether the situations below are examples of source monitoring (S) or reality monitoring (R).

_____ (a) You become convinced that you broke your arm when you were five years old, but your mother tells you that it never happened.

_____ (b) You attribute a funny story to your good friend Tom when in fact it was Fred, whom you don't really care for, who told you the story.

_____ (c) You believe that you received an "A" in high school algebra, but your transcript shows a "C."

Answers: 14-1. origins, common **14-2.** (a) R, (b) S, (c) R.

FORGETTING: WHEN MEMORY LAPSES

15. Describe Ebbinghaus's forgetting curve and three measures of retention.

15-1. Ebbinghaus's forgetting curve, using nonsense syllables and himself as the subject, showed that forgetting was most rapid in the (first/second) nine hours after learning the material. Later research has shown that the dramatic decline is (the same/much less) when more meaningful material is involved.

15-2. Which of the three different methods of measuring forgetting is illustrated in each of the following situations?

(a) You are asked to identify a suspect in a police lineup.

(b) You time yourself while learning 20 new French words. After a week, you find you have forgotten some of the words, and you again time yourself while learning the list a second time.

(c) You are asked to draw a floor plan of your bedroom from memory.

Answers: 15-1. first, much less **15-2.** (a) recognition, (b) relearning, (c) recall.

16. Explain how forgetting may be due to ineffective encoding.

16-1. Why are most people unable to recognize things that they have seen on many occasions, such as a Canadian penny?

16-2. What is another name for information loss due to ineffective coding of this kind?

16-3. Why is semantic coding better than phonemic coding for enhancing future recall of written material?

Answers: 16-1. They never encoded the correct figure in their memories. **16-2.** pseudoforgetting **16-3.** Semantic coding will lead to deeper processing and more elaborate associations.

17. Compare and contrast decay and interference as potential causes of forgetting.

17-1. Two other theories of forgetting propose additional factors that may be involved in retrieval failure. One theory holds that retrieval failure may be due to the impermanence of the memory storage itself. This is the notion behind the ______________ theory of forgetting. Decay theory is best able to explain retrieval failure in ______________ memory and to a lesser extent in (short-term/long-term) memory.

17-2. The other theory attributes retrieval failure to other information already in the memory or to information arriving at a later time. This is the notion behind the ______________ theory of forgetting. According to interference theory, the failure may be caused by interference from information already in the memory, a phenomenon called ______________ interference, or the failure may be caused by interference occurring after the original memory was stored, a phenomenon called ______________ interference. Interference is most likely to occur when the materials being stored are very (similar/different).

Answers: 17-1. decay, sensory store, short-term **17-2.** interference, proactive, retroactive, similar.

18. Explain how forgetting may be due to factors in the retrieval process.

18-1. Breakdowns in the retrieval process can occur when the encoding specificity principle is violated. This means there has been a mismatch between the original memory code and the ______________ cue being used to retrieve the information. A common instance of this violation is seen when one attempts to retrieve a semantically coded word with (semantic/phonemic) retrieval cues.

18-2. Retrieval failure may also occur when there is a poor fit between initial encoding processing and the processing required by the measure of retention. In other words, the two kinds of processing are not transfer-______________.

18-3. Sigmund Freud felt that some breakdowns in the retrieval process could be attributed to purposeful suppression of information by unconscious forces, a phenomenon called ______________ forgetting. Freud called motivated forgetting ______________.

Answers: 18-1. retrieval, phonemic **18-2.** appropriate **18-3.** motivated, repression.

19. Summarize evidence for the view that most recovered memories of childhood sexual abuse are genuine.

19-1. Those who argue that most of these recovered memories are genuine assert that the frequency of sexual abuse in childhood is (less/more) widespread than most people realize.

19-2. What did the 17-year follow-up study find regarding 129 female children who had emergency treatment for sexual abuse?

Answers: 19-1. more **19-2.** 38% failed to report the original incident.

20. Summarize evidence for the view that most recovered memories of childhood sexual abuse are inaccurate.

20-1. How do the skeptics of these recovered memories of childhood sexual abuse explain their origin?

20-2. What is the only way to tell for certain if a recovered memory is genuine or a pseudomemory?

Answers: 20-1. Some suggestible people are convinced by persuasive therapists (that these events must have happened). **20-2.** Through independent corroborative evidence.

IN SEARCH OF THE MEMORY TRACE: THE PHYSIOLOGY OF MEMORY

21. Summarize evidence on the biochemistry and neural circuitry underlying memory.

21-1. Which of the following biochemical changes have been implicated in the physiology of memory?

(a) alterations in synaptic transmission at specific sites

(b) induced changes in RNA

(c) hormones that can either facilitate or impair memory storage

(d) interference with protein synthesis

21-2. Answer the following questions regarding the neural circuitry of memory.

(a) What caused a rabbit to lose its memory of a conditioned eye blink?

(b) What neural changes were found in rats that learned to run a series of mazes?

(c) What does research with long-term potentiation (LTP) tell us about how memory is stored?

(d) What is long-term depression (LTD), and what is it relevant to?

(e) What is thought to be the relevance of neurogenesis to memory?

Answers: 21-1. a, c, d **21-2.** (a) Destruction of an area in the cerebellum. (b) Increased growth of neuronal dendritic trees. (c) Specific memories may have specific localized dedicated neural circuits. (d) Long-term depression involves a decrease in neural excitability along a pathway, and it may be related to forgetting. (e) Neurogenesis may enhance memory, and a lack of neurogenesis may impair memory; also, it is speculated that neurogenesis allows memories to be "time-stamped" (i.e., newer cells are associated with newer memories).

22. Distinguish between two types of amnesia, and identify the anatomical structures implicated in memory.

22-1. Amnesia cases due to head injury provide clues about the anatomical basis of memory. There are two basic types of head-injury amnesia. Memory loss of events prior to the injury is called ______________ amnesia. Memory loss of events following the injury is called ______________ amnesia.

22-2. What general region of the brain appears to play a major role in the consolidation of memories?

22-3. Consolidation is a hypothesized process that involves the gradual conversion of information into durable memory ______________ stored in long-term memory. These memories are consolidated in the hippocampal region and then stored (<u>in the hippocampus/all over the cortex</u>).

22-4. The neural basis for working memory may involve several areas. The central executive may especially involve the ______________ cortex, whereas the phonological loop and the visuospatial sketchpad may involve areas within the left and right hemispheres, respectively.

Answers:22-1. retrograde, anterograde **22-2.** the entire hippocampal region **22-3.** codes, all over the cortex **22-4.** prefrontal.

ARE THERE MULTIPLE MEMORY SYSTEMS?

23. Distinguish between implicit versus explicit memory and their relationship to declarative and procedural memory.

23-1. Identify whether the two following situations are examples of implicit or explicit memory.

(a) After studying for your history test, you were able to easily recall the information during the exam.

(b) While studying for your history exam, you unexpectedly recall an incident from the previous summer.

23-2. Another division of memory systems has been hypothesized for declarative memory and procedural memory. Identify these two divisions from the descriptions given below.

(a) This system allows you to drive a car or play a piano with minimal attention to the execution of movements that are required.

(b) This system allows you to explain how to drive a car or play the piano to a friend.

23-3. It has been suggested that there is an apparent relationship between implicit memory and ______________ memory and between explicit memory and ______________ memory.

Answers: 23-1. (a) explicit, (b) implicit **23-2.** (a) procedural, (b) declarative **23-3.** procedural, declarative.

24. Explain the distinctions between episodic memory versus semantic memory and prospective versus retrospective memory.

24-1. It has also been hypothesized that declarative memory can be further subdivided into semantic and episodic memory. Identify these two kinds of memory from the following descriptions:

(a) This kind of memory acts like an encyclopedia, storing all of the factual information you possess.

(b) This kind of memory acts like an autobiography, storing all of your personal experiences.

24-2. According to the Featured Study, episodic memory may be intimately related to our ability to imagine the ______________. According to the constructive ______________ ______________ hypothesis, remembering the past and simulating the future (are/are not) highly similar and therefore utilize similar neural processes. Schachter and Addis showed that participants using words to remember a past event and those using words to imagine a future event both showed activation in similar brain regions when measured on an _______________ machine.

24-3. Still another possibility is that we have separate memory systems for prospective and retrospective memory. The distinction here is between our ability to remember events from the past or previously learned information, _______________ memory, and our ability to remember or perform actions in the future, _______________ memory. The fact that _______________ memory is constructive in nature makes it highly suited to humans' ability to imagine future events.

24-4. Which form of prospective memory appears to give us the most trouble when we try to retrieve it: memory of event-based tasks or memory of time-based tasks?

Answers: 24-1. (a) semantic, (b) episodic **24-2.** future, episodic simulation, are, MRI **24-3.** retrospective, prospective, episodic **24-4.** memory of time-based tasks.

PUTTING IT IN PERSPECTIVE

25. Explain how this chapter highlighted three of the text's unifying themes.

25-1. Three unifying themes were especially noteworthy in this chapter: the subjectivity of experience, psychology's theoretical diversity, and multifactorial causation. The text mentions two areas in which subjectivity may influence memory. Identify them below.

(a) We often see only that which gets the focus of our _______________.

(b) Every time we tell of a particular experience, details are added or subtracted because of the _______________ nature of memory.

25-2. The numerous debates about the nature of memory storage, the causes of forgetting, and the existence of multiple memory systems nicely illustrate psychology's _______________ _______________.

25-3. Since the memory of a specific event can be influenced by many factors, operating in each of the three memory stores, it is obvious that memory, like most behaviour, has _______________ _______________.

Answers: 25-1. (a) attention (b) reconstructive **25-2.** theoretical diversity **25-3.** multifactorial causation.

PERSONAL APPLICATION * IMPROVING EVERYDAY MEMORY

26. Discuss the importance of rehearsal, distributed practice, and interference in efforts to improve everyday memory.

26-1. The text lists three general strategies for improving everyday memory. Identify which strategy is being employed in the following examples.

(a) Most persons can remember their phone number because of extensive _______________.

(b) Willie Nurd, the bookworm, always takes breaks between study periods when changing subject matter. Willie must realize the importance of ______________ practice.

(c) Ajax never studies any material other than mathematics on the day of his math exams in order to minimize ______________.

26-2. The serial position effect means that words in the middle of a list will need (more/less) of our attention.

Answers: 26-1. (a) rehearsal, (b) distributed (c) interference **26-2.** more.

27. Discuss the value of deep processing and good organization in efforts to improve everyday memory.

27-1. Answering questions such as these is much better than simply underlining the same material in the text because it forces you to engage in ______________ ______________.

27-2. Outlining material from textbooks can enhance retention because it leads to better ______________ of the material.

Answers: 27-1. deep processing **27-2.** organization.

28. Describe some verbal and visual mnemonic devices that can be used to improve everyday memory.

28-1. Specific strategies for enhancing memory are called ______________ devices. Examples of strategies that do not employ visual images are listed below. See if you can identify which strategy is being employed in each illustration.

(a) Using the phrase "My Very Excellent Mother Just Sells Nuts Under Protest" to remember the names and positions of the planets illustrates the use of an ______________.

(b) International Business Machines is easily identified by its ______________, IBM.

(c) The phrase "One two three four, I left my keys in the drawer" illustrates the use of ______________.

(d) Since you are going to the store, your roommate asks you to bring her a bar of Ivory soap, a box of Kleenex, and a Snickers bar. You then make up a story that begins, "On my way to the Ivory Coast to check on the latest shipment of Kleenex, I..." You're making use of a ______________ method as a mnemonic device.

28-2. Three techniques involving visual imagery can also serve as helpful mnemonic devices: the link method, the method of loci, and the keyword method. Identify these examples:

(a) You want to remember the name of your bus driver, Ray Blocker, who has especially large forearms. You form an image of a man using his large arms to block light rays from his face.

(b) You want to remember to buy bananas, eggs, milk, and bread. You visualize walking in your front door and tripping on a bunch of bananas. Stumbling forward into the hallway, you notice broken eggs on the table, etc.

(c) You imagine yourself using a banana to break eggs, which you then pour into a bowl of milk and bread.

Answers: 28-1. mnemonic, (a) acrostic, (b) acronym, (c) rhyming, (d) narrative **28-2.** (a) keyword method, (b) method of loci, (c) link method.

CRITICAL THINKING APPLICATION *** UNDERSTANDING THE FALLIBILITY OF EYEWITNESS ACCOUNTS**

29. Explain how hindsight bias and overconfidence contribute to the frequent inaccuracy of eyewitness testimony.

29-1. The frequent inaccuracy of eyewitness testimony is due in part to the reconstructive nature of memory, source monitoring, and the misinformation effect. In addition, the text points out that still another factor is our tendency to mould our interpretation of the past to fit how events actually turned out. This is called ____________ ____________.

29-2. The failure to seek disconfirming evidence can often lead to the ____________ effect, which is still another reason for the frequent inaccuracy of eyewitness testimony.

Answers: 29-1. hindsight bias **29-2.** overconfidence

Review of Key Terms

Anterograde amnesia
Attention
Chunk
Clustering
Conceptual hierarchy
Connectionist models
Consolidation
Decay theory
Declarative memory system
Dual-coding theory
Elaboration
Encoding
Encoding specificity principle
Episodic memory system
Explicit memory
Flashbulb memories
Forgetting curve
Hindsight bias
Implicit memory
Interference theory
Keyword method
Levels-of-processing theory
Link method
Long-term memory (LTM)
Long-term potentiation (LTP)
Method of loci
Misinformation effect
Mnemonic devices
Nondeclarative memory system
Overlearning
Parallel distributed processing (PDP) models
Proactive interference
Procedural memory system
Prospective memory
Reality monitoring
Recall
Recognition
Rehearsal
Relearning
Repression
Retention
Retrieval
Retroactive interference
Retrograde amnesia
Retrospective memory
Schema
Self-referent encoding
Semantic memory system
Semantic network
Sensory memory
Serial-position effect
Short-term memory
Source monitoring
Source-monitoring error
Storage
Tip-of-the-tongue phenomenon
Transfer-appropriate processing

______________________ **1.** Putting coded information into memory.

______________________ **2.** Maintaining coded information in memory.

______________________ **3.** Recovering information from memory stores.

______________________ **4.** The process of focusing awareness on a narrowed range of stimuli or events.

______________________ **5.** Involves remembering to perform actions in the future.

______________________ **6.** Involves remembering events from the past or previously learned information.

______________________ **7.** The initial processing of information is similar to the type of processing required by the subsequent measure of retention.

______________________ **8.** Assume that cognitive processes depend on patterns of activation in highly interconnected computational networks that resemble neural networks (note: <u>two</u> key terms apply to this definition).

______________________ **9.** Memory that involves the intentional recollection of previous experiences.

______________________ **10.** A theory that proposes that deeper levels of processing result in longer-lasting memory codes.

______________________ **11.** Involves linking a stimulus to other information at the time of encoding.

______________________ **12.** A theory that memory is enhanced by forming both semantic and visual codes since either can lead to recall.

______________________ **13.** Preserves information in its original sensory form for a very brief time.

______________________ **14.** A limited-capacity memory store that can maintain unrehearsed information for 20 to 30 seconds.

______________________ **15.** The process of repetitively verbalizing or thinking about new information.

______________________ **16.** A group of familiar stimuli stored as a single unit.

______________________ **17.** An unlimited capacity memory store that can hold information over lengthy periods of time.

______________________ **18.** Unusually vivid and detailed recollections of momentous events.

______________________ **19.** Occurs when subjects show better recall of items at the beginning and end of a list than of items in the middle.

______________________ **20.** Memory for factual information.

______________________ **21.** Memory for actions, skills, and operations.

______________________ **22.** Memory made up of chronological, or temporally dated, recollections of personal experiences.

______________________ **23.** Memory that contains general knowledge that is not tied to the time when the information was learned.

______________________ **24.** The tendency to remember similar or related items in a group.

______________________ **25.** These consist of concepts joined together by links that show how the concepts are related.

______________________ **26.** A long-lasting increase in neural excitability at synapses along a specific neural pathway.

______________________ **27.** An organized cluster of knowledge about a particular object or sequence of events.

_______________ **28.** The attempt to mould our interpretation of the past to fit how it actually turned out.

_______________ **29.** A temporary inability to remember something you know accompanied by the feeling that it's just out of reach.

_______________ **30.** A curve graphing retention and forgetting over time.

_______________ **31.** The proportion of material remembered.

_______________ **32.** The ability to remember information without any cues.

_______________ **33.** Requires the selection of previously learned information from an array of options (e.g., multiple-choice tests).

_______________ **34.** Requires the memorization of information a second time to determine how much time or effort is saved.

_______________ **35.** Attributes forgetting to the impermanence of memory storage.

_______________ **36.** Attributes forgetting to competition from other material.

_______________ **37.** Occurs when new information impairs the retention of previously learned information.

_______________ **38.** Occurs when previously learned information impairs the retention of new information.

_______________ **39.** States that the value of a retrieval cue depends on how well it corresponds to the memory code.

_______________ **40.** Involves purposeful suppression of memories (motivated forgetting).

_______________ **41.** A theoretical process involving the gradual conversion of information into durable memory codes stored in long-term memory.

_______________ **42.** The loss of memory of events that occurred prior to a brain injury.

_______________ **43.** The loss of memory of events that occur after a brain injury.

_______________ **44.** Strategies for enhancing memory.

_______________ **45.** The continued rehearsal of material after it has apparently been mastered.

_______________ **46.** Involves forming a mental image of items to be remembered in a way that connects them together.

_______________ **47.** A mnemonic device that involves taking an imaginary walk along a familiar path.

_______________ **48.** Involves associating a concrete word with an abstract word and generating an image to represent the concrete word.

_______________ **49.** A multilevel classification system based on common properties among items (e.g., cats, animals, living things).

_______________ **50.** Is apparent when retention is exhibited on a task that does not require intentional remembering.

_______________ **51.** The process of deciding how or whether information is personally relevant.

_______________ **52.** The process of making attributions about the origins of memories.

_______________ **53.** The process of deciding whether memories are based on external or internal sources.

_______________ **54.** An error that occurs when a memory derived from one source is attributed to another.

______________________ **55.** Another term for the procedural memory system that houses memory for actions, skills, and operations.

______________________ **56.** When recall of an event is altered by introducing misleading post-event information.

Answers: 1. encoding **2.** storage **3.** retrieval **4.** attention **5.** prospective memory **6.** retrospective memory **7.** transfer-appropriate processing **8.** connectionist models and parallel distributed processing (PDP) **9.** explicit memory **10.** levels-of-processing theory **11.** elaboration **12.** dual-coding theory **13.** sensory memory **14.** short-term memory (STM) **15.** rehearsal **16.** chunk **17.** long-term memory (LTM) **18.** flashbulb memories **19.** serial position effect **20.** declarative memory system **21.** procedural memory system **22.** episodic memory system **23.** semantic memory system **24.** clustering **25.** semantic networks **26.** long-term potentiation **27.** schema **28.** hindsight bias **29.** tip-of-the-tongue phenomenon **30.** forgetting curve **31.** retention **32.** recall **33.** recognition **34.** relearning **35.** decay theory **36.** interference theory **37.** retroactive interference **38.** proactive interference **39.** encoding specificity principle **40.** repression **41.** consolidation **42.** retrograde amnesia **43.** anterograde amnesia **44.** mnemonic devices **45.** overlearning **46.** link method **47.** method of loci **48.** keyword method **49.** conceptual hierarchy **50.** implicit memory **51.** self-referent encoding **52.** source monitoring **53.** reality monitoring **54.** source-monitoring error **55.** nondeclarative memory system **56.** misinformation effect.

Review of Key People

Richard Atkinson & Richard Shiffrin	Marcia Johnson	Brenda Milner
Fergus Craik & Robert Lockhart	Elizabeth Loftus	Endel Tulving
Herman Ebbinghaus	George Miller	

______________________ **1.** Proposed three progressively deeper levels for processing incoming information.

______________________ **2.** Influential in the development of the model of three different kinds of memory stores (sensory, STM, and LTM).

______________________ **3.** She and her colleagues proposed the notions of source and reality monitoring.

______________________ **4.** Demonstrated that the reconstructive nature of memory can distort eyewitness testimony.

______________________ **5.** Used nonsense syllables to become famous for his forgetting curve.

______________________ **6.** One of his many contributions was the encoding specificity principle.

______________________ **7.** Proposed the concept of chunking for storing information in short-term memory.

______________________ **8.** Followed the case of HM, who had his hippocampus removed.

Answers: 1. Craik & Lockhart **2.** Atkinson & Shiffrin **3.** Johnson **4.** Loftus **5.** Ebbinghaus **6.** Tulving **7.** Miller **8.** Milner.

Self-Quiz

1. Which of the following is not one of the three basic human memory processes?
a. storage
b. retrieval
c. decoding
d. encoding

2. Which one of the three levels of processing would probably be employed when attempting to memorize the following three-letter sequences: WAB WAC WAD?
a. structural
b. semantic
c. phonemic
d. chunking

3. According to Paivio's dual-coding theory:
a. words are easier to encode than images
b. abstract words are easier to encode than concrete words
c. visual imagery may hinder the retrieval of words
d. it should be easier to remember the word *banana* than the word *justice*

4. Retrieval from long-term memory is usually best when the information has been stored at which level of processing?
a. structural
b. semantic
c. phonemic
d. chunking

5. Which of the memory stores can store the least amount of information?
a. sensory store
b. short-term memory
c. long-term memory

6. Which of the following sequences of words would be most subject to a clustering effect?
a. FAN HEAVEN JUSTICE CHAIR
b. HOUSE VACATION MOUSE STATISTIC
c. BLUE DOG CAMEL YELLOW
d. CONVERSE ICICLE CONCEPT THINKING

7. According to Hasher and Zacks, the two ways in which we can process information are called:
a. effortful versus automatic
b. inattentive versus attentive
c. sensory versus perceptual
d. bottom-up versus top-down

8. When you attempt to recall the name of a high school classmate by imagining yourself back in the English class with her, you are making use of:
a. retrieval cues
b. context cues
c. schemas
d. recognition cues

9. You recall being lost in a shopping mall at the age of five, but your parents assure you that it never happened. Errors like this are most likely due to:
a. ineffective encoding
b. a reality-monitoring error
c. a source-monitoring error
d. the misinformation effect

10. Taking this particular self-test measures your:
a. constructive errors
b. reconstructive errors
c. recall
d. recognition

11. Ineffective encoding of information may result in:
a. the primacy effect
b. the recency effect
c. pseudoforgetting
d. chunking

12. Decay theory is best able to explain the loss of memory in:
a. sensory store
b. long-term memory
c. short-term memory
d. repressed memory

13. When you violate the encoding specificity principle, you are likely to experience an inability to:
a. encode information
b. store information
c. retrieve information
d. form a visual image of the material you want to retrieve

14. Which of the following statements is the most accurate as to the authenticity of the recall of repressed memories?
a. Research confirms that they are authentic.
b. Research confirms that they are not authentic.
c. Research cannot confirm or deny their authenticity.

15. Which of these appear to be intimately related?
a. implicit and procedural memory
b. implicit and semantic memory
c. explicit and procedural memory
d. implicit and declarative memory

16. It is very easy to recall the name of your high school because it has been subjected to extensive:
a. deep processing
b. clustering
c. chunking
d. rehearsal

17. The failure to seek out disconfirming evidence can often lead to
a. the overconfidence effect
b. the reconstructive bias
c. the hindsight bias
d. a source monitoring error

18. The amnesia experienced by a perpetrator of a violent crime may be a result of:
a. encoding specificity
b. elaborative rehearsal
c. parallel distributed processing
d. semantic networks

Answers: 1. c **2.** a **3.** d **4.** b **5.** b **6.** c **7.** a **8.** b **9.** b **10.** d **11.** c **12.** a **13.** c **14.** c **15.** a **16.** d **17.** a **18.** a.

InfoTrac Keywords

Amnesia

Flashbulb Memories

Misinformation Effect

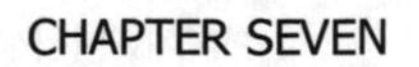

Chapter Eight
LANGUAGE AND THOUGHT

Review of Key Ideas

THE COGNITIVE REVOLUTION IN PSYCHOLOGY

1. Describe the "cognitive revolution" in psychology.

1-1. Answer the following questions regarding the cognitive revolution in psychology.

(a) In what decade did this revolution get underway?

(b) Why were earlier cognitive approaches abandoned?

(c) What topics did the cognitive revolution open up for cognitive psychologists to study?

Answers: 1-1. (a) the 1950s (b) Because of the limitations of introspection and the rise of behaviourism. (c) memory, language, problem solving, decision making, and reasoning.

LANGUAGE: TURNING THOUGHTS INTO WORDS

2. Outline the key properties of language.

2-1. Language is characterized by four properties: it is symbolic, semantic, generativc, and structured. Identify these properties in the following statements.

(a) Applying rules to arrange words into phrases and sentences illustrates the ____________ property of language.

(b) Using words or geometric forms to represent objects, actions, or events illustrates the ____________ property of language.

(c) Making different words out of the same letters, such as NOW and WON, illustrates the ____________ property of language.

(d) Giving the same meaning to different words, such as *chat*, *katz*, and *cat*, illustrates the ____________ aspect of language.

2-2. Identify the following parts (units) of language.

(a) With around 40 of these basic sounds, you can say all of the words in the English language: ____________.

(b) Phonemes are combined into these smallest units of meaning in a language, which may include root words as well as prefixes and suffixes: ____________.

(c) The component of language concerned with understanding the meaning of words and word combinations is called ____________.

(d) These rules specify how words can be combined into phrases and sentences: ____________.

Answers: 2-1. (a) structured, (b) symbolic, (c) generative, (d) semantic **2-2.** (a) phonemes, (b) morphemes, (c) semantics, (d) syntax.

3. Outline the development of human language during the first year.

3-1. Answer the following questions regarding the development of language during the first year of life.

(a) Even at two months of age, infants show a preference for ____________ sounds, reflecting what Werker has called a "perceptual bias."

(b) What are a child's three major vocalizations during the first six months of life?

(c) What is the range in months for the babbling stage of language development?

(d) What gradually occurs as the babbling stage progresses?

(e) One view of babbling is that it is a ____________ achievement, reflecting the brain's increasing control over motor operations required for speech. Another view is that babbling is a ____________ achievement, reflecting the infant's increased ability to produce natural language.

Answers: 3-1. (a) speech, (b) crying, laughing, and cooing (c) 6 to 18 months (d) The babbling increasingly resembles spoken language. (e) motor, linguistic.

4. Describe children's early use of single words and word combinations.

4-1. What does the text mean when it states that the receptive vocabulary of toddlers is much larger than their productive vocabulary?

4-2. Identify the following phenomena observed in children's early use of language.

(a) What phenomenon is illustrated when a child calls all four-legged creatures "doggie"?

(b) What phenomenon is illustrated when a child correctly communicates his or her desire to know where the family dog is simply by asking, "Doggie?"

(c) What phenomenon is illustrated when a child complains to her mother, "Doggie eat cookie"?

(d) What phenomenon is illustrated when a child says, "Doggie runned away"?

(e) What phenomenon is illustrated when a child puns, "I love your I's"?

(f) Children begin to appreciate irony and sarcasm between the ages of _____ and _____.

(g) Solve the following anagram, which best describes how children acquire language skills: WSYLIFT ____________

Answers: 4-1. They can understand more spoken words than they can reproduce themselves.
4-2. (a) overextensions, (b) holophrases, (c) telegraphic speech, (d) overregularization, (e) metalinguistic awareness, (f) 6, 8, (g) SWIFTLY.

5. Describe the purpose, findings, and interpretation of the Featured Study on infant babbling.

5-1. Petitto and Marentette (1991) tested whether the maturation of speech production mechanisms (i.e., a motor achievement) or the maturation of a brain-based language capacity (i.e., a linguistic achievement) was behind infant babbling. They tested these alternative possibilities by studying _____________ infants who use a nonspeech language, American _____________ _____________, and comparing them with hearing infants.

5-2. They predicted that if babbling represents a linguistic achievement, then it (should/should not) appear in deaf infants (albeit in a different form).

5-3. Results revealed that deaf infants showed evidence of _____________ babbling. In addition, the babbling by deaf infants resembled babbling for hearing infants in terms of progression through stages and time course. Petitto and Marentette concluded that babbling does not reflect _____________ mechanisms involved in speech production but rather reflects the developing _____________ _____________ of the infant.

Answers: 5-1. deaf, Sign Language **5-2.** should **5-3.** manual, motor, language capacity.

6. Summarize the effect of bilingualism on language and cognitive development and the factors that influence the learning of a second language.

6-1. What does research comparing monolingual and bilingual children show with respect to their language and cognitive development?

6-2. What are some disadvantages and advantages of bilingualism?

6-3. What are the three hypotheses that account for the cognitive advantages of bilingualism?

6-4. For minority students, what drawbacks are there of immersion in the majority language?

6-5. What three factors positively influence the learning of a second language?

Answers: 6-1. They are largely similar in their rate of development (in both areas). **6-2.** On some tasks, bilinguals may have a slight disadvantage on language-processing speed, but they may have advantage on tasks emphasizing cognitive flexibility, analytical reasoning, selective attention, and metalinguistic awareness. **6-3.** First, bilingual children may develop control over executive processes earlier than monolingual children. Second, as adults, enhanced executive control of bilinguals should give them advantages on tasks emphasizing executive function. Third, bilinguals should show delayed decline of executive processes as a function of aging. **6-4.** Undermining self-esteem and heritage language proficiency. **6-5.** Starting at an early age, becoming acculturated, and one's motivation and attitude toward the group whose language is being learned.

7. Summarize evidence on language acquisition in animals.

7-1. Indicate whether each of the following is true (T) or false (F).

_______ (a) Researchers have been able to teach chimpanzees to use symbols to communicate.

_______ (b) Kanzi the chimp appears to comprehend both words and their relations to one another through structure.

_______ (c) Language acquisition in chimpanzees appears to be very similar to language acquisition in children.

_______ (d) Research using PET scans suggests that chimpanzees have an area in the left hemisphere analogous to Broca's area in humans.

Answers: 7-1. (a) T, (b) T, (c) F, (d) T.

8. Discuss the possible evolutionary basis of language.

8-1. What evolutionary advantage might language have given human populations as compared to the Neanderthals (who, many believe, lacked the language capabilities found in human beings)?

Answers: 8-1. The Neanderthals became extinct (and we're still here).

9. Compare and contrast the behaviourist, nativist, and interactionist perspectives on the acquisition of language.

9-1. Identify the following perspectives on the acquisition of language.

(a) This perspective places great emphasis on the role of reinforcement and imitation.

(b) This perspective assumes that children make use of a language acquisition device (LAD) to acquire transformational rules, which enable them to easily translate between surface structure and deep structure.

(c) This interactionist perspective argues that language development is tied to progress in thinking and general cognitive development.

(d) This interactionist perspective argues that language development is directed to some extent by the social benefits children derive from interaction with mature language users.

(e) This interactionist theory proposes that the neural circuits supporting language emerge gradually in response to language learning experiences.

9-2. Which perspective places greatest emphasis on:

(a) nurture ______________

(b) nature ______________

(c) nature interacting with nurture ______________

Answers: 9-1. (a) behaviourist, (b) nativist, (c) cognitive theories, (d) social communication theories, (e) emergentist theories **9-2.** (a) behaviourist, (b) nativist, (c) interactionist.

10. Discuss culture and language and the status of the linguistic relativity hypothesis.

10-1. What is the major idea behind Benjamin Whorf's linguistic relativity hypothesis?

10-2. What did Eleanor Rosch's experiment show when she compared the colour recognition ability of English-speaking people with that of Dani people, who have only two words for colour?

10-3. While language does not appear to invariably determine thought, it might exert some influence over the way we approach an idea. In other words, one's language may make it either ______________ or more ______________ to think along certain lines.

Answers: 10-1. Language determines thought. **10-2.** She found no difference in the ability to deal with colours. **10-3.** easier, difficult.

PROBLEM SOLVING: IN SEARCH OF SOLUTIONS

11. List and describe the three types of problems proposed by Greeno.

11-1. Greeno has proposed three types of problems (arrangement, inducing structure, and transformation). Identify each of these types from the descriptions given below.

(a) This type of problem requires the problem solver to discover the relations among the parts of the problem.

(b) This type of problem requires the problem solver to place the parts in a way that satisfies some specific criterion.

(c) This type of problem requires the problem solver to carry out a sequence of changes or rearrangements in order to reach a specific goal.

11-2. Which types of Greeno's problems are represented in the following situations?

(a) Which two three-letter English words can be made from the letters TBU?

(b) Fill in the missing word in "Grass is to green as snow is to ______________."

(c) You need to take your child to a pediatrician, your dog to the veterinarian, and your mother to the hairdresser, all within a limited time period. You think to yourself, "I'll take the kid and the dog and pick up Mom. Mom can stay with the kid at the doctor's office while I take the dog to the vet. Then I'll..."

11-3. Which type of problem is often solved in a sudden burst of insight?

Answers: 11-1. (a) arrangement, (b) inducing structure, (c) transformation **11-2.** (a) inducing structure, (b) white, arrangement, (c) transformation **11-3.** arrangement.

12. Explain how irrelevant information and functional fixedness can hinder problem solving.

12-1. Which of the barriers to effective problem solving, irrelevant information or functional fixedness, are you overcoming when you:

(a) make a financial decision without first consulting your horoscope?

(b) use a page of newspaper as a wedge to keep a door open?

Answers: 12-1. (a) irrelevant information, (b) functional fixedness.

13. Explain how mental set and unnecessary constraints can hinder problem solving.

13-1. Which of the barriers to effective problem solving, mental set or unnecessary constraints, are you overcoming when you:

(a) colour outside the lines to create a more interesting picture?

(b) teach an old dog a new trick?

Answers: 13-1. (a) unnecessary constraints, (b) mental set.

14. Describe a variety of general problem-solving strategies.

14-1. The text describes a variety of different problem-solving techniques, or_____________. Which of these heuristics (means/ends analysis, forming subgoals, working backward, searching for analogies, or changing the representation of the problem) would be most applicable in solving the following problems?

(a) While opening your car door, you drop the keys. The keys hit your foot and bounce underneath the car, too far to reach. It has stopped raining, so you close your umbrella and ponder how to get your keys.

(b) You have accepted the responsibility of chairing the homecoming celebration at your school.

(c) Alone at night in the office, you observe that the ink cartridge is missing from a printer you want to use. After obtaining a new cartridge, you can't figure out how to install it correctly. Glancing around, you see a similar printer with the cartridge installed.

(d) As an entering freshman in college, you have already chosen a field of study and a specific graduate school you wish to attend. Now all you have to do is accomplish this goal.

(f) You have agreed to become the campaign chairwoman for a friend who wants to run for student body president. Obviously, your goal is to make your friend look like a good choice to students, but which heuristic do politicians often employ here?

Answers: 14-1. heuristics (a) search for analogies (the umbrella can be used as a rake), (b) form subgoals, (c) work backward (see how the cartridge comes out), (d) means/ends analysis, (e) change the representation of the problem (make the opponents look like a bad choice).

15. Discuss the distinction between field independence and dependence.

15-1. Answer the following true–false questions regarding the distinctions between field-dependent and field-independent persons.

________ (a) Field-dependent persons are more likely to use internal cues to orient themselves in space.

________ (b) Field-independent persons are more likely to recognize the component parts of a problem rather than just seeing it as a whole.

Answers: 15-1. (a) F, (b) T.

16. Discuss cultural variations in cognitive style as they relate to problem solving.

16-1. Answer the following true–false questions regarding cultural variations in cognitive style.

________ (a) Persons living in cultures that depend on hunting and gathering for their subsistence are generally more field dependent than persons living in more sedentary agricultural societies.

________ (b) Persons raised in cultures with lenient child-rearing practices and an emphasis on personal autonomy tend to be more field independent.

16-2. Nisbett and others have proposed that East Asian cultures focus on context and relationships among elements in a field, which they call a ______________ cognitive style, whereas people from Western cultures focus on objects and their properties, rather than context, which they call an _______________ cognitive style. They conclude that these cultural disparities in cognitive style are (substantial/minimal).

Answers: 16-1. (a) F, (b) T **16-2.** holistic, analytical, substantial.

DECISION MAKING: CHOICES AND CHANCES

17. Compare the additive and elimination-by-aspects approaches to selecting an alternative.

17-1. Indicate which of these two approaches to decision making would be best in the following situations:

(a) The task is complex and there are numerous alternatives to choose from.

(b) You want to allow attractive attributes to compensate for unattractive attributes.

Answers: 17-1. (a) elimination-by-aspects, (b) additive.

18. Identify some "quirks" to people's decisions, and explain the factors that individuals typically consider in risky decision making.

18-1. Answer the following true–false questions regarding various quirks in people's decision making.

________ (a) Evaluations of the attributes of options being compared (e.g., features of two bicycles one is choosing between) tend to be very stable.

________ (b) Comparative evaluations tend to yield different results than separate evaluations.

________ (c) Decisions about products can be swayed by such features as brand familiarity.

18-2. What differentiates risky decision making from other kinds of decision making?

18-3. What is the most you can know when making a risky decision?

18-4. What two things must be known in order to calculate the expected value of making a risky decision when gambling with money?

18-5. How does the concept of subjective utility explain why some persons still engage in risky decision making when the expected value predicts a loss?

Answers: 18-1. (a) F, (b) T, (c) T **18-2.** The outcome is uncertain. **18-3.** The probability of a particular outcome. **18-4.** The average amount of money you could expect to win or lose with each play and the probability of a win or loss. **18-5.** The personal worth of the outcome may outweigh the probability of losing.

19. Describe the availability and representativeness heuristics.

19-1. Estimating the probability of an event on the basis of how often one recalls it has been experienced in the past is what Tversky and Kahneman call a/an ____________ heuristic.

19-2. When most people are asked if there are more words that begin with *N* or words that have *N* as the third letter, they apply the availability heuristic and guess incorrectly. Explain why they do this.

19-3. Estimating the probability of an event on the basis of how similar it is to a particular model or stereotype of that event is what Tversky and Kahneman call a/an ____________ heuristic.

19-4. "Steve is very shy. He has a high need for structure and likes detail. Is Steve more likely to be a salesperson or a librarian?" When persons are given this problem, they usually guess that he is a librarian, even though there are many more salespersons than there are librarians. Explain why they do this.

Answers: 19-1. availability **19-2.** Because they can immediately recall many more words that begin with *N* than words having *N* as the third letter. **19-3.** representativeness **19-4.** Because they employ the representativeness heuristic, and Steve fits the stereotype of a librarian.

20. Describe base rate neglect and the conjunction fallacy and their causes.

20-1. Identify which type of flawed reasoning, base rate neglect or the conjunction fallacy, is being described below.

(a) Estimating that the odds of two uncertain events happening together are greater than the odds of either event happening alone.

(b) Guessing that Steve (in 19-4) is a librarian and not a salesperson.

(c) Which of these two errors in judgment is a misapplication of the representativeness heuristic?

Answers: 20-1. (a) conjunction fallacy, (b) base rate neglect, (c) base rate neglect.

21. Explain evolutionary theorists' evaluation of cognitive research on flaws in human decision strategies.

21-1. What are two arguments put forth by evolutionary psychologists concerning research conducted on humans' decision-making abilities?

21-2. According to Cosmides and Tooby, cognitive research may reveal poor human performance only because studies tend to involve ____________ problems that have no ____________ significance.

21-3. According to Gigerenzer, humans employ "fast and frugal" heuristics in their reasoning, including the ____________ heuristic, which leads us to infer that a recognized alternative has a higher value. These tend to be employed when people do not have the time, resources, or cognitive capacities to make optimal decisions.

21-4. According to __________ -__________ theories, we sometimes employ shortcuts when making decisions, in line with Gigerenzer's fast and frugal heuristics, but at other times we engage in more elaborate, effortful, controlled judgments.

Answers: 21-1. They argue that such research has imposed an unrealistic standard of rationality and that such research has framed problems in ways incompatible with the evolved mind. **21-2.** artificial, adaptive **21-3.** recognition **21-4.** dual-process.

PUTTING IT IN PERSPECTIVE

22. Explain how this chapter highlighted four of the text's themes.

22-1. Indicate which one of the four unifying themes (the interaction of heredity and the environment; behaviour is shaped by cultural heritage; the empirical nature of psychology; and the subjectivity of experience) is best represented by the following statements.

(a) Psychologists developed objective measures for higher mental processes thus bringing about the cognitive revolution.

(b) The manner in which questions are framed can influence cognitive appraisal of the questions.

(c) Neither pure nativist theories nor pure nurture theories appear to adequately explain the development of language.

(d) The ecological demands of one's environment appear to somewhat affect one's cognitive style.

Answers: 22-1. (a) the empirical nature of psychology, (b) the subjectivity of experience, (c) the interaction of heredity and the environment, (d) behaviour is shaped by cultural heritage.

PERSONAL APPLICATION * UNDERSTANDING PITFALLS IN REASONING ABOUT DECISIONS

23. Explain what is meant by the gambler's fallacy and the law of small numbers.

23-1. Identify which type of flawed reasoning, the gambler's fallacy or the law of small numbers, is being described below.

(a) The belief that a small sampling of cases can be as valid as a large sampling of cases.

(b) The belief that the odds of a chance event increase if the event hasn't occurred recently.

Answers: 23-1. (a) the law of small numbers, (b) the gambler's fallacy.

24. Describe the propensity to overestimate the improbable and seek confirming evidence.

24-1. What flaw in reasoning often results from intense media coverage of dramatic, vivid, but infrequent, events.

24-2. What omission leads to confirmation bias when making decisions?

24-3. How is confirmation bias related to belief perseverance?

Answers: 24-1. the propensity to overestimate the improbable **24-2.** failure to seek out disconfirming evidence **24-3.** Disconfirming evidence is subjected to little skeptical evaluation.

25. Discuss the overconfidence effect and the effects of framing on decisions.

25-1. Answer the following true–false questions regarding the overconfidence effect.

________ (a) We are much less subject to this effect when making decisions about ourselves than about more worldly matters.

________ (b) Scientists are not generally prone to this effect when making decisions about information in their own fields.

________ (c) In the study of college students cited in the text, it was observed that the gap between personal confidence and actual accuracy of decisions increased as the confidence level increased.

25-2. Asking persons if they would prefer their glass of wine to be half-full or half-empty illustrates the general idea behind the____________ of questions.

25-3. Are persons more likely to take risky options when the problem is framed so as to obtain gains or when it is framed so as to cut losses?

Answers: 25-1. (a) F, (b) F, (c) T **25-2.** framing **25-3.** When it is framed so as to cut losses.

CRITICAL THINKING APPLICATION * SHAPING THOUGHT WITH LANGUAGE: "ONLY A NAÏVE MORON WOULD BELIEVE THAT"

26. Describe some language manipulation strategies that people use to shape others' thoughts.

26-1. State which language manipulation strategy is being used in each of the following situations.

(a) A politician says that his opponent "has an IQ somewhat below room temperature."

(b) Pet owners have their pets "put to sleep" when they become terminally ill.

(c) Only someone unbelievably stupid would be against more gun control legislation.

(d) Insurance companies sell "life insurance" policies rather than "death benefits" policies.

26-2. Research examining semantic slanting shows that an organization is best advised to slant its objectives so as to be (for/against) something when attempting to accomplish its goal.

Answers: 26-1. (a) name calling, (b) semantic slanting, (c) anticipatory name calling, (d) semantic slanting **26-2.** for

Review of Key Terms

Acculturation
Algorithm
Availability heuristic
Belief perseverance
Bilingualism
Cognition
Confirmation bias
Conjunction fallacy
Decision making
Fast mapping
Field dependence–independence
Framing
Functional fixedness
Gambler's fallacy
Heuristic
Insight
Language
Language acquisition device (LAD)
Linguistic relativity
Mean length of utterance (MLU)
Mental set
Metalinguistic awareness
Morphemes
Overextension
Overregularization
Phonemes
Problem solving
Problem space
Representativeness heuristic
Risky decision making
Semantics
Syntax
Telegraphic speech
Theory of bounded rationality
Trial and error
Underextension

_______________ **1.** The component of language concerned with understanding the meaning of words and word combinations.

_______________ **2.** A collection of symbols, and rules for combining those symbols, that can be used to create an infinite variety of messages.

_______________ **3.** The smallest units of sound in a spoken language.

_______________ **4.** The smallest units of meaning in a language.

_______________ **5.** The rules that specify how words can be combined into phrases and sentences.

_______________ **6.** Using a word incorrectly to describe a wider set of objects or actions than it is meant to.

_______________ **7.** Using a word to describe a narrower set of objects than it is meant to.

_______________ **8.** Single-word utterances that represent the meaning of several words.

_______________ **9.** The ability to reflect on the use of language.

_______________ **10.** Consists of the acquisition of two languages that employ different speech sounds, vocabulary, and grammatical rules.

_______________ **11.** The degree to which a person is socially and psychologically integrated into a new culture.

_______________ **12.** Basing the estimated probability of an event on the ease with which relevant instances come to mind.

_______________ **13.** Basing the estimated probability of an event on how similar it is to the typical prototype of that event.

_______________ **14.** The mental processes involved in acquiring knowledge.

_______________ **15.** The tendency to perceive an item only in terms of its most common use.

_______________ **16.** The sudden discovery of a correct solution to a problem following incorrect attempts.

_______________ **17.** A strategy for solving problems.

_______________ **18.** The process by which children map a word on an underlying concept after only one exposure to the word.

_______________ **19.** The average of youngsters' spoken statements (measured in morphemes).

_______________ **20.** Generalizing grammatical rules to irregular cases where they do not apply.

_______________ **21.** Making decisions under conditions of uncertainty.

_______________ **22.** A hypothetical innate mechanism or process that facilitates the learning of language.

_______________ **23.** Persisting in using problem-solving strategies that have worked in the past.

_______________ **24.** The theory that one's language determines one's thoughts.

_______________ **25.** The active efforts to discover what must be done to achieve a goal that is not readily attainable.

_______________ **26.** Trying possible solutions sequentially and discarding those that are in error until one works.

_______________ **27.** Evaluating alternatives and making choices among them.

_______________ **28.** How issues are posed or how choices are structured.

_______________ **29.** A methodical, step-by-step procedure for trying all possible alternatives in searching for a solution to a problem.

_______________ **30.** The tendency to hang on to beliefs in the face of contradictory evidence.

_______________ **31.** The tendency to seek information that supports one's decisions and beliefs while ignoring disconfirming evidence.

_______________ **32.** Occurs when people estimate that the odds of two uncertain events happening are greater than the odds of either event happening alone.

_______________ **33.** Refers to individuals' tendency to rely primarily on either external or internal frames of reference when orienting themselves in space.

_______________ **34.** The belief that the odds of a chance event increase if the event hasn't occurred recently.

_______________ **35.** Refers to the set of possible pathways to a solution considered by the problem solver.

_______________ **36.** Asserts that people tend to use simple strategies in decision making that focus only on a few facets of available options and often result in "irrational" decisions that are less than optimal.

Answers: 1. semantics **2.** language **3.** phonemes **4.** morphemes **5.** syntax **6.** Overextension **7.** underextension **8.** telegraphic speech **9.** metalinguistic awareness **10.** bilingualism **11.** acculturation **12.** availability heuristic **13.** representativeness heuristic **14.** cognition **15.** functional fixedness **6.** insight **17.** heuristic **18.** fast mapping **19.** mean length of utterance (MLU) **20.** overregularization **21.** risky decision making **22.** language acquisition device (LAD) **23.** mental set **24.** linguistic relativity **25.** problem solving **26.** trial and error **27.** decision making **28.** framing **29.** algorithm **30.** belief perseverance **31.** confirmation bias **32.** conjunction fallacy **33.** field dependence–independence **34.** gambler's fallacy **35.** problem space **36.** theory of bounded rationality.

Review of Key People

Ellen Bialystok	Wallace Lambert	Herbert Simon
Noam Chomsky	Laura-Ann Petitto	B. F. Skinner
Leda Cosmides & John Tooby	Steven Pinker	Janet Werker
Daniel Kahneman & Amos Tversky	Sue Savage-Rumbaugh	

_______________ 1. Won the Nobel Prize for his research on decision making and artificial intelligence.

_______________ 2. Proposed that children learn language through the established principles of learning.

_______________ 3. Proposed that children learn language through a biologically built-in language acquisition device.

_______________ 4. Co-researchers who showed that people base probability estimates on heuristics that do not always yield reasonable estimates of success.

_______________ 5. Along with her colleagues, she taught the chimp Kanzi to communicate in a way that made use of all the basic properties of language.

_______________ 6. Argues that human language ability is a species-specific trait that is the product of natural selection.

_______________ **7.** Argue that the human mind has evolved to solve specific adaptive problems.

_______________ **8.** Showed that infants have a perceptual bias to selectively attend to speech sounds.

_______________ **9.** Studied babbling in deaf and hearing infants.

_______________ **10.** Studies the effects of bilingualism on children's cognition.

_______________ **11.** A McGill scholar who has studied French immersion.

Answers: 1. Simon **2.** Skinner **3.** Chomsky **4.** Kahneman & Tversky **5.** Savage-Rumbaugh **6.** Pinker **7.** Cosmides & Tooby **8.** Werker **9.** Petitto **10.** Bialystok **11.** Lambert.

Self-Quiz

1. In what decade did the cognitive revolution in psychology occur?
a. the 1920s
b. the 1970s
c. the 1950s
d. the 1990s

2. Which of the following is not one of the basic properties of language?
a. generative
b. symbolic
c. structured
d. alphabetical

3. The word SLOW would be an example of a:
a. metalinguistic
b. phoneme
c. syntactical unit
d. morpheme

4. When a child says that TUB and BUT are constructed of the same three letters, he or she is showing an awareness of:
a. morphemes
b. phonemes
c. metalinguistics
d. syntax

5. Which of the following statements is incorrect?
a. A chimp has learned to sign (ASL) more than 150 words.
b. Children and chimps appear to learn language in a similar manner.
c. A chimp has shown comprehension for both words and their relation to one another.
d. The ability to use language may not be unique to humans.

6. The fact that children appear to learn rules, rather than specific word combinations, when acquiring language skills argues most strongly against which theory of language development?
a. cognitive
b. behaviourist
c. nativist
d. social communication

7. Which one of Greeno's problems is exemplified by the anagram?
a. arrangement
b. inducing structure
c. transformation
d. chunking

8. Which barrier to problem solving are you overcoming when you use a piece of paperclip as a temporary replacement for the screw that fell out of your glasses?
a. irrelevant information
b. functional fixedness
c. mental set
d. unnecessary constraints

9. Which of the following heuristics would you probably employ if assigned the task of carrying out a school election?
a. work backward
b. representativeness
c. search for analogies
d. form subgoals

10. Field-independent persons are most likely to come from cultures that:
a. encourage strict child-rearing practices
b. have a stable agricultural base
c. encourage lenient child-rearing practices
d. stress conformity

11. When faced with having to choose among numerous alternatives, most persons will opt for:
a. an elimination-by-aspects approach
b. an additive approach
c. a means/end analysis
d. a subjective-utility model

12. Most persons mistakenly believe that more people die from tornadoes than from asthma. This is because they mistakenly apply:
a. the means/end analysis
b. the compensatory decision model
c. the availability heuristic
d. the representativeness heuristic

13. Failure to actively seek out contrary evidence may lead to:
a. overestimating the improbable
b. the conjunction fallacy
c. the gambler's fallacy
d. the confirmation bias

14. People generally prefer a choice that provides an 80% chance of success over one that provides a 19% chance of failure. This illustrates the effect of:
a. the availability heuristic
b. the representativeness heuristic
c. framing
d. mental set

15. Owners of automobile junkyards prefer to use the term *automobile recycling centres*. This is an example of the use of:
a. framing
b. semantic slanting
c. anticipatory name calling
d. subjective utility

16. The Featured Study revealed that deaf infants babble (albeit with their hands) in a manner that shows similar developmental progression and timing as hearing infants. This finding suggests that babbling reflects a/an:

a. motor achievement
b. unimportant achievement
c. linguistic achievement
d. behavioural achievement

Answers: 1. c **2.** d **3.** d **4.** c **5.** b **6.** b **7.** a **8.** b **9.** d **10.** c **11.** a **12.** c **13.** d **14.** c **15.** b. **16.** c.

InfoTrac Keywords

Bilingualism

Mental Set

Risky Decision Making

Chapter Nine
INTELLIGENCE AND PSYCHOLOGICAL TESTING

Review of Key Ideas

KEY CONCEPTS IN PSYCHOLOGICAL TESTING

1. List and describe the principle categories of psychological tests.

1-1. Most psychological tests can be placed into one of two very broad categories. These two categories are: _______________ _______________ tests and _______________ tests.

1-2. There are three categories of mental ability tests. Below are examples of each of these categories. Identify them.

(a) The ACT and SAT tests you may have taken before entering college are examples of _______________ tests.

(b) The exams you frequently take in your introductory psychology class are examples of _______________ tests.

(c) Tests used to demonstrate general intellectual giftedness are examples of _______________ tests.

1-3. Personality tests allow an individual to compare himself or herself to other persons with respect to particular personality ____________. Personality tests generally (do/do not) have right and wrong answers.

Answers: 1-1. mental ability, personality **1-2.** (a) aptitude, (b) achievement, (c) intelligence **1-3.** characteristics (or traits), do not.

2. Explain the concepts of standardization and test norms.

2-1. Developing test norms and uniform procedures for use in the administration and scoring of a test is the general idea behind test _______________.

2-2. In order to interpret a particular score on a test, it is necessary to know how other persons score on this test. This is the purpose of test _______________. An easy method for providing comparisons of test scores is to convert the raw scores into _______________ scores.

2-3. The sample of people that the norms are based on is called the _______________ group.

Answers: 2-1. standardization **2-2.** norms, percentile **2-3.** standardization.

3. Explain the meaning of test reliability and how it is estimated.

3-1. The ability of a test to produce consistent results across subsequent measurements of the same persons is known as its _______________. Psychological tests (are/are not) perfectly reliable.

3-2. Re-administering the same test to the same group of persons a week or two following the original testing (test-retest) allows one to estimate the _______________ of a test. If a test is highly reliable, then a person's scores on the two different administrations will be very similar. The amount of similarity can be assessed by means of the _______________ coefficient. The closer the correlation comes to 1.0 the (more/less) reliable the test is.

Answers: 3-1. reliability, are not **3-2.** reliability, correlation, more.

4. Explain the three types of validity and how they are assessed.

4-1. The ability of a test to actually measure what it claims to measure is known as its _______________. The term *validity* is also used to refer to the accuracy or usefulness of the _______________ based on a test.

4-2. There are three general kinds of validity. Identify each of these kinds from the descriptions given below.

(a) This kind of validity will tend to be high when, for example, scores on the ACT and SAT actually predict success in college.

(b) This kind of validity will be of particular importance to you when taking your exams for this class. It will be high if the exam sticks closely to the explicitly assigned material.

(c) This kind of validity is more vague than the other two kinds and refers to the ability of a test to measure abstract qualities, such as intelligence.

4-3. As with the estimation of reliability, the estimation of validity makes use of the _______________ _______________.

Answers: 4-1. validity, inferences (or decisions) **4-2.** (a) criterion-related validity, (b) content validity, (c) construct validity **4-3.** correlation coefficient.

THE EVOLUTION OF INTELLIGENCE TESTING

5. Summarize the contributions of Galton and Binet to the evolution of intelligence testing.

5-1. Identify each of the men mentioned above from the following descriptions of their contributions.

(a) This man developed the first useful intelligence test. His tests were used to predict success in school, and scores were expressed in terms of mental age: _______________.

(b) This man began the quest to measure intelligence. He assumed that intelligence was mainly inherited and could be measured by assessing sensory acuity. He also invented correlation and percentile test scores: _______________.

Answers: 5-1. (a) Binet, (b) Galton.

6. Summarize the contributions of Terman and Wechsler to the evolution of intelligence testing.

6-1. Identify each of the men mentioned above from the following descriptions of their contributions.

(a) This man revised Binet's tests to produce the Stanford–Binet Intelligence Scale, the standard for all future intelligence tests. He also introduced the intelligence quotient (IQ): _______________.

(b) This man developed the first successful test of adult intelligence, the WAIS. He also developed new intelligence tests for children: _______________.

(c) In developing his new intelligence tests, this man added many nonverbal items, which allowed for the separate assessment of both verbal and nonverbal abilities. He also replaced the IQ score with one based on the normal distribution: _______________.

Answers: 6-1. (a) Terman (b) Wechsler (c) Wechsler.

BASIC QUESTIONS ABOUT INTELLIGENCE TESTING

7. Explain the meaning of an individual's score on a modern intelligence test.

7-1. Answer the following questions regarding intelligence test scores.

(a) In what manner is human intelligence assumed to be distributed?

(b) What percentage of people have an IQ score below 100?

(c) What percentage of persons would score two or more standard deviations above the mean? (Hint: See Figure 9.7 on page 380 of the text.)

Answers: 7-1. (a) It forms a normal distribution. (b) 50%, (c) 2%.

8. Describe the reliability and validity of modern IQ test scores.

8-1. Answer the following questions about the reliability of modern intelligence tests.

(a) What reliability estimates (correlation coefficients) are found for most modern intelligence tests?

(b) What might be a problem here with respect to an individual's test score?

8-2. Answer the following questions with respect to the validity of modern intelligence tests.

(a) What is the correlation between IQ tests and grades in school?

(b) What is the correlation between IQ tests and the number of years of schooling that people complete?

(c) What might be a general problem with assuming intelligence tests are a valid measure of general mental ability?

Answers: 8-1. (a) They are in the low .90s. (b) Temporary conditions, such as high anxiety, could lower the score. **8-2.** (a) .40s and .50s, (b) .60 to .80, (c) They principally focus on mental abilities conducive to academic success and ignore other kinds of intelligence.

9. Discuss how well intelligence tests predict vocational success.

9-1. In what way is IQ related to occupational achievement?

9-2. What are some limitations concerning the ability of IQ scores to predict performance within a particular occupation?

Answers: 9-1. People who score high on IQ tests are more likely to end up in high-status jobs than are those who score low. **9-2.** Only about 25% of variation in job performance is predicted by IQ; the validity of supervisor ratings as a measure of job performance has been questioned; and minority groups may be disadvantaged by the use of IQ tests for job performance.

10. Discuss the use of IQ tests in non-Western cultures.

10-1. Which of the following statements best summarizes the history of IQ testing in non-Western cultures?

a. Most Western and non-Western cultures have successfully adapted the IQ tests to their own cultures.

b. Many non-Western cultures have different conceptions of what intelligence is and do not necessarily accept Western notions as to how it can be measured.

Answers: 10-1. b.

EXTREMES OF INTELLIGENCE

11. Describe how mental retardation (or intellectual disability) is defined and divided into various levels.

11-1. In addition to having subnormal mental abilities (IQ scores of less than 70 to 75), what else is included in the definition of mental retardation?

11-2. There are four levels of mental retardation: mild, moderate, severe, and profound. Identify each of these levels from the descriptions given below:

(a) These persons have IQ scores below 20 and require total care.

(b) These persons have IQ scores between 50 and 75 and may become self-supporting citizens after leaving school and becoming adults.

(c) These persons have IQ scores between 35 and 50 and can be semi-independent in a sheltered environment.

(d) These persons have IQ scores between 20 and 35 and can help to contribute to their self-support under total supervision.

Answers: 11-1. The individual must show deficiencies in adaptive (everyday living) skills originating before age 18. **11-2.** (a) profound, (b) mild, (c) moderate, (d) severe.

12. Discuss what is known about the causes of mental retardation.

12-1. Although there are more than 350 organic syndromes associated with retardation, including Down syndrome, _______________ X syndrome, phenylketonuria, and hydrocephaly, organic causes account for only about _____% of retardation cases.

12-2. There are two general hypotheses as to the causes of the remaining 75% of retardation cases, most of which are diagnosed as mild. One theory is that retardation results from subtle _______________ defects that are difficult to detect. The other theory suggests that retardation is caused by a variety of unfavourable _______________ conditions.

Answers: 12-1. fragile, 25 **12-2.** (a) physiological, environmental.

13. Discuss the role of IQ tests in the identification of gifted children.

13-1. Answer the following questions regarding gifted children:

(a) What method is used almost exclusively to identify gifted children?

(b) What is the lowest IQ score that is generally needed to qualify children as gifted?

Answers: 13-1. (a) scores on IQ tests, (b) 130.

14. Describe the characteristics of the gifted and factors relating to adult achievements of the gifted.

14-1. Answer the following questions regarding the characteristics of the gifted.

(a) What did Terman's long-term study of gifted children show with respect to the physical, social, and emotional development of these children?

(b) Ellen Winner took a special look at profoundly gifted (IQ above 180) children. What did she estimate to be the incidence of interpersonal and emotional problems in these children when compared to other children?

(c) What three factors must interact and be present to an exceptional degree in order to produce the rarest form of giftedness, according to Renzulli?

(d) What is meant by the term "hidden gifted"?

(e) In addition to intensive training and hard work, what other factor may be necessary to achieve extraordinary achievement?

Answers: 14-1. (a) They were above average in all three areas. (b) It's about twice as high in the profoundly gifted children. (c) intelligence, motivation, creativity (in any order), (d) children with very high IQ scores but who are underachieving in school, (e) rare, innate talent.

HEREDITY AND ENVIRONMENT AS DETERMINANTS OF INTELLIGENCE

15. Summarize the empirical evidence that heredity affects intelligence.

15-1. Below are the mean correlations for the intelligence of four different groups of children: *siblings reared together, fraternal twins reared together, identical twins reared apart*, and *identical twins reared together.* Match the group with the appropriate correlation.

.86 ____________________ .60 ____________________

.72 ____________________ .44 ____________________

15-2. What do the above correlations tell us about the role of heredity on intelligence?

Answers: 15-1. (.86) identical twins reared together, (.72) identical twins reared apart, (.60) fraternal twins reared together, (.44) siblings reared together **15-2.** That heredity plays a significant role in intelligence.

16. Discuss estimates of the heritability of intelligence and their limitations.

16-1. The consensus estimate of experts is that the heritability ratio for human intelligence hovers around 50%. What does this mean?

16-2. What are the limitations of heritability estimates?

Answers: 16-1. 50% of the variation in intelligence in a particular group is estimated to be due to heredity (leaving 50% due to environmental factors). **16-2.** Heritability is a group statistic and may give misleading results when applied to particular individuals; the heritability of a trait can vary from one group to another; and there really is no single value that represents any true heritability of IQ.

17. Describe various lines of research that indicate that environment affects intelligence.

17-1. What cumulative effects on intelligence have been found among children reared in deprived environments?

17-2. What effects on intelligence have been found among children moved from deprived environments to more enriched environments?

17-3. Answer the following questions regarding the "Flynn effect."

(a) What did Flynn's research show with respect to generational changes in IQ scores since 1930 in the industrialized world?

(b) Can these generational changes be attributed to heredity?

Answers: 17-1. There is a gradual decrease in intelligence (across time). **17-2.** There is a gradual increase in intelligence (across time). **17-3.** (a) Scores have been steadily rising. (b) no.

18. Using the concept of reaction range, explain how heredity and the environment interact to affect intelligence.

18-1. The notion behind the concept of reaction range is that heredity places an upper and lower _______________ on how much an individual can vary, with respect to a characteristic such as intelligence. This means that a child's IQ can vary significantly depending on the kind of _______________ he or she experiences. The major point here is that the limits for intelligence are determined by _______________ factors, and the movement within these limits is determined by _____________ factors.

18-2. Thus far, molecular genetics research (has/has not) advanced as quickly as expected, likely reflecting the fact that (many/few) genes are likely to influence intelligence and the fact that the influence of any one gene is likely to be (small/large).

Answers: 18-1. limit, environment, genetic (or hereditary), environmental. **18-2.** has not, many, small.

19. Discuss heritability and socioeconomic disadvantage as alternative explanations for cultural differences in average IQ.

19-1. Two explanations for the cultural differences in IQ scores are listed below. Tell what each of these explanations means.

(a) Jensen's heritability explanation.

(b) Socioeconomic disadvantage.

19-2. What evidence is consistent with the socioeconomic disadvantage explanation?

Answers: 19-1. (a) The cultural differences are due to heredity, (b) The cultural differences are due to environmental factors. **19-2.** Average IQ scores among children from lower social classes tend to be about 15 points below those among children of middle- and upper-class homes.

20. Discuss the possible contributions of stereotype vulnerability and cultural bias to ethnic differences in average IQ.

20-1. Steele's theory of stereotype vulnerability holds that a widely held stereotype, that certain racial groups are mentally inferior, acts on the members of these groups so as to make them (more/less) vulnerable (i.e., they tend to underperform) when confronted with tests assessing intellectual ability. Steele believes that this same vulnerability (does/does not) exist for women entering domains dominated by men. Research so far (does/does not) support the theory of stereotype vulnerability.

20-2. What did the text conclude about the possible effects of cultural bias with respect to ethnic differences in IQ scores?

Answers: 20-1. more, does, does **20-2.** The IQ gap may reflect differences in knowledge due to disparities in exposure to information. However, such cultural bias produces only weak and inconsistent effects.

NEW DIRECTIONS IN THE ASSESSMENT AND STUDY OF INTELLIGENCE

21. Describe some new trends in the assessment of intelligence.

21-1. The notion that intelligence is a function of general mental abilities, Spearman's *g*, dominated early thinking in test development. However, other researchers began to conclude that intelligence involves (few/multiple) abilities. Cattell and Horn believe that intelligence should be divided into intelligence that involves reasoning ability, memory capacity, and speed of information processing, which they call _______________ intelligence, and intelligence that involves ability to apply acquired knowledge and skills in problem solving, which they call _______________ intelligence.

21-2. As test developers have begun to turn away from tests designed to measure general intelligence, what kinds of tests are replacing them?

21-3. Which biologically oriented approach to measuring intelligence, reaction time or inspection time, appears to be the more promising?

21-4. What has recent research revealed concerning (a) brain size and intelligence and (b) longevity and intelligence?

Answers: 21-1. multiple, fluid, crystallized **21-2.** tests of specific mental abilities **21-3.** inspection time **21-4.** (a) The average correlation between brain size and intelligence is about .35. (b) Higher IQ scores early in life predict greater longevity, or "smarter people live longer."

22. Describe Sternberg's and Gardner's theories of intelligence and the concept of emotional intelligence.

22-1. Sternberg's triarchic theory proposes that intelligence is composed of three basic parts. Match these parts with their individual functions:

SUBTHEORY	FUNCTION
____ Contextual	(a) Emphasizes the role played by society.
____ Experiential	(b) Emphasizes the cognitive processes underlying intelligence.
____ Componential	(c) Emphasizes the interplay between intelligence and experience.

22-2. Which of these three subtheories contains three underlying subcomponents (metacomponents, performance components, and knowledge-acquisition components)?

22-3. In a recent addition to his theory, Sternberg has proposed three facets of what he calls "successful intelligence." Match these three facets with their respective descriptions.

FACETS (INTELLIGENCE)	DESCRIPTIONS
____ Analytical	(a) Ability to deal effectively with everyday problems.
____ Creative	(b) Ability to generate new ideas.
____ Practical	(c) Abstract reasoning, evaluation, and judgment.

22-4. Gardner has proposed eight relatively distinct human intelligences. What does his research show with respect to a *g* factor among these separate intelligences?

22-5. The ability to perceive and express emotion, assimilate emotion in thought, understand and reason with emotion, and regulate emotion is the general idea behind _____________ intelligence. Parker has suggested that emotional intelligence may be particularly helpful when it comes to coping with ____________ ____________.

Answers: 22-1. a, c, b **22-2.** componential **22-3.** c, b, a **22-4.** There does not appear to be a *g* factor; i.e., people display a mix of strong, weak, and intermediate abilities **22-5.** emotional, stressful events.

PUTTING IT IN PERSPECTIVE

23. Discuss how the chapter highlighted three of the text's unifying themes.

23-1. Answer the following questions about the three unifying themes (cultural factors shape behaviour; psychology evolves in a sociohistorical context; and heredity and environment jointly influence behaviour).

(a) What theme is exemplified by the controversy over the book *The Bell Curve*?

(b) What theme is exemplified by the different views about the nature of intelligence held by Western and non-Western cultures?

(c) What theme is exemplified by the extensive research using twin studies, adoption studies, and family studies?

Answers: 23-1. (a) Psychology evolves in a sociohistorical context. (b) Cultural factors shape behaviour. (c) Heredity and environment jointly influence behaviour.

PERSONAL APPLICATION * UNDERSTANDING CREATIVITY

24. Discuss popular ideas about the nature of creativity.

24-1. Popular notions about creativity would have us believe that creative ideas arise from nowhere, occur in a burst of insight, are not related to hard work, and are unrelated to intelligence. What does the text say about these notions?

Answers: 24-1. They are all false.

25. Describe creativity tests, and summarize how well they predict creative achievement.

25-1. Most tests of creativity attempt to assess (conventional/divergent) thinking, such as the following: List as many uses as you can for a book. Creativity scores are based on the ______________ of alternatives generated and the originality and ______________ of the suggested alternatives.

25-2. Creativity tests are rather (good/mediocre) predictors of creativity in the real world. One reason for this is that they attempt to treat creativity as a (specific/general) trait, while research evidence seems to show it is related to quite ______________ domains.

Answers: 25-1. divergent, number, usefulness (utility) **25-2.** mediocre, general, specific.

26. Discuss associations between creativity and personality, intelligence, and mental illness.

26-1. What two traits appear to be at the core of the personality characteristics common to creative people?

26-2. What is the intelligence level of most highly creative people?

26-3. What form of mental illness appears to be associated with creative achievement?

Answers: 26-1. independence and nonconformity **26-2.** average to above average **26-3.** mood disorders.

CRITICAL THINKING APPLICATION * THE INTELLIGENCE DEBATE, APPEALS TO IGNORANCE AND REIFICATION

27. Explain how appeals to ignorance and reification have cropped up in numerous debates about intelligence.

27-1. Tell whether the following statements represent examples of appeals to ignorance or to reification.

(a) He doesn't do very well in college because he's lacking in intelligence.

(b) If only 25% of the cases of mental retardation can be attributed to biological causes, the remaining 75% must be due to environmental factors.

(c) The downside to creativity is that it can lead to mood disorders.

(d) More money should be spent on research to find the accurate heritability coefficient of intelligence.

Answers: 27-1. (a) reification, (b) appeals to ignorance, (c) appeals to ignorance, (d) reification.

Review of Key Terms

Achievement tests
Aptitude tests
Construct validity
Content validity
Convergent thinking
Correlation coefficient
Creativity
Criterion-related validity
Crystallized intelligence
Deviation IQ scores
Divergent thinking
Emotional intelligence
Factor analysis
Fluid intelligence
Heritability ratio
Intelligence quotient (IQ)
Intelligence tests
Mental age
Mental retardation
Normal distribution
Percentile score
Personality tests
Psychological test
Reaction range
Reification
Reliability
Standardization
Test norms
Validity

________________ **1.** A standardized measure of a sample of a person's behaviour.

________________ **2.** Tests that measure general mental ability.

________________ **3.** Tests that measure various personality traits.

________________ **4.** Tests that assess talent for specific kinds of learning.

________________ **5.** Tests that gauge the mastery and knowledge of various subject areas.

________________ **6.** The development of uniform procedures for administering and scoring tests, including the development of test norms.

________________ **7.** Data that provide information about the relative standing of a particular test score.

________________ **8.** Number indicating the percentage of people who score above or below a particular test score.

________________ **9.** The measurement consistency of a test.

________________ **10.** The ability of a test to measure what it was designed to measure.

________________ **11.** The degree to which the content of a test is representative of the domain it is supposed to measure.

________________ **12.** The degree to which the scores on a particular test correlate with scores on an independent criterion (test).

________________ **13.** The degree to which there is evidence that a test measures a hypothetical construct.

________________ **14.** A score indicating the mental ability typical of a chronological age group.

________________ **15.** Mental age divided by chronological age and multiplied by 100.

____________________ **16.** A symmetrical, bell-shaped curve that describes the distribution of many physical and psychological attributes.

____________________ **17.** Scores that translate raw scores into a precise location in the normal distribution.

____________________ **18.** Subnormal, general mental ability accompanied by deficiencies in everyday living skills originating prior to age 18.

____________________ **19.** An estimate of the percentage of variation in a trait determined by genetic inheritance.

____________________ **20.** Genetically determined limits on intelligence.

____________________ **21.** Method that uses the correlation among many variables to identify closely related clusters.

____________________ **22.** The ability to apply acquired knowledge and skills to problem solving.

____________________ **23.** Includes reasoning ability, memory capacity, and speed of information processing.

____________________ **24.** The generation of ideas that are original, novel, and useful.

____________________ **25.** Thinking that attempts to narrow down a list of alternatives to a single best solution.

____________________ **26.** Thinking that attempts to expand the range of alternatives by generating many possible solutions.

____________________ **27.** A numerical index of the degree of relationship between two variables.

____________________ **28.** Occurs when a hypothetical abstract concept is given a name and then treated as though it were a concrete, tangible object.

____________________ **29.** The ability to perceive and express emotion, assimilate emotion in thought, understand and reason with emotion, and regulate emotion.

Answers: 1. psychological test **2.** intelligence tests **3.** personality tests **4.** aptitude tests **5.** achievement tests **6.** standardization **7.** test norms **8.** percentile score **9.** reliability **10.** validity **11.** content validity **12.** criterion-related validity **13.** construct validity **14.** mental age **15.** intelligence quotient **16.** normal distribution **17.** deviation IQ scores **18.** mental retardation **19.** heritability ratio **20.** reaction range **21.** factor analysis **22.** crystallized thinking **23.** fluid thinking **24.** creativity **25.** convergent thinking **26.** divergent thinking **27.** correlation coefficient **28.** reification **29.** emotional intelligence.

Review of Key People

Alfred Binet	Arthur Jensen	Robert Sternberg
Sir Francis Galton	Sandra Scarr	Lewis Terman
Howard Gardner	Claude Steele	David Wechsler
		Ellen Winner

____________________ **1.** Developed the Stanford–Binet Intelligence Scale.

____________________ **2.** Developed the first successful test of adult intelligence.

____________________ **3.** Postulated a cognitive triarchic theory of intelligence.

____________________ **4.** Proposed a reaction range model for human intelligence.

____________________ **5.** Developed the first useful intelligence test.

____________________ **6.** Postulated a heritability explanation for cultural differences in intelligence.

____________________ **7.** Began the quest to measure intelligence.

______________________ **8.** Proposed a stereotype vulnerability theory as an explanation for racial differences on IQ test scores.

______________________ **9.** Has suggested the existence of a number of relatively autonomous human intelligences.

______________________ **10.** Argued that moderately gifted children are quite different than profoundly gifted children.

Answers: 1. Terman **2.** Wechsler **3.** Sternberg **4.** Scarr **5.** Binet **6.** Jensen **7.** Galton **8.** Steele **9.** Gardner **10.** Winner.

Self-Quiz

1. This self-test you are now taking is an example of:
a. an aptitude test
b. an achievement test
c. an intelligence test
d. a criterion-related test

2. Which of the following statistics is generally used to estimate reliability and validity?
a. the correlation coefficient
b. the standard deviation
c. the percentile score
d. the median

3. What kind of validity do tests such as the SAT and ACT particularly strive for?
a. content validity
b. construct validity
c. absolute validity
d. criterion-related validity

4. With respect to modern intelligence tests:
a. validity is generally higher than reliability
b. reliability and validity are about the same
c. reliability is generally higher than validity
d. I have no idea what you're talking about

5. People in which of the following mentally retarded (or intellectual disability) groups can often pass for normal as adults?
a. mild
b. moderate
c. profound
d. both mild and moderate

6. What percentage of mental retardation cases have been definitely linked to organic causes?
a. approximately 25%
b. approximately 50%
c. approximately 75%
d. approximately 90%

7. Terman's long-term study of gifted children found that they tended to excel in:
a. physical development
b. social development
c. emotional development
d. all three areas

8. Which of the following groups shows the lowest correlation with respect to intelligence?
a. fraternal twins reared together
b. fraternal twins reared apart
c. identical twins reared apart
d. siblings reared together

9. If the heritability ratio for intelligence is 80%, this means that for you, heredity determines 80% of your intelligence and environment determines 20%. This statement is:
a. true
b. false

10. The "Flynn effect" arises from the observation that the general intelligence in industrialized societies:
a. has been rising across time
b. has been declining across time
c. has remained steady across time
d. is primarily affected by heredity and not environment

11. The rate of mental retardation (or intellectual disability) is somewhere between:
a. 1% and 3%
b. 10% and 15%
c. 6% and 10%
d. .01% and .05%

12. Which of the following explanations for racial differences in intelligence is best supported by research evidence?
a. Jensen's heritability theory
b. cultural bias in IQ tests
c. socioeconomic disadvantage
d. Watson's differential conditioning theory

13. Steele's theory of stereotype vulnerability is an attempt to explain:
a. why Asian–Americans score higher than average on IQ tests
b. why African–Americans score lower than average on IQ tests
c. why cultural bias must necessarily be inherent in all intelligence tests
d. why the general intelligence in a population declines across time

14. Spearman's *g* implies that:
a. most kinds of intelligence are highly related
b. most kinds of intelligence are not highly related
c. intelligence is highly correlated with personality characteristics
d. intelligence is primarily genetic in origin

15. Most tests of creativity emphasize:
a. convergent thinking
b. divergent thinking
c. bursts of insight
d. getting at unconscious thought processes

16. What form of mental illness frequently has been found to be associated with outstanding creativity?
a. anxiety disorders
b. antisocial personality
c. schizophrenia
d. mood disorders

17. Which of the following statements is an example of reification?
a. Birds of a feather flock together.
b. Creative people are born, not raised.
c. She gets good grades in school because she is intelligent.
d. Intelligence tests are only moderate predictors of vocational success.

18. Which of the following terms means the same as mental retardation?
a. mental disability
b. intellectual disability
c. cognitive limitation
d. intellectual limitation.

Answers: 1. b **2.** a **3.** d **4.** c **5.** a **6.** a **7.** d **8.** d **9.** b **10.** a **11.** a **12.** c **13.** b **14.** a **15.** b **16.** d **17.** c **18.** b.

InfoTrac Keywords

Achievement Tests

Aptitude Tests

Intelligence Tests

Chapter Ten
MOTIVATION AND EMOTION

Review of Key Ideas

MOTIVATIONAL THEORIES AND CONCEPTS

1. **Define motivation and compare drive, incentive, and evolutionary approaches to understanding motivation.**

1-1. Motivation is defined as involving __________ -__________ behaviour.

1-2. Drive theories are based on the idea that organisms strive to maintain a state of ________________ or physiological equilibrium. For example, organisms are motivated to maintain water balance: When deprived of water, they experience thirst. Thirst is a ________________ to return to a state of water equilibrium.

1-3. A drive is a state of tension. According to drive theories, organisms are motivated to seek drive or tension ________________.

1-4. Theories that emphasize the pull from the external environment are known as ________________ theories. For example, we may be motivated to eat, not as a function of hunger but as a result of the smell or appearance of food. Incentive theories (operate/do not operate) according to the principle of homeostasis.

1-5. From the point of view of evolutionary theory, all motivations, such as the needs for affiliation, dominance, achievement, and aggression, as well as needs for food and water, occur because they have ________________ value for the species. Organisms with adaptive sets of motivational characteristics are more likely to pass their ________________ on to the next generation.

1-6. Place the name of the theoretical approach described below (drive, incentive, or evolutionary) in the blanks.

______________ Emphasizes homeostasis, the pressure to return to a state of equilibrium.

______________ Actions result from attempts to reduce internal states of tension.

_____________ Emphasizes "pull" from the environment (as opposed to "push" from internal states).

_____________ Motivations arise as a function of their capacity to enhance reproductive success, to pass genes to the next generation.

_____________ Motivation to pursue a goal or object depends on the *value* of the object and one's *expectancy* of success at obtaining it.

Answers: 1-1. goal-directed **1-2.** homeostasis (balance), drive **1-3.** reduction **1-4.** incentive, do not operate **1-5.** adaptive (survival, reproductive), genes **1-6.** drive, drive, incentive, evolutionary, incentive.

2. Distinguish between the two major categories of motives found in humans.

2-1. Most theories of motivation distinguish between _______________ motives (e.g., for food, water, sex, warmth) and _______________ motives. Biological needs are generally essential for the _______________ of the group or individual.

2-2. Social motives (e.g., for achievement, autonomy, affiliation) are acquired as a result of people's experiences. While there are relatively few biological needs, people theoretically may acquire an unlimited number of _______________ needs.

Answers: 2-1. biological, social, survival **2-2.** social.

THE MOTIVATION OF HUNGER AND EATING

3. Summarize evidence of the physiological factors implicated in the regulation of hunger.

3-1. Within the brain, the major structure implicated in eating behaviour is the _______________.

3-2. Researchers used to think that eating was controlled by "on" and "off" centres in the hypothalamus. When the lateral hypothalamus (LH) was destroyed, animals stopped eating, as if hunger had been turned off like a switch. When the ventromedial hypothalamus (VMH) was destroyed, animals started to eat. While these structures are still considered important in hunger regulation, researchers now believe that eating is controlled to a greater extent by (complex neural circuits/simple anatomical centres).

3-3. In addition, researchers have changed their conclusions about the relative importance of various structures. According to current thinking, which of the following areas of the hypothalamus plays the most important role in hunger?

a. lateral hypothalamus (LH)

b. ventromedial hypothalamus (VMH)

c. paraventricular nucleus (PVN)

3-4. Much of the food we consume is converted into _______________, a simple sugar that is an important source of energy.

3-5. Based on research findings about glucose, Mayer proposed the theory that there are specialized neurons in the brain, which he called ________________, that function to monitor blood glucose. Lower levels of glucose, for example, are associated with a/an (increase/decrease) in hunger.

3-6. For cells to extract glucose from the blood, the hormone ________________ must be present. Insulin will produce a/an (increase/decrease) in the level of sugar in the blood, with the result that the person experiences a/an (increase/decrease) in the sensation of hunger.

3-7. More recently, a regulatory hormone called leptin has been discovered, a hormone produced by (fat cells/neurons) and circulated to the hypothalamus in the bloodstream. Higher levels of the hormone ________________ reflect a higher level of fat in the body, which is associated with a/an (increase/decrease) in the sensation of hunger.

Answers: 3-1. hypothalamus **3-2.** complex neural circuits **3-3.** c. **3-4.** glucose **3-5.** glucostats, increase **3-6.** insulin, decrease, increase **3-7.** fat cells, leptin, decrease.

4. Summarize evidence on how the availability of food and other cues, culture, learning, and stress influence hunger.

4-1. Hunger is based not only on a physiological need, but on external factors such as the appearance, tastiness, and availability of food. Thus, some aspects of hunger motivation support the (drive/incentive) approach to motivation. Sometimes we eat, according to this research, simply because food is available. There is also evidence that as you eat a specific food, its incentive value declines, a phenomenon called ____________-____________ ____________.

4-2. Social cues also play a role in our eating. The ____________ ____________ model suggests that social norms, as revealed by the behaviour of others around us, affect our eating. Most typically, people eat (more/less) when others are nearby.

4-3. Although we have some innate taste preferences (e.g., for fat), it is also clear that ________________ affects what we eat. For example, taste preferences and aversions may be learned by pairing a taste with pleasant or unpleasant experiences, the process of ________________ conditioning.

4-4. In addition, we are more likely to eat food that we see others eating, especially if the others are parents or friends. Thus, food preferences are acquired not only through conditioning but through the process of ________________ learning.

4-5. Our environments also provide frustrating circumstances that create ________________, a factor that may also trigger eating in many people. Although stress and increased eating are linked, it's not clear why the relationship occurs.

Answers: 4-1. incentive, sensory-specific satiety **4-2.** inhibitory norm, less **4-3.** learning (environment, culture), classical **4-4.** observational **4-5.** stress.

5. Discuss obesity and the factors that contribute to its development.

5-1. Obesity is usually defined in relation to the __________ __________ index (BMI; weight in kilograms divided by height in metres squared). A BMI of over ______ is often used as an indicator of obesity. The overall rate of obesity in Canada is _______%. Obesity rates in Canada have ______________ over the past two decades. A group revealing a substantially increasing rate of obesity is ______________.

5-2. Evolutionary theorists propose that in our ancestral past, when faced with the likelihood of famine, people evolved a capacity to overeat. Overeating, as a hedge against food shortages, had ______________ value. In many areas of the world, food is no longer scarce, but our tendency to overeat remains. In terms of our physiological needs, (very few/most) people overeat, and because of differences in makeup, some become overweight.

5-3. It is clear that many factors affect body weight and that some of the most important are genetic. For example, Stunkard et al. (1986) found that adopted children were much more similar in BMI to their (biological/adoptive) parents than to their (biological/adoptive) parents, even though they were brought up by the latter.

5-4. The most striking finding of the Stunkard et al. (1990) study with twins was that (identical/fraternal) twins reared apart were more similar in BMI than (identical/fraternal) twins reared in the same family environment. This research supports the idea that (genetics/environment) play(s) a major role in body weight.

5-5. The concept of set point may help explain why body weight remains so stable. The theory proposes that each individual has a "natural" body weight that is set, in large part, by the person's (genetics/environment).

5-6. According to __________-__________ theory, individual differences in body weight are in large part due to differences in genetic makeup. This theory asserts that the body actively defends a (wide range/ particular) body weight by, for example, increasing hunger or decreasing metabolism.

5-7. Settling-point theory is a bit more optimistic: Individuals who make long-term changes in eating or exercise will drift downward to a lower ______________ point without such active resistance. The settling-point view also asserts that this balance is achieved as a result of (a wide variety of/genetic) factors.

5-8. According to the concept of dietary restraint, the world is divided into two types of people: unrestrained eaters, who eat as much as they want when they want; and ______________ eaters, who closely monitor their food intake and frequently go hungry.

5-9. While restrained eaters are constantly on guard to control their eating, at times they may lose control and eat to excess. In other words, restraint may be disrupted or ______________, with the result that people overeat. This may include overeating just before they initiate a ______________ (i.e., in anticipation of food deprivation). Paradoxically, then, restraint in eating may contribute to obesity. Restrained eaters are also more sensitive to the media's portrayal of ______________ images of the thin body type.

Answers: 5-1. body mass, 30, 15, doubled, children **5-2.** survival (adaptive), most **5-3.** biological, adoptive **5-4.** identical , fraternal, genetics **5-5.** genetics **5-6.** set-point, particular **5-7.** settling, a wide variety of **5-8.** restrained **5-9.** disinhibited, diet, idealized.

6. Describe eating disorders and some factors associated with them.

6-1. The disorder that involves self-starvation is _______________ nervosa, and the disorder that involves binge eating and purging is _______________ nervosa. About _____% of Canadian women will develop an eating disorder, and the prevalence is (increasing/decreasing).

6-2. Factors such as an overemphasized thin _______________ and pressures to be _______________ contribute to eating disorders, in addition to other biological, psychological, developmental, and social factors. Excessive physical exercise may contribute to a version of eating disorder called _______________ anorexia.

Answers: 6-1. anorexia, bulimia, 3, increasing **6-2.** ideal, thin, activity.

SEXUAL MOTIVATION AND BEHAVIOUR

7. Describe survey findings concerning the sexual activities of young Canadians.

7-1. According to recent Canadian surveys, about ______% of 15- to 17-year-olds and ______% of 20- to 24-year-olds have engaged in sexual intercourse. Engaging in sex at an early age is correlated with _______________ _______________ partners and (among girls) weak __________-__________. Having sex without using a condom is (rare/not uncommon), with ______% of sexually active 20- to 24-year-olds reporting such behaviour.

Answers: 7-1. 28, 80, multiple sexual, self-concepts, not uncommon, 44.

8. Describe the impact of hormones in regulating animal and human sexual behaviour.

8-1. Hormones are clearly linked to sexual behaviour. For example, castrated rats have no sexual interest, but if they are injected with the hormone _______________, their sexual motivation revives.

8-2. The major female sex hormones are called _______________, and the major male sex hormones _______________. Both of these gonadal hormones occur in both sexes, however. Higher levels of the hormone _______________, a key androgen, are related to higher levels of sexual activity in (males only/females only/both sexes).

8-3. In general, the impact of hormones on sexual activity in humans appears to be (relatively modest/quite strong).

Answers: 8-1. testosterone **8-2.** estrogens, androgens, testosterone, both sexes **8-3.** relatively modest.

9. Discuss parental investment theory and findings on human gender differences in sexual activity.

9-1. Triver's parental investment theory asserts that a species' mating patterns are determined by the investment each sex must make to produce and nurture offspring. Since human females are the ones who are pregnant for nine months and breastfeed the offspring, their _______________ in the child is, by this analysis, greater than that of human males.

9-2. According to this viewpoint, the sex that makes the smaller investment will *compete* for mating opportunities with the sex that makes the larger investment, and the sex that makes the larger investment will be more *selective* of partners. Thus, males of many mammalian species, including human beings, seek to maximize their reproductive potential by mating with (as many/as few) females as possible. Females, on the other hand, optimize their reproductive potential by being (selective/unrestricted) in mating.

9-3. In line with predictions from parental investment theory and evolutionary theory in general, Buss's research showed that _______________ placed a higher value on potential partners' status and financial prospects, whereas _______________ placed a higher value on youthfulness and physical attractiveness. These findings (did/did not) emerge across cultures.

Answers: 9-1. investment **9-2.** as many, selective **9-3.** women, men, did.

10. Describe the Featured Study on judging mate potential.

10-1. The study by Roney and colleagues examined whether women could draw meaningful inferences about males' _______________ and _______________ _______________ from facial cues. Women rated the level of masculinity, parental potential, and other attributes of a men through facial photos.

10-2. Results showed that ratings of masculinity correlated significantly with males' actual _______________ levels, and ratings of parental potential (e.g., how much the man liked children) correlated with males' scores on a test of their interest in infants. Finally, women's ratings of masculinity correlated with their estimates of males' (short/long)-term mate potential, whereas women's ratings of parental potential correlated with their estimates of males' (short/long)-term mate potential.

Answers: 10-1. masculinity, parental potential **10-2.** testosterone, short, long.

11. Summarize evidence on the impact of erotic materials, including aggressive pornography, on human sexual behaviour.

11-1. Findings on the relationship between exposure to erotic materials and sexual activity have been inconsistent and open to interpretation. One fairly consistent finding, however, has been that erotic materials (increase/decrease) the likelihood of sexual activity for a few hours after exposure.

11-2. In the Zillman and Bryant studies described, male and female undergraduate subjects were exposed to relatively heavy doses of pornography over a period of weeks. One of the effects was that *attitudes* involving sexual practices became more (liberal/conventional). Another was that subjects became (more/less) satisfied with their partners' appearance and sexual performance.

11-3. In general, researchers (have/have not) found a link between exposure to erotic materials and sex crimes.

11-4. Several studies have found that pornography depicting violence against women (decreases/increases) men's tendency to be aggressive toward women. In these laboratory studies, aggression is defined as willingness to deliver electric shock to other subjects.

11-5. Other studies have found that exposure to aggressive pornography makes sexual coercion or rape seem (less/more) offensive to the participants, a troublesome finding in view of current information about the prevalence of rape.

Answers: 11-1. increase **11-2.** liberal, less **11-3.** have not **11-4.** increases **11-5.** less.

12. Summarize evidence on the nature of sexual orientation and on how common homosexuality is.

12-1. Sexual orientation refers to a person's preference for emotional and sexual relationships with individuals of the other sex, the same sex, or either sex. Those who prefer relationships with the other sex are termed _______________, with the same sex _______________, and with either sex _______________.

12-2. Because people may have experienced homosexuality in varying degrees, it seems reasonable to consider sexual orientation as a/an (continuum/all-or-none distinction). In part because of this definitional problem, and in part due to prejudice against homosexuals, it is difficult to determine precisely the proportion of homosexuals in the population. A frequently cited statistic is 10%, but recent surveys place the proportion somewhere between _____% and _____%.

Answers: 12-1. heterosexuals (straights), homosexuals (gays or lesbians), bisexuals **12-2.** continuum, 5, 8.

13. Summarize evidence on the determinants of sexual orientation.

13-1. What factors determine sexual orientation? Psychoanalysts thought the answer involved some aspect of the parent–child relationship. Behaviourists assumed that it was due to the association of same-sex stimuli with sexual arousal. Thus, both psychoanalytic and behavioural theorists proposed (environmental/biological) explanations of homosexuality.

13-2. Extensive research on the upbringing of homosexuals has (supported/not supported) the idea that homosexuality is primarily explainable by environmental factors.

13-3. Recent studies have produced evidence that homosexuality is in part genetic. Which of the following types of studies have supported this conclusion? (Place Y for yes or N for no in the blanks.)

____ Studies of hormonal differences between heterosexuals and homosexuals.

____ Studies of twins and adopted children.

____ Autopsy studies of the hypothalamus.

13-4. Subjects in one of the studies described were gay men who had an identical twin brother, a fraternal twin brother, or an adopted brother. For each of the categories, what percentage of the brothers of the subjects were also gay? Place the percentages in the appropriate blanks: 11%, 22%, 52%.

____ Identical twins

____ Fraternal twins

____ Adopted brothers

13-5. Many theorists also suspect that secretions of ______________ during prenatal development may be involved. For example, some research has found that women exposed prenatally to high ______________ levels are more likely to be homosexual.

13-6. While much of the evidence points toward biological factors, the fact that identical twins turn out to share sexual orientation only half of the time suggests that ______________ factors are involved in some way. Exactly what those factors might be is unknown, however.

13-7. There is also some evidence of greater ______________ (malleability) in females' sexuality than in males'. For example, lesbian and bisexual women may change their sexual orientation over the course of their adult years.

Answers: 13-1. environmental **13-2.** not supported **13-3.** N, Y, Y **13-4.** 52%, 22%, 11% (Note that a companion study for lesbians found similar results.) **13-5.** hormones, androgen **13-6.** environmental **13-7.** plasticity.

14. Outline the four phases of the human sexual response.

14-1. Write the names of the four phases of the human sexual response in the order in which they occur. (Hint: I made up a mnemonic device that's hard to forget. The first letter of each phase name produces EPOR, which happens to be ROPE spelled backward.)

(a) ______________________

(b) ______________________

(c) ______________________

(d) ______________________

14-2. In the blanks below write the first letter of the phase name that correctly labels the description.

____ Rapid increase in arousal (respiration, heart rate, blood pressure, etc.)

____ Vasocongestion of blood vessels in sexual organs; lubrication in female

____ Continued arousal, but at a slower place

____ Tightening of the vaginal entrance

____ Pulsating muscular contractions and ejaculation

____ Physiological changes produced by arousal subside

____ Includes a refractory period for men

Answers: 14-1. (a) excitement, (b) plateau, (c) orgasm, (d) resolution **14-2.** E, E, P, P, O, R, R.

ACHIEVEMENT: IN SEARCH OF EXCELLENCE

15. Describe the achievement motive, and discuss how individual differences in the need for achievement influence behaviour.

15-1. People with high achievement motivation have a need to:

a. master difficult challenges

b. outperform others

c. excel and compete

d. all of the above

15-2. What is the relationship between estimates of achievement motive in a country and the economic growth of that county?

15-3. The procedure used for measuring need for achievement involves subjects telling stories about pictures shown in the _______________ _______________ _______________.

15-4. How do people who score high on need for achievement differ from those who score low?

Answers: 15-1. d **15-2.** Countries with estimated high achievement motivation have higher economic growth (and greater productivity in general). **15-3.** Thematic Apperception Test **15-4.** They tend to work hard, compete, be persistent, delay gratification, and be successful in their careers.

16. Explain how situational factors influence achievement strivings.

16-1. According to Atkinson's elaboration of McClelland's views, achievement-oriented behaviour is determined not only by (1) achievement motivation but by (2) the _______________ that success will occur and (3) the _______________ value of success.

16-2. As the difficulty of a task increases, the _______________ of success at the task decreases. At the same time, success at harder tasks may be more satisfying, so the _______________ value of the task is likely to increase. When the incentive value and probability of success are weighed together, people with a high need for achievement would tend to select tasks of (extreme/moderate) difficulty.

16-3. In addition to success, Atkinson has included fear of failure as a factor. People vary not only in their motivation to succeed but in their motivation to avoid _______________.

16-4. The motivation to avoid failure may either stimulate achievement or inhibit achievement. Explain.

Answers: 16-1. probability, incentive **16-2.** probability, incentive, moderate **16-3.** failure **16-4.** One may achieve in order to avoid failure on a task; thus, fear of failure may lead to achievement. On the other hand, one may avoid failure by not pursuing the task at all; thus, fear of failure could also lead to lack of achievement.

THE ELEMENTS OF EMOTIONAL EXPERIENCE

17. Describe the cognitive component of emotion.

17-1. The word *cognition* refers to thoughts, beliefs, or conscious experience. When faced with an ugly-looking insect (or, for some people, the edge of a cliff or making a speech in public), you might say to yourself, "This is terrifying (or maybe disgusting)." This thought or cognition has an evaluative aspect: We assess our emotions as pleasant or unpleasant. Thus, one component of emotion is the thinking or _______________ component, which includes _______________ in terms of pleasantness–unpleasantness.

Answers: 17-1. cognitive, evaluation.

18. Describe the physiological underpinnings of emotion.

18-1. The second component of emotion is the _______________ component, primarily actions of the _______________ nervous system. Your encounter with the insect might be accompanied by changes in heart rate, breathing, or blood pressure—or by increased electrical conductivity of the skin, known as the _______________ skin response (GSR).

18-2. Lie detectors don't actually detect lies; they detect _______________ reflected by changes in heart rate, respiration, and GSR. Emotion does not necessarily reflect lying: Some people can lie without showing emotional arousal, and others show arousal when asked incriminating questions. Advocates claim that polygraphs are about 85% to 90% accurate; recent research (supports/does not support) this claim. In most courtrooms, polygraph results (are/are not) considered reliable enough to be used as evidence.

18-3. Recent evidence suggests that the brain structure known as the _______________ plays a central role in emotion.

18-4. The amygdala doesn't process emotion by itself but is at the core of a complex set of neural circuits. Sensory information relating to fear arrives at the thalamus and from there is relayed along two pathways, to the nearby _______________ and also to areas in the _______________.

18-5. The amygdala processes information extremely rapidly, which has clear _______________ value for the organism in threatening situations. The cortex responds more slowly but in greater detail, and relays potentially moderating information to the amygdala. While the hub of this vigilance system seems to be the ______________, both pathways are useful in assessing threat.

18-6. Additional brain areas involved in emotion include the ______________ cortex (which contributes to voluntary control of emotional reactions), the ______________ cortex (implicated in pain-related emotional distress), and the ______________ ______________ pathway (which plays a major role in pleasurable emotions associated with rewarding events). The (right/left) hemisphere plays a relatively large role in the perception of others' emotions and the experience of positive emotions, whereas the (right/left) hemisphere plays a relatively large role in the experience of negative emotions.

Answers: 18-1. physiological, autonomic, galvanic **18-2.** emotion (autonomic arousal), does not support, are not **18-3.** amygdala, fear **18-4.** amygdala, cortex **18-5.** survival (adaptive), amygdala **18-6.** prefrontal, cingulate, mesolimbic dopamine, right, left.

19. Discuss the body language of emotions and the facial feedback hypothesis.

19-1. We communicate emotions not only verbally but ______________, through our postures, gestures, and, especially, in our facial ______________.

19-2. Ekman and Friesen found that there are ______________ fundamental facial expressions of emotion: happiness, sadness, anger, fear, surprise, and disgust. Children who have been blind since birth frown and smile just like sighted children, which supports the idea that basic facial expressions are largely (learned/innate).

19-3. According to some researchers, facial expressions not only reflect emotions but help create them. This viewpoint, known as the __________-__________ hypothesis, asserts that facial muscles send signals to the brain that help produce the subjective experience of emotion. For example, turning up the corners of your mouth will tend to make you feel ______________.

Answers: 19-1. nonverbally (through body language), expressions **19-2.** six, innate **19-3.** facial-feedback, happy.

20. Discuss cross-cultural similarities and variations in emotional experience.

20-1. Ekman and Friesen asked people in different cultures to label the emotion shown on photographs of faces. What did they find?

20-2. Different cultures show striking similarities in other aspects of emotional experience as well. For example, regardless of culture, meeting with friends tends to trigger one emotion and encountering failure another. Thus, certain types of ______________ trigger the same emotions across cultures.

20-3. While there are similarities in emotional expression across cultures, there are also striking differences. For example, certain word labels for emotion (e.g., sadness, anxiety, remorse) (occur/do not occur) in all cultures. However, recent evidence suggests that cultural disparities in naming emotions may not necessarily reflect differences in emotional processing.

20-4. Although people in different cultures tend to show the same basic expressions of emotion, when they do so is governed by different cultural norms. What emotions are you "supposed" to show at a funeral or when watching a sporting event? The unwritten rules that regulate our display of emotion, known as _______________ rules, vary considerably across cultures.

Answers: 20-1. People from very different cultures, including cultures that have had virtually no contact with the West, show considerable agreement in labelling photographs of facial expressions with approximately six basic emotions. These data support the idea that emotional expression is largely universal. **20-2.** events (experiences, situations) **20-3.** do not occur **20-4.** display.

THEORIES OF EMOTION

21. Compare and contrast the James–Lange and Cannon–Bard theories of emotion, and explain how Schachter reconciled these conflicting views in his two-factor theory.

21-1. Suppose you saw a rat in your room (and assume that you are afraid of rats). Why would you be afraid? One would think that the process would be as follows: First, you would be consciously aware of your fear of the rat, and then you would experience the autonomic or visceral arousal that accompanies fear. The James–Lange theory reverses this process: We first experience the (visceral arousal/conscious fear), and then we experience (visceral arousal/conscious fear).

21-2. According to the James–Lange theory, then, fear and other emotions occur not as a result of different conscious experiences but as a result of different patterns of _______________ activation.

21-3. The Cannon–Bard theory argued that a subcortical structure in the brain (they thought it was the thalamus) simultaneously sends signals to both the cortex and the autonomic nervous system. According to this theory:

a. conscious fear would precede autonomic arousal

b. autonomic arousal would precede conscious fear

c. autonomic arousal and conscious fear would occur at the same time

21-4. According to Cannon–Bard, emotion originates in:

a. subcortical structures

b. the autonomic nervous system

c. conscious awareness

21-5. The Cannon–Bard theory contends that different emotions (e.g., fear, joy, love, anger) are accompanied by:

a. different patterns of autonomic arousal.

b. nearly identical patterns of autonomic arousal

c. neither of the above

21-6. Schachter's two-factor view is similar to the James–Lange theory in that (visceral arousal/conscious experience) is thought to precede the mental awareness of an emotion. The theory is similar to the Cannon–Bard theory in that (general autonomic arousal/ different autonomic responses) is assumed to account for a wide variety of emotions.

21-7. Since arousal is in large part the same regardless of the emotion, according to Schachter, we feel different emotions as a result of inferences we make from events in the environment. Hence, the two factors in Schachter's theory are ______________ (roughly the same for all emotions) and ______________ (people's interpretation of the arousal based on the situation).

21-8. To review the three theories, label each of the following with the name of a theory:

(a) __________________ The subjective experience of emotion is caused by different patterns of autonomic arousal.

(b) __________________ Emotions cannot be distinguished on the basis of autonomic arousal; general autonomic arousal causes one to look for an explanation or label.

(c) __________________ Love is accompanied by an autonomic pattern different from that of hate.

(d) __________________ The subjective experience of emotion is caused by two factors: arousal and cognition.

(e) __________________ Emotions originate in subcortical brain structures; different emotions produce almost identical patterns of autonomic arousal.

(f) __________________ Ralph observes that his heart pounds and that he becomes a little out of breath at times. He also notices that these signs of arousal occur whenever Mary is around, so he figures that he must be in love.

21-9. In what sense does Schachter's theory reconcile the James–Lange and Cannon–Bard theories?

Answers: 21-1. visceral arousal, conscious fear **21-2.** autonomic (visceral) **21-3.** c **21-4.** a **21-5.** b **21-6.** visceral arousal, general autonomic arousal **21-7.** arousal, cognition **21-8.** (a) James–Lange, (b) Schachter's two-factor, (c) James–Lange (d) Schachter's two-factor (e) Cannon–Bard (f) Schachter's two-factor **21-9.** Schachter's view is similar to the James–Lange theory in that arousal is thought to precede the conscious experience of emotion; it is similar to the Cannon–Bard theory in that there is assumed to be just one general physiological arousal response rather than a different visceral response for each emotion. Since arousal is in large part the same regardless of the emotion, Schachter proposed that we feel different emotions as a result of inferences we make from events in the environment.

22. Summarize the evolutionary perspective on emotion.

22-1. By preparing an organism for aggression and defence, the emotion of anger helps an organism survive. The emotions of fear, surprise, and interest have similar functions. From an evolutionary perspective, all emotions developed because of the _______________ value they have for a species.

22-2. Evolutionary theorists view emotions primarily as a group of (innate/learned) reactions that have been passed on because of their survival value. They also believe that emotions originate in subcortical areas, parts of the brain that evolved before the cortical structures associated with higher mental processes. In the view of evolutionary theorists, emotion evolved before thought and is largely (dependent on/independent of) thought.

22-3. How many basic, inherited emotions are there? The evolutionary writers assume that the wide range of emotions we experience are blends or variations in intensity of approximately _______________ innate or prewired primary emotions.

Answers: 22-1. survival (adaptive) **22-2.** innate, independent of **22-3.** eight (between six and ten).

PUTTING IT IN PERSPECTIVE

23. Explain how this chapter highlighted five of the text's unifying themes.

23-1. Five of the text's unifying themes were prominent in this chapter. Indicate which themes fit the following examples by writing the appropriate abbreviations in the blanks below: C for cultural contexts, SH for sociohistorical context, T for theoretical diversity, HE for heredity and environment, and MC for multiple causation.

(a) Achievement behaviour is affected by achievement motivation, the likelihood of success, the likelihood of failure, and so on. ____

(b) Display rules in a culture tell us when and where to express an emotion. ____

(c) Changing attitudes about homosexuality have produced more research on sexual orientation; in turn, data from the research has affected societal attitudes. ____

(d) Body weight seems to be influenced by set point, blood glucose, and inherited metabolism. It is also affected by eating habits and acquired tastes, which vary across cultures. ____, ____, and ____.

(e) The James–Lange theory proposed that different emotions reflected different patterns of physiological arousal; the Cannon–Bard theory assumed that emotions originate in subcortical structures; Schachter viewed emotion as a combination of physiological arousal and cognition ____.

Answers: 23-1. (a) MC (b) C (c) SH (d) HE, MC, C (e) T.

PERSONAL APPLICATION * EXPLORING THE INGREDIENTS OF HAPPINESS

24. Summarize information on factors that do not predict happiness.

24-1. Indicate whether each of the following statements is true (T) or false (F).

____ (a) There is very little correlation between income and happiness.

____ (b) Younger people tend to be happier than older people.

____ (c) People who have children tend to be happier than those without children.

____ (d) People with high IQ scores tend to be happier than those with low IQ scores.

____ (e) There is a negligible correlation between physical attractiveness and happiness.

24-2. List five factors discussed in your text that have little or no relationship to happiness.

Answers: 24-1. (a) T, (b) F, (c) F, (d) F, (e) T **24-2.** money (income), age, parenthood (either having or not having children), intelligence, physical attractiveness.

25. Summarize information on factors that are moderately or strongly correlated with happiness.

25-1. Indicate whether each of the following statements is true (T) or false (F).

____ (a) One of the strongest predictors of happiness is good health.

____ (b) Social support and friendship groups are moderately related to happiness.

____ (c) Religious people tend to be somewhat happier than nonreligious people.

____ (d) Marital status is strongly related to happiness; married people tend to be happier than single people.

____ (e) Job satisfaction tends to be strongly related to general happiness; people who like their jobs tend to be happy.

____ (f) Differences in personality have a negligible relationship to happiness; introverts, on the average, are just as happy as extraverts.

25-2. List four factors that are moderately correlated with happiness and three that are strongly correlated.

Answers: 25-1. (a) F (People adapt, so there is only a moderate relationship between health and happiness.), (b) T, (c) T, (d) T, (e) T, (f) F (People who are extraverted, optimistic, and have high self-esteem tend to be happier.) **25-2.** Moderately related: health, social activity (friendship), religion, and culture. Strongly related: marriage, work (job satisfaction), and personality.

26. Explain four conclusions that can be drawn about the dynamics of happiness.

26-1. One conclusion about happiness is that how we feel about our health, wealth, job, and age are more important than the facts of our situation. In other words, the objective realities are less important than our ________________ reactions.

26-2. In addition, the extent of our happiness depends on the comparison group. Generally, people compare themselves to others who are similar in some dimension, such as friends or neighbours. In the final analysis, our happiness is relative to the ________________ to which we compare ourselves.

26-3. A third conclusion is that people are generally bad at predicting what makes them happy, as shown in research on _______________ _______________. For example, students might overestimate the pleasure they are likely to feel by obtaining a very high grade in a course.

26-4. A fourth conclusion is that our baseline for judging pleasantness and unpleasantness constantly changes. When good things happen, we shift our baselines (what we feel we "need" or want) upward; when bad things happen, we shift down. In other words, people _______________ to changing circumstances by changing their baselines of comparison, a process termed _______________ adaptation.

Answers: 26-1. subjective **26-2.** group (people) **26-3.** affective forecasting **26-4.** adapt (adjust), hedonic.

CRITICAL THINKING APPLICATION * ANALYZING ARGUMENTS: MAKING SENSE OUT OF CONTROVERSY

27. Describe the key elements in arguments.

27-1. In logic, an *argument* is a series of statements that claims to prove something (whether it does or not). Arguments are composed of two major parts, a *conclusion* and one or more *premises*. The _______________ are statements intended to present evidence or proof. The _______________ supposedly derives from or is proved by the premises.

27-2. Consider this logical argument: "Any field of study that uses the scientific method is a science. Psychology uses the scientific method. Thus, psychology is a science." Label the parts of the argument below (C for conclusion and P for premise).

____ Any field of study that uses the scientific method is a science.

____ Psychology uses the scientific method.

____ Psychology is a science.

Answers: 27-1. premises, conclusion **27-2.** P, P, C. Note that this is an example of a valid argument. One may or may not agree with the premises (e.g., they may define science differently), but the conclusion logically follows from the premises.

28. Explain some common fallacies that often show up in arguments.

28-1. Read over the section on common logical fallacies described in your text. Then match the examples with the appropriate terms. (Suggestion: Use the abbreviations in parentheses. Note that there are five fallacies and seven examples; two fallacies are used twice.)

irrelevant reasons (IR)

circular reasoning (CR)

slippery slope (SS)

weak analogies (WA)

false dichotomy (FD)

(a) ____ Having trouble sleeping causes great difficulty in our lives because insomnia is a major problem for people.

(b) ____ People with insomnia should use the herb melatonin because insomnia is an enormous problem in our country.

(c) ____ Vitamin C is extremely effective in slowing the aging process. I know it is effective because I have taken it for many years. Obviously, the reason I take Vitamin C is that it works to reduce aging.

(d) ____ If we don't stop communism in Vietnam now, it will spread next to Laos, then to Cambodia, and then to the entire Southeast Asian peninsula.

(e) ____ We saw what happened when Chamberlain gave in to Hitler. The same thing will happen again unless we stand up to the tyranny in the Middle East.

(f) ____ We can fight in the Balkans now, or we can prepare for World War III.

(g) ____ Ralph bought a blender on a Tuesday in Peoria, and it lasted a long time. If I buy a blender on a Tuesday in Peoria, it should also last a long time.

Answers: 28-1. (a) CR. The premise and conclusion are the same. (b) IR. Insomnia may be a problem, but that does not lead to the conclusion that the herb melatonin should be taken. (c) CR. The conclusion, the first statement, is simply a restatement of the premise, which is the last statement. (d) SS. The argument is that if you allow one thing to happen, then a series of other things will inevitably happen. In fact, there may be no necessary connection between the events. (e) WA. While the two situations may have a degree of similarity, they are also likely to be sufficiently dissimilar to make the argument invalid. (f) FD. The choice seems to be between the two options, but, logically, these are not the only choices. We may also do both, or neither. (g) WA. While the situations share some elements in common, this does not mean that they share all elements or that some elements cause others.

Review of Key Terms

Achievement motive	Estrogens	Motivation
Affective forecasting	Galvanic skin response (GSR)	Obesity
Androgens	Glucose	Orgasm
Argument	Glucostats	Polygraph
Assumptions	Hedonic adaptation	Premises
Bisexuals	Heterosexuals	Refractory period
Body mass index (BMI)	Homeostasis	Set-point theory
Collectivism	Homosexuals	Settling-point theory
Display rules	Incentive	Sexual orientation
Drive	Individualism	Subjective well-being
Emotion	Lie detector	Vasocongestion

____________________ **1.** Goal-directed behaviour that may be affected by needs, wants, interests, desires, and incentives.

____________________ **2.** Cultural norms that regulate the expression of emotions.

____________________ **3.** One or more premises that are used to provide support for a conclusion.

____________________ **4.** The reasons presented in an argument to persuade someone that a conclusion is true.

____________________ **5.** Premises in an argument that are assumed but for which no proof or evidence is offered.

____________________ **6.** A measure of weight that controls for variations in height; weight in kilograms divided by height in metres, squared.

____________________ **7.** Refers to cultures that put group goals ahead of personal goals and defines a person's identity in terms of the groups to which a person belongs.

____________________ **8.** Blood sugar.

____________________ **9.** Neurons that are sensitive to glucose.

____________________ **10.** A hormone secreted by the pancreas needed for extracting glucose from the blood.

____________________ **11.** Refers to cultures that put personal goals ahead of group goals and defines a person's identity in terms of the personal attributes.

____________________ **12.** Proposes that the body monitors fat-cell levels to keep them (and weight) fairly stable.

____________________ **13.** The condition of being overweight.

____________________ **14.** The principal class of female sex hormones.

____________________ **15.** The principal class of male sex hormones.

____________________ **16.** A state of physiological equilibrium or stability.

____________________ **17.** An internal state of tension that motivates an organism to reduce tension.

____________________ **18.** Engorgement of the blood vessels.

____________________ **19.** Sexual climax.

____________________ **20.** A time following orgasm during which males are unresponsive to sexual stimulation.

____________________ **21.** Whether a person prefers emotional–sexual relationships with members of the same sex, the other sex, or either sex.

_______________ **22.** People who seek emotional–sexual relationships with members of the same sex.

_______________ **23.** People who seek emotional–sexual relationships with members of the other sex.

_______________ **24.** People who seek emotional–sexual relationships with members of either sex.

_______________ **25.** Efforts to predict one's emotional reactions to future events.

_______________ **26.** Individuals' personal perceptions of their overall happiness and life satisfaction.

_______________ **27.** The need to master difficult challenges and to excel in competition with others.

_______________ **28.** An increase in the electrical conductivity of the skin related to an increase in sweat gland activity.

_______________ **29.** A reaction that includes cognitive, physiological, and behavioural components.

_______________ **30.** The technical name for the "lie detector."

_______________ **31.** The informal name for polygraph, an apparatus that monitors physiological aspects of arousal (e.g., heart rate, GSR).

_______________ **32.** An external goal that motivates behaviour.

_______________ **33.** The view that body weight is determined by a wide variety of factors and that the body does not defend a particular point.

Answers: 1. motivation **2.** display rules **3.** argument **4.** premises **5.** assumptions **6.** body mass index (BMI) **7.** collectivism **8.** glucose **9.** glucostats **10.** hedonic adaptation **11.** individualism **12.** set point theory **13.** obesity **14.** estrogens **15.** androgens **16.** homeostasis **17.** drive **18.** vasocongestion **19.** orgasm **20.** refractory period **21.** sexual orientation **22.** homosexuals **23.** heterosexuals **24.** bisexuals **25.** affective forecasting **26.** subjective well-being **27.** achievement motive **28.** galvanic skin response (GSR) **29.** emotion **30.** polygraph **31.** lie detector **32.** incentive **33.** settling-point theory.

Review of Key People

John Atkinson
David Buss
Walter Cannon
Paul Ekman & Wallace Friesen
William James
Joseph LeDoux
William Masters & Virginia Johnson
David McClelland
Henry Murray
Judith Rodin
Stanley Schachter

_______________ **1.** Proposed that emotions arise in subcortical areas of the brain.

_______________ **2.** Compiled an influential catalogue of common social needs; also devised the TAT.

_______________ **3.** Prominent evolutionary theorist who explored, among many other topics, gender differences in human mate preferences.

_______________ **4.** Proposed that eating, on the part of obese people, is controlled by external cues; devised the two-factor theory of emotion.

_______________ **5.** Stressed the importance of the amygdala as the core of a set of interacting neural circuits that process emotion.

_______________ **6.** Did the groundbreaking work on the physiology of the human sexual response.

_______________ **7.** Is responsible for most of the early research on achievement motivation.

_______________ **8.** Emphasized additional factors in an elaboration of McClelland's theory of achievement motivation.

_______________ **9.** In a series of cross-cultural studies, found that people can identify six or so basic emotions from facial expressions.

_______________ **10.** Thought that emotion arose from one's perception of variations in autonomic arousal.

_______________ **11.** Studied the cues that can elicit hunger processes.

Answers: 1. Cannon **2.** Murray **3.** Buss **4.** Schachter **5.** LeDoux **6.** Masters & Johnson **7.** McClelland **8.** Atkinson **9.** Ekman & Friesen **10.** James **11.** Rodin.

Self-Quiz

1. Which of the following are most likely to be similar in BMI (body mass index)?
a. identical twins brought up in different family environments
b. fraternal twins brought up in the same family environment
c. parents and their adopted children
d. adopted siblings brought up in the same family environment

2. The subjective feeling of hunger is influenced by:
a. the amount of glucose in the bloodstream
b. secretion of insulin by the pancreas
c. external cues, including odour and appearance of food
d. all of the above

3. What is the effect of insulin on blood glucose?
a. Glucose level increases.
b. Glucose level decreases.
c. Glucose changes to free fatty acids.
d. CCK increases.

4. According to this theory, the sex that makes the larger investment in offspring (bearing, nursing, etc.) will be more selective of partners than the sex that makes the smaller investment.
a. adaptation level theory
b. parental investment theory
c. investment differentiation theory
d. social learning theory

5. Which of the following theories proposes that the body actively defends a particular body weight by adjusting metabolism and hunger?
a. set-point theory
b. settling-point theory
c. adaptation level theory
d. parental investment theory

6. Which of the following would best reflect the James–Lange theory of emotion?
a. The subjective experience of emotion is caused by thinking about the cause of autonomic arousal.
b. The conscious experience of emotion is caused by different patterns of autonomic arousal.
c. Emotion originates in subcortical structures, which send signals to both the cortex and autonomic nervous system.
d. Cognitive awareness of emotion precedes autonomic arousal.

7. The fact that identical twins are more likely to share sexual orientation than fraternal twins suggests that sexual orientation is:
a. due to the environment
b. in part genetic
c. largely chemical
d. primarily hormonal

8. Cultural norms that indicate which facial expressions of emotion are appropriate on what occasions are termed:
a. display rules
b. parental investments
c. investment differentiations
d. social scripts

9. According to the evolutionary theories, men seek as partners women who:
a. are similar to them in important attitudes
b. have a good sense of humour
c. are beautiful, youthful, and in good health
d. have good financial prospects

10. What test is generally used to measure need for achievement?
a. the TAT
b. the GSR
c. the Rorschach
d. the MMPI

11. Evidence regarding facial expression in different cultures suggests that:
a. the two-factor theory accounts for nonverbal behaviour
b. facial expression of emotion is to some extent innate
c. emotions originate in the cortex
d. learning is the major factor in explaining basic facial expressions

12. Which of the following proposed that emotion arises from one's perception or interpretation of autonomic arousal?
a. Schachter
b. Cannon–Bard
c. LeDoux
d. McClelland

13. Which of the following theories asserts that thinking or cognition plays a relatively small role in emotion?
a. two-factor theory
b. James–Lange theory
c. achievement theory
d. evolutionary theory

14. Of the following, which has been found to be most strongly associated with happiness?
a. physical attractiveness
b. health
c. job satisfaction
d. general intelligence

15. Someone exhorts people to take action against company policy, as follows: "We can oppose these changes, or we can live out our lives in poverty." This type of argument reflects which of the following fallacies?
a. slippery slope
b. weak analogy
c. false dichotomy
d. circular reasoning

16. Which eating disorder involves binging and purging?
a. obesity
b. bulimia nervosa
c. anorexia nervosa
d. all of the above

17. Obesity is most often determined with which kind of measure?
a. a self-report obesity scale
b. the set-point scale
c. weight in kilograms
d. body mass index

18. Our attempt to predict our emotional reactions to future events is called:
a. emotional expectations
b. affective forecasting
c. emotionometer
d. emotional predictions

19. The heritability of happiness is approximately:
a. 20%
b. 30%
c. 40%
d. 50%

Answers: **1.** a **2.** d **3.**b **4.** b **5.** a **6.** d **7.** b **8.** a **9.** c **10.** a **11.** b **12.** a **13.** d **14.** c **15.** c **16.** b **17.** d **18.** b **19.** d.

InfoTrac Keywords

Bisexuals
Lie Detector
Motivation
Galvanic Skin Response

Chapter Eleven
HUMAN DEVELOPMENT ACROSS THE LIFE SPAN

Review of Key Ideas

1. Define development.

1-1. Development is the sequence of ___________-___________ changes that occur as a person progresses from conception to death. It includes both the ______________ and ______________ changes that take place as people grow older.

Answers: 1-1. age-related, biological, behavioural.

PROGRESS BEFORE BIRTH: PRENATAL DEVELOPMENT

2. Outline the major events of the three phases of prenatal development.

2-1. Each box below represents one month in the typical pregnancy; each short line at the top of the boxes represents one week. Indicate the beginning and end of each phase of prenatal development by placing the appropriate capital letters from the diagram in the blanks after the descriptions below.

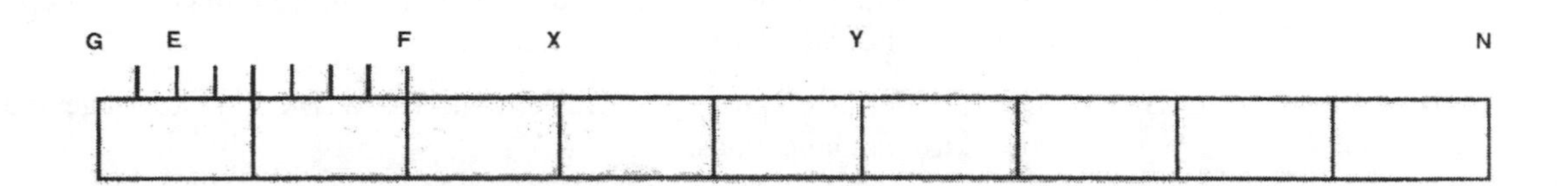

(a) The germinal stage begins at conception, represented by point ________ in the diagram, and ends at point ________.

(b) The embryonic stage begins at point ________ and ends at point ________.

(c) The fetal stage begins at point ________ and ends at point ________.

2-2. List the names of the three phases of prenatal development in the order in which they occur. In the parentheses at the right, indicate the age ranges encompassed by each stage.

(a) ______________________________ ( )

(b) ______________________________ ( )

(c) ______________________________ ( )

2-3. Match each stage in the previous question with the descriptions below. Use the letters G, E, and F to represent the germinal, embryonic, and fetal stages, respectively.

(a) ____ The placenta begins to form.

(b) ____ At the end of this stage, the organism begins to have a human appearance; it is about an inch in length.

(c) ____ The zygote begins to implant in the uterine wall; about one in five are rejected.

(d) ____ Muscles and bones develop, and physical movements occur.

(e) ____ Most major birth defects probably have their origins in this stage.

(f) ____ The age of viability (about 22 to 26 weeks after conception) occurs during this stage.

Answers: 2-1. (a) G, E, (b) E, F, (c) F, N **2-2.** (a) germinal (birth to two weeks), (b) embryonic (two weeks to two months), (c) fetal (two months to nine months) **2-3.** (a) G, (b) E, (c) G, (d) F, (e) E, (f) F.

3. Summarize the impact of environmental factors on prenatal development.

3-1. Indicate whether the following statements concerning environmental factors and fetal development are true (T) or false (F).

____(a) Severe malnutrition increases the risk of birth complications and neurological deficits.

____(b) Few, if any, drugs consumed by a pregnant woman are able to pass through the placental barrier.

____(c) Recent studies indicate that moderate drinking during pregnancy produces no risk for the developing fetus.

____(d) Marijuana use by a pregnant woman may lead to attention/impulsivity problems in the child.

____(e) Heavy drinking of alcohol by a pregnant woman may produce microcephaly, heart defects, and retardation in her child.

____(f) Smoking during pregnancy is related to increased risk of miscarriage and other birth complications.

____(g) The placenta screens out many but not all infectious diseases.

____(h) Genital herpes is usually transmitted during the birth process, when newborns come into contact with their mothers' lesions.

____(i) AIDS is transmitted primarily during the birth process, when newborns come into contact with their mothers' blood cells.

____(j) Good quality prenatal care is associated with fewer premature births and higher infant survival rates.

Answers: 3-1. (a) T, (b) F, (c) F, (d) T, (e) T, (f) T, (g) T, (h) T, (i) T, (j) T.

THE WONDROUS YEARS OF CHILDHOOD

4. Describe general trends and principles and cultural variations in motor development.

4-1. In the space below, describe the two basic trends in motor development described in the text.

Cephalocaudal trend:

Proximodistal trend:

4-2. The average ages at which children display various behaviours and abilities are referred to as developmental _______________. While these averages provide useful information, they don't reflect variability, and the age at which children display certain behaviours or abilities varies (enormously/very little) across children.

4-3. Thus, with regard to the behaviour of walking up steps, for example, which of the following is true?

a. Children walk up steps at approximately the same age.

b. Many normal children walk up steps well after or well before the average age indicated.

4-4. The process that underlies the developmental norms is *maturation*. What is maturation? (Be specific with regard to thc factors of heredity and environment.)

4-5. Cross-cultural research has revealed a considerable degree of consistency between cultures in terms of when and in what order motor skills appear. In general, early motor development is much more dependent on (maturation/culture) than is later motor development. As children in a culture grow older, however, the motor skills that they acquire depend to a greater extent on (maturation/culture).

Answers: 4-1. Head to foot: children tend to gain motor control of the upper body before the lower body. Centre outward: the tendency to gain control of the torso before the limbs. **4-2.** norms, enormously **4-3.** b **4-4.** *Maturation* refers to developmental changes that occur in an organism as a result of *genetic*, as opposed to *environmental*, factors. **4-5.** maturation, culture.

5. Summarize the findings of Thomas and Chess's longitudinal study of infant temperament.

5-1. Identify the following designs by indicating whether they are longitudinal or cross-sectional.

(a) ______________________ In this experimental design, researchers compare groups of subjects of differing ages at a single point in time.

(b) ________________________ This design measures a single group of subjects over a period of time.

5-2. Using a longitudinal design, Thomas and Chess identified three basic temperaments, described below. Place the names of these temperamental styles in the appropriate blanks.

(a) ________________________ Happy, regular in sleep and eating, adaptable.

(b) ________________________ Less cheery, less regular in sleep and eating, more wary of new experiences.

(c) ________________________ Glum, erratic in sleep and eating, irritable.

5-3. The largest group of children (about 40%) were of the ________________________ temperament, another 15% were ________________________, and 10% were in the ________________________ category. The remaining 35% showed mixtures of these three temperaments.

5-4. What is the major result and conclusion from the Thomas and Chess study?

Answers: 5-1. (a) cross-sectional, (b) longitudinal **5-2.** (a) easy, (b) slow to warm up, (c) difficult **5-3.** easy, slow to warm up, difficult **5-4.** Temperament remains somewhat stable across age. A child's temperament at three months tends to predict temperament at age 10 years. This stability suggests that temperament has a strong biological basis.

6. Summarize theories of attachment and research on patterns of attachment, and their effects.

6-1. Newborn babies do not form attachments to their mothers immediately. They begin to show a strong preference for their mothers, often crying when they are separated from them, beginning at about _______________ months of age.

6-2. The emotional distress that occurs when some infants are separated from their caregivers is called _______________ anxiety. This distress peaks at about _______________ months of age and then begins to decline.

6-3. Early research by Harlow questioned the behaviourist assumption that early attachment reflects reinforcement effects by showing that a "substitute mother" monkey that provides _______________ _______________ is preferred over one that provides food.

6-4. Bowlby argued that there was likely a _______________ basis for attachment. He stated that infants are biologically programmed to emit behaviours that elicit protective, caring responses from adults, and that adults are biologically programmed to respond with warmth, love, and protection.

6-5. Research by Ainsworth and her colleagues indicates that attachments between mothers and their infants tend to fall into three categories. Label each of the following with the pattern of attachment described: *secure, anxious–ambivalent, avoidant, or disorganized–disoriented.*

(a) ______________________ The infant is anxious even when the mother is near, becomes very agitated when she leaves, and is not comforted when the mother returns.

(b) ______________________ The infant seeks little contact with the mother and is not distressed when she leaves.

(c) ______________________ The infant plays comfortably when the mother is present, is upset when the mother leaves, but is quickly calmed by her when she returns.

(d) ______________________ The infant appears confused about whether he or she should approach or avoid the mother.

6-6. Although one cannot assume a causal relationship, attachment in infancy has been found to be related to behaviour in later childhood. For a number of desirable characteristics, including social skills, persistence, curiosity, leadership, and cognitive development, it appears that children who experienced a ______________ attachment have the advantage.

Answers: 6-1. six to eight **6-2.** separation, 14 to 18 **6-3.** contact comfort **6-4.** biological **6-5.** (a) anxious–ambivalent, (b) avoidant, (c) secure, (d) disorganized–disoriented **6-6.** secure.

7. Discuss daycare and culture in relation to attachment.

7-1. Does daycare affect infant–mother attachment? Belsky reports that daycare for more than 20 hours per week increases the likelihood that a/an (insecure/secure) attachment will form between mother and infant.

7-2. Belsky's findings must be put in perspective, however. Mark the following statements true (T) or false (F).

____ The proportion of insecure attachments found in the Belsky studies is only slightly higher than the U.S. norm.

____ The preponderance of other studies suggests that daycare is not harmful to children's attachment relationships.

____ Considering the deprived child-rearing conditions in many homes, daycare can have beneficial effects on some children's social development.

7-3. Separation anxiety occurs at roughly the same ages across different cultures. There are cross-cultural differences, however, in the proportion of infants who fall into the three attachment categories (see Figure 11.7 in your text).

(a) Which cultural sample (U.S., Germany, or Japan) showed the highest proportion of *avoidant* attachments? ______________________

(b) Which cultural sample evidenced virtually *no avoidant attachments* at all?

____

(c) Which cultural sample showed the highest levels of *anxious–ambivalent* attachments?

____

(d) Which two countries had the highest proportion of *secure* attachments?

_______________________ and _______________________

Answers: 7-1. insecure **7-2.** T, T, T **7-3.** (a) Germany, (b) Japan, (c) Japan, (d) Japan, U.S.

8. Explain the evolutionary perspective on attachment.

8-1. Bowlby assumed that attachment between parent and child had important _______________ value for the child.

8-2. Contemporary theorists emphasize that parent–child attachments may enhance _______________ fitness, by promoting the social and emotional maturation of the child so that he or she may engage in successful mating.

Answers: 8-1. survival **8-2.** reproductive.

9. Outline the basic tenets of Erikson's theory, and describe his stages of childhood personality development.

9-1. Erikson's theory is clearly derived from Freudian psychoanalytic theory. Freud asserted that there are five childhood stages that determine the adult's personality. In contrast, Erikson proposed that there are _______________ stages that influence personality across an individual's (childhood/entire lifespan).

9-2. Erikson described four childhood stages and four adult stages. In the spaces below, write the names of the crises that mark the four *childhood* stages, and indicate in the parentheses the approximate ages at which the crises are supposed to occur.

(a) _______________ vs. _______________ ( )

(b) _______________ vs. _______________ ( )

(c) _______________ vs. _______________ ( )

(d) _______________ vs. _______________ ( )

9-3. Below are descriptions of several individuals. In what childhood stage would they have acquired these characteristics, according to Erikson? Use the letters from the question above to indicate the stages.

____ Jack has trouble functioning effectively in the world outside his family; he is unproductive, and he lacks a sense of competence.

____ Kristi is insecure and suspicious of everyone.

____ Larry was torn between being independent of his family and avoiding conflict; as an adult, he feels guilty and lacks self-esteem.

____ From an early age, Maureen's parents never seemed satisfied with what she did. Maureen is plagued by a sense of shame and self-doubt.

9-4. As you may have noted in responding to the previous item, a weakness of Erikson's theory is that it attempts to account for very (few/many) aspects of personality. Thus, the theory cannot explain the enormous individual _______________ between people.

Answers: 9-1. eight, entire lifespan **9-2.** (a) trust vs. mistrust (first year), (b) autonomy vs. shame and doubt (second year), (c) initiative vs. guilt (ages three to six), (d) industry vs. inferiority (age six through puberty) **9-3.** d, a, c, b **9-4.** few, differences (variation).

10. Outline Piaget's stages of cognitive development, and discuss the strengths and weaknesses of Piaget's theory.

10-1. The diagram below represents Piaget's four main stages of development. Write the names of the stages in the appropriate blanks.

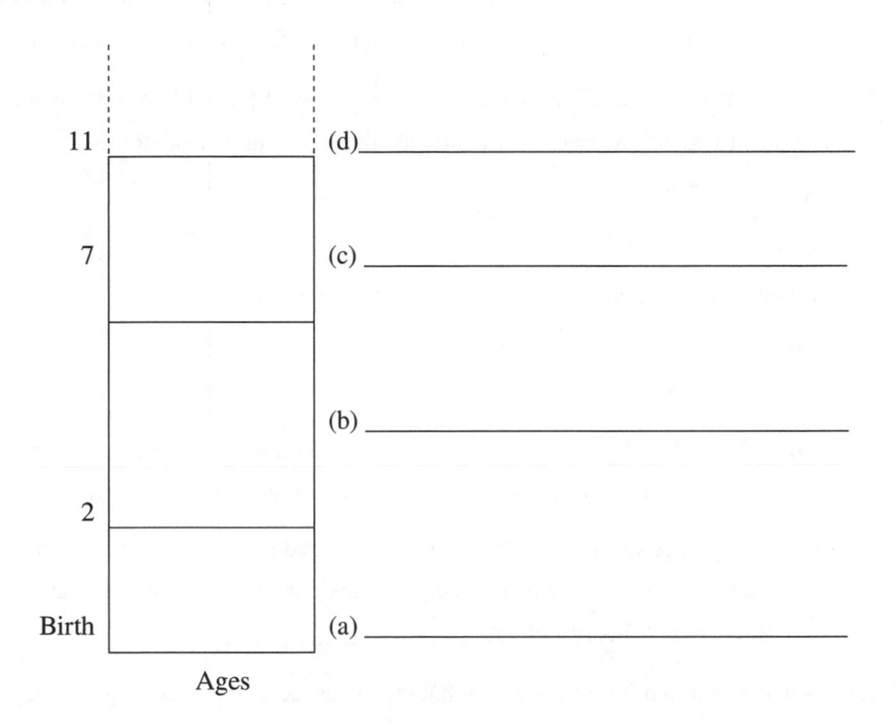

10-2. The stages of development are marked by changes in children's thinking processes brought about by two major processes. If the child interprets a new experience in terms of an *existing* mental structure, then _______________ is operating. On the other hand, if the child interprets an experience by *changing* his thinking strategy, then the child has used

__________________.

10-3. Following is a list of characteristics of children's thinking during various stages. Identify the stage by placing the correct letter (from in question 10-1) in the blank.

(a) ____ At the end of this stage, the child is beginning to develop the capacity for symbolic thought (to think in terms of mental images).

(b) ____ At the beginning of this stage, the child's behaviour is dominated by reflexes and the ability to coordinate sensory input and movement.

(c) ____ The child understands conservation and can handle hierarchical classification but tends not to use abstractions.

(d) ____ The child's thought processes are abstract and systematic.

(e) ____ Object permanence occurs toward the end of this stage.

(f) ____ During the first part of this stage, "out of sight, out of mind" might describe the child's reaction to hidden objects.

(g) ____ When water is poured from a wide beaker into a taller beaker, children say there is now more water in the taller beaker.

(h) ____ The child demonstrates a lack of understanding of conservation.

(i) ____ The child shows the shortcomings of centration, irreversibility, egocentrism, and animism.

(j) ____ For the first time, the child in this stage is mentally able to undo an action and also is able to focus on more than one feature of a problem at the same time.

10-4. When my (R.S.) daughter Vanessa was about five, I placed two rows of stones on the grass, as illustrated below. Each row contained the same number of stones.

Row A: * * * * * * * *

Row B: * * * * * * * *

I then spread out one row so that it took up more space:

Row A: *   *   *   *   *   *   *   *

Row B: * * * * * * * *

(a) I then asked Vanessa to point to the row that now had more stones. If Vanessa behaved like other preoperational children, which row would she point to? ________________

(b) The preoperational child has not yet mastered the principle that physical quantities remain constant in spite of changes in their shape or, in this case, arrangement. What is the name of this principle? __________________

10-5. Some research has demonstrated that certain aspects of Piaget's theory may be incorrect in detail. For example, while Piaget argued that development is discontinuous (i.e., made up of discrete stages), some evidence points to ________________ in development. Also, there is some evidence that object permanence and some aspects of conservation may develop (earlier/later) than Piaget had thought.

10-6. Piaget also had little to say about individual ________________ in development or about so-called ________________ of stages, in which elements of an earlier stage may appear in a later one.

10-7. Piaget thought that people of all cultures would pass through the stages at the same time; subsequent research has found that this (is/is not) the case. While the *sequence* of stages appears to be relatively invariant across cultures, the ________________ that children follow in passing through these stages varies considerably across cultures. Nonetheless, Piaget's brilliance, the novelty of his approach, and the wealth of research that his theory inspired assure his place in history.

Answers: 10-1. (a) sensorimotor, (b) preoperational, (c) concrete operations, (d) formal operations **10-2.** assimilation, accommodation **10-3.**(a) a, (b) a, (c) c, (d) d, (e) a, (f) a, (g) b, (h) b, (i) b, (j) c **10-4.** (a) Row A (at which point Samantha, then 8 and in the stage of concrete operations, was astonished by her sister's choice and informed her that there were the same number in both!) (b) conservation **10-5.** continuity, earlier **10-6.** differences, mixing **10-7.** is not, timetable (age, time).

11. Describe neo-Piagetian views on cognitive development.

11-1. Pascual-Leone used ________________ ________________ concepts in his reinterpretation of Piaget's developmental stages. He argued that cognitive development involves an increase in information processing capacity. ______-________________ (similar to working memory) refers to the maximum number of mental concepts that can be kept in mind at one time. Gifted children have (higher/lower) M-capacity than do nongifted children.

11-2. Case presented a neo-Piagetian view in which he suggested that cognitive development does not involve a single general intellectual factor but, rather, involves ________________ skills that may show uneven development.

Answers: 11-1. information processing, M-capacity, higher **11-2.** distinct (discrete).

12. Describe how Vygotsky's sociocultural theory differs from Piaget's views.

12-1. First, whereas Piaget argued that cognitive development is primarily fuelled by children's active exploration of the world, Vygotsky argued that cognitive development is fuelled by ________________ ________________.

12-2. Second, whereas Piaget viewed cognitive development as a universal process, Vygotsky argued that ________________ exerts a significant influence over how cognitive growth unfolds.

12-3. Third, whereas Piaget viewed children's mastery of ________________ as just another aspect of cognitive development, Vygotsky argued that language acquisition plays a central role. For example, he argued for an important role of ________________ ________________ in children's ability to plan strategies, regulate their actions and accomplish their goals.

12-4. According to Vygotsky, a child's zone of proximal development is the gap between what a learner can accomplish ________________ and what he or she can achieve with guidance from more skilled partners. ________________ occurs when the assistance provided to a child is adjusted as learning progresses.

Answers: 12-1. social interaction **12-2.** culture **12-3.** language, private speech **12-4.** alone, scaffolding.

13. Summarize evidence that suggests that some cognitive abilities could be innate.

13-1. When infants look at a stimulus that is presented repeatedly, the strength of their responses gradually decreases. They spend less and less time looking at the stimulus, and their heart and respiration rates decrease. This reduction in response strength is known as

________________. When a new stimulus is presented, response strength increases, a process known as ________________.

13-2. By using the habituation–dishabituation technique, researchers can tell when a child is able to discriminate between different events. For example, at three to four months of age, infants understand that (write true [T] or false [F] for each of the following):

____ Objects on slopes roll down rather than up.

____ One solid object cannot pass through another.

____ Objects move in continuous paths.

13-3. In another demonstration of the cognitive abilities of young children, five-month-old infants were shown a display in which an object was added to or subtracted from others behind a screen. Remarkably, the children exhibited surprise, indicated by the response of (habituation/dishabituation), when the expected number of objects was not there. This result suggests that infants (are/are not) able to add and subtract small numbers.

13-4. Because these cognitive abilities occur at such an early age, before infants would have had much chance to learn them, some theorists have concluded that these capacities are largely (acquired/innate).

13-5. Two groups of theorists favour an explanation in terms of innate cognitive abilities: the *nativists* and the *evolutionary psychologists*. Of these theoretical positions, it is primarily the (nativists/evolutionary theorists) who are interested in explaining why these abilities are innately programmed.

13-6. Why would we be prewired to understand addition and subtraction? The (nativists/evolutionary theorists) assert that basic addition and subtraction abilities had clear ________________ value in a hunting, foraging, and social-bargaining society.

Answers: 13-1. habituation, dishabituation **13-2.** T, T, T **13-3.** dishabituation, are **13-4.** innate **13-5.** evolutionary theorists **13-6.** evolutionary theorists, survival (adaptive).

14. Describe the concepts of critical and sensitive periods in development.

14-1. A critical period is a limited time span when it is optimal for certain capacities to emerge because the organism is especially ________________ to certain experiences. A sensitive period suggests an optimal period for acquisition, but acquisition could occur at a later point. Many argue that these periods may apply to our acquisition of ________________ and ________________ abilities.

Answers: 14-1. responsive, language, musical.

15. Describe what is meant by a child's theory of mind.

15-1. "Theory of mind" refers to children's understanding about the mind and how it works, and how children conceive of ________________ ________________ thought processes, knowledge, beliefs, and feelings.

15-2. An experimenter shows a child a candy box and asks what it contains. The child responds, "Candy." In fact, when the box is opened, the child sees that it contains crayons. The child is then asked what he would expect another child to say when the other child is shown the closed box.

(a) Suppose the first child is five years old. What would he say the second child will say when shown the closed box: "candy" or "crayons"? ____________________

(b) Suppose a three-year-old child is asked the same question. He says that candy is in the box, and when the box is opened, he sees it contains crayons. What does he say the second child will say is in the closed box? ____________________

(c) Once shown that the box contains crayons, the three-year-old is also asked what he originally said. What does he say he said: "candy" or "crayons"?

____

15-3. Why does the three-year-old child respond this way? Because most children under four years do not understand that there can be a difference between *beliefs* and *external reality.* In other words, they cannot yet appreciate the possibility that people can hold ________________ beliefs that do not accurately reflect reality.

15-4. Between ages three and four, children make the connection between mental states and external reality. They develop the understanding that beliefs (may not/will always) reflect external reality. The understanding of false belief is a necessary condition for the child moving from a ________________ theory of mind (i.e., viewing the mind like a recording device) toward the more mature ________________ theory of mind (i.e., viewing the mind as a constructive interpreter of reality).

Answers: 15-1. another person's **15-2.** (a) candy, (b) crayonsm (c) crayons **15-3.** false **15-4.** may not, copy, interpretive.

16. Outline Kohlberg's stages of moral development, and summarize the strengths and weaknesses of Kohlberg's theory.

16-1. Kohlberg's theory includes three moral levels, each with two stages, for a total of six stages. Indicate which of the three moral levels is described in each of the following statements.

(a) Acts are considered wrong because they are punished or right because they lead to positive consequences: ____________________.

(b) Individuals at this level conform very strictly to society's rules, which they accept as absolute and inviolable: ____________________.

(c) This level is characterized by situational or conditional morality, such that stealing might be considered wrong in one circumstance but permissible in another: ____________________.

16-2. The central ideas of Kohlberg's theory have received a fair amount of support. Research has found that children (do/do not) tend to progress through Kohlberg's stages in the order that he indicated. As children get older, stages 1 and 2 reasoning tend to decrease, while stages 3 and 4 reasoning tend to _______________.

16-3. There have also been several criticisms of Kohlberg's theory. First, individuals may show characteristics of several different stages at the same time. In other words, as was true of other stage theories, there tends to be a "_______________" of stages.

16-4. Second, researchers have focused too heavily on (Kohlberg's/newly created) dilemmas, which tends to narrow the scope of research on moral reasoning.

16-5. Third, it may be the case that Kohlberg's theory is much more (value-free/culture-specific) than he had supposed. The theory may reflect a liberal, individualistic ideology most characteristic of modern _______________ nations.

16-6. Fourth, Gilligan has argued that males and females are socialized differently, such that women develop a morality of _______________ and men a morality of _______________. Because the latter is classified within a higher stage of reasoning, Gilligan argues that Kohlberg's stages are biased in favour of _______________.

Answers: 16-1. (a) preconventional (b) conventional (c) postconventional **16-2.** do, increase **16-3.** mixing **16-4.** Kohlberg's **16-5.** culture-specific, Western **16-6.** care, justice, males.

THE TRANSITION OF ADOLESCENCE

17. Describe the major events of puberty.

17-1. Match the descriptions with one of the appropriate terms: pubescence, puberty, secondary sex characteristics, menarche, and adolescence.

(a) ____________________ The approximately two-year span preceding puberty that is marked by rapid growth in height and weight and during which secondary sex characteristics appear.

(b) ____________________ Physical features that distinguish one sex from another but that are not essential for reproduction (e.g., facial hair in males, breasts in females).

(c) ____________________ The stage during which sexual functions essential for reproduction reach maturity; includes menarche in females and the production of sperm in males.

(d) ____________________ The first occurrence of menstruation.

(e) ____________________ The transitional period between childhood and adulthood that includes early physical changes (puberty) and later cognitive and social changes.

Answers: 17-1. (a) pubescence, (b) secondary sex characteristics, (c) puberty, (d) menarche, (e) adolescence.

18. Describe changes taking place in the teen brain.

18-1. There is evidence that growth of the ________________ matter seems to increase steadily from childhood into puberty, reflecting the fact that neurons are becoming more ________________. Grey matter decreases in volume, reflecting synaptic ________________.

18-2. Most of these changes appear to take place in the ______________ ______________, which has been characterized as an ______________ ______________ centre crucial to planning, emotional regulation, and inhibition of responses. Immaturity of the prefrontal cortex may be related to adolescents' tendency to engage in risky behaviour.

Answers: 18-1. white, myelinated, pruning **18-2.** prefrontal cortex, executive control.

19. Evaluate the assertion that adolescence is a time of turmoil.

19-1. How tumultuous is adolescence? With regard to suicide and other indicants of stress, current data indicate that (mark each of the following statements true [T] or false [F].):

____ (a) Most 12- to 13-year-old Canadian youths report being happy with their lives.

____ (b) Suicide among adolescents has increased over the past few decades.

____ (c) The rate of adolescent suicide attempts is greater for males than females.

____ (d) The suicide rate among First Nations Canadians is higher than for the general Canadian population.

____ (e) In general, adolescents encounter somewhat more storm and stress than do people in other periods of life.

Answers: 19-1. (a) T, (b) T, (c) F, (d) T, (e) T.

20. Describe the Featured Study on Canadian First Nations youth.

20-1. Chandler and Lalonde examined whether differences in suicide rates across various groups of First Nations Canadians reflected differences in cultural ______________ between these groups. A lack of cultural continuity could contribute to a lack of ______________ continuity, thereby leading to higher suicide rates.

20-2. Chandler and Lalonde used a set of cultural ______________ (e.g., self-governance, land claims, and control over education, health, or emergency services) to determine the degree of cultural continuity in various First Nations communities. They found that suicide rates were (higher/lower) in those communities whose cultural practices helped to preserve and restore Native culture. That is, cultural continuity promoted ______________ continuity and the ability to inhibit self-destructive thoughts and actions.

Answers: 20-1. continuity, personal (self) **20-2.** markers, lower, personal.

21. Discuss some common patterns of identity formation in adolescence.

21-1. Adolescence is a period of change, so it is readily understandable that adolescents tend to focus on the struggle for ________________, the question of "Who am I?"

21-2. Recall that Erik Erikson described four crises that mark childhood. What is the crisis that marks adolescence, according to Erikson? ________________ vs. ________________

21-3. Marcia (1966, 1980) has described four orientations or statuses that individuals may adopt in attempting to resolve identity. In order of increasing maturity, these are identity diffusion, foreclosure, achievement, and moratorium.

(a) One possible status is simply to take on the values and roles prescribed by one's parents, the status of identity ________________. While this may temporarily resolve the crisis, in the long run, the individual may not be comfortable with the adopted identity.

(b) Another status involves a period of experimentation with various ideologies and careers and a delay in commitment to any one, termed identity ________________.

(c) If the experimentation and lack of commitment become permanent, the individual is said to be in a status of identity ________________.

(d) On the other hand, if the consideration of alternatives leads to conviction about a sense of self, one takes on the status referred to as identity ________________.

21-4. The statuses are not stages that adolescents pass through in an orderly manner. In fact, recent research has found that (very few/most) adolescents shift back and forth among the four identity statuses. In addition, most individuals reach the last stage, identity ________________, at a later age than Marcia had supposed.

Answers: 21-1. identity **21-2.** identity, confusion **21-3.** (a) foreclosure, (b) moratorium, (c) diffusion, (d) achievement **21-4.** most, achievement.

22. Summarize arguments for "emerging adulthood" as a new developmental stage.

22-1. Arnett has argued that a transitional stage of life occurs between the ages of ______ and ______. The features of this stage include a subjective sense that one is between the stages of adolescence and adulthood, a sense of great ________________, a tendency toward self-________________, and identity formation.

Answers: 22-1. 18, 25, optimism, focus.

THE EXPANSE OF ADULTHOOD

23. Summarize evidence on the stability of personality and the prevalence of the midlife crisis.

23-1. Do people change throughout their lifetimes, or does personality tend to remain the same?

Research evidence supports the conclusion that:

a. Personality is stable across one's lifetime.

b. Personality changes across one's lifetime.

c. Both of the above.

d. Neither of the above.

23-2. The explanation for these apparently contradictory findings is that some personality traits do appear to _______________ as people grow older, while others remain _______________. Also, Vaillant has argued that _______________ tends to remain stable, whereas character (lifestyle and life choices) can change considerably.

23-3. Two influential studies conducted in the 1970s asserted that people experience a period of emotional turmoil sometime between ages 35 and 45, a transitional phase known as the _______________ _______________.

23-4. The midlife crisis, described as a period of reappraisal and assessment of time left, was thought by Gould and Levinson to be a transitional phase that affected (a minority/most) adults. More recently, a large number of other investigators, using more objective methods, have found that (very few/most) people go through a midlife crisis.

Answers: 23-1. c **23-2.** change, stable (the same), temperament **23-3.** midlife crisis **23-4.** most, very few.

24. Outline Erikson's stages of development in adulthood.

24-1. In the spaces below, write the names of the crises that mark Erikson's three stages of adulthood. In the parentheses, indicate the approximate period of adulthood during which the crises are supposed to occur.

(a) _______________ vs. _______________ ( )

(b) _______________ vs. _______________ ( )

(c) _______________ vs. _______________ ( )

24-2. Following are descriptions of the crises occurring in each of the above stages. Indicate the stages by placing the letters (a, b, or c from the previous question) in the appropriate blanks.

____ Concern for helping future generations versus a self-indulgent concern for meeting one's own desires.

____ Concern for finding meaning in the remainder of one's life versus a preoccupation with earlier failures and eventual death.

____ Concern for developing a capacity for intimacy with others versus a strategy in which others are manipulated as a means to an end.

Answers: 24-1. (a) intimacy vs. isolation (early adulthood), (b) generativity vs. self-absorption (middle adulthood), (c) integrity vs. despair (aging years) **24-2.** b, c, a.

25. Describe typical transitions in family relations during the adult years.

25-1. In part due to shifting social and economic trends, remaining single or postponing marriage is a much more acceptable option today than it was a few decades ago. Nonetheless, over ______% of Canadian adults eventually marry. Since the 1980s, the number of common-law relationships in Canada has been (decreasing/increasing). Since 1997, the rate of divorce in Canada has been (increasing/decreasing).

25-2. In general, the level of happiness in marriage tends to be U-shaped. That is, spouses' overall satisfaction with marital life tends to be highest at both the beginning and end and reach a low point toward the ________________ of the family cycle.

25-3. What causes the drop in marital satisfaction during the middle years? To some degree it coincides with the burdens of child-rearing. The decline begins to occur (only after/even before) the first child is born, however, so other factors appear to be involved as well.

25-4. Although most couples rate parenthood as a very positive experience, the birth of a child is frequently quite stressful. Adolescence, while not as contentious a period as previously believed, (does/does not) bring an increase in parent–child conflict. The effects of this conflict appear to be more adverse for the (children/parents).

25-5. Marital satisfaction tends to (decrease/increase) as the children grow up and leave home. While the "empty nest" syndrome may briefly occur, it seems to have little lasting negative impact.

Answers: 25-1. 90, increasing, decreasing **25-2.** middle **25-3.** even before **25-4.** does, parents **25-5.** increase.

26. Describe the physical changes associated with aging and the evidence on Alzheimer's disease.

26-1. As we age, our physical and cognitive characteristics change. Indicate which of the following physical traits *increase* and which *decrease* by placing checkmarks in the appropriate blanks.

Physical changes	Increases	Decreases
Proportion of body fat:	______	______
Overall weight:	______	______
Number of neurons in the brain:	______	______
Visual acuity:	______	______
Ability to see close:	______	______
Hearing:	______	______

26-2. The ending of the menstrual cycle and loss of fertility among women is referred to as ________________. Most women experience some physical discomfort during menopause (e.g., hot flashes), but the emotional distress (does/does not) appear to be especially severe.

26-3. Men (also/do not) go through a comparable experience. Testosterone levels begin to decline at middle age, and the eventual loss is (slight/substantial). The change occurs gradually, however, and is not comparable to the relatively sudden onset of menopause in women.

26-4. An abnormal condition marked by loss of memory and other cognitive abilities is termed a _______________. Dementia occurs in approximately _____ % of individuals over age 75. Thus, dementia (is/is not) a normal part of the aging process.

26-5. The disorder known as _______________ disease accounts for approximately 60% of dementia. This disease is accompanied by a (slight/widespread) loss of neurons, beginning in the hippocampus and spreading to other areas of the brain.

26-6. Alzheimer's usually begins (before/after) age 65 and is initially marked by the rapid forgetting of newly acquired information. Eventually, victims may fail to recognize familiar people and become disoriented and unable to care for themselves. A cure for Alzheimer's (does/does not) appear to be close at hand. Causes likely include genetic factors, and protective factors are thought to include regular _______________ and participation in stimulating _______________ activities.

Answers: 26-1. Body fat and overall weight increase (except that overall weight may decrease somewhat after the mid-50s); the rest decrease **26-2.** menopause, does not **26-3.** do not, substantial **26-4.** dementia, 15–20, is not **26-5.** Alzheimer's, widespread **26-6.** after, does not, exercise, cognitive.

27. Describe how intelligence and memory change in later adulthood.

27-1. With regard to changes in cognitive ability that may accompany aging, which of the following are true (T) and which are (F)?

____ (a) Average test scores in cognitive ability show some decline after age 60.

____ (b) For the majority of people, the decline in general intelligence that occurs in later years is relatively slight.

____ (c) Crystallized intelligence is more likely to decline with aging than fluid intelligence.

____ (d) The memory loss that accompanies aging is relatively severe for the majority of people.

____ (e) The type of general cognitive loss that occurs with aging is thought to involve processing speed.

____ (f) Problem-solving ability generally remains unimpaired as people age if they are given additional time to compensate for reduced speed.

Answers: 27-1. (a) T, (b) T, (c) F, (d) F, (e) T, (f) T.

PUTTING IT IN PERSPECTIVE

28. Explain how this chapter highlighted the text's unifying themes.

28-1. The behaviour of a child is the result of the child's genetic inheritance and its environment, which includes the behaviour of the child's parents. In turn, the behaviour of the parents toward the child is affected both by the child's inherited characteristics and by the behaviour of the child. Thus, behaviour is the result not of heredity or environment operating separately but of an _______________ between the two factors.

28-2. To understand the concept of *interaction*, consider this problem: There is a form of mental retardation that results from phenylketonuria, an inherited inability to metabolize a common amino acid in milk. When fed milk, children born with phenylketonuria become mentally retarded. Is this type of retardation an inherited disorder?

a. Yes, it's genetic.

b. No, it's caused by the environment.

c. A certain proportion of the causal factors are hereditary, and the remainder are due to the environment.

d. The disorder results from heredity and environment operating jointly.

28-3. This chapter has been concerned with changes in human behaviour across the life span. The theme being stressed here is that these changes result from an *interaction* of heredity and environment. In your own words, explain how the interaction operates.

Answers: 28-1. interaction **28-2.** d. (This disorder might at first seem to be inherited since there is a genetic trait involved. But the retardation does not occur if the infant is not fed milk products, which involves the environment. The point is that this disorder, like behaviour in general, cannot be attributed solely to nature or to nurture or even to relative weights of each; it is a function of an *interaction* between the two.) **28-3.** The interaction of heredity and environment refers to the fact that we are a product of both factors. It means more than that, however. Heredity and environment don't operate separately. Interaction means that the genetic factors affect the operation of the environment and that environmental factors affect genetic predispositions. The influence of one factor *depends on* the effects of the other.

PERSONAL APPLICATION * UNDERSTANDING GENDER DIFFERENCES

29. Summarize evidence on gender differences in behaviour, and discuss the significance of these differences.

29-1. Which gender tends to show more of (or score higher on tests of) the following abilities or traits? Circle the correct answer at the right.

Cognitive

verbal skills	Males	Females	Neither
mathematical skills	Males	Females	Neither
visual–spatial skills	Males	Females	Neither

Social

aggression	Males	Females	Neither
sensitivity to nonverbal cues	Males	Females	Neither
risk-taking	Males	Females	Neither
sexually permissive attitudes	Males	Females	Neither
assertiveness	Males	Females	Neither
anxiety	Males	Females	Neither
nurturance	Males	Females	Neither

29-2. There is an enormous overlap between the genders with regard to these traits. There are, of course, many females who are more aggressive than the average male and many males who are more sensitive to nonverbal cues than the average female. Thus, it is important to note that the differences referred to in this section are differences between group ________________ and that the size of the differences is relatively ________________.

Answers: 29-1. cognitive: females, males, males; social: males, females, males, males, males, females, females **29-2.** averages (means), small.

30. Explain how biological factors are thought to contribute to gender differences.

30-1. For evolutionary theorists, the relative invariance of gender differences found across cultures reflects natural selection. From this perspective, males are more sexually active and permissive than females because reproductive success for males is maximized by seeking (few/many) sexual partners. Greater aggressiveness has survival value for males because it enhances their ability to acquire material ________________ sought by females selecting a mate.

30-2. Evolutionary theorists also assert that ability differences between the genders reflect the division of labour in our ancestral past. Males were primarily the hunters and females the gatherers, and the adaptive demands of hunting may have produced males' superiority at most ________________ tasks.

30-3. The evolutionary view of gender is certainly an interesting and plausible explanation of the remarkable similarity in gender differences across cultures. The viewpoint has its critics, however. For one thing, there are reasonable ________________ theories of gender differences; for another, the evolutionary explanation is relatively (easy/difficult) to test empirically.

30-4. Concerning other biological factors, several studies indicate that hormones contribute to shaping gender differences. For example, females exposed prenatally to high levels of an ________________-like drug given to their mothers during pregnancy tend to show more male-typical behaviour than do other females.

30-5. Recent studies have also found that normal aging men given testosterone to enhance their sexual function tend to show increases in ________________ perception. While these correlational studies involving hormones support the role of biology in gender development, it is important to note that they are based on (small/large) samples of people who have (normal/abnormal) conditions.

30-6. Other biological evidence indicates that males depend more heavily on the left hemisphere for verbal processing and the right for spatial processing than do females. That is, males may tend to exhibit more cerebral ________________ than females. This finding has been linked to another finding: that females have larger ________________ callosums (the connecting sheath of axons between hemispheres) than do males.

30-7. Results from studies of specialization and of gender differences in the corpus callosum have not been consistent, however. In addition, it would be difficult to see how gender differences in *specialization* could account for gender differences in *ability*, that is, the superiority of males on ______________–______________ tasks and the superiority of females on ________________ tasks.

Answers: 30-1. many, resources **30-2.** spatial (visual–spatial) **30-3.** alternative, difficult **30-4.** androgen **30-5.** spatial (visual–spatial), small, abnormal **30-6.** specialization, corpus **30-7.** visual–spatial, verbal.

31. Explain how environmental factors are thought to contribute to gender differences.

31-1. Many researchers remain convinced that gender differences are largely shaped by the environment. One of the ways that children learn gender roles is from the consequences for their behaviour, the rewards and punishments that they receive in the process known as ________________ conditioning.

31-2. Children also acquire information by seeing what others do, the process of ________________ learning. While children imitate both males and females, they are more likely to imitate the behaviour of (same-sex/opposite-sex) models.

31-3. In addition to operant conditioning and observational learning, children are active participants in their own gender-role socialization, the process referred to as ________________-socialization. First, once they discover (at age five or six) that being a boy or girl is a permanent condition, they will then ________________ themselves as boys or girls. Second, following classification in terms of gender, children will ________________ characteristics and behaviours associated with their gender. Third, they will bring their ________________ in line with their values by engaging in "sex-appropriate" behaviours.

31-4. Whether through operant conditioning, observational learning, or self-socialization, the major forces for gender-role socialization occur in three main areas of the child's environment: in their ________________, in ________________, and in the ________________.

Answers: 31-1. operant **31-2.** observational (modelling), same-sex **31-3.** self, classify (categorize), value, behaviour **31-4.** families, schools, media.

CRITICAL THINKING APPLICATION * ARE FATHERS ESSENTIAL TO CHILDREN'S WELL–BEING?

32. Explain the argument that fathers are essential for healthy development and some criticism of this line of reasoning.

32-1. Over the past several decades in the U.S., the percentage of children brought up without fathers in the home has steadily increased, from about 17% in 1960 to more than 35% today. During the same period, there has also been a dramatic (decrease/increase) in teen pregnancy, juvenile delinquency, violent crime, drug abuse, eating disorders, and family dysfunction in general.

32-2. Further, fatherless children are two to three times more likely than fathered children to drop out of high school, become a teenage parent, or become a juvenile delinquent. In other words, father absence (causes/is correlated with) a host of unfortunate cultural trends.

32-3. Based on the association between father absence and social problems, some writers have asserted that the presence of a father is essential for a child's well-being. As you are by now well aware, however, one (can/cannot) infer causation on the basis of correlational data alone.

32-4. Among the reasonable alternative explanations for the correlational relationship described are the following. Father absence frequently occurs when the parents ________________, so it is possible that this factor, rather than father absence, may cause the negative effects referred to.

32-5. Or, since father absence is much more frequent in (low-income/high-income) families, it is possible that poverty, rather than father absence, may cause some (or all) of the negative effects.

32-6. In your continued critical thinking about the assertions discussed, recall also the fallacies in reasoning introduced in Chapter 10: irrelevant reasons, circular reasoning, slippery slope, weak analogies, and false dichotomy. Which of these apply to the following assertions? Use the abbreviations IR, CR, SS, WA, or FD.

(a) ____ If present trends continue, our society could be on the verge of social suicide.

(b) ____ To tolerate the trend of fatherlessness is to accept the inevitability of continued societal recession.

Answers: 32-1. increase **32-2.** is correlated with **32-3.** cannot **32-4.** divorce **32-5.** low-income **32-6.** (a) SS. The argument is that if we allow one event to happen, then other events will inevitably follow on this slippery slope that will lead to disaster. (b) FD. The statement may have elements of more than one fallacy, but the author really is posing a dichotomy: either we reduce father absence or else we will face social decline. Of course, we could do both (reduce father absence *and* face social decline) or neither.

Review of Key Terms

Accommodation
Age of viability
Animism
Assimilation
Attachment
Centration
Cephalocaudal trend
Cognitive development
Conservation
Cross-sectional design
Dementia
Development
Developmental norms
Dishabituation
Egocentrism
Embryonic stage
Family life cycle
Fetal alcohol syndrome
Fetal stage
Gender
Gender differences
Gender roles
Gender stereotypes
Germinal stage
Habituation
Irreversibility
Longitudinal design
Maturation
Menarche
Midlife crisis
Motor development
Object permanence
Placenta
Prenatal period
Primary sex characteristics
Proximodistal trend
Puberty
Pubescence
Scaffolding
Secondary sex characteristics
Separation anxiety
Sex
Socialization
Stage
Temperament
Zygote

____________________ **1.** The sequence of age-related changes that occurs as a person progresses from conception to death.

____________________ **2.** The period of pregnancy, extending from conception to birth.

____________________ **3.** The first two weeks after conception.

____________________ **4.** The structure that connects the circulation of the fetus and the mother but that blocks passage of blood cells.

____________________ **5.** The second stage of prenatal development, lasting from two weeks after conception until the end of the second month.

____________________ **6.** The third stage of prenatal development, lasting from two months after conception through birth.

____________________ **7.** The age at which the baby can first survive in the event of a premature birth.

____________________ **8.** A collection of congenital problems associated with a mother's excessive use of alcohol during pregnancy.

____________________ **9.** Changing existing mental structures to explain new experiences, a concept from Piaget's theory of cognitive development.

____________________ **10.** Developmental changes in muscular coordination required for physical movement.

____________________ **11.** The head-to-foot direction of motor development.

____________________ **12.** The centre-outward direction of motor development.

____________________ **13.** The average ages at which people display certain behaviours and abilities.

____________________ **14.** Characteristic mood, energy level, and reactivity.

____________________ **15.** One group of subjects is observed over a long period of time.

____________________ **16.** Investigators compare groups of subjects of differing ages at a single point in time.

____________________ **17.** A difficult, turbulent period of doubt and reappraisal of one's life that may occur at midlife.

____________________ **18.** Emotional distress displayed by an infant when separated from a person with whom it has formed an attachment.

_________________________ **19.** Culturally constructed distinctions between femininity and masculinity.

_________________________ **20.** Widely held beliefs about females' and males' abilities, personality traits, and social behaviour.

_________________________ **21.** Development of thinking, reasoning, remembering, and problem solving.

_________________________ **22.** The gradual reduction in response strength that occurs when people are repeatedly exposed to some event.

_________________________ **23.** The increase in response strength that occurs when people are exposed to a new stimulus event.

_________________________ **24.** A mental capacity that involves recognizing that objects continue to exist even when they are no longer visible.

_________________________ **25.** Piaget's term for the awareness that physical quantities remain constant in spite of changes in their shape or appearance.

_________________________ **26.** The Piagetian term for the tendency to focus on just one feature of a problem and neglect other important features.

_________________________ **27.** The inability to cognitively visualize reversing an action.

_________________________ **28.** Thinking characterized by a limited ability to share another person's viewpoint.

_________________________ **29.** A sequence of stages that families tend to progress through.

_________________________ **30.** Interpreting new experiences in terms of mental structures already available, a concept from Piaget's theory of cognitive development.

_________________________ **31.** The attribution of lifelike qualities to inanimate objects.

_________________________ **32.** A developmental period during which certain behaviours and capacities occur.

_________________________ **33.** The biologically based categories of male and female.

_________________________ **34.** A close, emotional bond of affection between an infant and its caregiver.

_________________________ **35.** Physical features associated with gender that are not directly needed for reproduction.

_________________________ **36.** The physical structures necessary for reproduction.

_________________________ **37.** The two-year span preceding puberty, marked by the appearance of secondary sex characteristics and by rapid growth.

_________________________ **38.** The first occurrence of menstruation.

_________________________ **39.** The stage during which reproductive functions reach maturity.

_________________________ **40.** An abnormal condition marked by multiple cognitive deficits; more prevalent in older adults but not a product of normal aging.

_________________________ **41.** Developmental changes that reflect one's genetic blueprint rather than environment.

_________________________ **42.** A one-celled organism created by the process of fertilization, the union of sperm and egg.

_________________________ **43.** Behavioural differences between females and males.

_________________________ **44.** When the assistance provided to a child is adjusted as learning progresses.

_________________________ **45.** The acquisition of norms, roles, and behaviours expected of people in a particular group.

______________________ **46.** Expectations concerning what appropriate behaviour is for each sex.

Answers: 1. development **2.** prenatal period **3.** germinal stage **4.** placenta **5.** embryonic stage **6.** fetal stage **7.** age of viability **8.** fetal alcohol syndrome **9.** accommodation **10.** motor development **11.** cephalocaudal trend **12.** proximodistal trend **13.** developmental norms **14.** temperament **15.** longitudinal design **16.** cross-sectional design **17.** midlife crisis **18.** separation anxiety **19.** gender **20.** gender stereotypes **21.** cognitive development **22.** habituation **23.** dishabituation **24.** object permanence **25.** conservation **26.** centration **27** irreversibility **28.** egocentrism **29.** family life cycle **30.** assimilation **31.** animism **32.** stage **33.** sex **34.** attachment **35.** secondary sex characteristics **36.** primary sex characteristics **37.** pubescence **38.** menarche **39.** puberty **40.** dementia **41.** maturation **42.** zygote **43.** gender differences **44.** scaffolding **45.** socialization **46.** gender roles.

Review of Key People

Mary Ainsworth	Robbie Case	Juan Pascual-Leone
Jay Belsky	Erik Erikson	Jean Piaget
John Bowlby	Lawrence Kohlberg	Alexander Thomas & Stella Chess

______________________ **1.** Conducted a major longitudinal study in which they identified three basic styles of children's temperament.

______________________ **2.** Conducted research on daycare.

______________________ **3.** Theorized that there are critical periods in human infants' lives during which attachments must occur for normal development to take place.

______________________ **4.** Partitioned the life span into eight stages, each accompanied by a psychosocial crisis.

______________________ **5.** Pioneered the study of children's cognitive development.

______________________ **6.** Developed a stage theory of moral development.

______________________ **7.** Described three categories of infant–mother attachment.

______________________ **8.** A neo-Piagetian theorist who used the concept of M-capacity.

______________________ **9.** A neo-Piagetian theorist who emphasized that cognitive capacity involved numerous discrete skills that may show uneven development.

Answers: 1. Thomas & Chess **2.** Belsky **3.** Bowlby **4.** Erikson **5.** Piaget **6.** Kohlberg **7.** Ainsworth **8.** Pascual-Leone **9.** Case.

Self-Quiz

1. Which prenatal period begins at the second week and ends at the second month of pregnancy?
a. germinal stage
b. embryonic stage
c. fetal stage
d. seminal stage

2. In which prenatal stage do most major birth defects probably have their origins?
a. germinal stage
b. embryonic stage
c. fetal stage
d. seminal stage

3. A child is shown a candy box. When asked what he thinks is in it, he says, "Candy." He is then shown that the candy box actually contains crayons. He is then asked what he thinks another child will say when shown the same closed box. He says that he thinks the next child will say, "Crayons." What would be the best guess about the age of the child?
   a. 3 years
   b. 5 years
   c. 6 years
   d. 7 years

4. In their Featured Study, Chandler and Lalonde examined whether a lack of cultural continuity within First Nations bands in B.C. would be associated with:
   a. suicide
   b. violence
   c. educational attainment
   d. all of the above

5. What is the major conclusion from Thomas and Chess's longitudinal study of temperament?
   a. Children's temperaments tend to go through predictable stages.
   b. The temperament of the child is not a good predictor of the temperament of the adult.
   c. Opposites attract.
   d. Children's temperaments tend to be consistent over the years.

6. The crisis occurring in the first year, according to Erikson, is one involving:
   a. trust versus mistrust
   b. initiative versus guilt
   c. industry versus inferiority
   d. identity versus conformity

7. During which stage in Piaget's system is the child first able to handle conservation problems and hierarchical classification problems?
   a. sensorimotor
   b. preoperational
   c. concrete operations
   d. formal operations

8. A child in the early sensorimotor period is shown a ball, which she watches intensely. The ball is then hidden under a pillow. What will the child do?
   a. Ask "Where is the pillow?"
   b. Stare at the pillow but not pick it up.
   c. Move the pillow and pick up the ball.
   d. Ignore the pillow, as if the ball didn't exist.

9. Who developed a stage theory of moral development?
   a. Piaget
   b. Kohlberg
   c. Gould
   d. Bowlby

10. Which of the following cognitive capacities is most likely to decline as a function of aging?
   a. fluid intelligence
   b. crystallized intelligence
   c. problem-solving ability
   d. specialized intelligence

11. Some researchers have found that very young children (e.g., five months old) appear to be aware of the addition or subtraction of objects from behind a screen. The technique used in these studies was:
a. sensory preconditioning
b. self-socialization
c. classical conditioning
d. habituation–dishabituation

12. Which of the following factors tends to be accompanied by a drop in ratings of marital satisfaction?
a. childlessness during early married life
b. the birth of the first child
c. the first child's departure for college
d. when the last child leaves home

13. Females tend to score higher than males on tests of:
a. verbal ability
b. mathematical ability
c. visual–spatial ability
d. cerebral specialization

14. Females exposed to high levels of androgen during prenatal development tend to show:
a. more male-typical behaviour than other females
b. more stereotypic female behaviour than other females
c. less cerebral specialization than other females
d. a larger corpus callosum than other females

15. Once children discover that their gender is permanent, they are likely to want to engage in behaviour that is "sex appropriate," as defined by their culture. This process is referred to as:
a. operant conditioning
b. observational learning
c. self-socialization
d. classical conditioning

16. According to Lalonde and Chandler, for a child to develop an interpretive theory of mind, he or she must understand the idea of:
a. conservation
b. permanence
c. false belief
d. reversibility

17. The idea of a zone of proximal development was put forth by:
a. Piaget
b. Erikson
c. Harlow
d. Vygotsky

18. A brain area that is believed to mature through adolescence and that is thought to be related to the willingness of teens to engage in risky behaviour is:
a. the prefrontal cortex
b. the hippocampus
c. the cingulate cortex
d. the mesolimbic dopamine pathway

19. According to Arnett, all of the following are characteristic of emerging adulthood *except*:
a. pessimism about the future
b. self-focus
c. a subjective feeling of being between adolescence and adulthood
d. identity formation

Answers: **1.** b **2.** b **3.** a **4.** a **5.** d **6.** a **7.** c **8.** d **9.** b **10.** a **11.** d **12.** b **13.** a **14.** a **15.** c **16.** c **17.** d **18.** a **19.** a.

InfoTrac Keywords

Dementia
Fetal Alcohol Syndrome
Gender Stereotypes
Puberty
Temperament

Chapter Twelve

PERSONALITY: THEORY, RESEARCH, AND ASSESSMENT

Review of Key Ideas

THE NATURE OF PERSONALITY

1. Define the construct of personality in terms of consistency and distinctiveness.

1-1. I could always tell when my colleague across the hall (now retired) had finished for the day, because I could hear squeaking as he carefully moved his computer table under his bookcase. And I knew what followed: he closed and reshelved his books, sorted the papers on his desk into two piles, and slid the pens and pencils into his desk drawer bin. The fact that my colleague engaged in the *same behaviours* every day illustrates the feature of personality termed ________________.

1-2. When I'm done, on the other hand, I usually just stand up and walk out, leaving my somewhat (some would say very) messy desk behind. The fact that my colleague and I *differ* with respect to office neatness illustrates the feature of personality termed ________________.

Answers: 1-1. consistency (stability) **1-2.** distinctiveness (behavioural differences).

2. Explain what is meant by a personality trait, and describe the five-factor model of personality.

2-1. A consistent or durable disposition to behave in a particular way is referred to as a personality ________________. Personality trait descriptions frequently consist of a series of ________________, such as *anxious*, *excitable*, *shy*, *aggressive*, and so on.

2-2. There are an enormous number of trait words that could be used to describe people. Gordon Allport, for example, listed several thousand. Raymond Cattell reduced Allport's list to just ________________ traits. More recently, McCrae and Costa have described an even simpler model involving only ________________ traits, the so-called Big Five theory.

2-3. Research has shown that the Big Five traits do correlate with important life outcomes. For example, ________________ correlates with higher grades and reduced mortality, and ________________ correlates with a greater likelihood of divorce.

2-4. Some researchers maintain that more than five factors are needed to describe personality. Of the various models, however, the dominant conception of personality structure is currently the ________________ ________________ theory.

2-5. Below are listed some of the adjectives that describe each of the five factors: neuroticism, extraversion, openness to experience, agreeableness, and conscientiousness. List the name of each of the factors next to the descriptions. (The five factors are relatively easy to remember using the acronym OCEAN).

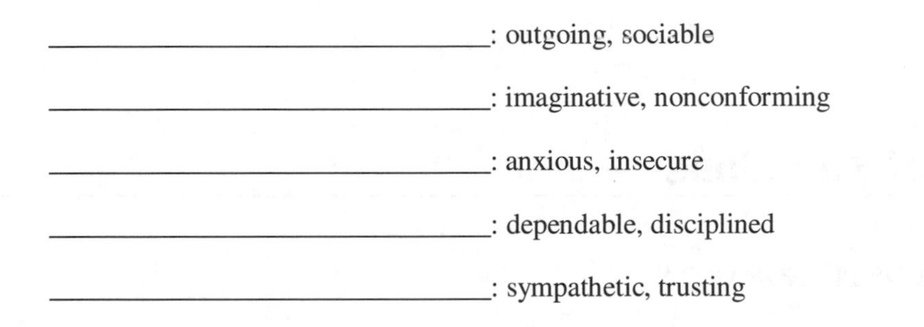

______________________________: outgoing, sociable

______________________________: imaginative, nonconforming

______________________________: anxious, insecure

______________________________: dependable, disciplined

______________________________: sympathetic, trusting

Answers: 2-1. trait, adjectives **2-2.** 16, five **2-3.** conscientiousness, neuroticism **2-4.** Big Five (five-factor) **2-5.** extraversion, openness to experience, neuroticism, conscientiousness, agreeableness.

PSYCHODYNAMIC PERSPECTIVES

3. List and describe the three components into which Freud divided the personality, and indicate how these are distributed across three levels of awareness.

3-1. The following is a schematic illustration of the three Freudian structures of personality. Label each structure.

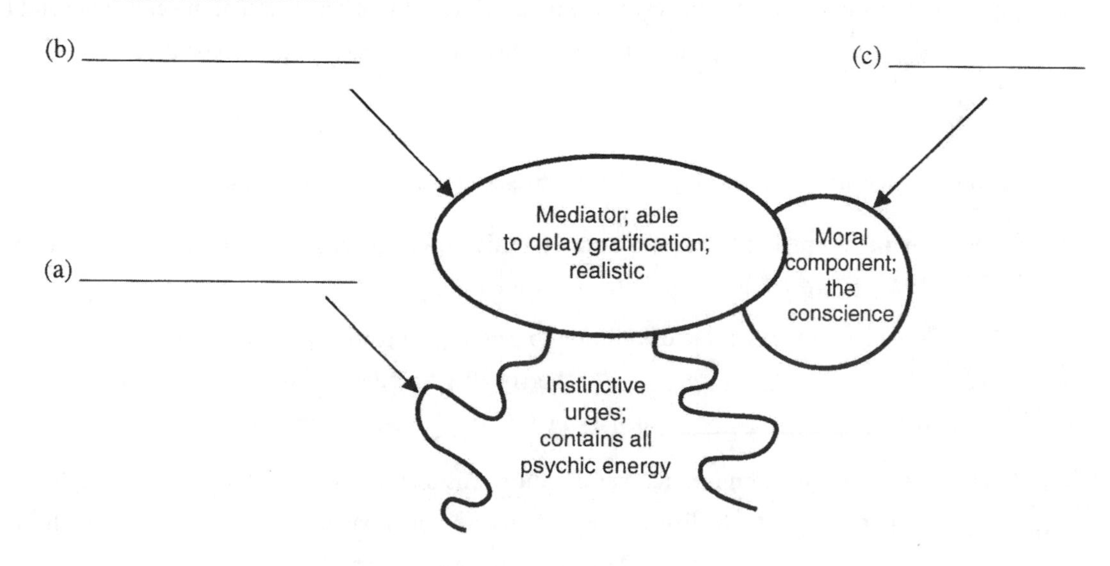

3-2. Freud superimposed levels of consciousness on the psychic structures. The following illustration makes clear that two of the structures exist at all three levels, while one is entirely unconscious. Label the levels.

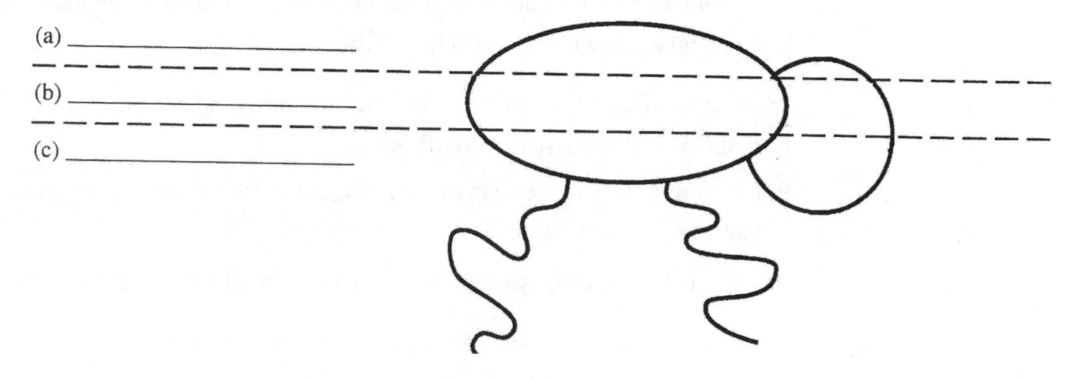

Answers: 3-1. (a) id, (b) ego, (c) superego **3-2.** (a) conscious, (b) preconscious, (c) unconscious. (The diagram shows that the ego emerges from the id, and that the superego grows out of the ego.)

4. Explain the preeminence of sexual and aggressive conflicts in Freud's theory, and describe the operation of defence mechanisms.

4-1. Freud believed that most of our conflicts arise from ________________ and ________________ urges. Conflicts relating to these areas were preeminent in his mind because (1) they are subject to subtle social ________________ and, for that reason, are a source of confusion; and (2) they are less likely to be immediately gratified and more apt than other urges to be ________________.

4-2. Following is a list of the defence mechanisms. Match each with the correct description by placing the appropriate letters in the blanks.

A. rationalization
B. repression
C. projection
D. displacement
E. reaction formation
F. regression
G. identification

____ A return to an earlier, less mature stage of development.

____ Forming an imaginary or real alliance with a person or group; becoming like them.

____ Creating false but reasonable-sounding excuses.

____ Pushing distressing thoughts into the unconscious.

____ Attributing one's own thoughts, feelings, or conflicts to another.

____ Expressing an emotion that is the exact opposite of the way one really, but unconsciously, feels.

____ Diverting emotional feelings from their original source to a substitute target.

4-3. Using five of the letters from the previous question, match the defence mechanisms with the following examples.

____ After John and Marsha break up, John says he hates Marsha; this statement helps him defend against his real feelings of affection.

____ "Society is filled with perverts," says the preacher, but later evidence suggests that he is the one with the sexual conflicts.

____ In reaction to the stress of entering college, Alice starts acting like a grade-school kid.

____ Bruce acts like John Wayne, and he owns tapes of all the Duke's movies.

____ Mary is angry at her mother, so she kicks her baby brother.

Answers: 4-1. sexual, aggressive, norms (rules, controls), frustrated (thwarted, unfulfilled) **4-2.** F, G, A, B, C, E, D **4-3.** E, C, F, G, D.

5. Outline Freud's psychosexual stages of development and their theorized relations to adult personality.

5-1. List Freud's stages of psychosexual development, in the order in which they are supposed to occur, in the blanks below. Place the ages in the parentheses.

(a) ______________________________ ( )

(b) ______________________________ ( )

(c) ______________________________ ( )

(d) ______________________________ ( )

(e) ______________________________ ( )

5-2. The following behaviours or personality characteristics are supposed to result from fixation at a particular psychosexual stage. Place the names of the correct stages in the blanks.

(a) She has problems with anger control, is hostile toward people in authority, and defies any attempt at regulation of her behaviour. ___________________

(b) He eats too much, drinks too much, and smokes. ___________________

(c) He has occasional outbursts of hostility toward his father that he can't understand. In family arguments he sides with his mother. ___________________

5-3. The Oedipus complex occurs during the ________________ stage, between the ages of ________________ and ________________. This complex theoretically involves an erotically tinged attraction toward the (same-sex/opposite-sex) parent and a strong hostility toward the (same-sex/opposite-sex) parent. Resolution of the Oedipus complex involves (increasing/stopping) both the child's erotic attraction and the child's hostility.

Answers: 5-1. (a) oral (first year), (b) anal (second year), (c) phallic (ages three through five), (d) latency (age five to puberty), (e) genital (puberty onward) **5-2.** (a) anal, (b) oral, (c) phallic **5-3.** phallic, three, five, opposite-sex, same-sex, stopping.

6. Summarize the revisions of Freud's theory proposed by Jung and Adler.

6-1. Freud devised the theory and method of treatment termed *psychoanalysis*. To differentiate his approach from Freud's, Jung called his theory ________________ ________________. Like Freud, Jung emphasized the unconscious determinants of personality. Unlike Freud, he proposed that the unconscious consists of two layers, a ________________ unconscious and a ________________ unconscious. The personal unconscious is similar to Freud's unconscious, but it has less emphasis on sexuality. The collective unconscious is a repository of inherited, ancestral memories that Jung termed ________________.

6-2. Jung's major contribution to psychology is considered by many to be his description of two major personality types: ________________, reserved, contemplative people who tend to be concerned with their own internal world of thoughts, and ________________, outgoing people who are more interested in the external world of others.

6-3. For Freud, the driving energy behind the human personality was sexuality; for Jung, it may have been the collective unconscious. For Adler, it was striving for ________________ and the attempt to overcome childhood feelings of inferiority. Efforts to overcome imagined or real inferiorities involve ________________ through development of one's abilities. While Adler considered compensation to be a normal mechanism, he saw ________________ as an abnormal attempt to conceal feelings of inferiority.

6-4. Adler is associated with the term ________________ ________________, an exaggerated feeling of inadequacy, supposedly caused by parental pampering or neglect in early childhood. Adler also thought that ________________ ________________ (that is, whether one is an only child, first-born, second-born, etc.) had a major effect on personality.

6-5. Adler's concept of birth order has created considerable interest. Initial data failed to support Adler's hypotheses, but Frank Sulloway's recent analyses of decades of research concludes that birth order (<u>is/is not</u>) a factor in personality. Referring to the ______________ ______________ trait theory, Sulloway proposed, for example, that first-borns are more conscientious but less agreeable than later-borns. (<u>Not all/All other</u>) research on birth order has supported Sulloway's conclusions, and the topic is of current interest to many researchers.

Answers: 6-1. analytical psychology, personal, collective, archetypes **6-2.** introverts, extraverts **6-3.** superiority, compensation, overcompensation **6-4.** inferiority complex, birth order **6-5.** is, Big Five, not all.

7. **Summarize the strengths and weaknesses of the psychodynamic approach to personality.**

7-1. Psychoanalytic formulations have had a major impact on the field of psychology. List the three contributions discussed in your text.

7-2. Psychoanalytic formulations have also been extensively criticized. After each of the following statements, list the particular criticism, from the discussion in your text, that the statement invites.

(a) Freud proposed that females develop weaker superegos and that they have a chronic sense of inferiority caused by penis envy. ____________________

(b) Although he discussed some characteristics associated with the psychosexual stages, Freud didn't really specify which events, occurring during which childhood stages, produce which sets of personality traits. ____________________

(c) Claims of support for the theories are based largely on clinical case studies and clinical intuition. ____________________

Answers: 7-1. The discovery that *unconscious forces* can influence behaviour, that *internal conflict* may generate psychological distress, and that *early childhood experiences* influence the adult personality **7-2.** (a) sexism, (b) vague (untestable ideas), (c) inadequate (or weak) evidence.

BEHAVIOURAL PERSPECTIVES

8. **Discuss how Skinner's principles of operant conditioning can be applied to the structure and development of personality.**

8-1. Which of the following processes plays an important part in Skinner's ideas about human behaviour?

a. mental conflict

b. the mind

c. free will

d. none of the above

8-2. According to Skinner, much of our behaviour is affected by reinforcement, punishment, or extinction—in other words, by the environmental __________________ that follow our behaviour. For example, if some individuals behave in a consistently aggressive manner (i.e., have aggressive personality traits), they do so because they have been __________________ for behaving aggressively in the past.

8-3. Skinner recognized that there are differences between people and that people behave relatively consistently over time. Distinctiveness and consistency occur, however, not because of what's going on in an individual's *mind* but because of what has occurred previously in their ________________.

8-4. Thus, for Skinner, personality is not mental, but environmental. People's minds don't change; their environment changes. Skinner makes a strong case for the point of view that our behaviour is caused, or ________________, rather than free, and that the determinants are largely ________________ rather than genetic.

Answers: 8-1. d **8-2.** consequences (stimuli, events), reinforced **8-3.** environment **8-4.** determined, environmental.

9. Describe Bandura's social cognitive theory, and compare it to Skinner's viewpoint.

9-1. In what respect is Bandura's point of view similar to Skinner's?

9-2. Three of the major differences between Bandura's and Skinner's viewpoints involve the concepts listed below. Carefully define and explain these concepts and indicate how they represent a difference from Skinner's position.

(a) reciprocal determinism:

(b) observational learning:

(c) self-efficacy:

9-3. According to Bandura, whom do we imitate and in what circumstances?

Answers: 9-1. It is similar in that Bandura believes that personality is largely shaped through learning. **9-2.** (a) *Reciprocal determinism* refers to the point of view that not only does environment determine behaviour, as Skinner asserted, but behaviour determines environment, and, further, that behaviour, environment, and mental processes all mutually affect one another. (b) *Observational learning* is the process through which we learn behaviours by observing the consequences of someone else's (i.e., a model's) behaviour. For example, we learn not only by being reinforced, as Skinner proposed, but by observing someone else being reinforced. (c) *Self-efficacy* is a belief in our ability to perform certain behaviours. This belief affects whether we undertake those behaviours and how well we perform them. Skinner makes no allowance for mentalistic concepts such as self-efficacy. **9-3.** We tend to imitate models whom we like, consider attractive and powerful, and view as similar to ourselves, and whom we observe being reinforced.

10. Identify Mischel's major contribution to personality theory, and indicate why his ideas have generated so much controversy.

10-1. Mischel's major contribution to personality theory is his contention that human behaviour is determined to a much greater extent by the ________________ than by ________________.

10-2. Why is this such a controversial idea for personality theory?

10-3. What do advocates of the *interactional* approach argue?

Answers: 10-1. situation (situational factors), personality (personality traits) **10-2.** The notion is controversial because the very definition of personality involves the word *consistency*. Mischel's findings suggest that behaviour is not as consistent as personality theorists may have thought, that it is strongly affected by an ever-changing situation. **10-3.** They argue that personality traits interact with situational factors to produce behaviour.

11. Summarize the strengths and weaknesses of the behavioural approach to personality.

11-1. The major strengths of the behavioural approach have been its commitment to empirical ________________ and its identification of important ________________ determinants of behaviour.

11-2. The major weaknesses of the behavioural approach, according to its critics, have been its overdependence on research involving ________________ subjects, its denial of free will and of the importance of ________________ processes, and its view of personality as nothing more than a collection of behaviours or ________________ associations.

Answers: 11-1. research, environmental (empirical) **11-2.** animal, cognitive, stimulus–response.

HUMANISTIC PERSPECTIVES

12. Explain how humanism was a reaction against both the behavioural and psychodynamic approaches, and discuss the assumptions of the humanistic view.

12-1. The humanistic movement reacted against the behavioural approach because of its mechanistic view of personality and its emphasis on ________________ research, and against the psychoanalytic approach because of its emphasis on ________________ drives.

12-2. The humanistic viewpoint found fault with both movements because they stressed ________________, or absolute causation. The humanists also thought that the behaviourists and the Freudians failed to recognize the (unique/common) qualities of human behaviour.

12-3. Humanistic psychology emphasizes the (similarities/differences) between human beings and the other animal species, believes we (are controlled by/can rise above) our biological heritage, asserts that we are largely (rational/irrational) creatures, and maintains that a person's (subjective/objective) view of the world is more important than _______________ reality.

Answers: 12-1. animal, primitive (animalistic) **12-2.** determinism, unique **12-3.** differences, can rise above, rational, subjective, objective.

13. Identify the single structural construct in Rogers's person-centred theory, and summarize his view of personality development.

13-1. Who are you? What are you like? What are your unique qualities? What is your typical behaviour? Your answers to these questions are likely to reflect what Rogers called the _______________.

13-2. Although Ralph tends to be a submissive and somewhat lazy person (and that is the way his friends, family, and co-workers describe him), he views himself as hard-working and dynamic, a leader both on the job and at home.

(a) What is Ralph's self-concept?

(b) Is his self-concept congruent or incongruent?

(c) According to Rogers, what parental behaviour may have led to this incongruence?

(d) According to Rogers, what parental behaviour would have resulted in Ralph's achieving congruence rather than incongruence?

13-3. Define the following Rogerian concepts.

(a) conditional love:

(b) unconditional love:

13-4. What is defensiveness for Rogers?

Answers: 13-1. self or self-concept **13-2.** (a) that he is hard-working, dynamic, and a leader, (b) incongruent, (c) conditional love or acceptance, (d) unconditional love or acceptance **13-3.** (a) affection given conditionally, the condition being that the child or adult must live up to another's expectations, (b) affection given without conditions, full acceptance of the person not dependent on what he or she is or does. **13-4.** Defensiveness is related to Roger's incongruence. As with Freud's theory, people defend against anxiety by distorting or denying reality. For Rogers, defensiveness arises when people defend their self-concepts against inconsistent experiences.

14. Describe the results of the Featured Study on the effects of a "significant other" on self-concept.

14-1. Using the views of others to judge ourselves has been called reflective _________________. Baldwin examined whether such a process operates even when we are _________________ reminded of a significant person in our lives at the point of making such appraisals.

14-2. In the first study, graduate students rated the quality of their own research ideas after being subliminally primed with either a disapproving face of their _________________ _________________ or an approving face of another psychologist. Results showed that being exposed to a subliminally presented disapproving face of someone of significance led students to make more (positive/negative) ratings of their own research ideas.

14-3. In the second study, female Catholic students first read a passage that portrayed a permissive attitude toward sexuality. They were then exposed subliminally to a disapproving face of either the _________________ or a stranger. They then rated themselves in the areas of anxiety, morality, and competency. Results showed that the participants rated themselves more (positively, negatively) when exposed to the disapproving face of the Pope compared to the disapproving stranger's face. These findings support the idea that our current self-concepts can be affected by evaluations of us provided by significant others.

Answers: 14-1. appraisal, subliminally **14-2.** research supervisor, negative **14-3.** Pope, negatively.

15. Explain Maslow's hierarchy of needs, and summarize his findings on the characteristics of self-actualizing people.

15-1. Maslow proposed that human needs are arranged in a hierarchy, usually depicted as a pyramid, with the most basic, physiological needs at the _________________ and higher-level needs closer to the _________________.

15-2. The lower-level needs would include needs for food, water, and factors related to survival and security. Next in the hierarchy would be a need for acceptance by others. Higher-level needs, called _________________ needs, would include the need for knowledge and aesthetic beauty. At the top of the pyramid is the need for ______________-______________, the need to express one's full potential.

15-3. A higher-level need would be activated only after a lower-level need is satisfied. For example, a need for knowledge would be activated (before/after) needs for esteem, belongingness, and several lower-level needs had been reasonably well satisfied.

15-4. Maslow referred to a need to fulfill one's potential in his concept of ______________-_________________. For example, if a woman had the talent and strong desire to become a mathematician but followed the urging of others and became a nurse instead (or vice versa), she would not be _______________-_________________.

15-5. Maslow proposed that people who are self-actualized have exceptionally healthy personalities. Which of the following, according to Maslow, are characteristic of self-actualized people? Place Y in the blank if the description applies, N if it does not.

____ are spontaneous

____ have more profound emotional experiences than others

____ are uncomfortable being alone

____ are not dependent on others for approval

____ thrive on their work

____ are extreme in personality (e.g., either conforming or rebellious)

Answers: 15-1. bottom, top **15-2.** growth, self-actualization **15-3.** after **15-4.** self-actualization, self-actualized **15-5.** Y, Y, N, Y, Y, N.

16. Summarize the strengths and weaknesses of the humanistic approach to personality.

16-1. To its credit, the humanistic movement called attention to the possibility that a person's ________________ views may be more important than objective reality. The movement also emphasized the importance of the ________________, or self-concept, and stressed the study of the (normal/abnormal) personality.

16-2. Critics have also identified several weaknesses of the humanistic formulations. Match the weaknesses listed below with the statements by placing the appropriate letters in the blanks.

a. poor testability

b. unrealistic view of human nature

c. inadequate evidence

____ Humanistic psychologists tend to scorn research, so little experimental support for their views has emerged.

____ Even without research, some of the descriptions, such as of self-actualized personalities, have an idealized, perfectionistic ring.

____ Humanistic ideas are frequently difficult to define, so research on some concepts is difficult or impossible.

Answers: 16-1. subjective, self, normal **16-2.** c, b, a.

BIOLOGICAL PERSPECTIVES

17. Describe Eysenck's theory of personality.

17-1. According to Eysenck, individual differences in personality can be understood in terms of a hierarchy of traits. At the top of the hierarchy are three fundamental higher-order traits from which all other traits derive: _________________, _________________, and _________________.

17-2. Eysenck asserted that a major factor in personality involves the ease with which people can be _________________. Eysenck believed that differences in conditionability, like personality differences in general, are to a large extent (environmentally/genetically) determined.

17-3. Conditionability, in turn, is related to extraversion–introversion. According to Eysenck, (extraverts/introverts) have higher levels of physiological arousal, a characteristic that makes them (more/less) readily conditioned.

17-4. Why would conditionability be related to introversion? Because easily conditioned people could be readily conditioned to fear social situations. People who fear social situations may be classified as _________________.

Answers: 17-1. extraversion, neuroticism, psychoticism (you can remember these with the acronym PEN) **17-2.** conditioned, genetically **17-3.** introverts, more **17-4.** introverts.

18. Summarize behavioural genetics research on personality and its conclusions.

18-1. The most important and conclusive result from the various twin studies is the finding that the personalities of (identical/fraternal) twins reared (together/apart) were more similar than those of (identical/fraternal) twins reared (together/apart). This outcome has been found with several dependent measures, including the factors of the Big Five personality inventory as well as peer ratings.

18-2. Approximately what percentage of the variance in personality is assumed to be caused by genetic factors?

a. 10% to 20%

b. 20% to 40%

c. 40% to 60%

d. 60% to 80%

18-3. How important a determinant of personality is family environment, according to the results of these studies?

a. of very little importance

b. of about the same importance as heredity

c. more important than heredity

18-4. The twin studies have had a major impact on the way psychologists think about the causes of human behaviour. Why are the results so important and so surprising?

18-5. Is the family environment an unimportant factor? Obviously, opinions still differ on this issue, for a couple of reasons. First, the same family environment may be received (exactly the same way/very differently) by different children. Second, family environment may not be as homogeneous as has been assumed: children in the same family (may not be/are always) treated the same way. Research on this issue continues.

Answers: 18-1. identical, apart, fraternal, together. This is the most important comparison because, even though the fraternal twins shared the same environment, their common environment did not make them nearly as similar as twins who did not have a common environment *but who shared the same genes.* **18-2.** c **18-3.** a **18-4.** Theories of development and personality have tended to stress the importance of the environment, especially the family environment; the recent twin studies find heredity to be very important and family environment to be of little importance. Thus, the results are contrary to the expectations of most of us and of much of the theorizing in the field of personality. **18-5.** very differently, may not be.

19. Outline Buss's explanation for why the Big Five traits are important.

19-1. As group animals, we gain an advantage by being able to predict the behaviour of other human beings. That is, the ability to recognize the Big Five characteristics in others has ________________ value for our species.

19-2. The Big Five traits are neuroticism, extraversion, openness to experience, agreeableness, and conscientiousness. In terms of survival value, it is useful to know who in a group will fulfill their commitments, the trait of ________________; who will fall apart under stress, the trait of ________________; who will be a good problem solver, the trait of ________________, and so on.

19-3. The fact that these traits appear as dimensions across a variety of cultures attests to their importance. For Buss, our ability to ________________ these traits in others also has adaptive significance. MacDonald, also an evolutionary theorist, asserts that it is the traits themselves, not just the ability to ________________ them, that had adaptive value in our evolutionary past.

Answers: 19-1. adaptive (survival, evolutionary) **19-2.** conscientiousness, neuroticism, openness to experience **19-3.** recognize, recognize.

20. Summarize the strengths and weaknesses of the biological approach to personality.

20-1. People frequently blame parents for children's personalities. I recently asked a friend of mine why she thought a mutual acquaintance was so obnoxious. She said, "Well, raised with such crazy parents, what would you expect?" I asked, "Is that an argument for environment or heredity?" That is one of the benefits of the twin studies: They put data in place of speculation. But what are some of the weaknesses of the biological approach? First, heritability ratios should be regarded only as ________________ that will vary depending on sampling and other procedures. Second, there is no truly comprehensive biological ________________ of personality.

Answers: 20-1. estimates, theory.

A CONTEMPORARY EMPIRICAL APPROACH TO PERSONALITY: TERROR MANAGEMENT THEORY

21. Discuss the essentials of terror management theory.

21-1. According to terror management theory, because humans have the ability to be aware of the inevitability of death, feelings of ________________, alarm, and terror arise when people think about their mortality.

21-2. This crisis is solved by ________________. Worldviews give people a sense of being part of an enduring legacy, or a sense of meaning, that can soothe fear of death.

21-3. Confidence in the validity of one's cultural worldview and seeing oneself as living up to the standards of one's worldview provides a sense of __________-______________. Therefore, self-esteem serves as an ________________ ________________.

Answers: 21-1. anxiety **21-2.** culture **21-3.** self-esteem, anxiety buffer.

22. Discuss applications of terror management theory.

22-1. Under conditions of mortality ________________, people may be motivated to defend their cultural worldview. This can fuel ________________ (e.g., evaluating people from different ethnic backgrounds more negatively). The defence of one's worldview and the preservation of self-esteem may also motivate excessive ________________. Bodily ________________ may be downplayed under conditions of mortality salience, such as reduced engagement in health-protective behaviours, as people will be motivated to deny their animal nature.

Answers: 22-1. salience, prejudice, materialism, concerns.

CULTURE AND PERSONALITY

23. Summarize research on the cross-cultural validity of the five-factor model and on cultural variations in conceptions of self.

23-1. For a decade or so after World War II, researchers using the Freudian model attempted to find a modal personality type representative of each culture. This attempt was (successful/not successful).

23-2. With the current increased attention to cultural factors, interest in the relationship between personality and culture has again surfaced, and the new data have revealed both cross-cultural similarities and differences. With regard to similarity, precisely the same "___________ ___________" personality factors tend to emerge in different cultures. With regard to differences, a comparison of 51 cultures revealed cultural disparities in average trait scores across different countries. For example, Brazilians scored high on ________________, and Australians scored high on ________________.

23-3. With regard to differences, research by Markus and Kitayama clearly indicates that the individualistic orientation characteristic of the West is not universal across cultures. While

North Americans tend to value (independence/connectedness), Asians value (interdependence/uniqueness) among people. Similarly, while North American parents encourage their children to (stand out/blend in), Asian parents emphasize taking pride in the accomplishments of (each individual/the group).

Answers: 23-1. not successful **23-2.** Big Five, neuroticism, extraversion **23-3.** independence, interdependence, stand out, the group.

PUTTING IT IN PERSPECTIVE

24. Explain how the chapter highlighted three of the text's unifying themes.

24-1. We've just discussed one of the three themes emphasized in this chapter, that our behaviour is influenced by our cultural heritage. Two other themes prominently demonstrated in the area of personality are that the field is theoretically ________________ and that psychology evolves in a ________________ context.

24-2. Freudian, behavioural, and biological perspectives of personality assume that behaviour is determined; the ________________ perspective does not. The biological perspective stresses genetic inheritance; the behavioural perspective stresses (heredity/environment). As these examples illustrate, the study of personality has produced an enormous amount of theoretical ________________.

24-3. Concerning sociohistorical context, it is clear that theories of personality have strongly affected our culture. For example, the Surrealist art movement, begun in the 1920s, derives directly from ________________ psychology, as do other movements in literature and the arts. And the current debate on the effects of media violence is, to a large extent, a product of research in social ________________ theory.

24-4. In turn, culture has affected psychology. For example, it seems quite likely that the sexually repressive climate of Victorian Vienna caused Freud to emphasize the ________________ aspects of human behaviour; and it is clear, from Freud's own description, that World War I influenced his development of the second Freudian instinct, the ________________ instinct. Thus, psychology evolves in a ________________ context.

Answers: 24-1. diverse, sociohistorical **24-2.** humanistic, environment, diversity **24-3.** psychoanalytic (Freudian), learning **24-4.** sexual, aggression, sociohistorical.

PERSONAL APPLICATION * UNDERSTANDING PERSONALITY ASSESSMENT

25. Outline the four principal uses of personality tests.

25-1. In the blanks next to their descriptions, fill in the four principal uses of personality tests.

(a) Psychological ________________: Measuring personality traits in empirical studies.

(b) ________________: Advising people on career plans and decisions.

(c) ________________ selection: Choosing employees in business and government.

(d) Clinical ________________: Assessing psychological disorders.

Answers: 25-1. (a) research, (b) counselling, (c) personnel, (d) diagnosis.

26. Describe the MMPI, 16PF, and NEO Personality Inventory, and summarize the strengths and weaknesses of self-report inventories.

26-1. The MMPI, 16PF, and NEO Personality Inventories are (projective/self-report) tests. All three tests are also used to measure (single/multiple) traits.

26-2. Identify which tests (MMPI, 16PF, or NEO) are described by each of the following.

(a) _______ Originally designed to diagnose psychological disorders.

(b) _______, _______ Originally designed to assess the normal personality.

(c) _______ Contains 187 items.

(d) _______ Contains 567 items.

(e) _______ Measures the Big Five personality traits.

(f) _______ Includes four validity scales to help detect deception.

26-3. The major strength of self-report inventories, in comparison with simply asking a person what they are like, is that they provide a more precise and more (objective/personal) measure of personality.

26-4. The major weakness of self-report inventories is that they are subject to several sources of error, including the following: (1) Test-takers may intentionally fake responses, that is, may engage in deliberate ________________. (2) While not realizing it, people may answer questions in ways to make themselves "look good," the ________________ ________________ bias. (3) In addition, some people tend either to agree or to disagree with nearly every statement on a test, a source of error involving ________________ sets.

Answers: 26-1. self-report, multiple **26-2.** (a) MMPI, (b) 16PF, NEO, (c) 16PF, (d) MMPI, (e) NEO, (f) MPI **26-3.** objective **26-4.** deception, social desirability, response.

27. Describe the projective hypothesis, and summarize the strengths and weaknesses of projective tests.

27-1. If you have ever looked at clouds and described the images you've seen, you've done something similar to taking a projective test. If you thought that the images you saw reflected something about your personality, then you also accepted the *projective hypothesis.* The projective hypothesis is the idea that people will tend to ________________ their characteristics onto ambiguous stimuli, so that what they see reveals something about their personalities and problems.

27-2. Two major projective tests are the Rorschach, a series of ________________, and the TAT, a series of simple ________________.

27-3. The advantages of projective tests are that (1) since the way the tests are interpreted is not at all obvious, it is difficult for people to engage in intentional ________________; and (2) projective tests may help tap problems or aspects of personality of which people are ________________.

27-4. The major weakness of projective tests concerns ________________ scoring, inadequate norms, cultural bias, and poor ________________ and validity. Clinicians often find information from projective tests to be (useful/useless). Some have suggested that, given their poor scientific evidence, projective tests should be referred to as instruments or techniques rather than tests.

Answers: 27-1. project **27-2.** inkblots, pictures (scenes) **27-3.** deception, unconscious (unaware) **27-4.** inconsistent, reliability, useful.

28. Describe advantages and disadvantages of personality testing on the Internet.

28-1. Advantages of Internet-based testing include the fact that tests can be completed ________________ with reduced ________________. Also, information such as answer-________________ and how long questions are pondered before being answered can be measured. Online tests can also be completed by ________________ residents who lack access to psychologists.

28-2. Disadvantages of online testing include ________________ of test item content, verifying the ________________ of respondents, and whether results obtained from online testing are equivalent to what is found from paper-and-pencil versions of the tests. With respect to this latter issue, results thus far suggest that results from online tests (are/are not) similar to those obtained from offline counterparts.

Answers: 28-1. quickly, costs, changing, rural **28-2.** security, identity, are.

CRITICAL THINKING APPLICATION * HINDSIGHT IN EVERYDAY ANALYSES OF PERSONALITY

29. Discuss how hindsight bias affects everyday analyses of personality, as well as some theoretical analyses of personality.

29-1. I (R.S.) am writing this sentence following a period of very substantial decline in the stock market. Somewhat surprising, to me at least, is the fact that my colleagues say they saw it coming. If everyone saw it coming, why didn't everyone sell last year? Or the year before? Because we didn't see it coming. Rather, once exposed to information, we are inclined to believe that we already knew it, the cognitive tendency known as ________________ ________________.

29-2. You may recall from Chapter 11 the experiment with the three-year-old and the candy box. The child first guesses that candy is in the candy box. After the child sees that crayons are in the candy box, the three-year-old will usually insist that he or she always thought there were crayons in the box. The five-year-old doesn't make this mistake, but these data suggest that _______________ _______________ begins early, that from a young age we reconstruct past events in terms of _______________ information.

29-3. Suppose you meet someone who is achievement motivated and fiercely independent. You learn that this person was brought up by adoptive parents who were somewhat distant and undemonstrative. Would you connect the events, thinking that the parent's child-rearing style accounted for their child's independence? Or suppose that the person brought up by these parents is depressed and chronically unemployed. Would you connect the parenting and personality in this case, too? You might, because people tend to interpret _______________ events in terms of _______________ _______________, which is a definition of *hindsight bias*.

29-4. What is hindsight bias? Write a definition in the space below.

29-5. In what way might psychoanalytic interpretations involve hindsight bias?

29-6. How might evolutionary theory's account of the emergence of the Big Five traits reflect hindsight bias?

Answers: 29-1. hindsight bias (By the way, this week the market recovered a bit. I knew it would!) **29-2.** hindsight bias, present (current, outcome, recent) **29-3.** past (previous), present information (outcomes, current information) **29-4.** Once we know something, we tend to reinterpret past events in terms of that information. Or, once exposed to information, we tend to think we knew it all along. Or knowing the outcome of events tends to bias our recall and interpretation of those events. **29-5.** Once the analyst is exposed to an individual's personality, he or she can easily explain how the person's childhood experiences could account for present behaviour. **29-6.** Once exposed to the fact that the Big Five traits appear worldwide, a theorist can fairly easily explain why that might be the case. If a dozen entirely different traits had emerged, one could imagine that there could be an evolutionary explanation for that occurrence as well.

Review of Key Terms

Archetypes
Behaviourism
Collective unconscious
Compensation
Conscious
Defence mechanisms
Displacement
Ego
Extraverts
Factor analysis
Fixation
Hierarchy of needs
Hindsight bias
Humanism
Id
Identification
Incongruence
Introverts
Model
Need for self-actualization
Observational learning
Oedipal complex
Personal unconscious
Personality
Personality trait
Phenomenological approach
Pleasure principle
Preconscious
Projection
Projective tests
Psychodynamic theories
Psychosexual stages
Rationalization
Reaction formation
Reality principle
Reciprocal determinism
Regression
Repression
Self-actualizing persons
Self-concept
Self-efficacy
Self-enhancement
Self-report inventories
Striving for superiority
Superego
Terror management theory
Unconscious

_______________ **1.** An individual's unique constellation of consistent behavioural traits.

_______________ **2.** A characteristic that represents a durable disposition to behave in a particular way in a variety of situations.

_______________ **3.** A systematic arrangement of needs, according to priority, in which basic, physiological needs must be met before social or growth needs are aroused.

_______________ **4.** All the diverse theories, descended from the work of Sigmund Freud, that focus on unconscious mental forces.

_______________ **5.** The primitive, instinctive component of personality that operates according to the pleasure principle.

_______________ **6.** The id's demands for immediate gratification of its urges.

_______________ **7.** The decision-making component of personality that operates according to the reality principle.

_______________ **8.** The ego's delay of gratification of the id's urges until appropriate outlets and situations can be found.

_______________ **9.** The moral component of personality that incorporates social standards about what represents right and wrong.

_______________ **10.** Consists of whatever you are aware of at a particular point in time.

_______________ **11.** Contains material just beneath the surface of awareness that can be easily retrieved.

_______________ **12.** Contains thoughts, memories, and desires that are well below the surface of conscious awareness.

_______________ **13.** The series of largely unconscious Freudian reactions that protect a person from unpleasant emotions such as anxiety or guilt.

_______________ **14.** The defence mechanism that pushes distressing thoughts and feelings into the unconscious or keeps them from emerging into consciousness.

_______________ **15.** Attributing your own thoughts, feelings, or motives to another.

_______________ **16.** Creating false but plausible excuses to justify unacceptable behaviour.

_______________ **17.** Diverting emotional feelings (usually anger) from their original source to a substitute target.

_______________ **18.** Behaving in a way that is exactly the opposite of one's true (but unconscious) feelings.

_______________ **19.** Reverting to immature patterns of behaviour.

_______________ **20.** Bolstering self-esteem by forming an imaginary or real alliance with some person or group.

_______________ **21.** Developmental periods with a characteristic sexual focus that leave their mark on adult personality.

_______________ **22.** A failure to move forward from one stage to another as expected.

_______________ **23.** Characterized by erotically tinged desires for one's opposite-sex parent and hostility toward one's same-sex parent.

_______________ **24.** Jungian concept referring to the structure that holds material that is not in one's awareness because it has been repressed or forgotten.

_______________ **25.** A storehouse of latent memory traces inherited from our ancestral past.

_______________ **26.** Emotionally charged images and thought forms that have universal meaning.

______________________ **27.** People who tend to be preoccupied with the internal world of their own thoughts, feelings, and experiences.

______________________ **28.** People who tend to be interested in the external world of people and things.

______________________ **29.** An Adlerian concept referring to a universal drive to adapt, to improve oneself, and to master life's challenges.

______________________ **30.** Efforts to overcome imagined or real inferiorities by developing one's abilities.

______________________ **31.** Personality tests that ask people a series of questions about their characteristic behaviour.

______________________ **32.** A statistical procedure that identifies clusters of variables that are highly correlated with one another.

______________________ **33.** A theoretical orientation based on the premise that scientific psychology should study only observable behaviour.

______________________ **34.** The assumption that internal mental events, external environmental events, and overt behaviour all influence one another.

______________________ **35.** Learning that occurs when an organism's responding is influenced by the observation of others.

______________________ **36.** A person whose behaviour is observed by another.

______________________ **37.** Our belief about our ability to perform behaviours that should lead to expected outcomes.

______________________ **38.** A theoretical orientation that emphasizes the unique qualities of humans, especially their freedom and potential for personal growth.

______________________ **39.** Approach that assumes we have to appreciate individuals' personal, subjective experiences to truly understand their behaviour.

______________________ **40.** A collection of beliefs about one's own nature, unique qualities, and typical behaviour.

______________________ **41.** A Rogerian concept referring to the degree of disparity between one's self-concept and one's actual experience.

______________________ **42.** The need to fulfill one's potential.

______________________ **43.** People with exceptionally healthy personalities, marked by continued personal growth.

______________________ **44.** The biased interpretation of past events in terms of present information.

______________________ **45.** A theory concerning how people manage the anxiety associated with anticipating their own inevitable deaths.

______________________ **46.** Tests that ask participants to respond to vague, ambiguous stimuli in ways that may reveal the subjects' needs, feelings, and personality traits.

______________________ **47.** The tendency to focus on positive feedback, exaggerate one's strengths, and see oneself as above average.

Answers: 1. personality **2.** personality trait **3.** hierarchy of needs **4.** psychodynamic theories **5.** id **6.** pleasure principle **7.** ego **8.** reality principle **9.** superego **10.** conscious **11.** preconscious **12.** unconscious **13.** defence mechanisms **14.** repression **15.** projection **16.** rationalization **17.** displacement **18.** reaction formation **19.** regression **20.** identification **21.** psychosexual stages **22.** fixation **23.** Oedipal complex **24.** personal unconscious **25.** collective unconscious **26.** archetypes **27.** introverts **28.** extraverts **29.** striving for superiority **30.** compensation **31.** self-report inventories

32. factor analysis **33.** behaviourism **34.** reciprocal determinism **35.** observational learning **36.** model **37.** self-efficacy **38.** humanism **39.** phenomenological approach **40.** self-concept **41.** incongruence **42.** need for self-actualization **43.** self-actualizing persons **44.** hindsight bias **45.** terror management theory **46.** projective tests **47.** self-enhancement.

Review of Key People

Alfred Adler	Hans Eysenck	Walter Mischel
Albert Bandura	Sigmund Freud	Delroy Paulhus
David Buss	Carl Jung	Carl Rogers
Norman Endler	Abraham Maslow	B. F. Skinner

____________________ **1.** The founder of psychoanalysis.

____________________ **2.** Developed the theory called analytical psychology; anticipated the humanists' emphasis on personal growth and self-actualization.

____________________ **3.** Founder of an approach to personality called individual psychology.

____________________ **4.** Modern behaviourism's most prominent theorist, recognized for his theories of operant conditioning.

____________________ **5.** A contemporary behavioural theorist who elaborated the concept of observational learning.

____________________ **6.** His chief contribution to personality theory has been to focus attention on the extent to which situational factors govern behaviour.

____________________ **7.** One of the fathers of the human potential movement, he called his approach a person-centred theory.

____________________ **8.** The humanist who developed a theory of self-actualization.

____________________ **9.** Proposed that conditionability and introversion–extraversion are largely genetically determined.

____________________ **10.** Studied birth order and personality, cultural differences in self-enhancement, and response sets in self-report personality inventories.

____________________ **11.** Advocated an interactional (personality traits interacting with situational factors) approach to personality.

____________________ **12.** Adopted an evolutionary view toward the existence of the Big Five personality traits.

Answers: 1. Freud **2.** Jung **3.** Adler **4.** Skinner **5.** Bandura **6.** Mischel **7.** Rogers **8.** Maslow **9.** Eysenck **10.** Paulhus **11.** Endler **12.** Buss.

Self-Quiz

1. Personality traits are characterized by
a. consistency and distinctiveness
b. charm and wit
c. change as a function of the situation
d. lack of individual differences

2. Someone attributes his thoughts or feelings or conflicts to someone else. For example, although he chronically interrupts people, he thinks that other people interrupt him. What Freudian defence mechanism is illustrated?
a. rationalization
b. reaction formation
c. regression
d. projection

3. Which of the following is entirely unconscious, according to Freud?
a. the id
b. the ego
c. the superego
d. the archetype

4. Although Osmo, at an unconscious level, has great hatred for Cosmo, he believes that he likes Cosmo and, to the outside world, gives all the appearance of liking him. Which defence mechanism is Osmo using?
a. regression
b. reaction formation
c. projection
d. rationalization

5. The Oedipal complex occurs during the:
a. oral stage
b. anal stage
c. phallic stage
d. genital stage

6. Which of the following concepts did Carl Jung originate?
a. id
b. superego
c. inferiority complex
d. introversion–extraversion

7. Which of the following did Adler emphasize in his theory of personality?
a. striving for superiority
b. castration anxiety
c. introversion–extraversion
d. the collective unconscious

8. Much of the behaviour that we call personality results from reinforcement and observational learning, according to:
a. Jung
b. Skinner
c. Bandura
d. Adler

9. Which of the following tends to emphasize freedom and personal growth in its view of human behaviour?
a. the psychoanalytic approach
b. the biological approach
c. the behavioural approach
d. the humanistic approach

10. According to Rogers, what causes incongruence?
a. an inherited sense of irony
b. conditional acceptance or affection
c. unconditional acceptance or affection
d. unconditioned stimuli

11. Herb had the desire and potential to be a violinist but became, instead, a trader in hog futures. He decided never to touch the violin again. What is wrong with Herb, according to Maslow?
a. He suffers from incontinence.
b. He suffers from castration anxiety.
c. He has not achieved self-actualization.
d. He has an inferiority complex.

12. Which of the following views personality in terms of the adaptive significance to the Big Five traits?
a. Abraham Maslow
b. William James
c. the behavioural approach
d. the evolutionary approach

13. Your friend spends money like water. When you learn that he is from a poverty-stricken background, you attribute his spending patterns to his earlier deprivation. According to the critical thinking analysis, you are likely to do this because of:
a. hindsight bias
b. a self-serving attribution
c. the consistency and distinctiveness of personality
d. circular reasoning

14. According to Mischel, what is the major factor that predicts human behaviour?
a. childhood experience
b. specifics of the situation
c. extraversion and introversion
d. central and peripheral traits

15. You are asked to tell stories about a series of pictures. Which test is being administered to you?
a. Rorschach
b. MMPI
c. TAT
d. 16PF

16. The Featured Study examined the impact of ________________ on how we view ourselves.
a. evaluations of others
b. genetics
c. person–situation interactions
d. the drive for self-actualization

17. The Featured Study showed that subliminally presented images of a scowling significant other can lead one to:
a. try harder on an exam
b. avoid that particular person
c. scowl right back at them
d. make more negative self-ratings

18. According to terror management theory, self-esteem serves as a(n):
a. measure of our social acceptability
b. anxiety buffer
c. measure of our status
d. depression buffer

Answers: 1. a **2.** d **3.** a **4.** b **5.** c **6.** d **7.** a **8.** c **9.** d **10.** b **11.** c **12.** d **13.** a **14.** b **15.** c **16.** a **17.** d **18.** b.

InfoTrac Keywords

Defence Mechanisms
Extraverts (see extraversion or introversion)
Oedipal Complex
Puberty
Personality Trait
Projective Tests

Chapter Thirteen
STRESS, COPING, AND HEALTH

Review of Key Ideas

THE NATURE OF STRESS

1. **Define stress, describe the biopsychosocial model, and explain why an understanding of stress is important in health psychology.**

1-1. Stress is defined as any circumstances that ________________ or are perceived to threaten one's well-being and that thereby tax one's ________________ abilities.

1-2. The biopsychosocial model holds that ________________ illness is caused by a complex interaction of biological, psychological, and ________________ factors.

1-3. Health psychology examines how psychosocial factors relate to health and to the causation, prevention, and treatment of ________________. An important psychosocial factor is ________________.

Answers: 1-1. threaten, coping **1-2.** physical, sociocultural **1-3.** illness, stress.

2. **Discuss the impact of minor stressors.**

2-1. While some forms of stress arise from unusual, traumatic crises, most stress arises from (infrequent/everyday) problems. These minor hassles appear to be detrimental to mental health because of the ________________ nature of stress.

Answers: 2-1. everyday, cumulative.

3. **Describe the nature of our appraisals of stress.**

3-1. The text defines stress as any circumstances that threaten or are perceived to threaten one's well-being, and thereby they tax one's coping abilities. This definition would indicate that the sources of stress are quite (subjective/objective). Or to put it another way, stress lies in the mind of the ________________.

Answers: 3-1. subjective, beholder (or individual).

MAJOR TYPES OF STRESS

4. Describe frustration as a form of stress.

4-1. Which of the following three situations best illustrates what is meant by frustration?

a. Your family moves from a large city to a rather small, rural community.

b. You are late for an appointment and stuck in a traffic jam.

c. You are forced to choose between two good movies on television.

4-2. If you picked choice *b*, then you have caught on that frustration always involves the ________________ of the pursuit of some goal.

Answers: 4-1. b **4-2.** thwarting (or blocking).

5. Identify the three basic types of conflict, and discuss which types are most troublesome.

5-1. Many persons do not want to pay their income taxes, but, on the other hand, they don't want to go to jail either. These persons are faced with an ________________–________________ conflict.

5-2. Getting married has both positive and negative aspects that make it an excellent example of an ________________–________________ conflict.

5-3. Consider the problem of the student who has to choose between scholarships for two different universities. Since he cannot accept both, he's faced with an ________________–________________ conflict.

5-4. Now that you have correctly identified the three basic types of conflict, list them below in their order of troublesomeness, beginning with the least troublesome.

(a) ________________

(b) ________________

(c) ________________

Answers: 5-1. avoidance–avoidance **5-2.** approach–avoidance **5-3.** approach–approach **5-4.** (a) approach–approach, (b) approach–avoidance, (c) avoidance–avoidance.

6. Summarize evidence on life change and pressure as forms of stress.

6-1. The Social Readjustment Rating Scale (SRRS) measures the stress induced by ________________ in daily living routines. The developers of this scale theorized that all kinds of life changes, both pleasant and unpleasant, would induce stress. Early research showed that high scores on the SRRS were correlated with psychological disturbances and many kinds of physical ________________.

6-2. Later research began to indicate that high scores on the SRRS were primarily the result of (pleasant/unpleasant) events. At the present time, research seems to indicate that change by itself (is/is not) inevitably stressful.

6-3. There are two kinds of pressure. One is the pressure to get things accomplished, or the pressure to ________________. The other is the pressure to abide by rules, or the pressure to ________________.

6-4. Which appears to have the strongest influence on mental health: life changes or pressure?

6-5. Academic pressure may undermine academic ________________ and lead to ________________ behaviours such as alcohol use. Such pressure is often ___________-________________.

Answers: 6-1. changes, illness **6-2.** unpleasant, is not **6-3.** perform, conform **6-4.** pressure **6-5.** performance, escape, self-imposed.

RESPONDING TO STRESS

7. Identify some common emotional responses to stress, and discuss the effects of emotional arousal.

7-1. The text describes three different dimensions of negative emotions that are particularly likely to be triggered by stress. Identify which of these dimensions is most likely to be present in the following situations.

(a) The emotions in this dimension are likely to be found as a person begins to feel more and more helpless and unable to cope (e.g., you detect signs that your lover is going to leave you).

(b) The emotions in this dimension are likely to be found as a person begins to feel increasingly put upon and treated unfairly (e.g., you are being falsely accused of a deed you didn't commit).

(c) The emotions in this dimension are likely to be found as a person faces increasing degrees of conflict or uncertainty (e.g., you're driving on a highway, and the fog is gradually becoming thicker).

7-2. What did the study of emotional responding in the weeks following 9/11 show?

7-3. According to broaden-and-build theory, positive emotions can promote resilience via three routes: First, positive emotions can broaden people's scope of ________________ and increase their creativity and problem solving. Second, positive emotions can undermine the lingering effects of ________________ ________________. Third, positive emotions promote rewarding ________________ ________________.

7-4. What does the inverted-U hypothesis say about what happens to the optimal arousal level as tasks become more complex?

Answers: 7-1. (a) dejection, sadness, and grief (b) annoyance, anger, and rage (c) apprehension, anxiety, and fear **7-2.** Although many participants reported negative emotions, positive emotions such as gratitude and love also emerged, and the frequency of positive emotions correlated positively with resilience. **7-3.** attention, negative emotions, social interactions **7-4.** The optimal arousal level decreases.

8. Describe the fight-or-flight response and the three stages of the general adaptation syndrome.

8-1. What division of the autonomic nervous system mediates the fight-or-flight response?

8-2. Although the body's fight-or-flight response appears to be an evolutionary carry-over from our past, why is it perhaps of more harm than help to modern human beings?

8-3. Indicate which of the three stages of the general adaptation syndrome is being described in each of the following.

(a) This is the initial stage, in which the body prepares for the fight-or-flight response.

(b) This is the second stage, in which the body stabilizes its physiological changes as it begins to effectively cope with the stress.

(c) This is the third stage, in which the body's resources are becoming depleted, and the harmful physiological effects of stress can create "diseases of adaptation."

Answers: 8-1. sympathetic nervous system **8-2.** Because most stressful situations generally require a more complex response than simple fight or flight. **8-3.** (a) stage of alarm, (b) stage of resistance, (c) stage of exhaustion.

9. Discuss the two major pathways along which the brain sends signals to the endocrine system in response to stress.

9-1. Fill in the missing parts in the diagram on the next page, detailing the two major pathways along which the brain sends signals to the endocrine system.

CEREBRAL CORTEX

(a) ________________

SYMPATHETIC NS

PITUITARY GLAND

ACTH

(b) ____________________ (GLAND)

(c) ________________ (GLAND)

CATECHOLAMINES

Increases heart rate, respiration, etc.

CORTICOSTEROIDS

Increases energy, inhibits tissue inflammation, etc.

Answers: 9-1. (a) hypothalamus, (b) adrenal medulla, (c) adrenal cortex.

10. Describe some relatively unhealthy coping responses that are common.

10-1. Answer the following questions regarding giving up and blaming oneself as responses to stress.

(a) What syndrome often results from giving up in response to exposure to unavoidable stressful events?

(b) What are potential advantages of giving up?

(c) What phenomenon often accompanies blaming oneself in response to stress?

10-2. Answer the following questions regarding aggression and self-indulgence as responses to stress.

(a) Which of these responses is illustrated by the saying "When the going gets tough, the tough go shopping?" ________________

(b) Which of these responses is frequently, but not always, triggered by frustration?

____

(c) Which of these responses is linked to gambling? ________________

(d) Which of these responses is linked to Internet addiction? ________________

10-3. What is a common fault with both of these behavioural responses to stress?

Answers: 10-1. (a) learned helplessness, (b) People who can disengage from unattainable goals report better health, lower stress hormones, and lower evidence of inflammation. (c) catastrophic thinking **10-2.** (a) self-indulgence (b) aggression (c) self-indulgence (d) self-indulgence **10-3.** They divert effort away from finding solutions to problems.

11. Explain how defence mechanisms work and discuss the value of defensive coping and constructive coping.

11-1. Indicate whether each of the following statements regarding defensive coping is true (T) or false (F).

__________ (a) Although they are largely unconscious, defence mechanisms can operate at any level of consciousness.

__________ (b) Only neurotic persons use defensive mechanisms.

__________ (c) Defence mechanisms are used to shield against emotional discomfort that often occurs with stress, particularly anxiety.

11-2. One shortcoming of defensive coping is that it avoids the real problem. What other consequence might arise here?

11-3. What conclusion does the text draw regarding small versus extreme positive illusions?

11-4. In contrast to defensive coping, constructive coping refers to relatively ________________ efforts that people make to deal with stressful events. Characteristics of constructive coping include confronting problems ________________, making reasonably realistic appraisals of stress and coping resources, learning to recognize and at times inhibit disruptive ________________ reactions, and taking steps to ensure that one's body is not especially vulnerable to stress.

Answers: 11-1. (a) T, (b) F, (c) T **11-2.** health-related risks (poor health) **11-3.** Small positive illusions may be beneficial while extreme illusions may be harmful. **11-4.** healthful, directly, emotional.

THE EFFECTS OF STRESS ON PSYCHOLOGICAL FUNCTIONING

12. Discuss the effects of stress on task performance and the burnout syndrome.

12-1. Baumeister's theory as to why stress affects task performance is that pressure to perform makes us self-conscious, and this elevated self-consciousness disrupts our ________________. The term we commonly use for this is ________________ under pressure. Research shows that this phenomenon is quite (rare/common) among normal persons.

12-2. Indicate whether each of the following statements regarding the burnout syndrome is true (T) or false (F).

__________ (a) Burnout is related to only a few highly stressful occupations.

__________ (b) The onset of burnout is usually sudden.

Answers: 12-1. attention, choking, common **12-2.** (a) F, (b) F.

13. Discuss some of the psychological problems and disorders that may result from stress.

13-1. Answer the following questions regarding post-traumatic stress syndrome.

(a) What is unique about post-traumatic stress disorder?

(b) What are some of the common causes of this syndrome, besides combat experience?

13-2. In addition to alcohol abuse and unhappiness, what four other psychological problems appear to be related to chronic stress? (One of them has to do with school, two have to do with sleep, and one involves intimate relationships.)

13-3. Stress has also been implicated in the onset of serious psychological disorders. In addition to schizophrenia, what three other disorders are mentioned in the text?

Answers: 13-1. (a) It is caused by a single episode of extreme stress. (b) being exposed to trauma in one's occupation as a police officer or paramedic or a similar position; being exposed to rape, robbery, assault, seeing someone die, serious automobile accidents, major natural disasters **13-2.** poor academic performance, insomnia, nightmares, sexual difficulties **13-3.** anxiety disorders, depression, eating disorders.

THE EFFECTS OF STRESS ON PHYSICAL HEALTH

14. Describe the evidence linking personality factors to coronary heart disease.

14-1. What is the principal cause of coronary heart disorder?

14-2. Indicate whether the following characteristics are found in Type A or Type B persons.

__________ (a) easygoing

__________ (b) competitive

__________ (c) impatient

__________ (d) amicable

__________ (e) hostile

14-3. According to McCann's ______________–______________ hypothesis, early achievers are at risk for early ______________, likely reflecting the Type (A/B) behaviour pattern.

14-4. Which aspect of the Type A behaviour seems to be most highly related to coronary heart disease?

Answers: 14-1. arteriosclerosis **14-2.** (a) Type B, (b) Type A, (c) Type A, (d) Type B, (e) Type A **14-3.** precocity–longevity, death, B **14-4.** hostility (anger).

15. Summarize the evidence linking emotional reactions and depression to heart disease.

15-1. Research has shown that negative emotions (can/cannot) trigger acute symptoms of heart disease.

15-2. Mental stress can trigger increases in the ________________ that is thought to contribute to cardiovascular risk.

15-3. The Featured Study examined whether depression can increase ________________ mortality by following participants' health and mortality over a period of four years. Participants were classified as to whether they had cardiac disease at the beginning of the study or not and whether they developed ________________ or not. Results showed that the mortality rate was (increased/decreased) for those who exhibited depression and that this was true whether or not participants had cardiac disease when the study was initiated. This study suggests that it is most likely that depression (contributed to/was a result of) cardiac disease.

Answers: 15-1. can **15-2.** inflammation **15-3.** cardiac, depression, increased, contributed to.

16. Discuss how stress affects immune functioning.

16-1. Research has found stress to be related to numerous diseases and disorders. What appears to be a common factor that relates stress to so many disorders?

Answers: 16-1. Stress appears to suppress the immune system temporarily.

FACTORS MODERATING THE IMPACT OF STRESS

17. Discuss how social support moderates the impact of stress.

17-1. What two areas of our health appear to benefit from having strong social support groups?

17-2. With respect to physical health, social support can reduce ________________. Those with a strong sense of ________________ report better physical and mental health. However, social ________________ are not the same as social support; that is, negative interactions with others predict lower health.

Answers: 17-1. Mental and physical health. **17-2.** mortality, community, bonds.

18. Discuss how personality factors are related to stress resistance.

18-1. What difference was found between optimists and pessimists, with respect to good physical health?

18-2. The personality characteristic of ________________ was found to be related to longevity in a recent study from a sample of Terman's gifted children, probably because this personality trait fosters better ________________ ________________.

Answers: 18-1. Optimists were more likely to enjoy good physical health. **18-2.** conscientiousness, health habits.

HEALTH-IMPAIRING BEHAVIOUR

19. Discuss the negative impact of smoking, poor nutrition, and lack of exercise on physical health.

19-1. Answer the following questions regarding the negative impact of smoking on physical health.

(a) How many fewer years can a 25-year-old male smoker expect to live than a 25-year-old nonsmoker?

(b) What are the two most frequent diseases that kill smokers?

(c) What appears to happen with respect to readiness to give up as smokers cycle through periods of abstinence and relapse?

19-2. Answer the following questions true (T) or false (F).

__________ (a) Among North Americans, most deficiencies in diet are because of inability to afford appropriate food.

__________ (b) Regular exercise appears to increase longevity.

__________ (c) Alcohol is the most damaging of all the recreational drugs.

__________ (d) Exercise can reduce chronic inflammation.

Answers: 19-1. (a) eight years (or 8.3 years), (b) lung cancer and heart disease, (c) Readiness to give up smoking builds gradually. **19-2.** (a) F, (b) T, (c) T, (d) T.

20. Discuss the relationship between behavioural styles and AIDS.

20-1. What two bodily fluids are most likely to transmit AIDS?

20-2. What two general groups have the highest incidence of AIDS in North America?

20-3. In the world as a whole, which form of transmission, gay and bisexual sex or heterosexual sex, is most common?

20-4. How can one virtually guarantee that he or she will not contract AIDS?

Answers: 20-1. blood and semen **20-2.** Gay and bisexual males and intravenous drug users. **20-3.** heterosexual transmission **20-4.** Stay with only one sexual partner (known to prefer this same lifestyle), and don't use intravenous drugs.

21. Explain how health-impairing lifestyles develop.

21-1. The text lists four complementary explanations as to why health-impairing lifestyles develop. Given the hints below, list these four reasons.

(a) slowly

(b) immediate

(c) delayed

(d) "not me"

Answers: 21-1. (a) They develop slowly. (b) The pleasure they provide is immediate. (c) The health-impairing consequences are delayed. (d) The consequences are likely to happen to others (but "not me").

REACTIONS TO ILLNESS

22. Discuss individual differences in willingness to seek medical treatment.

22-1. Indicate whether the following statements regarding individual differences in willingness to seek medical treatment are true (T) or false (F).

______ (a) Delay in seeking treatment is perhaps the biggest problem.

______ (b) The perception of pain and illness is very subjective.

Answers: 22-1. (a) T, (b) T.

23. Describe some barriers to effective patient–provider communication and ways to overcome these problems.

23-1. Which of the following factors appear to be a barrier to effective patient–provider communication?

a. economic realities

b. medical jargon

c. patient forgetfulness

d. patient evasiveness

e. patient passivity

f. all of the above

23-2. What does the text recommend as the best way to improve patient–provider communication?

Answers: 23-1. f **23-2.** Don't be a passive consumer of medical advice.

24. Discuss the extent to which people tend to adhere to medical advice.

24-1. The text lists three reasons for failure to comply with medical advice. One is that patients often fail to completely ________________ treatment instructions. A second is that the treatment may prove to be quite ________________. The third reason is not directly related to either instructions or treatment, but rather to the attitude toward the ________________. A negative attitude makes compliance (more/less) likely.

Answers: 24-1. understand, unpleasant (or aversive), physician (or doctor), less.

PUTTING IT IN PERSPECTIVE

25. Explain how this chapter highlighted two of the text's unifying themes.

25-1. The fact that the amount of stress in any given situation primarily lies in the eyes of the beholder nicely illustrates the theme that experience is ________________.

25-2. The fact that stress interacts with numerous other factors that affect health illustrates the theme of multifactorial ________________.

Answers: 25-1. subjective **25-2.** causation.

PERSONAL APPLICATION * IMPROVING COPING AND STRESS MANAGEMENT

26. Summarize Albert Ellis's ideas about controlling one's emotions.

26-1. The main idea behind Albert Ellis's rational–emotive therapy is that stress is largely caused by ________________ thinking. Therefore, by changing one's catastrophic thinking and taking a more rational approach, one can reduce the amount of _______________ being experienced.

26-2. Ellis illustrates this theory by postulating an A–B–C series of events. Describe below what each item refers to.

(A) activating event:

(B) belief:

(C) consequence:

26-3. Since the emotional turmoil in the A–B–C sequence is caused by the B (belief) system, effort must be directed toward changing irrational beliefs. Ellis proposed two techniques for doing this. One must first learn to _______________ instances of irrational beliefs. Then one must learn to actively _______________ these irrational beliefs.

Answers: 26-1. catastrophic, stress **26-2.** (A) the activating event that precedes the stress, (B) one's belief about the event, (C) the emotional consequences that result from the belief **26-3.** detect, dispute.

27. Discuss the adaptive value of humour, releasing pent-up emotions, managing hostility, and forgiving others.

27-1. What dual role does humour appear to play in easing stress from difficult situations?

27-2. Why might writing or talking about a problem with a sympathetic friend prove useful when experiencing stress?

27-3. What two common benefits were found among people who learned to manage hostility and people who practised forgiveness?

Answers: 27-1. It allows for both redefining the problem in a less threatening way and releasing the tension. **27-2.** It may help to release pent-up tension. **27-3.** Both mental and physical health improved.

28. Discuss the adaptive value of relaxation and exercise.

28-1. Complete the following statements regarding the adaptive value of relaxation and exercise.

(a) A quiet environment, a mental device, a passive attitude, and a comfortable position are conditions that facilitate _______________.

(b) Eating a balanced diet, getting adequate sleep and exercise, and avoiding overeating and using harmful drugs can help to minimize _______________.

Answers: 28-1. (a) learning to relax (b) physical vulnerability.

CRITICAL THINKING APPLICATION * THINKING RATIONALLY ABOUT HEALTH STATISTICS AND DECISIONS

29. Describe some important considerations in evaluating health statistics and making health decisions.

29-1. Which kind of faulty statistical reasoning (correlation is no assurance of causation, statistical significance is not equivalent to practical significance, and failure to consider base rates) is illustrated by the following statements?

(a) Using cell phones may cause brain cancer.

(b) Since heart disease and depression are correlated, heart disease must cause depression.

(c) In a large sample population, it was observed that the prevalence of hypertension was statistically significantly higher in individuals with higher sodium intakes. Therefore, everyone should reduce their sodium intake.

29-2. In addition to seeking information to reduce uncertainty, what other two basic principles of quantitative reasoning does the text suggest?

29-3. What should one do after reaching a decision and initiating action?

Answers: 29-1. (a) failure to consider base rates (and also forgetting that correlation is no assurance of causation), (b) correlation is no assurance of causation, (c) statistical significance is not equivalent to practical significance **29-2.** Make risk–benefit assessments and list alternative courses of action. **29-3.** Continue to re-evaluate the decision (in light of treatment progress, new options, etc.).

Review of Key Terms

Acquired immune deficiency syndrome (AIDS)
Acute stressors
Aggression
Approach–approach conflict
Approach–avoidance conflict
Avoidance–avoidance conflict
Biopsychosocial model
Burnout
Catastrophic thinking
Catharsis
Chronic stressors
Conflict
Constructive coping
Coping
Defence mechanisms
Fight-or-flight response
Frustration
General adaptation syndrome
Health psychology
Immune response
Internet addiction
Learned helplessness
Life changes
Optimism
Post-traumatic stress disorder (PTSD)
Pressure
Psychosomatic diseases
Rational–emotive therapy
Social support
Stress
Type A personality
Type B personality

_______________ 1. Holds that physical illness is caused by a complex interaction of biological, psychological, and sociocultural factors.

_______________ 2. Concerned with how psychosocial forces relate to the promotion and maintenance of health, and the causation, prevention, and treatment of illness.

_______________ 3. Any circumstances that threaten or are perceived to threaten our well-being and thereby tax our coping abilities.

_______________ 4. A passive behaviour produced by exposure to unavoidable aversive events.

_______________ 5. Occurs in any situation in which the pursuit of some goal is thwarted.

_______________ 6. Occurs when two or more incompatible motivations or behavioural impulses compete for expression.

_______________ 7. Occurs when a choice must be made between two attractive goals.

_______________ 8. Occurs when a choice must be made between two unattractive goals.

_______________ 9. Occurs when a choice must be made whether to pursue a single goal that has both attractive and unattractive aspects.

_______________ 10. Any noticeable alterations in one's living circumstances that require readjustment.

_______________ 11. Expectations or demands that one should behave in a certain way.

_______________ 12. A physiological reaction to threat in which the autonomic nervous system mobilizes an organism for either attacking or fleeing an enemy.

_______________ 13. A model of the body's stress response consisting of three stages: alarm, resistance, and exhaustion.

_______________ 14. An active effort to master, reduce, or tolerate the demands created by stress.

_______________ 15. Involves any behaviour that is intended to hurt someone, either physically or verbally.

_______________ 16. Consists of spending an inordinate amount of time on the Internet and the inability to control online use.

_______________ 17. Largely unconscious reactions that protect a person from unpleasant emotions such as anxiety and guilt.

_______________ 18. Relatively healthy efforts to deal with stressful events.

_______________ 19. Involves physical, mental, and emotional exhaustion that is attributable to work-related stress.

_______________ 20. Disturbed behaviour that emerges after a major stressful event is over.

_______________ 21. A behaviour pattern marked by competitive, aggressive, impatient, hostile behaviour.

_______________ 22. A behaviour pattern marked by relaxed, patient, easygoing, amicable behaviour.

_______________ 23. The body's defensive reaction to invasion by bacteria, viral agents, or other foreign substances.

_______________ 24. Various types of aid and succour provided by members of one's social network.

_______________ 25. A general tendency to expect good outcomes.

_______________ **26.** An approach to therapy that focuses on altering clients' patterns of irrational thinking to reduce maladaptive emotions and behaviour.

_______________ **27.** The release of emotional tension.

_______________ **28.** Unrealistic and pessimistic appraisal of stress that exaggerates the magnitude of a problem.

_______________ **29.** Physical ailments caused, in part, by psychological factors, especially emotional distress.

_______________ **30.** A disorder in which the immune system is gradually weakened and eventually disabled by the human immunodeficiency virus (HIV).

_______________ **31.** Threatening events that have a relatively long duration and no readily apparent time limit.

_______________ **32.** Threatening events that have a relatively short duration and a clear endpoint.

Answers: **1.** biopsychosocial model **2.** health psychology **3.** stress **4.** learned helplessness **5.** frustration **6.** conflict **7.** approach–approach conflict **8.** avoidance–avoidance conflict **9.** approach–avoidance conflict **10.** life changes **11.** pressure **12.** fight-or-flight response **13.** general adaptation syndrome **14.** coping **15.** aggression **16.** Internet addiction **17.** defence mechanisms **18.** constructive coping **19.** burnout **20.** post-traumatic stress disorder **21.** Type A personality **22.** Type B personality **23.** immune response **24.** social support **25.** optimism **26.** rational–emotive therapy **27.** catharsis **28.** catastrophic thinking **29.** psychosomatic diseases **30.** acquired immune deficiency syndrome (AIDS) **31.** chronic stressors **32.** acute stressors.

Review of Key People

Walter Cannon	Thomas Holmes & Richard Rahe	Martin Seligman
Robin DiMatteo	Janice Kiecolt-Glaser	Hans Selye
Albert Ellis	Richard Lazarus	Shelley Taylor
Meyer Friedman	Neal Miller	

_______________ **1.** Observed that minor hassles were more closely related to mental health than were major stressful events.

_______________ **2.** Noted for his extensive investigations of the three types of conflict.

_______________ **3.** These researchers developed the Social Readjustment Rating Scale.

_______________ **4.** One of the first theorists to describe the fight-or-flight response.

_______________ **5.** Coined the word *stress* and described the general adaptation syndrome.

_______________ **6.** Found a connection between coronary risk and Type A behaviour.

_______________ **7.** The developer of rational–emotive therapy.

_______________ **8.** Researched the notion that "positive illusions" promote well-being.

_______________ **9.** A leading expert on patient behaviour.

_______________ **10.** Has conducted research linking stress to temporary suppression of the immune system.

_______________ **11.** Has conducted research on optimism versus pessimism and on learned helplessness.

Answers: 1. Lazarus **2.** Miller **3.** Holmes & Rahe **4.** Cannon **5.** Selye **6.** Friedman **7.** Ellis **8.** Taylor **9.** DiMatteo **10.** Kiecolt-Glaser **11.** Seligman.

Self-Quiz

1. Which of the following statements regarding stress is incorrect?
a. Stress is a subjective experience.
b. The effects of stress are cumulative.
c. Minor hassles may prove more stressful than major ones.
d. One should seek to avoid all stress.

2. You've been invited to dinner at a nice restaurant on the final night of a TV miniseries you've been watching and thus find yourself confronted with:
a. pressure
b. frustration
c. an approach–avoidance conflict
d. an approach–approach conflict

3. The week of final exams subjects most students to what kind of stress?
a. pressure
b. change
c. frustration
d. conflict

4. High scores on the Social Readjustment Rating Scale were found to be correlated with psychological disturbances and:
a. Type A behaviour patterns
b. physical illness
c. pessimistic attitudes
d. all of the above

5. According to optimal-arousal theories, which of the following situations would be least affected by a high optimal-arousal level?
a. taking a psychology exam
b. typing a term paper
c. buttoning a shirt
d. learning to drive a car

6. The general adaptation syndrome shows that the body:
a. gradually adapts to a particular stress
b. gradually adapts to all form of stress
c. may gradually weaken and die from continued stress
d. can react rapidly to all forms of stress

7. Which of the following organs is involved in both of the body's two major stress pathways?
a. the adrenal gland
b. the sympathetic nervous system
c. the pituitary gland
d. the pineal gland

8. Aggression is frequently triggered by:
a. helplessness
b. frustration
c. loneliness
d. change

9. Which of the following behavioural responses to stress may result in Internet addiction?
a. defensive coping
b. self-indulgence
c. positive illusions
d. giving up

10. Rape and seeing someone die are two of the principal causes of:
a. post-traumatic stress disorder
b. burnout
c. learned helplessness
d. coronary heart disease

11. Smoking is to lung cancer as Type A behaviour is to:
a. coronary heart disease
b. AIDS
c. defensive coping
d. mental disorders

12. One of the key links between stress and physical illness may be that the body's response to stress:
a. increases the optimal-arousal level
b. suppresses the immune system
c. decreases the optimal-arousal level
d. suppresses the adrenal gland

13. Health-impairing lifestyles appear to develop:
a. rapidly
b. unconsciously
c. slowly
d. as a defence against stress

14. A major idea behind rational–emotive therapy is that stress is caused by:
a. conflict
b. frustration
c. pressure
d. catastrophic thinking

15. Analyzing the possible gains and losses before undertaking a health-treatment program is an example of:
a. seeking information to reduce uncertainty
b. listing alternative courses of action
c. making a risk–benefit analysis
d. analyzing base rates

16. Threatening events that have a short duration and a clear endpoint are called:
a. chronic stressors
b. acute stressors
c. brief stressors
d. hassles

Answers: 1. d **2.** d **3.** a **4.** b **5.** c **6.** c **7.** a **8.** b **9.** b **10.** a **11.** a **12.** b **13.** c **14.** d **15.** c **16.** b.

InfoTrac Keywords

Constructive Coping
Health Psychology
Internet Addiction
Type A Personality
Type B Personality

Chapter Fourteen
PSYCHOLOGICAL DISORDERS

Review of Key Ideas

ABNORMAL BEHAVIOUR: MYTHS, REALITIES, AND CONTROVERSIES

1. **Describe the medical model of abnormal behaviour.**

1-1. A model is a metaphor or theory that is useful in describing some phenomenon. For example, the computer is frequently used as a model of thinking. The *medical model* uses physical illness as a model of psychological disorders. Under the medical model, maladaptive behaviour is referred to as mental ________________.

1-2. The term *mental illness* is so familiar to all of us that we rarely think about the meaning of the concept and whether or not the analogy with disease is a good one. Among the model's critics, Thomas Szasz asserts that words such as *sickness*, *illness*, and *disease* are correctly used only in reference to the ________________, and that it is more appropriate to view abnormal behaviour as a deviation from accepted social ________________ than as an illness.

1-3. The text takes an intermediate position. While there are problems with the medical model, it may be of value as long as one understands that it is just a/an ________________ and not a true explanation.

1-4. The medical concepts of *diagnosis*, *etiology*, and *prognosis* have proven valuable in the study of abnormality. For each of the following definitions, identify the appropriate term (diagnosis, etiology, or prognosis):

(a) ________________________: The apparent causation and developmental history of an illness.

(b) ________________________: A forecast about the probable course of an illness.

(c) ________________________: Distinguishing one illness from another.

Answers: 1-1. illness (disease, sickness) **1-2.** body, norms (behaviour, standards) **1-3.** analogy (model) **1-4.** (a) etiology, (b) prognosis, (c) diagnosis.

2. Explain the most commonly used criteria of abnormality.

2-1. What does abnormal mean? The three criteria most frequently used are *deviance*, *maladaptive behaviour*, and *personal distress*.

(a) ________________________: Does not *conform* to cultural norms or standards.

(b) ________________________: Behaviour that *interferes with* the individual's social or occupational functioning.

(c) ________________________: Intense *discomfort* produced by depression or anxiety.

2-2. Following are three statements that describe a person with a particular type of disorder. Which criterion of abnormal behaviour is illustrated by each statement? Place the letters from the list above in the appropriate blanks.

____ Ralph washes his hands several dozen times a day. His hand-washing interferes with his work and prevents him from establishing normal friendships.

____ Even if Ralph's hand-washing compulsion did not interfere with his work and social life, his behaviour still would be considered strange. That is, most people do not do what he does.

____ It is also the case that Ralph's skin is very raw, and he becomes extremely anxious when he does not have immediate access to a sink.

2-3. In some cultures, hearing voices or speaking with gods may be valued. In our culture, however, such behaviour is likely to be considered abnormal. While the major categories of disorder may transcend culture, our assessments of abnormality are nonetheless value judgments, which are strongly influenced by our ________________. Thus, one of the problems involved in defining abnormality is that there are no criteria for psychological disorders that are entirely ________________-free.

Answers: 2-1. (a) deviance (b) maladaptive behaviour (c) personal distress **2-2.** b, a, c **2-3.** culture (society), value (culture).

3. List three stereotypes of people with psychological disorders.

3-1. In the space below, list three stereotypes of people with psychological disorders:

(a) The disorders are ________________.

(b) People with the disorders are ________________ and dangerous.

(c) People with the disorders behave in a bizarre manner and are very ________________ from normal people.

Answers: 3-1. (a) incurable, (b) violent, (c) different.

4. Describe Rosenhan's study of mental hospital admissions.

4-1. What type of people did Rosenhan seek to have admitted to mental hospitals?

4-2. Once they were admitted, did the pseudopatients continue to complain of hearing voices, or did they behave normally?

4-3. What proportion of the pseudopatients were admitted to the hospital?

4-4. Indicate true (T) or false (F) for each of the following statements.

____ (a) Once the patients no longer claimed to hear voices, the professional staff rapidly recognized that they were not abnormal.

____ (b) Most of the pseudopatients were dismissed within a couple of days.

____ (c) The diagnosis for most of the pseudopatients was that they suffered from a relatively mild form of mental disorder.

4-5. What is the major implication to be drawn from Rosenhan's study?

Answers: 4-1. normal individuals **4-2.** behaved normally **4-3.** all of them (Eight people sought admission to mental hospitals in five states, and all of them were admitted.) **4-4.** (a) F, (b) F (The shortest stay was seven days, the longest 52 days, and the average 19 days.), (c) F (Most were diagnosed with schizophrenia, a severe form of mental illness.) **4-5.** The major implication is that it is difficult, even for mental health professionals, to distinguish normal from abnormal behaviour. (The study may also be interpreted to mean that there is a bias toward seeing abnormality where it may not exist or that abnormality is easily feigned.)

5. List the five diagnostic axes of DSM-IV.

5-1. Below are descriptions of the five axes of the DSM-IV classification system. Label each with the correct axis number (I through V).

(a) ____ Notes concerning the severity of stress experienced by the individual in the past year

(b) ____ Estimates of the individual's current level of adaptive functioning (social and occupational)

(c) ____ Diagnosis of most types of mental disorders

(d) ____ Diagnosis of long-running personality disorders or mental retardation

(e) ____ Listing of physical disorders

Answers: 5-1. (a) IV, (b) V, (c) I, (d) II, (e) III.

6. **Discuss estimates of the prevalence of psychological disorders.**

6-1. Epidemiological studies assess the _______________ of various disorders. Prevalence is the _______________ of people who suffer from a disorder across a specific period of time. For our purposes, *lifetime* prevalence is most interesting.

6-2. What percentage of people will exhibit a mental disorder at some point during their lifetime? If drug-related disorders are included, estimates range from one-third to, more recently, ______%. The estimates are complicated by several factors, but recent studies do suggest that there (has been/has not been) a genuine increase in lifetime prevalence.

6-3. Figure 14.5 in the text shows one-year prevalence information for mood, anxiety, and substance disorders in Canada. Women had higher rates of _______________ and _______________ disorders than did men, whereas men had higher rates of _______________ _______________ disorders than did women.

Answers: 6-1. prevalence, percentage (proportion) **6-2.** 51%, has been **6-3.** mood, anxiety, substance dependence.

ANXIETY DISORDERS

7. **List five types of anxiety disorders and describe the symptoms associated with each.**

7-1. List the names of the five anxiety syndromes in the spaces below. As hints, the initial letters of some keywords are listed at the left.

GAD: ____

PTSD: ____

PhD: ____

OCD: ____

PDA: ____________________ and ____________________

7-2. Match the anxiety disorders with the symptoms that follow by placing the appropriate letters (from the previous question) in the blanks.

(a) ______ Sudden, unexpected, and paralyzing attacks of anxiety

(b) ______ Not tied to a specific object or event

(c) ______ Senseless, repetitive rituals

(d) ______ Brooding over decisions

(e) ______ Fear of specific objects or situations

(f) ______ Persistent intrusion of distressing and unwanted thoughts

(g) ______ Associated with victims of violent crimes or disasters

(h) ______ Frequently includes fear of going out in public

(i) _______ Nightmares, flashbacks, and emotional numbing

(j) _______ Free-floating anxiety

Answers: 7-1. generalized anxiety disorder, post-traumatic stress disorder, phobic disorder, obsessive-compulsive disorder, panic disorder and agoraphobia **7-2.** (a) PDA (in this example, panic attacks), (b) GAD, (c) OCD, (d) GAD, (e) PhD, (f) OCD, (g) PTSD, (h) PDA (in this case, agoraphobia), (i) PTSD, (j) GAD.

8. Discuss the contribution of biological and cognitive factors, conditioning, and stress to the etiology of anxiety disorders.

8-1. Several types of studies suggest that there are inherited predispositions to anxiety disorders. For example, twin studies find higher concordance rates for anxiety among ________________ twins than ________________ twins.

8-2. Other biological evidence implicates disturbances at synapses using GABA for some types of anxiety disorders and of serotonin for panic attacks and obsessive-compulsive disorder. Thus, the body chemicals known as ________________ appear to play an important role in anxiety.

8-3. Conditioning, or learning, clearly plays a role as well. For example, if an individual is bitten by a dog, he or she may develop a fear of dogs through the process of ________________ conditioning. The individual may then avoid dogs in the future, a response maintained by ________________ conditioning.

8-4. People are more likely to be afraid of snakes than of hot irons. Using Seligman's notion of preparedness, explain why.

8-5. Two types of anecdotal evidence do not support the conditioning point of view. For example, people with phobias (<u>always can/frequently cannot</u>) recall a traumatic incident, and people who have experienced extreme traumas (<u>always/frequently do not</u>) develop phobias.

8-6. As discussed in Chapter 6, the conditioning models are being extended to include a larger role for cognitive factors. For example, children probably acquire fears by ________________ the behaviour of anxious parents.

8-7. In addition, cognitive theorists indicate that certain *thinking styles* contribute to anxiety. For example, as indicated in your text, the sentence "The doctor examined little Emma's growth" could refer either to height or to a tumour. People who are high in anxiety will tend to perceive the (<u>tumour/height</u>) interpretation. People's readiness to perceive threat, in other words, appears to be related to their tendency to experience ________________.

8-8. Finally, *stress* is related to anxiety disorders. Studies described in your text indicate that stress is related both to ________________ disorder and to the development of social ________________.

Answers: 8-1. identical, fraternal **8-2.** neurotransmitters **8-3.** classical, operant **8-4.** Preparedness is Seligman's notion that human beings have evolved to be more prepared or more ready to be conditioned to some stimuli than to others. We have evolved to be more afraid of snakes than of hot irons, the latter having appeared only relatively recently in our evolutionary history. (As a whole, research has provided only modest support for the idea of preparedness in acquisition of phobias.) **8-5.** frequently cannot, frequently do not **8-6.** observing **8-7.** tumour, anxiety **8-8.** panic, phobia.

SOMATOFORM DISORDERS

9. Compare and contrast the three somatoform disorders, and discuss their etiology.

9-1. For each of the following symptoms, indicate which disorder is described by placing the appropriate letters in the blanks: S for somatization, C for conversion, and H for hypochondriasis.

(a) ____ Serious disability that may include paralysis, loss of vision or hearing, loss of feeling, and so on.

(b) ____ Many different minor physical ailments accompanied by a long history of medical treatment.

(c) ____ Cannot believe the doctor's report that the person is not really ill.

(d) ____ Symptoms that appear to be organic in origin but don't match underlying anatomical organization.

(e) ____ Diverse physical complaints that vary with amount of life stress.

(f) ____ Usually does not involve disability so much as overinterpreting slight, possible signs of illness.

(g) ____ "Glove anesthesia"; seizures without loss of bladder control.

9-2. In the film *Hannah and Her Sisters,* Woody Allen is convinced that certain minor physical changes are a sign of cancer. When tests eventually find no evidence of cancer, he is sure the tests have been done incorrectly. Which of the somatoform disorders does this seem to represent? ________________

9-3. The somatoform disorders are associated with certain personality types, with particular cognitive styles, and with learning. Among personality types, the self-centred, excitable, and overly dramatic ________________ personalities are more at risk for developing these disorders. As with anxiety disorders, the trait of ________________ appears to be related to somatoform disorders.

9-4. With regard to cognitive factors, focusing excessive attention on internal ________________ factors, or believing that good health should involve a complete lack of discomfort, may also contribute to somatoform disorders.

9-5. With regard to learning, the sick role may be positively reinforced through, for example, ________________ from others or negatively reinforced by ________________ certain of life's problems or unpleasant aspects.

Answers: 9-1. (a) C, (b) S, (c) H, (d) C, (e) S, (f) H, (g) C **9-2.** hypochondriasis **9-3.** histrionic, neuroticism **9-4.** physiological **9-5.** attention (kindness, etc.), avoiding (escaping).

DISSOCIATIVE DISORDERS

10. Describe three dissociative disorders, and discuss their etiology.

10-1. The three dissociative disorders involve memory and identity. Two of the disorders involve fairly massive amounts of forgetting: dissociative ________________ and dissociative ________________.

10-2. People who have been in serious accidents frequently can't remember the accident or events surrounding the accident. This type of memory loss, which involves specific traumatic events, is known as dissociative ________________.

10-3. An even greater memory loss, in which people lose their memories for their entire lives along with their sense of identity, is termed dissociative ________________.

10-4. You may have seen media characterizations of individuals who can't remember who they are—what their names are, where they live, who their family is, and so on. While popularly referred to as amnesia, this type of dissociative disorder is more correctly called dissociative ________________.

10-5. A few years ago, there was a spate of appearances on talk shows by guests who claimed to have more than one identity or personality. This disorder is still widely known as ________________ -________________ disorder (MPD), but the formal name in the DSM-IV is ________________ ________________ disorder (DID). The disorder is also often (correctly/mistakenly) called schizophrenia.

10-6. What causes dissociative disorders? Dissociative amnesia and dissociative fugue are related to excessive ________________, but little else is known about why these extreme reactions occur in a tiny minority of people.

10-7. With regard to multiple-personality disorder, the diagnosis is controversial. Although many clinicians believe that the disorder is authentic, Spanos argues that it is the product of media attention and the misguided probings of a small minority of psychotherapists. In other words, Spanos believes that MPD (is/is not) a genuine disorder.

10-8. While the majority of people with multiple-personality disorders report having been emotionally and sexually ________________ in childhood, little is known about the causes of this controversial diagnosis. In fact, in a recent survey of American psychiatrists, only ________________ of those polled believed that there was enough scientific evidence to warrant including DID as a valid diagnostic category.

Answers: 10-1. amnesia, fugue **10-2.** amnesia **10-3.** fugue **10-4.** fugue **10-5.** multiple-personality, dissociative identity, mistakenly **10-6.** stress **10-7.** is not **10-8.** abused, one-quarter.

MOOD DISORDERS

11. Describe the two major mood disorders.

11-1. While the terms *manic* and *depressive* describe mood, they refer to a number of other characteristics as well, listed below. Using one or two words for each characteristic, describe the manic and depressive episodes. (Before you make the lists, review Table 14.1 on page 624 of the text and the sections on depressive and bipolar mood disorders.)

	Manic	*Depressive*
mood:	____________	____________
sleep:	____________	____________
activity:	____________	____________
speech:	____________	____________
sex drive:	____________	____________

11-2. Be sure to note that mania and depression are not the names of the two affective disorders. What is the name of the disorder accompanied only by depression? ________________ ________________ By both manic and depressive states? ________________ ________________

11-3. The DSM refers to persistent but relatively mild symptoms of depressive disorder as ________________ disorder, and to persistent but mild symptoms of bipolar disorder as ________________ disorder.

11-4. Prevalence data indicate that women are about ________________ as likely as men to suffer from depression. According to Moretti, women may be more sensitive to gaps between beliefs about themselves and an ________________ view of themselves held by others. According to Nolen-Hoeksema, this gender difference in depression prevalence occurs for several reasons, including women's greater likelihood of experiencing ________________ abuse and their tendency to (ignore/ruminate about) setbacks and problems.

Answers: 11-1. mood: euphoric (elated, extremely happy) vs. depressed (blue, extremely sad); sleep: goes without or doesn't want to vs. can't (insomnia); activity: very active vs. sluggish (slow, inactive); speech: very fast vs. very slow; sex drive: increased vs. decreased **11-2.** unipolar disorder (major depressive disorder), bipolar disorder **11-3.** dysthymic, cyclothymic **11-4.** twice, idealized, sexual, ruminate about.

12. Describe two additional subcategories of mood disorders.

12-1. ________________ ________________ disorder (SAD) is a subtype that follows a seasonal pattern. Perhaps ____% of depressed Canadians experienced the SAD subtype. Onset of SAD may be related to ________________ production and circadian rhythms. A treatment for SAD is ________________.

12-2. Another subtype of mood disorder is _______________ depression, a type of depression that follows _______________. Prevalence estimates suggest that _____ to _____% of women who have given birth may experience postpartum depression. Risk factors include previous episodes of depression, _______________, and adjustment problems.

Answers: 12-1. seasonal affective, 11, melatonin, phototherapy **12-2.** postpartum, childbirth, 10, 20, stress.

13. Discuss what is known about suicide and mood disorders.

13-1. Official statistics may underestimate the true rate of suicides, as many are disguised as _______________. And attempts outnumber completed suicides by a ratio of as much as _______________ to 1. Women attempt suicide (more/less) often than men, but men complete _______________ times as many suicides as women.

13-2. About _____% of people who complete suicide have a psychological disorder, most commonly a _______________ disorder.

Answers: 13-1. accidents, 20, more, four **13-2.** 90, mood.

14. Explain how genetic and neurochemical factors may be related to the development of mood disorders.

14-1. Twin studies implicate genetic factors in the development of mood disorders. In a sentence, summarize the results of these studies.

14-2. While the exact mechanism is not known, correlations have been found between mood disorders and abnormal levels of _______________ in the brain, including norepinephrine and serotonin.

Answers: 14-1. For mood disorders, the concordance rate for identical twins is much higher than that for fraternal twins (about 65% for the former compared to 15% for the latter). **14-2.** neurotransmitters (neurochemicals).

15. Explain how dispositional factors, cognitive factors, interpersonal factors, and stress may be related to the development of mood disorders.

15-1. _______________, or the setting of excessively high standards, is a dispositional factor associated with depression. According to Beck, two other personality dispositions are related to depression: _______________ individuals are highly invested in their interpersonal relationships whereas _______________ individuals are oriented toward their own achievement and independence. Finally, Blatt argues that _______________ and self-_______________ are two important dispositional variables associated with depression. Both Beck and Blatt argue that a congruency between a type of stressful event experienced and the type of specific personality disposition may promote depression. For example, failure on an exam for a person who is highly _______________ may promote depression.

15-2. Beck also emphasized cognitive factors in depression, including the negative _______________ _______________, reflecting depressed people's tendency to view themselves, their world, and their future in a negative fashion. Beck also argued that _______________ schemas may lead depressed people to selectively attend to negative information about the self.

15-3. Seligman's model of depression is referred to as the _______________ _______________ model. While he originally based his theory of depression on animal research, examining exposure to unavoidable aversive stimuli, he has more recently emphasized (cognitive/behavioural) factors. People with a _______________ explanatory style are particularly prone to depression. For example, people who attribute obstacles to (situational factors/personal flaws) are more likely to experience depression.

15-4. Building on the learned helplessness theory, the _______________ theory maintains that a pessimistic explanatory style is just one of several factors—stress and low self-esteem are others—that contribute to depression. For example, people who repetitively focus or _______________ about their depression are more likely to remain depressed.

15-5. With regard to interpersonal factors, depressed people tend to lack _______________ skills. How does this characteristic affect the ability to obtain reinforcers?

15-6. Why do we tend to reject depressed people?

15-7. What is the relationship between stress and the onset of mood disorders?

Answers: 15-1. perfectionism, sociotropic, autonomous, dependency, criticism, autonomous **15-2.** cognitive triad, depressive **15-3.** learned helplessness, cognitive, pessimistic (negative), personal flaws **15-4.** hopelessness, ruminate **15-5.** social (interpersonal). Lack of social skills makes it difficult to obtain certain reinforcers, such as good friends and desirable jobs. **15-6.** Because they are not pleasant to be around. Depressed people complain a lot, are irritable, and tend to pass their mood along to others. **15-7.** There is a moderately strong link between stress and the onset of mood disorders.

SCHIZOPHRENIC DISORDERS

16. Describe the general characteristics (symptoms) of schizophrenia.

16-1. Before we review the different types of schizophrenia, consider some general characteristics of the schizophrenic disorders, as follows.

(a) Delusions and irrational thought: Delusions are false (beliefs/perceptions) (e.g., the idea that one is a world-famous political figure who is being pursued by terrorists, when this is not in fact true).

(b) Deterioration of adaptive behaviour: The deterioration usually involves social relationships, work, and neglect of personal _________________.

(c) Hallucinations: Hallucinations are ________________ ________________ that occur in the absence of a real stimulus. The most common hallucinations are (auditory/ visual).

(d) Disturbed emotion: Emotional responsiveness may be disturbed in a variety of ways. The person may have little or no responsiveness, referred to as ______________ affect, or they may show ______________ emotional responses, such as laughing at news of a tragic death.

Answers: 16-1. (a) beliefs (b) hygiene (cleanliness) (c) sensory perceptions (perceptions, sensory experiences, perceptual distortions), auditory (d) flat (flattened, blunted), inappropriate (bizarre).

17. Describe two classification systems for schizophrenic subtypes, and discuss the course of schizophrenia.

17-1. Write the names of the four recognized subcategories of schizophrenia next to the descriptions that follow.

(a) ______________________ type: Particularly severe deterioration, incoherence, complete social withdrawal, aimless babbling and giggling, delusions centring on bodily functions.

(b) ______________________ type: Muscular rigidity and stupor at one extreme or random motor activity, hyperactivity, and incoherence at the other; now quite rare.

(c) ______________________ type: Delusions of persecution and grandeur.

(d) ______________________ type: Clearly schizophrenic but doesn't fit other three categories.

17-2. Several critics have asserted that there are no meaningful differences among the categories listed above and have proposed an alternative classification system. Nancy Andreasen and others have described a classification system consisting of only two categories, one that consists of ______________ symptoms and the other of ______________ symptoms.

17-3. In Andreasen's system, "positive" and "negative" do not mean pleasant and unpleasant. Positive symptoms *add* something to behaviour (like chaotic speech), and negative symptoms *subtract* something (like social withdrawal). Indicate which of the following are positive and which negative, by placing a P or an N in the appropriate blanks.

(a) ____ flattened emotions

(b) ____ hallucinations

(c) ____ bizarre behaviour

(d) ____ social withdrawal

(e) ____ apathy

(f) ____ nonstop babbling

(g) ____ doesn't speak

17-4. Theorists hoped that classification of schizophrenia into positive and negative symptoms would provide more meaningful categories in terms of etiology and prognosis. Some differentiation between the two types of symptoms has been found; for example, *positive* symptoms seem to be associated with (better/worse) adjustment prior to the onset of schizophrenia and a (better/worse) prognosis. All in all, however, this system (has/has not) produced a classification that can replace the traditional subtypes.

17-5. When does schizophrenia tend to emerge?

17-6. Mark the following true (T) or false (F).

____ (a) Schizophrenia may have either a sudden or gradual onset.

____ (b) A person with schizophrenia can never truly recover from the disorder.

____ (c) With high-quality care, about half of people with schizophrenia experience a significant degree of recovery.

____ (d) Males tend to have an earlier onset of schizophrenia than females.

____ (e) Males tend to have more hospitalizations and higher relapse rates than females.

Answers: 17-1. (a) disorganized, (b) catatonic, (c) paranoid, (d) undifferentiated **17-2.** positive, negative **17-3.** (a) N, (b) P, (c) P, (d) N, (e) N, (f) P, (g) N **17-4.** better, better, has not **17-5.** generally during adolescence and early adulthood **17-6.** (a) T, (b) F, (c) T, (d) T, (e) T.

18. Explain how genetic vulnerability, neurochemical factors, and structural abnormalities in the brain may contribute to the etiology of schizophrenia.

18-1. As with mood disorders, twin studies implicate genetic factors in the development of schizophrenia. In a sentence, summarize the general results of these studies.

18-2. As with mood disorders, neurotransmitter substances in the brain are implicated in the etiology of schizophrenia. Although the evidence is somewhat clouded, ______________ is thought to be involved. Recently, a link has emerged between ______________ use in adolescence and schizophrenia. It is thought that the key ingredient in marijuana (THC) may amplify neurotransmitter activity in ______________ circuits.

18-3. In addition to possible neurochemical factors, certain differences in brain structure may be associated with schizophrenia. One of these differences involves enlarged brain ______________, which are hollow, fluid-filled cavities in the brain. It is impossible to know at this point whether this brain abnormality is a cause of schizophrenia or a/an ______________.

18-4. Recent brain-imaging studies have also found abnormal metabolic activity in both the frontal and _______________ lobes of the cortex. In addition, the metabolic abnormalities in the prefrontal cortex coincide with a major pathway for the neurotransmitter _______________. Since dopamine is already implicated in schizophrenia, this finding supports the idea of a link between this area of the prefrontal cortex and schizophrenia.

Answers: 18-1. For schizophrenia, the concordance rate is higher for identical than for fraternal twins. (The actual concordance rates have been found to be about 48% for identical and 17% for fraternal twins. For comparison, the respective percentages found for mood disorders were about 67% and 15%.) **18-2.** dopamine (thought to be a factor, because most drugs useful in treating schizophrenia decrease dopamine activity in the brain), marijuana (cannabis), dopamine **18-3.** ventricles, effect (result, consequence) **18-4.** temporal, dopamine.

19. Summarize evidence on how neurodevelopmental processes, family dynamics, and stress may be related to the development of schizophrenia.

19-1. The _______________ hypothesis of schizophrenia maintains that schizophrenia is caused, in part, by early neurological damage that occurs either prenatally or during the birth process.

19-2. Among the causes of neurological damage are _______________ infections; _______________, which may occur, for example, during famine; and complications that occur during _______________.

19-3. Expressed emotion refers to the extent to which a patient's relatives are overly critical or protective or are in other ways overly emotionally involved with the patient. Patients returning to families that are high in expressed emotion have a relapse rate that is much (higher/lower) than that of patients returning to families low in expressed emotion.

19-4. What role does stress play in the etiology of schizophrenia? Stress is a fact of life, and it is obvious that not everyone who experiences stress develops schizophrenia. Current thinking is that stress may be a precipitating factor for people who are biologically, or for other reasons, already _______________ to schizophrenia.

Answers: 19-1. neurodevelopmental **19-2.** viral (flu), malnutrition (starvation), delivery (birth, the birth process) **19-3.** higher **19-4.** vulnerable (predisposed).

PERSONALITY DISORDERS

20. Discuss the nature of personality disorders, and describe the three broad clusters of such disorders.

20-1. The personality disorders, recorded on Axis II, are frequently (less/more) severe versions of disorders on Axis I. These disorders consist of relatively extreme and (flexible/inflexible) sets of personality traits that cause subjective distress or impaired functioning.

20-2. DSM-IV lists 10 disorders, classified into three clusters, as follows:

(a) _______________–fearful cluster

(b) _______________–eccentric cluster

(c) _______________–impulsive cluster

20-3. Match the clusters listed in the previous question with the following descriptions by placing the appropriate letters in the blanks.

____ Distrustful, aloof, unable to connect emotionally with others

____ Maladaptive efforts to control fear of social rejection

____ Overly dramatic or impulsive

20-4. A major problem with the classification of personality disorders is that there is an enormous overlap between the 10 _______________ disorders on Axis II and the disorders listed on Axis I. There is also considerable _______________ among the personality disorders themselves.

20-5. For example, one study found that the majority of patients diagnosed with a histrionic personality disorder (also/did not) fit the descriptions of one or more other personality disorders. This blurring of the lines makes diagnosis difficult, and some have questioned the wisdom of separating the two axes.

20-6. In hopes of remedying these problems, some theorists have suggested that rather than using nonoverlapping categories, personality disorders should be described in terms of continuous scores on a set of personality _______________. While this approach has many advocates, psychologists are not in agreement about which personality dimensions to use or even whether this approach has clinical utility.

Answers: 20-1. less, inflexible **20-2.** anxious, odd, dramatic **20-3.** b, a, c **20-4.** personality, overlap **20-5.** also **20-6.** dimensions (factors, traits).

21. Describe the antisocial personality disorder, and discuss its etiology.

21-1. The *antisocial* personality disorder is more extensively researched than are the other personality disorders and is described in detail in your text. Check the concepts from the following list that are likely to correctly describe this disorder.

____ sexually promiscuous

____ manipulative

____ feels guilty

____ impulsive

____ genuinely affectionate

____ lacks an adequate conscience

____ may appear charming

____ much more likely to occur in males than females

____ may be a con-artist, thug, or unprincipled business executive

21-2. A term often used interchangeably with antisocial personality disorder is _______________. Canadian psychologist Robert Hare devised a measure of psychopathy called the _______________ _______________–_______________.

21-3. What types of studies support the idea that biological factors are involved in the etiology of the antisocial personality?

21-4. What environmental factors seem to be related to development of an antisocial personality?

Answers: 21-1. All the terms describe the antisocial personality except for *feels guilty* and *genuinely affectionate.* **21-2.** psychopathy, Psychopathy Checklist-Revised **21-3.** Twin and adoption studies. (There also has been mixed support for Eysenck's idea that antisocial personalities are chronically lower in autonomic arousal and therefore less likely to develop conditioned inhibitions.) **21-4.** Studies suggest that erratic or ineffective parental discipline, abuse, or neglect may be involved. Since one or both parents may also exhibit antisocial characteristics, observational learning may also be a factor.

PSYCHOLOGICAL DISORDERS AND THE LAW

22. Explain the legal concept of insanity.

22-1. _______________ is an important legal concept because criminal acts must be _______________ but at times those with a mental disorder may lack _______________.

22-2. Building upon the earlier M'Naghten rule, which stated that insanity exists when a mental disorder makes a person unable to distinguish _______________ from _______________, Canadian law currently allows a designation of "not _______________ _______________ on account of mental disorder." Also, an individual unable to participate in his or her own defence because of a psychological disorder may be found "_______________ to stand trial." A defence that a defendant is not guilty because he or she was not in control of his or her behaviour for reasons other than mental disorder is referred to as _______________. Such reasons could include sleepwalking or a physical blow.

Answers: 22-1. insanity, intentional, intent **22-2.** right, wrong, criminally responsible, unfit, automatism.

CULTURE AND PATHOLOGY

23. Discuss the evidence on culture and pathology.

23-1. Your text divides viewpoints about culture and pathology into *relativists* and *panculturalists.* The _______________ believe that there are basic standards of mental health that are *universal* across cultures. The _______________ believe that psychological disorders *vary as a function of culture.*

23-2. Some data support the pancultural view. For example, most investigators agree that the three most serious categories of disorder, listed below, are universal:

____

____

____

23-3. On the other hand, in some cultures, hypochondria, somatization, generalized anxiety disorder, and some of the other (milder/more severe) disturbances are not considered full-fledged disorders.

23-4. In addition, some disorders exist in some cultures and not others. For example, the obsessive fear about one's penis withdrawing into one's abdomen is found only among Chinese males in Malaya; and, until recently, ______________ nervosa was found only in affluent Western societies.

23-5. In summary, are psychological disorders universal, or do they vary across cultures?

a. There are some universal standards of normality and abnormality.

b. There are some disorders that are specific to particular cultures.

c. Both of the above: Some aspects of psychopathology are universal; some vary as a function of culture.

Answers: 23-1. panculturalists, relativists **23-2.** schizophrenia, depression, bipolar disorder **23-3.** milder **23-4.** anorexia **23-5.** c.

PUTTING IT IN PERSPECTIVE

24. Explain how this chapter highlighted four of the text's unifying themes.

24-1. Below are examples of the highlighted themes. Indicate which theme fits each example by writing the appropriate abbreviations in the blanks: MC for multifactorial causation, HE for the interplay of heredity and environment, SH for sociohistorical context, and C for the influence of culture.

(a) Mood and schizophrenic disorders will occur if one has a genetic vulnerability to the disorder *and* if one experiences a considerable amount of stress. _____

(b) Psychological disorders are caused by neurochemical factors, brain abnormalities, styles of child-rearing, life stress, and so on. _____

(c) Anorexia nervosa occurs almost exclusively in affluent Western societies. _____

(d) Decades ago, homosexuality was classified as a disorder; in recent DSMs, it is not. _____ and _____

Answers: 24-1. (a) HE (b) MC (c) C (d) SH, C.

PERSONAL APPLICATION * UNDERSTANDING EATING DISORDERS

25. Describe the symptoms and medical complications of anorexia nervosa, bulimia nervosa, and binge-eating disorder.

25-1. What are the names of the two major categories of eating disorder? ________________ ________________ and ________________ ________________

25-2. The most obvious feature of anorexia nervosa is the drastic weight loss that accompanies the disorder. Other characteristics include an intense ________________ of gaining weight, a disturbed ________________ ________________ (they think they are fat, no matter how emaciated they become), and (struggling/refusal) to maintain normal weight.

25-3. There are two major subtypes of anorexia nervosa. The *restricting type* is characterized by ________________ or severely limiting food eaten; the *binge-eating/purging type* is characterized by binging and then ________________ (by vomiting, using laxatives and diuretics, and exercising excessively).

25-4. The weight loss that accompanies anorexia nervosa is substantial, typically 25–30% below normal weight. A critical diagnostic criterion for anorexia nervosa in women is amenorrhea, the loss of the ________________ cycle.

25-5. There are other consequences as well, including serious gastrointestinal difficulties, heart and circulatory problems, and osteoporosis, all of which may lead to death in approximately _______% of cases. Anorexia nervosa patients (usually/rarely) seek treatment on their own.

25-6. Bulimia nervosa shares many of the characteristics of the binge-eating/purging type of anorexia. Its main differentiating feature is the fact that people with bulimia maintain a (relatively normal/drastically decreased) body weight. They are also somewhat more likely to recognize that there is a problem and to cooperate with treatment.

25-7. Binge-eating disorder involves ________________ but not the purging, fasting, and excessive exercise seen in bulimia. It is (less/more) severe and (less/more) common than bulimia.

Answers: 25-1. anorexia nervosa, bulimia nervosa **25-2.** fear, body image, refusal **25-3.** restricting, purging **25-4.** menstrual **25-5.** 2–10, rarely **25-6.** relatively normal **25-7.** binging, less, more.

26. Discuss the history, prevalence, and gender distribution of eating disorders.

26-1. Anorexia nervosa was extremely (common/rare) and bulimia nervosa (omnipresent/nonexistent) prior to the middle of the 20th century. Obviously, culture has a great deal to do with these disorders; the combination of abundant food and the desire for thinness seems to have been a major impetus for the problem. Thus, eating disorders are in large part a product of (Western/developing) cultures.

26-2. Probably as a result of the greater pressure on women to fit the current fashion of thinness, about ______% of individuals with eating disorders are female. Studies suggest that about 1% of young women develop ________________ nervosa and about 2–3% develop ________________ nervosa. The onset of the disorders typically occurs (before/after) age

21. Therapeutic interventions claim some success, but it is estimated that only about ______% of patients with anorexia experience a full recovery. Bulimia has a recovery rate of about ______%.

Answers: 26-1. rare, nonexistent, Western **26-2.** 90–95, anorexia, bulimia, before, 40–50, 70.

27. Explain how genetic factors, personality, and culture may contribute to eating disorders.

27-1. Data from ________________ studies and studies of relatives of people with eating disorders suggest that there is some degree of genetic predisposition for the disorders.

27-2. There are also personality correlates of the disorders that may reflect an underlying vulnerability. For example, people who are impulsive, overly sensitive, and low in self-esteem are more likely to suffer from (bulimia/anorexia) nervosa. People characterized as neurotic, obsessive, and rigid are more likely to have (bulimia/anorexia) nervosa.

27-3. As mentioned previously, cultural values are clearly implicated as well. Over the last half of the 20th century, eating disorders (increased/decreased) in prevalence as the ideal body weight (increased/decreased). Although one cannot make causal conclusions, it seems likely that the cultural milieu is a major factor in eating disorders.

Answers: 27-1. twin **27-2.** bulimia, anorexia **27-3.** increased, decreased

28. Explain how family dynamics and disturbed thinking may contribute to eating disorders.

28-1. It is very difficult to sort out cause and effect in case and informal studies, but some theorists contend that parents who are (underinvolved/overly involved) in their children's lives unintentionally push their adolescent children to exert autonomy through pathological eating patterns. Other theorists contend that mothers pass along the thinness message by ________________ unhealthy dieting practices.

28-2. Disturbed thinking seems to accompany eating disorders, but whether it is a cause or a result of the disorders is hard to say. (For example, studies of food deprivation in volunteer subjects also find disturbed thinking processes.) In any case, the type of thinking may be characterized as ________________ thinking (e.g., If I am not thin, I am nothing; if I eat, I am not in control of my life.).

Answers: 28-1. overly involved, modelling (endorsing, agreeing with, passing on) **28-2.** rigid (all-or-none, dichotomous).

CRITICAL THINKING APPLICATION * WORKING WITH PROBABILITIES IN THINKING ABOUT MENTAL ILLNESS

29. Discuss how mental heuristics can distort estimates of cumulative and conjunctive probabilities.

29-1. Basing an estimate of probability on the similarity of an event to a prototype (or mental representation) is a distortion in thinking referred to as the ________________ heuristic.

29-2. Over a lifetime, what is the probability that someone will be afflicted with mental illness? Higher than most people think, about one chance in three. People underestimate this probability in part because when they think of mental illness, they think of severe disturbances, such as schizophrenia. When a ________________ such as this comes to mind, people tend to ignore information about ________________. This bias in our thinking is called the ________________ ________________.

29-3. In fact, the lifetime mental illness referred to could be schizophrenia, or obsessive-compulsive disorder, or phobia, or substance abuse disorder, or any of an enormous number of other disorders. Each "or" in this instance should involve (adding/subtracting) estimates of the appropriate probabilities, an example of (conjunctive/cumulative) probabilities. The representativeness heuristic, however, results in our estimating probabilities based on similarity to a ________________.

29-4. Here is another probability question: Which of the following is more likely?

a. having a phobia

b. having a phobia and being obsessive-compulsive

You don't have to know anything about these disorders or their actual probabilities to know that the answer is ____. In this example, you implicitly know that the likelihood of two events occurring together is less than that of either of these events occurring alone. This example illustrates "and" relationships or ________________ probabilities.

29-5. Sometimes the answer is not so apparent. Consider this question: John was reported to have been brain damaged at birth. At age 14, John's IQ was measured as 70. Of the following, which is most likely?

a. John wins a Nobel Prize at age 40.

b. John is given an experimental treatment for retardation; John wins a Nobel Prize at age 40.

c. John was mixed up with another baby; John's IQ test was scored incorrectly; John wins a Nobel Prize at age 40.

29-6. The answer to the previous question is another example of ________________ probabilities. If you, like most people that I have shown this problem, picked some answer other than *a*, you made the error known as the ________________ fallacy.

29-7. Why do we make the conjunction fallacy? In part, the mistake results, again, from our tendency to be influenced by prototypes, the ________________ heuristic. Even though we know that, logically, the likelihood of two events occurring together is less than the probability of either occurring alone, the additional "explanation" makes the combined result seem more reasonable. In fact, it is just another example of ________________ probabilities.

29-8. When you first read about mood disorders, or obsessive-compulsive disorder, or generalized anxiety disorder, or hypochondriasis, did you tend to think that each description might fit you or one of your friends? If so, you were probably influenced by the ________________ heuristic.

29-9. The availability heuristic involves the ease with which we can bring something to ________________. The more readily we can think of some event, the more likely it is to influence our judgment about its frequency or ________________.

29-10. Review. If one estimates probability based on a mental image or prototype, one is using the ________________ ________________. If we think that it is more likely that two events will occur together than that either will occur alone, we have made the error known as the ________________ ________________. If we base our estimate of probability on the ease with which something comes to mind, we are using the ________________ ________________.

Answers: 29-1. representativeness **29-2.** prototype (mental representation), probability, representativeness heuristic **29-3.** adding, cumulative, prototype **29-4.** a, conjunctive **29-5.** a **29-6.** conjunctive, conjunction **29-7.** representativeness, conjunctive **29-8.** availability **29-9.** mind, probability **29-10.** representativeness heuristic, conjunction fallacy, availability heuristic.

Review of Key Terms

Agoraphobia
Anorexia nervosa
Antisocial personality disorder
Anxiety disorders
Availability heuristic
Binge-eating disorder
Bipolar disorder
Bulimia nervosa
Catatonic schizophrenia
Comorbidity
Concordance rate
Conjunction fallacy
Conversion disorder
Culture-bound disorders
Cyclothymic disorder
Delusions
Diagnosis
Disorganized schizophrenia
Dissociative amnesia
Dissociative disorders
Dissociative fugue
Dissociative identity disorder (DID)
Dysthymic disorder
Eating disorders
Epidemiology
Etiology
Generalized anxiety disorder
Hallucinations
Hypochondriasis
Major depressive disorder
Medical model
Mood disorders
Multiple-personality disorder
Negative symptoms
Obsessive-compulsive disorder (OCD)
Panic disorder
Paranoid schizophrenia
Personality disorders
Phobic disorder
Positive symptoms
Postpartum depression
Prevalence
Prognosis
Representativeness heuristic
Schizophrenic disorders
Seasonal affective disorder
Somatization disorder
Somatoform disorders
Undifferentiated schizophrenia

________________ **1.** Proposes that it is useful to think of abnormal behaviour as a disease.

________________ **2.** Involves distinguishing one illness from another.

________________ **3.** Refers to the apparent causation and developmental history of an illness.

________________ **4.** A forecast about the possible course of an illness.

________________ **5.** An eating disorder characterized by fear of gaining weight, disturbed body image, refusal to maintain normal weight, and using dangerous measures to lose weight.

______________________ **6.** The study of the distribution of mental or physical disorders in a population.

______________________ **7.** Refers to the percentage of a population that exhibits a disorder during a specified time period.

______________________ **8.** A class of disorders marked by feelings of excessive apprehension and anxiety.

______________________ **9.** Disorder marked by a chronic high level of anxiety that is not tied to any specific threat.

______________________ **10.** Disorder marked by a persistent and irrational fear of an object or situation that presents no realistic danger.

______________________ **11.** Disorder that involves recurrent attacks of overwhelming anxiety that usually occur suddenly and unexpectedly.

______________________ **12.** Disorder marked by persistent, uncontrollable intrusions of unwanted thoughts and urges to engage in senseless rituals.

______________________ **13.** A fear of going out in public places.

______________________ **14.** One part of a two-category classification system of schizophrenia that includes behavioural excesses such as hallucinations, delusions, and bizarre behaviour.

______________________ **15.** A class of disorders involving physical ailments that have no authentic organic basis and are due to psychological factors.

______________________ **16.** Disorder marked by a history of diverse physical complaints that appear to be psychological in origin.

______________________ **17.** Disorder that involves a significant loss of physical function (with no apparent organic basis), usually in a single-organ system.

______________________ **18.** Disorder that involves excessive preoccupation with health concerns and incessant worrying about developing physical illnesses.

______________________ **19.** A class of disorders in which people lose contact with portions of their consciousness or memory, resulting in disruptions in their sense of identity.

______________________ **20.** A sudden loss of memory for important personal information that is too extensive to be due to normal forgetting.

______________________ **21.** The loss of memory of one's entire life along with one's sense of personal identity.

______________________ **22.** Older term, still widely used, that describes the coexistence in one person of two or more personalities.

______________________ **23.** The new term that replaced multiple-personality disorder in the DSM-IV.

______________________ **24.** A class of disorders marked by depressed or elevated mood disturbances that may spill over to disrupt physical, perceptual, social, and thought processes.

______________________ **25.** Severe disturbances in eating behaviour characterized by preoccupation with weight concerns and unhealthy efforts to control weight; includes the syndromes anorexia nervosa and bulimia nervosa.

______________________ **26.** A disorder marked by persistent feelings of sadness and despair and a loss of interest in previous sources of pleasure.

______________________ **27.** Disorder marked by the experience of both depressive and manic periods.

______ 28. Statistic indicating the percentage of twin pairs or other pairs of relatives who exhibit the same disorder.

______ 29. Estimating the probability of an event based on the ease with which relevant instances come to mind.

______ 30. A class of disorders marked by disturbances in thought that spill over to affect perceptual, social, and emotional processes.

______ 31. False beliefs that are maintained even though they clearly are out of touch with reality.

______ 32. Sensory perceptions that occur in the absence of a real, external stimulus or gross distortions of perceptual input.

______ 33. Type of schizophrenia dominated by delusions of persecution, along with delusions of grandeur.

______ 34. Type of schizophrenia marked by striking motor disturbances, ranging from muscular rigidity to random motor activity.

______ 35. Type of schizophrenia marked by a particularly severe deterioration of adaptive behaviour.

______ 36. Type of schizophrenia marked by idiosyncratic mixtures of schizophrenic symptoms.

______ 37. A class of disorders marked by extreme, inflexible personality traits that cause subjective distress or impaired social and occupational functioning.

______ 38. Disorder marked by impulsive, callous, manipulative, aggressive, and irresponsible behaviour; reflects a failure to accept social norms.

______ 39. An eating disorder characterized by binges but no purges, laxative use, or excessive exercise.

______ 40. A part of a two-category classification system of schizophrenia that includes behavioural deficits, such as flattened emotions, social withdrawal, and apathy.

______ 41. Chronic but relatively mild symptoms of bipolar disturbance.

______ 42. Abnormal syndromes found only in a few cultural groups.

______ 43. Chronic depression that is insufficient in severity to merit diagnosis of a major depressive episode.

______ 44. Estimating the probability of an event based on how similar the event is to a prototype.

______ 45. An error in thinking that involves estimating that the odds of two uncertain events happening together are greater than the odds of either event happening alone.

______ 46. An eating disorder that involves binge eating followed by unhealthy compensatory efforts such as vomiting, fasting, abuse of laxatives and diuretics, and excessive exercise.

______ 47. The coexistence of two or more disorders in the same individual.

______ 48. A type of depression occurring after childbirth.

______ 49. A mood disorder involving seasonal variation.

Answers: 1. medical model **2.** diagnosis **3.** etiology **4.** prognosis **5.** anorexia nervosa **6.** epidemiology **7.** prevalence **8.** anxiety disorders **9.** generalized anxiety disorder **10.** phobic disorder **11.** panic disorder **12.** obsessive-compulsive disorder **13.** agoraphobia **14.** positive symptoms **15.** somatoform disorders **16.** somatization disorder **17.** conversion disorder **18.** hypochondriasis **19.** dissociative disorders

20. dissociative amnesia **21.** dissociative fugue **22.** multiple-personality disorder **23.** dissociative identity disorder **24.** mood disorders **25.** eating disorders **26.** major depressive disorder **27.** bipolar disorder **28.** concordance rate **29.** availability heuristic **30.** schizophrenic disorders **31.** delusions **32.** hallucinations **33.** paranoid schizophrenia **34.** catatonic schizophrenia **35.** disorganized schizophrenia **36.** undifferentiated schizophrenia **37.** personality disorders **38.** antisocial personality disorder **39.** binge-eating disorder **40.** negative symptoms **41.** cyclothymic disorder **42.** culture-bound disorders **43.** dysthymic disorder **44.** representativeness heuristic **45.** conjunction fallacy **46.** bulimia nervosa **47.** comorbidity **48.** postpartum depression **49.** seasonal affective disorder.

Review of Key People

Nancy Andreasen	Robert Hare	Regina Schuller
Martin Antony	Susan Nolen-Hoeksema	Thomas Szasz
Aaron Beck	David Rosenhan	

________________ **1.** Critic of the medical model; argues that abnormal behaviour usually involves a deviation from social norms rather than an illness.

________________ **2.** Did a study on admission of pseudopatients to a mental hospital; concluded that our mental health system is biased toward seeing pathology where it doesn't exist.

________________ **3.** Studies the interface between psychology and Canadian law.

________________ **4.** Proposed an alternative approach to subtyping that divides schizophrenic disorders into just two categories, based on the presence of negative versus positive symptoms.

________________ **5.** Asserts that dissociative identity disorder (multiple-personality disorder) is not a genuine disorder but is the product of media attention and the probings of psychotherapists.

________________ **6.** Conducted research on the association between "rumination" and depression.

________________ **7.** Developed the Psychopathy Checklist–Revised.

________________ **8.** Studied different dimensions, or aspects, of obsessive-compulsive disorder.

Answers: 1. Szasz **2.** Rosenhan **3.** Schuller **4.** Andreasen **5.** Spanos **6.** Nolen-Hoeksema **7.** Hare **8.** Antony.

Self-Quiz

1. Which of the following concepts or people asserts that abnormal behaviour is best thought of as an illness?
a. the behavioural model
b. the medical model
c. Thomas Szasz
d. Arthur Staats

2. The concordance rate for mood disorders has been found to be about 65% among identical twins and 17% among fraternal twins. These data suggest that the mood disorders:
a. are caused primarily by stress
b. have an onset at an early age
c. are due primarily to family environment
d. are caused in part by genetic factors

3. In Rosenhan's study involving admission of pseudopatients to psychiatric facilities, most of the "patients" were:
a. diagnosed as seriously disturbed
b. diagnosed as suffering from a mild neurosis
c. dismissed within two days
d. misdiagnosed by the ward attendants but correctly diagnosed by the professional staff

4. An individual gets sudden, paralyzing attacks of anxiety and also fears going out in public away from his or her house. Which anxiety disorder does this describe?
a. generalized anxiety disorder
b. phobic disorder
c. obsessive-compulsive disorder
d. panic disorder and agoraphobia

5. Ralph cleans and scrubs the cupboards in his house seven times each day. Which anxiety disorder does this describe?
a. generalized anxiety disorder
b. phobic disorder
c. obsessive-compulsive disorder
d. panic disorder

6. Human beings may have evolved to be more easily conditioned to fear some stimuli than others. This is Seligman's notion of:
a. preparedness
b. anxiety differentiation
c. somatization
d. learned helplessness

7. Delusions and hallucinations are likely to characterize:
a. major depressive disorder
b. hypochondriasis
c. phobias
d. schizophrenia

8. Paralysis or loss of feeling that does not match underlying anatomical organization may be a symptom of:
a. somatization disorder
b. conversion disorder
c. hypochondriasis
d. malingering

9. A disorder that was extremely rare prior to the last half of the 20th century is the syndrome:
a. manic-depressive disorder
b. schizophrenia
c. obsessive-compulsive disorder
d. anorexia nervosa

10. The disorder marked by striking motor disturbances ranging from rigidity to random motor activity and incoherence is termed:
a. catatonic schizophrenia
b. multiple personality
c. dissociative disorder
d. paranoid schizophrenia

11. Which of the following are disorders that occur in all cultures?
a. generalized anxiety disorder and panic disorder
b. hypochondriasis, somatization, conversion disorder
c. schizophrenia, bipolar disorder, depression
d. bulimia and anorexia nervosa

12. A disorder characterized by amenorrhea (loss of the menstrual cycle) in women is the syndrome termed:
a. generalized anxiety disorder
b. bipolar disorder
c. anorexia nervosa
d. bulimia nervosa

13. An individual thinks he is Jesus Christ. He also believes that, because he is Christ, people are trying to kill him. Assume that this individual is not correct—he is not Christ, and people are not trying to kill him. Which of the following would be the most likely diagnosis?
a. multiple personality
b. paranoid schizophrenia
c. obsessive-compulsive disorder
d. catatonic schizophrenia

14. A Canadian court in 2008 declares that, because of a mental illness, an individual did not know right from wrong. The individual is likely to be found:
a. not criminally responsible on account of mental disorder
b. psychopathic
c. psychotic
d. not guilty by reason of insanity

15. Being careful not to make the conjunction fallacy, indicate which of the following is most probable:
a. Ralph is an alcoholic; Ralph wins a major world tennis tournament.
b. Ralph is an alcoholic; Ralph enters a treatment program; Ralph wins a major world tennis tournament.
c. Ralph is an alcoholic; Ralph enters a treatment program; Ralph has been sober for a year; Ralph wins a major world tennis tournament.
d. Ralph is an alcoholic; Ralph enters a treatment program; Ralph has been sober for a year; Ralph practices tennis 50 hours a week; Ralph wins a major world tennis tournament.

16. Canadian General Romeo Dallaire, winner of the Pearson Peace Medal in 2005, has suffered from which anxiety disorder?
a. phobic disorder
b. post-traumatic stress disorder
c. generalized anxiety disorder
d. panic disorder

17. The Featured Study revealed that the later development of depression can be predicted by earlier measurement of:
a. negative thinking
b. traumatic experiences
c. exposure to others who are depressed
d. all of the above

Answers: 1. b **2.** d **3.** a **4.** d **5.** c **6.** a **7.** d **8.** b **9.** d **10.** a **11.**c **12.** c **13.** b **14.** a **15.** a **16.** b **17.** a.

InfoTrac Keywords

Agoraphobia
Anorexia Nervosa
Availability Heuristic
Hypochondriasis (see hypochondria)
Major Depressive Disorder
Obsessive-compulsive Disorder
Paranoid Schizophrenia
Somatoform Disorders

Chapter Fifteen
TREATMENT OF PSYCHOLOGICAL DISORDERS

Review of Key Ideas

THE ELEMENTS OF THE TREATMENT PROCESS

1. Identify the three major categories of therapy, and discuss how various demographic variables relate to the likelihood of treatment.

1-1. Even though she already owns more than a thousand pairs of shoes, Imelba cannot resist the urge to buy more. She checks the Yellow Pages and calls three different psychotherapists regarding possible treatment for her compulsion.

(a) One therapist tells her that treatment will require her to talk with the therapist so as to develop a better understanding of her inner feelings. This therapist probably belongs to the ________________ school of psychotherapy.

(b) Another therapist suggests that some form of medication may help alleviate her compulsion. This therapist probably pursues the ________________ approach to psychotherapy.

(c) The third therapist is of the opinion that her urge to buy shoes results from learning, and correcting it requires that she unlearn this compulsion. This therapist probably pursues the ________________ approach to psychotherapy.

1-2. Indicate whether the following statements about people who seek or choose not to seek psychotherapy are true (T) or false (F).

__________ (a) Fewer Canadians are committed to improving their mental health in the future than their physical health.

__________ (b) The two most common presenting symptoms are excessive anxiety and depression.

__________ (c) Persons seeking psychotherapy always have identifiable disorders.

___________ (d) Many people feel that seeking psychotherapy is an admission of personal weakness.

Answers: 1-1. (a) insight, (b) biomedical, (c) behavioural **1-2.** (a) T, (b) T, (c) F, (d) T.

2. Describe the various types of mental health professionals involved in the provision of psychotherapy.

2-1. Identify the following kinds of mental health professionals:

(a) Medically trained persons (physicians) who generally use biomedical and insight approaches to psychotherapy.

(b) Persons with doctoral degrees who emphasize behavioural and insight approaches to psychotherapy in treating a full range of psychological problems (two types).

(c) Nurses who usually work as part of the treatment team in a hospital setting.

(d) These persons often work with both the patient and family to reintegrate the patient back into society.

(e) Persons who usually specialize in particular types of problems, such as vocational, drug, or marital counselling.

Answers: 2-1. (a) psychiatrists, (b) clinical and counselling psychologists, (c) psychiatric nurses, (d) clinical social workers, (e) counsellors.

INSIGHT THERAPIES

3. Explain the logic of psychoanalysis, and describe the techniques by which analysts probe the unconscious.

3-1. Freud believed that psychological disturbances originate from unresolved conflicts deep in the unconscious levels of the mind. His theory of personality, which he called _______________, would be classified as an _______________ approach to psychotherapy. The psychoanalyst plays the role of psychological detective, seeking out problems thought to originate from conflicts left over from early _______________.

3-2. The psychoanalyst employs two techniques to probe the unconscious. One technique requires the patient to tell whatever comes to mind, no matter how trivial. This technique is called _______________ _______________. The other technique requires the patient to learn to remember his or her dreams, which are then probed for their hidden meaning by the psychoanalyst. This technique is called _______________ _______________.

Answers: 3-1. psychoanalysis, insight, childhood **3-2.** free association, dream analysis.

4. Discuss resistance and transference in psychoanalysis.

4-1. Freud believed most people (do/do not) want to know the true nature of their inner conflicts and will employ various strategies so as to offer _______________ to the progress of therapy. As therapy progresses, the patient often begins to relate to the therapist as though he or she was actually one of the significant persons (mother, father, spouse, etc.) in the patient's life. This phenomenon is called _______________.

Answers: 4-1. do not, resistance, transference.

5. Identify the elements of therapeutic climate, and discuss therapeutic process in Rogers's client-centred therapy.

5-1. Client-centred therapy, as developed by Carl Rogers, holds that there are three important aspects necessary for a good therapeutic climate. These are *genuineness*, *unconditional positive regard*, and *empathy*. Match these terms with their correct definitions, as given below.

(a) _________________________: The ability to truly see the world from the client's point of view and to communicate this understanding to the client.

(b) _________________________: The therapist's openness and honesty with the client.

(c) _________________________: The complete and nonjudgmental acceptance of the client as a person, without necessarily agreeing with what the client has to say.

5-2. The major emphasis for client-centred therapy is to provide feedback and _______________ as the client expresses his or her thoughts and feelings. The idea here is that the client (does/does not) need direct advice. What is needed is help in sorting through personal confusion in order to gain greater _______________ into true inner feelings.

5-3. An important extension of client-centred therapy is _______________-_______________ couples therapy, which addresses _______________ issues within a partnership as well as underlying _______________.

Answers: 5-1. (a) empathy, (b) genuineness, (c) unconditional positive regard **5-2.** clarification, does not, insight (or understanding) **5-3.** emotion-focused, relationship, emotions.

6. Discuss therapies inspired by positive psychology.

6-1. Fava and colleagues developed ____________-____________ therapy, which seeks to enhance a client's self-acceptance, purpose in life, autonomy and personal growth. It has been used in the treatment of _____________ and _____________ disorders. Another approach, developed by Seligman and colleagues, is _____________ psychotherapy, which teaches clients to recognize their _____________, appreciate their blessings, savour positive experiences, _____________ those who have wronged them, and find _____________ in their lives. Positive psychotherapy can be an effective treatment for depression.

Answers: 6-1. well-being, mood, anxiety, positive, strengths, forgive, meaning.

7. Describe how group therapy is generally conducted, and identify some advantages of this approach.

7-1. When conducting group therapy, the therapist generally plays a/an (active/subtle) role, one that is primarily aimed at promoting _______________ cohesiveness. Participants essentially function as _______________ for each other, providing acceptance and emotional support.

7-2. Besides being less expensive, group therapy also has three other advantages: (1) the realization by the participants that their problems (are/are not) unique, (2) the opportunity to work in a safe environment to build _______________ skills, and (3) the fact that group therapy is particularly appropriate for (all/certain) kinds of problems.

Answers: 7-1. subtle, group, therapists **7-2.** are not, social, certain.

8. Discuss evidence on the efficacy of insight therapies and the role of common factors in therapy.

8-1. Evaluating the efficacy of therapies is challenging, in part because disorders can improve on their own, a phenomenon called _______________ _______________.

8-2. A large number of studies have suggested that insight therapies are superior to no treatment or placebo treatment, and are (equal to/better than) drug therapies. Most gains occur (early/late) in the treatment. About _____% of patients show clinically meaningful recovery within about 20 sessions.

8-3. With respect to mechanisms of _______________, it appears that _______________ _______________ account for much of the improvement experienced by clients receiving insight therapy. These factors include a therapeutic _______________, provision of emotional _______________ and _______________ by the therapist, the cultivation of _______________, the provision of a _______________, and the opportunity to express feelings, confront problems, gain new insights, and learn new patterns of behaviour.

Answers: 8-1. spontaneous remission **8-2.** equal to, early, 50 **8-3.** action, common factors, alliance, support, empathy, hope, rationale.

BEHAVIOUR THERAPIES

9. Summarize the general principles underlying behavioural approaches to therapy.

9-1. In contrast to insight therapists, who believe that pathological symptoms are signs of an underlying problem, behaviour therapists believe that the _______________ are the problem. Thus, behaviour therapists focus on employing the principles of learning to directly change maladaptive _______________. The two general principles underlying this approach are (1) one's behaviour is a product of _______________, and (2) what has been learned can be _______________.

Answers: 9-1. symptoms, behaviour, learning, unlearned.

10. Describe the goals and procedures of systematic desensitization and aversion therapy.

10-1. State whether the following situations would be most applicable to systematic desensitization or to aversion therapy.

(a) The treatment goal is to lessen the attractiveness of particular stimuli and behaviours that are personally or socially harmful.

(b) The treatment goal is to reduce irrational fears, such as those found in phobias and other anxiety disorders.

(c) The three-step treatment involves pairing an imagined anxiety hierarchy with deep muscle relaxation.

(d) Treatment involves presenting an unpleasant stimulus, such as electric shock, while a person is engaged in performing a self-destructive, but personally appealing, act.

(e) This would be the treatment of choice for students who are unduly anxious about public speaking.

Answers: 10-1. (a) aversion therapy, (b) systematic desensitization, (c) systematic desensitization, (d) aversion therapy, (e) systematic desensitization.

11. Describe the goals and techniques of social skills training.

11-1. As the name implies, social skills training is a behaviour therapy designed to improve a client's social or _______________ skills. Three different behavioural techniques are employed. First, one is required to watch closely the behaviour of socially skilled persons, a technique called _______________. Next, the client is expected to imitate and practice the behaviour he or she has just witnessed, a technique called behaviour _______________. Finally, the client is expected to perform in social situations requiring increasingly more difficult social skills, a technique called _______________.

Answers: 11-1. interpersonal, modelling, rehearsal, shaping.

12. Discuss the logic, goals, and techniques of cognitive therapy.

12-1. Answer the following questions regarding the logic, goals, and techniques of cognitive therapy.

(a) What is the origin of many psychological problems according to cognitive therapy?

(b) What is the primary goal of cognitive therapy?

(c) How do cognitive therapists go about trying to change a client's negative illogical thinking?

(d) What techniques from behaviour therapy do cognitive therapists frequently employ?

(e) What is the aim of mindfulness training?

Answers: 12-1. (a) "errors" in thinking, (b) to change the client's negative thoughts and maladaptive beliefs, (c) through identification and challenging the basis in reality of negative thoughts, (d) modelling, systematic monitoring of one's behaviour, and behavioural rehearsal, (e) Training in mindfulness emphasizes attention to, and nonjudgmental acceptance of, present-moment experience. For example, depressed patients might be taught to observe and accept their troubling thoughts or emotions without judging or elaborating on them.

13. Discuss evidence on the effectiveness of behaviour therapies.

13-1. Compared to the evidence in support of insight therapies, the evidence in favour of behaviour therapy is somewhat (weaker/stronger). It is important to remember, however, that behaviour therapies are best suited for treating (specific/general) psychological disorders, and that all of the various behavioural techniques (are/are not) equally effective.

Answers: 13-1. stronger, specific, are not.

BIOMEDICAL THERAPIES

14. Define biomedical therapy, and describe historical uses of surgical treatment of mental disorders.

14-1. Biomedical therapies are _______________ interventions intended to reduce symptoms associated with (physical/psychological) disorders. Biomedical therapies include psychosurgery, electroconvulsive shock therapy, and _______________ therapies.

14-2. The modern use of psychosurgery dates from the year ________, when a Swiss psychiatrist, Burckhardt, used the procedure to treat hallucinations. The prefrontal leucotomy was developed by Portuguese psychiatrist Moniz in the 19____, and was further developed in the 1940s by Walter ______________ in the U.S. Performance of lobotomies in Canada declined through the 1970s, and the technique has now fallen into disuse. A procedure that is used on occasion is the ______________, a treatment reserved for instances of obsessive-compulsive disorder that don't respond to other interventions.

Answers: 14-1. physiological, psychological, drug **14-2.** 1888, 30s, Freeman, cingulotomy.

15. Describe the principal categories of drugs used in the treatment of psychological disorders.

15-1. Valium and Xanax, popularly called tranquilizers, are used to treat psychological disorders in which anxiety is a major feature. Thus, they are collectively called ______________ drugs.

15-2. Another class of drugs is used to treat severe psychotic symptoms, such as hallucinations and confusion. These drugs are collectively called ______________ drugs.

14-3. Four classes of drugs (tricyclics, MAO inhibitors, selective serotonin reuptake inhibitors, and serotonin and norepinephrine reuptake inhibitors) have been found to be useful in alleviating depression. These drugs are collectively called ______________ drugs.

15-4. Drugs for bipolar disorder are known as ______________ *stabilizers.* They include lithium and ______________.

Answers: 15-1. antianxiety **15-2.** antipsychotic **15-3.** antidepressant **15-4.** mood, valproate.

16. Discuss evidence on the effects and problems of drug treatments for psychological disorders.

16-1. Drug therapies have proven useful in the treatment of many psychological disorders. However, they remain controversial for at least three reasons. Use the hints below to describe these three reasons.

(a) resolve problems

(b) two areas having to do with excess

(c) cure is worse than the disease

16-2. What problem exists between drug companies and researchers that may influence results regarding the effectiveness and side effects of drugs?

Answers: 16-1. (a) They alleviate rather than solve psychological problems. (b) They are overprescribed, and patients are overmedicated. (c) The side effects may be worse than the disease. **16-2.** The researchers are too financially dependent on the drug companies. This may be related to selective publication practices and adoption of research designs that exaggerate positive effects.

17. Describe the therapeutic effects and risks of ECT and describe newer brain stimulation techniques.

17-1. Answer the following questions about the nature, therapeutic effects, and risks of ECT.

(a) What is the physical effect of the electric shock on the patient?

(b) What general class of disorders warrants conservative use of ECT as a treatment technique?

(c) Why does ECT work?

(d) What is a short-term side effect of ECT?

17-2. Answer the following questions about newer brain stimulation techniques.

(a) What is transcranial magnetic stimulation?

(b) What is deep brain stimulation?

Answers: 17-1. (a) It produces convulsive seizures. (b) severe mood disorders (depression and mania), (c) It is unknown at this time. (d) It can produce intellectual impairment. **17-2.** (a) Transcranial magnetic stimulation involves enhancing or depressing activity in specific cortical areas. It has been used to reduce depression. (b) Deep brain stimulation involves implanting an electrode into the brain in order to deliver electrical current. It has been used to treat movement disorders such as Parkinson's disease.

CURRENT TRENDS AND ISSUES IN TREATMENT

18. Discuss the merits of blending or combining different approaches to therapy.

18-1. A significant trend in modern psychotherapy is to blend or combine many different treatment approaches. Psychologists who advocate and use this approach are said to be _______________. The chapter's Featured Study suggests there may be merit to this approach. In this study, four different groups of depressed patients were treated by either insight therapy (i.e., interpersonal therapy) with placebo medication, medication alone (the antidepressant nortriptyline), insight therapy along with medication, or placebo medication alone. The greatest improvement was found in patients treated by (drug therapy alone/ interpersonal therapy alone/both therapies combined).

Answers: 18-1. eclectic, both therapies combined.

19. Discuss the barriers that lead to underutilization of mental health services by ethnic minorities and possible solutions to the problem.

19-1. The text lists four general barriers (cultural, language, access, and institutional) to mental health services for ethnic minorities. Indicate which of these barriers is represented in the following statements.

_______________ (a) Many of the ethnic minorities are in low-paying jobs and without health insurance.

_______________ (b) Very few mental health facilities are equipped to provide culturally responsive services.

_______________ (c) There is a limited number of bilingual therapists.

_______________ (d) Psychotherapy was developed by whites in the Western world to treat whites in the Western world.

19-2. Canadian First Nations peoples are at elevated risk of depression, suicide, and substance abuse. Therapy settings that fail to include _______________ healing practices for such individuals tend to be ineffective (i.e., those settings create an _______________ barrier to treatment).

19-3. Overall, studies show that ethnic minorities are (more/less) likely to go to mental health facilities that are staffed by a higher proportion of people who share their ethnic identity. Individual therapists can also work toward building a strong _______________ _______________ with their ethnic clients, and interventions can be _______________ to be more compatible with specific ethnic groups' values and traditions.

Answers: 19-1. (a) access, (b) institutional, (c) language, (d) cultural **19-2.** indigenous, institutional **19-3.** more, therapeutic alliance, tailored (adapted, modified).

INSTITUTIONAL TREATMENT IN TRANSITION

20. Explain why people grew disenchanted with mental hospitals, and describe the community mental health movement.

20-1. After more than a century of reliance on state mental hospitals, the evidence began to grow that these institutions were not helping the patients; rather, in many instances, they were worsening their condition. What condition, unrelated to funding, was said to be responsible for this state of affairs?

20-2. In order to correct for these shortcomings, the community mental health movement arose as an alternative treatment option. These community based facilities emphasize (short-term/ long-term) therapy and getting patients stabilized and back into the community _______________.

Answers: 20-1. The removal of patients from their communities separated them from essential support groups. **20-2.** short-term, swiftly.

21. Describe the deinstitutionalization trend, and evaluate its effects.

21-1. The transferring of mental health care from large state institutions to community-based facilities is what is meant by the term _________________. As a result of deinstitutionalization, the number of mental patients in large institutional hospitals has _______________ remarkably. For example, in Canada, the number of beds per 100,000 people declined from four to one between 1964 and 1981. The length of stay by patients in mental hospitals has also _______________.

21-2. While deinstitutionalization has resulted in a decrease in the number of patients, as well as their length of stay, the number of admissions to psychiatric hospitals has actually _______________. This is because of a large number of readmissions for short-term care, which the text calls "the _______________ _______________ problem." In addition, many end up in _______________. Another problem brought about by deinstitutionalization is that a large number of discharged patients who have meagre job skills and no close support groups make up a substantial portion of the nation's _______________ persons.

Answers: 21-1. deinstitutionalization, declined, declined **21-2.** increased, revolving door, prisons, homeless.

PUTTING IT IN PERSPECTIVE

22. Explain how this chapter highlighted two of the text's unifying themes.

22-1. What point does the text make about how theoretical diversity influenced the treatment techniques employed by psychotherapy?

22-2. The approaches to psychotherapy discussed in this chapter are not universally accepted or used, and some are actually counterproductive in many cultures. Why is this?

Answers: 22-1. It has resulted in better treatment techniques (because of the many diverse approaches). **22-2.** Cultural factors influence psychological processes.

PERSONAL APPLICATION * LOOKING FOR A THERAPIST

23. Discuss where to seek therapy and the potential importance of a therapist's sex, professional background, and cost.

23-1. Most therapists (are/are not) in private practice. In addition to talking to friends and acquaintances, the text lists many places (Table 15.2) where one might seek psychotherapy. The general idea here is to _______________ around when looking for a therapist.

23-2. The text concludes that the kind of degree held by the psychotherapist (is/is not) crucial, although a verifiable degree indicating some kind of professional training is important. The sex of the therapist should be chosen according to the feelings of the _______________; it is unwise to engage a therapist whose sex makes the client feel uncomfortable.

23-3. Answer the following questions regarding the cost of psychotherapy.

(a) How does the cost of therapists involved in private practice compare with the fees charged by similar professional groups?

(b) Are the costs of seeing a psychologist covered by health care? What about the costs of seeing a psychiatrist?

Answers: 22-1. are not, shop **22-2.** is not, client **22-3.** (a) The costs are similar. (b) The services of a private-practice psychologist are not covered by health care, whereas the services of a psychiatrist are covered.

24. Discuss the importance of a therapist's theoretical approach.

24-1. Studies of the effectiveness of various theoretical approaches to therapy show they are (unequal/equal) in overall success. This equality of results among all theoretical approaches (does/does not) apply to all types of problems. The theoretical approach may make a difference for specific types of problems.

Answers: 24-1. equal, does not.

25. Summarize what one should look for in a prospective therapist and what one should expect out of therapy.

25-1. The text lists three areas to evaluate when looking for a therapist. Complete the following statements describing these areas.

(a) Can you talk to the therapist _______________?

(b) Does the therapist appear to have empathy and _______________?

(c) Does the therapist appear to be self-assured and _______________?

25-2. What should one consider before terminating therapy because of lack of progress?

25-3. What did the Ehrenbergs say about what to expect from psychotherapy?

Answers: 25-1. (a) openly (in a candid, nondefensive manner), (b) understanding, (c) confident **25-2.** The lack of progress may be due to resistance on the client's part. **25-3.** It takes time, effort, and courage.

CRITICAL THINKING APPLICATION * FROM CRISIS TO WELLNESS—BUT WAS IT THE THERAPY?

26. Explain how placebo effects and regression toward the mean can complicate the evaluation of therapy.

26-1. In addition to therapy itself, what other two factors can influence the outcome of a treatment program?

26-2. Which of these two factors is least affected by having only a small sample?

26-3. Which of these factors leads us to predict that persons who score the healthiest on a mental health questionnaire will actually score lower on this questionnaire following a brief therapy intervention?

Answers: 26-1. placebo effects and regression toward the mean **26-2.** placebo effects **26-3.** regression toward the mean.

Review of Key Terms

Antianxiety drugs
Antidepressant drugs
Antipsychotic drugs
Aversion therapy
Behaviour therapies
Biomedical therapies
Client-centred therapy
Cognitive-behavioural treatments
Cognitive therapy
Deep brain stimulation
Deinstitutionalization
Dream analysis
Eclecticism
Electroconvulsive therapy (ECT)
Free association
Group therapy
Insight therapies
Interpretation
Mental hospital
Mood stabilizers
Placebo effects
Psychiatrists
Psychoanalysis
Psychopharmacotherapy
Regression toward the mean
Resistance
Social skills training
Spontaneous remission
Systematic desensitization
Tardive dyskinesia
Transcranial magnetic stimulation
Transference

____________________ **1.** Delivering electrical current to brain tissue adjacent to an implanted electrode.

____________________ **2.** Physicians who specialize in the treatment of psychological disorders.

____________________ **3.** Therapies that involve verbal interactions intended to enhance a client's self-knowledge and thus produce healthful changes in personality and behaviour.

____________________ **4.** An insight therapy that emphasizes the recovery of unconscious conflicts, motives, and defences through techniques such as free association and transference.

____________________ **5.** A technique in which clients are urged to spontaneously express their thoughts and feelings with as little personal censorship as possible.

____________________ **6.** A technique for interpreting the symbolic meaning of dreams.

____________________ **7.** A therapist's attempts to explain the inner significance of a client's thoughts, feelings, memories, and behaviour.

____________________ **8.** A client's largely unconscious defensive manoeuvres intended to hinder the progress of therapy.

____________________ **9.** A process that occurs when clients start relating to their therapist in ways that mimic critical relationships in their lives.

____________________ **10.** An insight therapy that emphasizes providing a supportive emotional climate for clients who play a major role in determining the pace and direction of their therapy.

____________________ **11.** A therapy that emphasizes recognizing and changing negative thoughts and maladaptive beliefs.

____________________ **12.** The simultaneous treatment of several clients.

____________________ **13.** Therapies that involve the application of learning principles to change a client's maladaptive behaviours.

____________________ **14.** A behaviour therapy used to reduce anxiety responses through counterconditioning.

____________________ **15.** A behaviour therapy in which an aversive stimulus is paired with a stimulus that elicits an undesirable response.

____________________ **16.** Recovery from a disorder that occurs without formal treatment.

____________________ **17.** A behaviour therapy designed to improve interpersonal skills and that emphasizes shaping, modelling, and behavioural rehearsal.

______________ **18.** Therapies that use physiological interventions intended to reduce symptoms associated with psychological disorders.

______________ **19.** The treatment of mental disorders with drug therapy.

______________ **20.** Drugs that relieve tension, apprehension, and nervousness.

______________ **21.** Drugs that gradually reduce psychotic symptoms.

______________ **22.** A neurological disorder marked by chronic tremors and involuntary spastic movements.

______________ **23.** Drugs that gradually elevate mood and help bring people out of a depression.

______________ **24.** A chemical used to control mood swings in patients with bipolar disorder.

______________ **25.** A treatment in which electric shock is used to produce cortical seizure accompanied by convulsions.

______________ **26.** A medical institution specializing in thc provision of inpatient care for psychological disorders.

______________ **27.** Involves drawing ideas from two or more systems of therapy, instead of just committing to one system.

______________ **28.** Transferring the treatment of mental illness from inpatient institutions to community-based facilities that emphasize outpatient care.

______________ **29.** Occur when people's expectations lead them to experience some change, even though they receive a fake treatment.

______________ **30.** Occurs when people who score extremely high or low on some trait are measured a second time, and their new scores fall closer to the mean.

______________ **31.** Enhancing or depressing brain activity in specific regions of the cortex using a magnetic coil.

______________ **32.** The combination of verbal interventions and behaviour modification techniques.

Answers: 1. deep brain stimulation **2.** psychiatrists **3.** insight therapies **4.** psychoanalysis **5.** free association **6.** dream analysis **7.** interpretation **8.** resistance **9.** transference **10.** client-centred therapy **11.** cognitive therapy **12.** group therapy **13.** behaviour therapies **14.** systematic desensitization **15.** aversion therapy **16.** spontaneous remission **17.** social skills training **18.** biomedical therapies **19.** psychopharmacotherapy **20.** antianxiety drugs **21.** antipsychotic drugs **22.** tardive dyskinesia **23.** antidepressant drugs **24.** mood stabilizers **25.** electroconvulsive therapy (ECT) **26.** mental hospital **27.** eclecticism **28.** deinstitutionalization **29.** placebo effects **30.** regression toward the mean **31.** transcranial magnetic stimulation **32.** cognitive-behavioural techniques.

Review of Key People

Aaron Beck
Dorothea Dix
Keith Dobson
Hans Eysenck
Sigmund Freud
Les Greenberg
Donald Meichenbaum
Carl Rogers
Zindel Segal
Joseph Wolpe

______________ **1.** Developed a systematic treatment procedure, which he called psychoanalysis.

______________ **2.** The developer of client-centred therapy.

______________ **3.** Noted for his work in the development of cognitive therapy.

______________ **4.** His early research showed that insight therapies were ineffective.

______________ **5.** The developer of systematic desensitization.

______________ **6.** One of the early reformers who helped to establish North American mental hospitals.

______________ **7.** Studied the extent to which diversity training was provided in Canadian clinical psychology graduate programs.

______________ **8.** University of Waterloo psychologist who made important contributions to cognitive-behavioural therapy, including the use of *self-instructional training*.

______________ **9.** Developed emotions-focused couples therapy.

______________ **10.** Integrated ideas from cognitive therapy and mindfulness meditation.

Answers: **1.** Freud **2.** Rogers **3.** Beck **4.** Eysenck **5.** Wolpe **6.** Dix **7.** Dobson **8.** Meichenbaum **9.** Greenberg **10.** Segal.

Self-Quiz

1. Which of the following is not a true statement?
   a. People sometimes seek help for everyday problems.
   b. The two most common problems that lead to psychotherapy are sexual problems and depression.
   c. Persons seeking psychotherapy don't always have identifiable problems.
   d. Many people feel that seeking psychotherapy is an admission of personal weakness.

2. Which of the following mental health professionals must have medical degrees?
   a. psychiatric social workers
   b. clinical psychologists
   c. psychiatric nurses
   d. psychiatrists

3. Psychoanalysis is an example of what kind of approach to psychotherapy?
   a. insight
   b. learning
   c. biomedical
   d. a combination of learning and biomedical

4. When a client begins relating to his psychoanalyst as though she were his mother, we have an example of:
   a. transference
   b. free association
   c. catharsis
   d. restructuring

5. The major emphasis in client-centred therapy is to provide the client with
   a. interpretation of unconscious thinking
   b. cognitive restructuring
   c. feedback and clarification
   d. good advice

6. Which of the following is likely to be found in cognitive therapy?
   a. searching for negative illogical thinking
   b. dream interpretation
   c. free association
   d. an emphasis on childhood conflicts

7. Which therapists are likely to play the least active (most subtle) role in conducting therapy?
   a. behaviour therapists
   b. cognitive therapists
   c. group therapists
   d. psychoanalytic therapists

8. The newest category of antidepressants is called:
   a. monoamine oxidase inhibitors
   b. selective serotonin reuptake inhibitors
   c. serotonin and norepinephrine reuptake inhibitors
   d. tricyclic antidepressants

9. Which of the following therapies is most likely to see the symptom as the problem?
   a. psychoanalysis
   b. client-centred therapy
   c. cognitive therapy
   d. behaviour therapy

10. Which of the following therapies would be most likely to employ aversive conditioning?
    a. psychoanalysis
    b. behaviour therapy
    c. biomedical therapies
    d. client-centred therapy

11. Which of the following behaviour therapy techniques would most likely be used to treat a fear of flying?
    a. systematic desensitization
    b. aversive conditioning
    c. modelling
    d. biofeedback

12. Electroconvulsive therapy (ECT) is now primarily used to treat patients suffering from:
    a. anxiety
    b. phobias
    c. severe mood disorders
    d. psychosis

13. The Featured Study on treatment of depression revealed that which approach was most effective?
    a. drug therapy
    b. interpersonal therapy
    c. drug therapy + interpersonal therapy
    d. no approach was effective

14. Psychotherapists who combine several different approaches in their approach to therapy are said to be:
    a. enigmatic
    b. eclectic
    c. unspecific
    d. imaginative

15. The trend toward deinstitutionalization mainly came about because large mental institutions:
    a. were becoming too expensive
    b. were actually worsening the condition of many patients
    c. were overstaffed
    d. were becoming too political

16. Which of the following factors can affect the outcome of a treatment program?
    a. the efficacy of the treatment itself
    b. regression toward the mean
    c. placebo effects
    d. all of the above

17. Which of the following is NOT a biomedical therapy approach?
    a. psychosurgery
    b. drug therapy
    c. ECT
    d. cognitive-behavioural therapy

Answers: 1. b **2.** d **3.** a **4.** a **5.** c **6.** a **7.** c **8.** c **9.** d **10.** b **11.** a **12.** c **13.** c **14.** b **15.** b **16.** d **17.** d.

InfoTrac Keywords

Aversion Therapy
Deinstitutionalization
Electroconvulsive Therapy
Placebo Effects

Chapter Sixteen
SOCIAL BEHAVIOUR

Review of Key Ideas

1. Define *social psychology*.

1-1. Social psychology is the branch of psychology concerned with the way _______________ thoughts, feelings, and behaviours are influenced by _______________. The presence of others may be actual, _______________, or implied.

Answers: 1-1. individuals', others, imagined.

PERSON PERCEPTION: FORMING IMPRESSIONS OF OTHERS

2. Describe how various aspects of physical appearance may influence our impressions of others.

2-1. In general, we attribute _______________ personality characteristics to good-looking people. For example, we view attractive people as warmer, friendlier, better-adjusted, and more poised. We also believe that attractive people will have better lives, be better spouses, and be more _______________ in their careers. Research by Dion reveals that these perceptions are established (early in life/in adulthood).

2-2. For the most part, physical attractiveness has relatively little impact on judgments of honesty. People do tend to view baby-faced individuals (large eyes, rounded chin), however, as more _______________, helpless, and submissive than others. What about the notorious criminal, Baby-Faced Nelson? Well, recent data indicate that our *perception* of baby-faced people (is/is not) a good match for their actual traits.

2-3. Judgments of people's _______________ seem to be very important. Evidence suggests that perceptions of _______________ based on facial features are associated with objective measures of successful performance in important areas of life. Even _______________ judgments of others based on facial appearance can be quite accurate.

Answers: 2-1. positive (desirable, favourable), successful, early in life **2-2.** honest, is not **2-3.** faces, personality, instant.

3. Explain how schemas, stereotypes, and other factors contribute to subjectivity in person perception.

3-1. Briefly define the following:

(a) schemas:

(b) stereotypes:

3-2. Men are competitive; women are sensitive: These are stereotypes. Stereotypes are broad generalizations that tend to ignore the _______________ within a group. People who hold stereotypes do not necessarily assume that all members of a particular group have the same characteristics, but merely that there is an increased _______________ that they do.

3-3. Stereotypes might also produce a self-_______________ prophecy. For example, Word and colleagues showed that, when interviewing a black job applicant, white interviewers adopted a _______________ style (i.e., sitting farther away, making more speech errors, looking away). In a follow-up study, white job applicants interviewed with this nonimmediate style performed (less well/better) in the interview.

3-4. Whether probabilistic or absolute, schemas in general and stereotypes in particular direct our perception so that we tend to see the things we expect to see. Such selective perception results in an overestimation of the degree to which our expectations match actual events, a phenomenon referred to as _______________ correlation.

3-5. In one study, discussed in the text, subjects watched a videotape of a woman engaged in various activities (including drinking beer and listening to classical music). For one set of subjects, she was described as a librarian and for another as a waitress. What effect did the occupational labels have on subjects' recall of the woman's *activities*? Which of the following is/are true?

______ Subjects in the "librarian" condition tended to recall her listening to classical music.
______ Subjects in the "waitress" condition tended to recall her drinking beer.

3-6. The study just described illustrates subjectivity in person perception. The schemas, in this case the _______________ that we have about categories of people, affect how we perceive and what we remember.

Answers: 3-1. (a) clusters of ideas about people and events, (b) a type of schema; widely held beliefs about people based on group membership **3-2.** diversity (variability), probability
3-3. fulfilling, nonimmediate, less well **3-3.** illusory **3-5.** Both are true. **3-6.** stereotypes.

4. Explain the evolutionary perspective on bias in person perception.

4-1. How does one explain bias or prejudice in terms of evolution? To explain anything in terms of evolution, one assumes that the particular characteristic or trait had ________________ value in our evolutionary past. For example, the bias in favour of physical attractiveness might have signalled health, associated with ________________ potential in women and the ability to acquire ________________ in men. The stereotype of ____________-____________ individuals as submissive and honest could simply result from our adaptive reaction to infants.

4-2. Evolutionary theorists also assert that we needed a quick way to categorize people as friend or enemy or, in more technical terms, as members of our ________________ or members of the ________________.

4-3. The question still remains: How could prejudice and bias be adaptive? It must be clear that what was adaptive in our evolutionary past (is also/may not be) adaptive now. Nonetheless, from the point of view of evolutionary theory, cognitive mechanisms involving bias have been shaped by natural ________________.

Answers: 4-1. adaptive, reproductive, resources, baby-faced **4-2.** ingroup, outgroup **4-3.** may not be, selection.

ATTRIBUTION PROCESSES: EXPLAINING BEHAVIOUR

5. Explain what attributions are and why we make them.

5-1. Why are you reading this book? The search for causes of events and of our own and others' behaviour is termed ________________. For example, you might ________________ your reading behaviour to an upcoming test (or to personal interest, lust for knowledge, fear, etc.).

5-2. Attributions are inferences that people make about the ________________ of events and their own and others' behaviour.

5-3. Why do we make attributions? We seem to have a strong need to ________________ our experiences.

Answers: 5-1. attribution, attribute **5-2.** causes (origin, source) **5-3.** understand (explain).

6. Describe the distinction between internal and external attributions.

6-1. Which of the following involve internal and which external attributions? Label each sentence with an I or an E.

____ (a) He flunked because he's lazy.

____ (b) Our team lost because the officials were biased against us.

____ (c) The accident was caused by poor road conditions.

____ (d) He achieved by the sweat of his brow.

____ (e) Criminal behaviour is caused by poverty.

____ (f) His success is directly derived from his parents' wealth and influence.

Answers: 6-1. (a) I, (b) E, (c) E, (d) I, (e) E, (f) E.

7. Summarize Weiner's theory of attribution.

7-1. Weiner proposed that attributions are made, not only in terms of an internal–external dimension but also in terms of a stable–unstable dimension. Suppose that Sally makes a high score on an exam. She could attribute her score to her ability, an (internal/external) factor that is also (stable/unstable). If she attributed her success to her good mood, the attribution would be (internal/external) and (stable/unstable).

7-2. Or Sally may think she did well because these types of test are always easy, an (internal/external) and (stable/unstable) attribution. If she attributes her score to luck, the attribution would be (internal/external) and (stable/unstable).

Answers: 7-1. internal, stable, internal, unstable **7-2.** external, stable, external, unstable.

8. Describe several types of attributional bias and cultural variations in attributional tendencies.

8-1. Define or describe the following:

(a) fundamental attribution error:

(b) actor–observer bias:

(c) defensive attribution:

(d) self-serving bias:

8-2. Recent research has indicated that the attributional biases described above may not apply to all cultures. Since collectivist societies emphasize accomplishing the goals of the group over individual achievement, collectivist cultures are (less/more) likely to attribute others' behaviour to personal traits. In other words, people from collectivist cultures tend to be (less/more) prone to the fundamental attribution error.

8-3. Some evidence also indicates that people from collectivist societies would be more likely to attribute their successes to (the ease of a task/unusual ability). Similarly, they would be more likely to attribute their *failures* to (bad luck/lack of effort). Thus, in contrast with people from individualistic societies, people from collectivist cultures appear to be (less/more) prone to the self-serving bias.

Answers: 8-1. (a) the tendency for observers to attribute an individual's behaviour to *internal* rather than *external* factors, (b) the tendency for observers to attribute an actor's behaviour to internal rather than external factors, *and the tendency for actors to attribute their own behaviour to external causes* (Yes, there is overlap between these two concepts. The fundamental attribution error is part of the actor–observer bias.), (c) the tendency to attribute other people's misfortunes to internal causes; that is, the tendency to blame the victim, (d) the tendency to attribute our *successes* to internal factors and our *failures* to situational factors **8-2.** less, less **8-3.** the ease of a task, lack of effort, less.

CLOSE RELATIONSHIPS: LIKING AND LOVING

9. Summarize evidence on the role of physical attractiveness and similarity in attraction.

9-1. Physical attractiveness is the key determinant of romantic attraction for:

a. males

b. females

c. both males and females

9-2. The *matching hypothesis* asserts that people tend to date and marry others who are:

a. similar to them in attitudes and personality

b. approximately equal to them in physical attractiveness

c. both of the above

9-3. Do opposites really attract, or do we like people who are similar to us? An overwhelming amount of research supports the idea that we are attracted to people who are (similar to/ different from) us on several dimensions, especially in terms of attitudes and personality.

9-4. The similarity-attraction relationship extends to:

a. friendship

b. romantic relationships

c. both of the above

9-5. It is clear that similarity causes attraction: People are attracted to others who are similar. Does attraction also cause similarity? Some studies (also/do not) support this causal direction.

Answers: 9-1. c **9-2.** b **9-3.** similar to **9-4.** c **9-5.** also.

10. Summarize evidence on the role of similarity and reciprocity and romantic ideals in attraction.

10-1. We tend to like people who like us. We also tend to think that if we like others, they will like us. This is the principle of ________________ in attraction.

10-2. What do we get from reciprocal relationships? First, our friends frequently provide positive feedback that enhances the way we feel about ourselves, the self-________________ effect. Second, our friends may verify our own view of ourselves, the self-________________ effect.

10-3. In romantic relationships, people constantly evaluate their partners against various ideals. Studies have found that the *greater the difference* between people's perceptions of their partners and their ideals, the (more/less) satisfied they are with the relationship and the more likely it is to (continue/dissolve).

10-4. The perception of a partner is subjective, of course. People may exaggerate the good characteristics and overlook the bad. Some research has found that, among couples, individuals view their partners (more favourably/less favourably) than their partners view themselves. For example, suppose Jeff and Mary are a couple. Who would have the more favourable evaluation of Jeff? (Jeff/Mary)

10-5. Positive illusions about one's partner may make for a better relationship than will a cold view of reality. The happiest couples seem to be those who hold a reciprocated and (accurate/idealized) view of their partners.

Answers: 10-1. reciprocity **10-2.** enhancement, verification **10-3.** less, dissolve **10-4.** more favourably, Mary **10-5.** idealized.

11. Describe various distinctions regarding love, described by Berscheid and Hatfield and Sternberg.

11-1. Hatfield and Berscheid divide love into two types, the intense emotional and sexual feelings of ________________ love and the warm and tolerant affection of ________________ love.

11-2. Sternberg further divides companionate love into ________________, characterized by closeness and sharing, and ________________, an intention to maintain a relationship in the face of difficulties.

11-3. Research suggests that (passionate/companionate) love is a powerful motivational force that produces changes in people's thinking, emotion, and behaviour. But relationship stability is best predicted by ________________.

Answers: 11-1. passionate, companionate **11-2.** intimacy, commitment **11-3.** passionate, commitment.

12. Summarize the evidence on love as a form of attachment.

12-1. In Chapter 11 we discussed types of attachment styles between infants and their caregivers. What *general* conclusion did Hazen and Shaver reach concerning the association between types of infant attachment and the love relationships of adults?

12-2. Write the names of the three infant attachment styles next to the appropriate letters below.

S: ________________________

A–A: ________________________

A: ________________________

12-3. Using the letters from the previous question, identify the types of romantic relations predicted by the infant attachment styles.

____ As adults, these individuals tend to use casual sex as a way of getting physically close without the vulnerability of genuine intimacy and commitment.

____ These people experience more emotional highs and lows in their relationships, find conflict stressful, have more negative feelings after dealing with conflict.

____ These individuals easily develop close, committed, well-adjusted, long-lasting relationships.

12-4. Many now believe that adult attachment is best conceptualized with two dimensions: attachment ________________ (reflecting concerns about lovability and abandonment) and attachment ________________ (reflecting a lack of comfort with closeness and intimacy). Ultimately, ________________ types of adult attachment styles are yielded when high and low scores on the two dimensions are combined.

12-5. Adult attachment style is also related to patterns of sexuality. People with a secure attachment are (comfortable/uncomfortable) with their sexuality and (more/less) open to sexual exploration. Those with an ________________ attachment are more likely to consent to unwanted sexual acts and less likely to practice safe sex. Finally, those with an avoidant attachment are more likely to engage in ________________ sex and to use sex to manipulate a partner.

Answers: 12-1. The three types of infant-caretaker attachments (also described in Chapter 11) tend to predict the love relationships that children have as adults. **12-2.** secure, anxious–ambivalent, avoidant **12-3.** A, A–A, S **12-4.** anxiety, avoidance, four **12-5.** comfortable, more, anxious, casual.

13. Discuss cross-cultural research on romantic relationships and evolutionary analyses of mating patterns.

13-1. While there is considerable cross-cultural overlap in what the two sexes want in mates (e.g., kindness, intelligence, dependability), David Buss has found nearly universal differences as well. Buss's data indicate that ________________ want mates who can acquire resources that can be invested in children, while ________________ want mates who are beautiful, youthful, and in good health. These gender differences in mate preference appear to occur (in virtually all/only in Western) societies.

13-2. There are also differences among cultures in their views on the relationship between romantic love and marriage. The idea that one should be in love in order to marry is in large part an 18th-century invention of (Eastern/Western) culture. Arranged marriages, in which romantic love is less important, tend to be characteristic of (collectivist/individualist) societies.

13-3. A standard of attractiveness that has been found cross-culturally is facial ________________, which from an evolutionary point of view may be an index of health. Another standard of attractiveness that may transcend culture is women's ______________ -to-______________ ratio, which may be an index of reproductive potential.

13-4. In terms of mating preferences, men are generally more interested than women in seeking youthfulness and ________________ ________________ in their mates, while women are more interested than men in seeking traits such as ambition, social ________________, and financial potential in their mates.

13-5. Women's ________________ ________________ can also affect mating preferences. When they are most fertile, women prefer men who exhibit ________________ facial and bodily features, attractiveness, and dominance. And, men rate masculine males as more ________________ when their partners are in the fertile portion of their menstrual cycle.

Answers: 13-1. women, men, in virtually all **13-2.** Western, collectivist **13-3.** symmetry, waist, hip **13-4.** physical attractiveness, status **13-5.** menstrual cycle, masculine, threatening.

ATTITUDES: MAKING SOCIAL JUDGMENTS

14. Describe the components and dimensions of attitudes and correlates of attitude strength.

14-1. Do you favour gun control? Do you like expressionist art? Do you hate cottage cheese? Your answers would be *evaluations* and would also express your ________________ toward these objects of thought.

14-2. Attitudes are positive or negative ________________ of objects of thought. They may include three components: cognition (thought), affect (emotion), and behavioural predispositions. For example, people have attitudes toward cottage cheese. List the three possible components of attitudes next to the examples below.

________________ He likes cottage cheese.

________________ He eats cottage cheese.

________________ He thinks: "Cottage cheese seems kind of lumpy."

14-3. Attitudes also vary along various dimensions, as follows:

________________ The importance, vested interest, or knowledge about the attitude object.

________________ How easily the attitude comes to mind.

________________ The degree to which the attitude includes both positive and negative aspects.

14-4. Attitude strength is a function of several factors, including how ________________ the attitude is to the person, the extent to which the attitude involves a ________________ interest that directly affects them, and the degree of ________________ that they have about the attitude object.

Answers: 14-1. attitudes **14-2.** evaluations, affect, behaviour, cognition (Note that the components may be remembered as the ABCs of attitude.) **14-3.** strength, accessibility, ambivalence **14-4.** important, vested, information (knowledge).

15. Discuss the relations between attitudes and behaviour.

15-1. As LaPiere found in his travels with a Chinese couple, attitudes (are/are not) consistently good predictors of behaviour. One reason involves a failure to account for attitude ________________, the importance of the attitude for the person. In general, the stronger the attitude, the better it will predict ________________. Behaviour is also better predicted by attitudes that are highly ________________ and that are ________________ over time.

15-2. In addition, the actual situation is likely to present new information: possible embarrassment, pressure from others, the unanticipated pleasant or unpleasant aspects of the situation, and so on. In other words, the behavioural component is just a *predisposition* that may change as a function of norms or other constraints of the ________________.

Answers: 15-1. are not, strength, behaviour, accessible, stable **15-2.** situation.

16. Summarize evidence on source factors, message factors, and receiver factors that influence the process of persuasion.

16-1. If you are the *source* of a communication, the message giver:

(a) What factors mentioned in your text would you use to make yourself more *credible*? ________________ and ________________

(b) What else would you hope to emphasize about yourself? ____________________

16-2. With regard to *message* factors:

(a) Which is generally more effective, a one-sided message or a two-sided message? ________________

(b) In presenting your argument, should you use every argument that you can think of or emphasize just the stronger arguments? ________________

(c) Is simple repetition a good strategy, or should you say something just once? ________________

(d) If you repeat something often enough, people will come to believe it. What is the name of this effect? ________________

(e) Do fear appeals tend to work? _______ When? ________________

16-3. With regard to *receiver* factors in persuasive communications:

(a) If you know in advance that someone is going to attempt to persuade you on a particular topic, you will be (harder/easier) to persuade. This is the factor referred to as ________________.

(b) Resistance to persuasion is greater when an audience holds an attitude incompatible with the one being presented. In this case, the receiver will also tend to scrutinize arguments longer and with more skepticism, an effect referred to as ________________ bias.

(c) In addition, in part because they may be anchored in networks of other beliefs that may also require change, ________________ attitudes are more resistant to change.

Answers: 16-1. (a) expertise, trustworthiness, (b) likability (for example, by increasing your physical attractiveness or emphasizing your similarity with the message receiver) **16-2.** (a) In general, two-sided. (That's the kind of speech Mark Antony gave over the body of Caesar in Shakespeare's *Julius Caesar.*) (b) stronger only, (c) repetition (causes people to believe it's true, whether it is or isn't), (d) validity effect, (e) yes, *if* they arouse fear (and especially if the audience thinks the consequences are very unpleasant, likely to occur, and avoidable) **16-3.** (a) harder, forewarning (b) disconfirmation (c) stronger.

17. Discuss how learning processes can contribute to attitudes.

17-1. Following are examples that relate learning theory to attitude change. Indicate which type of learning—classical conditioning, operant conditioning, or observational learning—matches the example.

____________________ Ralph hears a speaker express a particular political attitude that is followed by thunderous applause. Thereafter, Ralph tends to express the same attitude.

____________________ Advertisers pair soft drinks (and just about any other product) with attractive models. The audience likes the models and develops a stronger liking for the product.

____________________ If you express an attitude that I like, I will agree with you, nod, say "mm-hmm," and so on. This will tend to strengthen your expression of that attitude.

Answers: 17-1. observational learning, classical conditioning, operant conditioning.

18. Explain how cognitive dissonance can account for the effects of counterattitudinal behaviour and effort justification.

(Dissonance is a truly complicated theory, but the following exercise should help. First read over the text, then see how you do on these questions. Here's a hint: Both problems that follow are contrary to commonsense ideas of reward and punishment; dissonance theory prides itself on making predictions contrary to these commonsense ideas. Item 18-1 indicates that we like behaviours accompanied by less, not more, reward; item 18-2 indicates that we like behaviours accompanied by more, not less, discomfort.)

18-1. Ralph bought a used car. However, the car uses a lot of gas, which he doesn't like because he strongly supports conserving energy. He rapidly concludes that conserving fuel isn't so important after all.

(a) Ralph has engaged in counterattitudinal behaviour. What were the two contradictory cognitions? (One is a thought about his *behaviour.* The other is a thought about an important *attitude.*)

(b) Suppose the car was a real beauty, a rare antique worth much more than the price paid. Alternatively, suppose that the car was only marginally worth what was paid for it. In which case would dissonance be stronger? In which case would the attitude about gas guzzling be more likely to change?

18-2. Suppose Bruce decides to join a particular club. One possible scenario is that (1) he must travel a great distance to attend, the club is very expensive, and he must give up much of his free time to become a member. Alternatively, suppose that (2) the travelling time is short, the club is inexpensive, and he need not give up any free time. In which case (1 or 2) will he tend to value his membership more, according to dissonance theory? Briefly, why?

Answers: 18-1. (a) I know I bought the car. I'm against the purchase of cars that waste gas. (b) The additional reward in the first situation produces less dissonance and will tend to leave Ralph's original attitude about gas consumption intact. Ralph's attitude about gas consumption will change more when there is less justification (in terms of the value of the car) for his action. As described in your text, we tend to have greater dissonance, and greater attitude change, when *less reward* accompanies our counterattitudinal behaviour. **18-2.** According to dissonance theory, he will value the membership more under alternative 1, even if the benefits of membership are slight, because people attempt to *justify the effort* expended in terms of the benefits received. (While dissonance is a genuine phenomenon with many of the characteristics that Festinger described in 1957, several other variables are operating, so it is difficult to predict when dissonance will occur.)

19. Relate self-perception theory and the elaboration likelihood model to attitude change.

19-1. At a cocktail party, Bruce eats caviar. When asked whether he likes caviar, he responds, "I'm eating it, so I guess I must like it." This example illustrates ____________-_______________ theory.

19-2. According to self-perception theory, people infer their attitudes by observing their own _______________. Thus, if people engage in a behaviour that is not accompanied by high rewards, they are likely to infer that they (enjoy/do not enjoy) the behaviour.

19-3. To illustrate the elaboration likelihood model: Suppose that you are to travel in Europe and must decide between two options: renting a car or travelling by train (on a Eurail pass). In the blanks below, indicate which persuasive route, central (C) or peripheral (P), is referred to in the examples.

____ On the basis of train brochures, showing apparently wealthy and dignified travellers dining in luxury on the train while viewing the Alps, you opt for the train.

____ Your travel agent is an expert who has advised many of your friends, and she strongly recommends that you take the train. You decide on the train.

____ A friend urges you to consider details you hadn't previously considered: traffic, waiting in line, additional cab fare, and so on. You seek additional information, and after weighing the relative expenses and conveniences for four travelling together, you decide to rent a car.

19-4. In the elaboration likelihood model, the route that is easier and that involves the least amount of thinking is the ________________ route. The route in which relevant information is sought out and carefully pondered is the ________________ route. Elaboration, which involves thinking about the various complexities of the situation, is more likely to occur when the ________________ route is used.

19-5. Elaboration leads to (more enduring/transient) changes in attitudes. In addition, elaboration (i.e., the more central route) is (more/less) likely to predict behaviour.

Answers: 19-1. self-perception **19-2.** behaviour, enjoy **19-3.** P, P, C **19-4.** peripheral, central, central **19-5.** more enduring, more.

CONFORMITY AND OBEDIENCE: YIELDING TO OTHERS

20. Summarize research on the determinants of conformity.

20-1. Briefly summarize the general procedure and results of the Asch line-judging studies.

20-2. Suppose there are six accomplices, one real subject, and that one of the accomplices dissents from the majority. What effect will this "dissenter" have on conformity by the real subject?

20-3. Several factors affect conformity, as you may have observed. For example, people are more likely to conform in ________________ situations, when the "correct" answer is very unclear.

Answers: 20-1. Subjects were asked to judge which of three lines matched a standard line, a judgment that was actually quite easy to make. Only one of the subjects was a real subject, however; the others were accomplices of the experimenter, who gave wrong answers on key trials. The result was that a majority of the real subjects tended to conform to the wrong judgments of the majority on at least some trials. **20-2.** Conformity will be dramatically reduced, to about one-fourth the frequency without a dissenter. **20-3.** ambiguous.

21. Describe the Featured Study on obedience to authority and the ensuing controversy generated by Milgram's research.

21-1. Two individuals at a time participated in Milgram's initial study, but only one was a real subject. The other "subject" was an accomplice of the experimenter, an actor. By a rigged drawing of slips of paper, the real subject became the ________________, and the accomplice became the _________________. There were a total of ______ subjects, or teachers, in the initial study.

21-2. The experimenter strapped the learner into a chair and stationed the teacher at an apparatus from which he could, supposedly, deliver electric shocks to the learner. The teacher was to start at 15 volts, and each time the learner made a mistake, the teacher was supposed to _________________ the level of shock by 15 volts—up to a level of 450 volts.

21-3. What percentage of the subjects continued to obey instructions, thereby increasing the shock all the way up to 450 volts? ______%

21-4. What is the major conclusion to be drawn from this study? Why are the results of interest?

21-5. As you might imagine, Milgram's studies on obedience were controversial, producing both detractors and defenders. Following are summaries of the objections, involving both *generality* and *ethics*, followed by possible counterarguments. Complete the counterarguments by selecting the appropriate alternatives.

(a) "Subjects in an experiment expect to obey an experimenter, so the results don't generalize to the real world."

The flaw in this argument, according to Milgram's defenders, is that in many aspects of the real world, including the military and business worlds, obedience (is not/is also) considered appropriate. So, Milgram's results (do/do not) generalize to the real world.

(b) "Milgram's procedure, by which subjects were allowed to think that they had caved in to commands to harm an innocent victim, was potentially emotionally damaging to the subjects. Milgram's experiment was unethical."
Milgram's defenders assert that the brief distress experienced by the subjects was relatively (slight/great), in comparison with the important insights that emerged.

Answers: 21-1. teacher, learner, 40 **21-2.** increase **21-3.** 65 **21-4.** The major conclusion is that ordinary people will tend to obey an authority, even when their obedience could result in considerable harm (and perhaps even death) to others. The result is of interest because it suggests that such obedience, as occurs in war atrocities (e.g., in World War II, at Mi Lai in Vietnam, in Cambodia, Rwanda, Yugoslavia, and throughout history), may not be due so much to the evil *character* of the participants as to pressures in the *situation*. (Milgram's results are also of interest because most people would not expect them: Even psychiatric experts predicted that fewer than 1% of the subjects would go all the way to 450 volts.) **21-5.** (a) is also, do (b) slight. (Many psychologists today share the critics' concerns, however, and the study has not been replicated since the 1970s.)

22. Discuss cultural variations in conformity and obedience.

22-1. As with other cross-cultural comparisons, replications in other countries yield some similarities and some differences. Indicate true (T) or false (F) for the following statements.

____ The obedience effect found by Milgram seems to be a uniquely North American phenomenon.

____ In replications of the Milgram studies in several European countries, obedience levels were even higher than those in North America.

____ Replications of the Asch line-judging studies have found that cultures that emphasize collectivism are more conforming than are those that emphasize individualism.

Answers: 22-1. F, T, T.

BEHAVIOUR IN GROUPS: JOINING WITH OTHERS

23. Discuss the nature of groups and the bystander effect.

23-1. The word *group* doesn't have the same meaning for social psychologists as it does for everyone else. As I look out across my social psychology class on a Tuesday morning, I might say to myself, "Hm, quite a large group we have here today." Actually, my class is *not* a group in social psychological terms because it lacks one, and perhaps two, of the essential characteristics of a group. A group consists of two or more individuals who (a) ________________ and (b) are ________________.

23-2. Which of the following are groups, as defined by social psychologists?

____ a husband and wife

____ the board of directors of a corporation

____ a sports team

____ spectators at an athletic event

____ shoppers at a mall

23-3. What is the bystander effect?

23-4. Why does the bystander effect occur? In part because the presence of onlookers not doing anything produces an ________________ situation (no one seems to be upset, so maybe it's not an emergency). In addition, the presence of others causes a ________________ of responsibility (we're all responsible, or someone else will do it).

Answers: 23-1. (a) interact (b) interdependent **23-2.** The first three are groups, and the last two are not. **23-3.** When people are in groups (or at least in the presence of others), they are less likely to help than when they are alone. Or the greater the number of onlookers in an emergency, the less likely any one of them is to assist the person in need. **23-4.** ambiguous, diffusion.

24. Summarize evidence on group productivity, including social loafing.

24-1. Individual productivity in large groups is frequently less than it is in small groups. Two factors contribute to this decreased productivity: a loss of ________________ among workers in larger groups (e.g., efforts of one person interfere with those of another) and decreased ________________ resulting from *social loafing*.

24-2. Social loafing is the reduction in ________________ expended by individuals working in groups compared to people working alone.

24-3. Social loafing doesn't always occur. People high in ________________ ________________ are less likely to engage in loafing than are those who score high on ________________ and ________________. In some situations in which members are convinced that individuals' personal contributions to productivity are readily ________________ and when group norms encourage ________________ and personal involvement, social loafing is (less/more) likely to occur. Social loafing is also less frequent in more cohesive groups. Social loafing is less common in (collectivist/individualistic) societies, for example.

Answers: 24-1. efficiency (coordination), effort **24-2.** effort **24-3.** achievement motivation, agreeableness, conscientiousness, identifiable, productivity, less, collectivist.

25. Describe group polarization and groupthink.

25-1. This problem should help you understand the concept of group polarization. Suppose that a group of five corporate executives meet to decide whether to *raise* or *lower* the cost of their product, and by how much. Before they meet as a group, the decisions of the five executives (expressed as a percentage) are as follows: +32%, +17%, +13%, +11%, and +2%. After they meet as a group, which of the following is most likely to be the result? Assume that group polarization occurs.

a. +30%, +10%, +3%, +3%, and +2%

b. +32%, +19%, +19%, +15%, and +13%

c. -3%, -1%, 0%, +9%, and +11%

d. -10%, -7%, -3%, 0%, and +2%

25-2. What is group polarization?

25-3. Have you ever been in a group when you thought to yourself, "This is a stupid idea, but my best friends seem to be going along with it, so I won't say anything." If so, you may have been in a group afflicted with groupthink. Groupthink is characterized by, among other things, an intense pressure to ________________ to group opinions accompanied by very low tolerance for dissent.

25-4. Groups afflicted with groupthink tend to ignore important information. Members are under pressure to avoid presenting conflicting views, and they (underestimate/overestimate) the unanimity of the group.

25-5. Recent evidence has also found that group members tend not to pool information. That is, they tend to:

a. discuss information that is commonly known among members

b. explore information that is unique to individual members

25-6. According to Janis, the major cause of groupthink is high group ________________, the group spirit or attraction that members have for the group. Other factors that may contribute to groupthink include *isolation*, (directive/nondirective) leadership, and *stress* accompanying the decision process.

25-7. Much of the support for groupthink consists of (laboratory studies/retrospective accounts). The theory is difficult to test in formal experiments, but it is a fascinating viewpoint that will undoubtedly inspire continued research.

25-8. Despite the phenomena of polarization and groupthink, groups have their advantages. For example, groups exhibit greater accuracy than ________________ on person perception tasks, and teams of physicians generate better ________________ than individual physicians. Similarly, teams of students perform better than individual students on ________________ tests, and groups are better than individuals in solving complicated logic problems.

Answers: 25-1. b **25-2.** Group polarization is the tendency for a group's decision to shift toward a *more extreme position* in the direction that individual members are *already leaning*. **25-3.** conform **25-4.** overestimate **25-5.** a **25-6.** cohesiveness, directive **25-7.** retrospective accounts **25-8.** individuals, diagnoses, academic.

SOCIAL NEUROSCIENCE

26. Define *social neuroscience*, and describe how it has been applied to social psychological phenomena.

26-1. Social neuroscience is an approach to research and theory in social psychology that ________________ models of neuroscience and social psychology to study the mechanisms of ________________ ________________.

26-2. One of the major topics within social neuroscience has been ______________ relations. For example, Cunningham studied the role of the ____________ in people's response to black and white faces. White participants showed greater activation in the amygdala in response to ______________ faces, especially under (lengthy/brief) presentation times. This was particularly true for participants previously judged to be ______________ biased.

Answers: 26-1. integrates, social behaviour **26-2.** ethnic, amygdala, black, brief, racially.

PUTTING IT IN PERSPECTIVE

27. Explain how the chapter highlighted three of the text's unifying themes.

27-1. This chapter again illustrates psychology's commitment to empirical research. When people hear the results of psychological studies, they frequently conclude that the research just confirms common sense. Dispute this view by listing and describing *at least one study* with results that are not predictable from commonsense assumptions.

27-2. Cross-cultural differences and similarities also reflect one of the unifying themes. People conform, obey, attribute, and love throughout the world, but the manner and extent to which they do so are affected by cultural factors. Important among these factors is the degree to which a culture has an ________________ or ________________ orientation.

27-3. Finally, the chapter provides several illustrations of the way in which our view of the world is highly subjective. For example, we tend to make ability and personality judgments based on people's physical ________________; see what we expect to see as a result of the cognitive structures, termed social ________________; distort judgments of physical lines based on pressures to ________________; and make foolish decisions when we become enmeshed in the group phenomenon, known as ________________.

Answers: 27-1. This chapter has described at least three studies that defy the predictions of common sense or of experts. (1) Concerning *Milgram's studies*, psychiatrists incorrectly predicted that fewer than 1% of the subjects would go to 450 volts. (2) Results from *cognitive dissonance* studies are frequently the opposite of common sense. For example, common sense would suggest that the more people are paid, the more they would like the tasks for which they receive payment; dissonance researchers found that the opposite is true; people paid *more* liked the tasks *less*. (3) Common sense might predict that the larger the number of people who see someone in need of help, the more likely any one is to offer help. Research on the *bystander effect* consistently finds the opposite result. **27-2.** individualistic, collectivistic **27-3.** attractiveness (appearance), schemas, conform, groupthink.

PERSONAL APPLICATION * UNDERSTANDING PREJUDICE

28. Relate person perception processes and attributional bias to prejudice.

28-1. Prejudice is a negative ________________ toward others based on group membership. Like other attitudes, prejudice may include affective, ________________, and behavioural components.

28-2. The cognitive component of prejudice may be composed of schemas about groups. This type of schema is frequently referred to as a ________________.

28-3. Stereotypes are part of the *subjectivity* of person perception. People tend to see what they expect to see, and when stereotypes are activated, people see and remember information that (is/is not) congruent with their stereotype.

28-4. Stereotypes are highly accessible and frequently activated automatically, so that even though people reject prejudiced ideas, stereotypes (cannot/may still) influence behaviour.

28-5. Our *attributional biases* are also likely to maintain or augment prejudice. For example, observers tend to attribute success in men to (ability/luck) but success in women to (ability/luck).

28-6. People may also attribute other people's behaviour to internal traits, the bias referred to as the ________________ attribution error.

28-7. When people experience adversity such as prejudice, we are also likely to attribute their misfortune to character flaws, a predisposition referred to as defensive attribution or ________________ ________________.

Answers: 28-1. attitude, cognitive **28-2.** stereotype **28-3.** is **28-4.** may still **28-5.** ability, luck **28-6.** fundamental **28-7.** victim blaming.

29. Relate principles of attitude formation and group processes to prejudice.

29-1. Attitudes are to a large extent learned. For example, if someone makes a disparaging remark about an ethnic group that is followed by approval, the approval is likely to function as a ________________ that increases that person's tendency to make similar remarks in the future. This is the learning process known as ________________ ________________. Or, if someone simply *observes* another person making such a remark, the observer may acquire the tendency to make similar remarks through the process known as ________________ ________________.

29-2. Explicit prejudice involves consciously held negative evaluations of an outgroup, whereas ________________ prejudice involves negative associations to an outgroup that are activated ________________, without control or intention.

29-3. Ingroup members view themselves as different from the outgroup in several ways. First, they tend to see their group as superior to outgroups, a tendency known as ________________. In addition, they see themselves as relatively diverse or heterogeneous and outgroup members as relatively ________________.

29-4. The tendency for ingroup members to see outgroup members as highly (dissimilar/similar) to one another is known as the illusion of outgroup ________________.

29-5. Ingroup favouritism is something that doesn't go away. Prejudice clearly exists in modern societies, but it tends to be of the more (subtle/blatant) form. By one estimate, only about _____% of people display the more extreme form of prejudice involving intense hatred and aggression.

Answers: 29-1. reinforcer, operant conditioning, observational learning (modelling) **29-2.** implicit, automatically **29-3.** ethnocentrism, homogeneous **29-4.** similar, homogeneity **29-5.** subtle, 10.

CRITICAL THINKING APPLICATION * WHOM CAN YOU TRUST? ANALYZING CREDIBILITY AND SOCIAL INFLUENCE TACTICS

30. Discuss some useful criteria for evaluating credibility and some standard social influence strategies.

30-1. We are constantly bombarded with information designed to persuade. Sometimes we are persuaded and happy about it, and sometimes we regret the outcome. How can we resist attempts at manipulation? Two tactics are discussed in this section: evaluating the ________________ of the source and learning about several widely used social ________________ strategies.

30-2. To assess credibility, consider these questions: Do they have a ________________ interest? If so, information they provide may not be objective. What are the source's ________________? Although degrees do not certify competence, they may indicate relevant training.

30-3. Is the information consistent with ________________ views on the issue? If not, one should ponder why others haven't arrived at the same conclusion. Finally, what was the ________________ of analysis used? One should be particularly skeptical if the source relies on anecdotes or focuses on small inconsistencies in accepted beliefs.

30-4. In addition, learn to recognize social influence strategies. Following are several scenarios. Identify each with one of the four strategies discussed: *foot-in-the-door*, *reciprocity*, *lowball*, or *scarcity*.

__________________ Scenario 1: Mail solicitation for a magazine subscription. "Enclosed is a packet of seeds, free of charge, just for you. We hope you enjoy the beautiful flowers they produce! Also, you will benefit from subscribing to *Outdoor Beauty* magazine. We've enclosed a free copy."

__________________ Scenario 2: Newspaper ad. "This weekend only—mammoth blowout car deals!! These beauties will go fast!!!! Don't miss this once-in-a-lifetime opportunity!!"

__________________ Scenario 3: A college development office calling alumni. First week: "We don't care about the amount, perhaps $5, just so that we can ensure full participation." You commit to $5. Next week: "Would you become one of our member donors with a contribution of $100?"

__________________ Scenario 4: On the phone with a wholesale camera salesman. "Yes, we do have the XXY Camera at $499.00 plus tax. We'll ship that this afternoon. Now, did you want the new lens or the old lens with that? The new lens would be an additional $99. Did you want the carrying case also?" (Your assumption was that the so-called extras were included in the original price.)

__________________ Scenario 5: Mail solicitation. First week: "Would you answer this brief survey for us? There are only 12 questions." Next week: "Thanks for responding to our survey! We desperately need money for this worthwhile (candidate, school, charity, etc.)."

__________________ Scenario 6: At the car dealer. "We've got a deal, $22,900 plus tax! You'll be very happy with this car! Let me check with my manager to see if that price includes the radio and CD player." (Fifteen minutes pass while the salesman supposedly checks.) "Well, I tried, but the manager won't budge. Fortunately, it's not much additional cost!"

Answers: 30-1. credibility, influence **30-2.** vested, credentials **30-3.** conventional, method **30-4.** reciprocity, scarcity, foot-in-the-door, lowball, foot-in-the-door, lowball.

Review of Key Terms

Attitudes
Attributions
Bystander effect
Channel
Cognitive dissonance
Collectivism
Commitment
Companionate love
Conformity
Defensive attribution
Discrimination
Ethnocentrism
External attributions
Foot-in-the-door technique
Fundamental attribution error
Group
Group cohesiveness
Group polarization
Groupthink
Illusory correlation
Individualism
Ingroup
Internal attributions
Interpersonal attraction
Intimacy
Lowball technique
Matching hypothesis
Message
Prejudice
Receiver
Obedience
Outgroup
Passionate love
Person perception
Reciprocity
Reciprocity norm
Self-serving bias
Social loafing
Social neuroscience
Social psychology
Social schemas
Source
Stereotypes

____________________ **1.** The branch of psychology concerned with the way individuals' thoughts, feelings, and behaviours are influenced by others.

____________________ **2.** The process of forming impressions of others.

____________________ **3.** Clusters of ideas about categories of social events and people, which we use to organize the world around us.

____________________ **4.** Widely held beliefs that people have certain characteristics because of their membership in a particular group.

____________________ **5.** Error that occurs when we estimate that we have encountered more confirmations of an association between social traits than we have actually seen.

____________________ **6.** Inferences that people draw about the causes of events, others' behaviour, and their own behaviour.

____________________ **7.** Attributing the causes of behaviour to personal dispositions, traits, abilities, and feelings.

____________________ **8.** Attributing the causes of behaviour to situational demands and environmental constraints.

____________________ **9.** The tendency of an observer to favour internal attributions in explaining the behaviour of an actor.

____________________ **10.** The tendency to blame victims for their misfortune so that we feel less likely to be victimized in a similar way.

____________________ **11.** The tendency to attribute our positive outcomes to personal factors and our negative outcomes to situational factors.

____________________ **12.** Liking or positive feelings toward another.

____________________ **13.** Getting people to agree to a small request to increase the chances that they will agree to a larger request later.

____________________ **14.** The observation that males and females of approximately equal physical attractiveness are likely to select each other as partners.

____________________ **15.** Liking those who show that they like us.

____________________ **16.** A complete absorption in another person that includes tender sexual feelings and the agony and ecstasy of intense emotion.

____________________ **17.** A warm, trusting, tolerant affection for another whose life is deeply intertwined with one's own.

____________________ **18.** Warmth, closeness, and sharing in a relationship.

______________________ **19.** The intent to maintain a relationship in spite of the difficulties and costs that may arise.

______________________ **20.** Positive or negative evaluation of objects of thought; may include cognitive, behavioural, and emotional components.

______________________ **21.** The person who sends a communication.

______________________ **22.** The person to whom the message is sent.

______________________ **23.** The information transmitted by the source.

______________________ **24.** The medium through which the message is sent.

______________________ **25.** The rule that we should pay back when we receive something from others; may be used in an influence strategy.

______________________ **26.** A tendency to evaluate people in outgroups less favourably than those in one's ingroup.

______________________ **27.** Situation that exists when related cognitions are inconsistent.

______________________ **28.** Yielding to real or imagined social pressure.

______________________ **29.** Involves getting someone to commit to an attractive deal before its hidden costs are revealed.

______________________ **30.** A form of compliance that occurs when people follow direct commands, usually from someone in a position of authority.

______________________ **31.** Involves putting group goals ahead of personal goals and defining one's identity in terms of the group one belongs to.

______________________ **32.** Involves putting personal goals ahead of group goals and defining one's identity in terms of personal attributes rather than group memberships.

______________________ **33.** Two or more individuals who interact and are interdependent.

______________________ **34.** The apparent paradox that people are less likely to provide needed help when they are in groups than when they are alone.

______________________ **35.** A reduction in effort by individuals when they work together, as compared to when they work by themselves.

______________________ **36.** Situation that occurs when group discussion strengthens a group's dominant point of view and produces a shift toward a more extreme decision in that direction.

______________________ **37.** Phenomenon that occurs when members of a cohesive group emphasize concurrence at the expense of critical thinking in arriving at a decision.

______________________ **38.** The group one belongs to and identifies with.

______________________ **39.** People who are not a part of the ingroup.

______________________ **40.** The strength of the liking relationships linking group members to each other and to the group itself.

______________________ **41.** A negative attitude held toward members of a group.

______________________ **42.** Behaving differently, usually unfairly, toward the members of a group.

______________________ **43.** Integrates models of neuroscience and social psychology to study social behaviour.

Answers: 1. social psychology **2.** person perception **3.** social schemas **4.** stereotypes **5.** illusory correlation **6.** attributions **7.** internal attributions **8.** external attributions **9.** fundamental attribution error **10.** defensive attribution **11.** self-serving bias **12.** interpersonal attraction **13.** foot-in-the-door technique **14.** matching hypothesis **15.** reciprocity **16.** passionate love **17.** companionate love **18.** intimacy **19.** commitment **20.** attitudes **21.** source **22.** receiver **23.** message **24.** channel **25.** reciprocity norm **26.** ethnocentrism **27.** cognitive dissonance **28.** conformity **29.** lowball technique **30.** obedience

31. collectivism **32.** individualism **33.** group **34.** bystander effect **35.** social loafing **36.** group polarization **37.** groupthink **38.** ingroup **39.** outgroup **40.** group cohesiveness **41.** prejudice **42.** discrimination **43.** social neuroscience.

Review of Key People

Solomon Asch	Leon Festinger	Irving Janis
Ellen Berscheid	Elaine Hatfield	Stanley Milgram
David Buss	Cindy Hazen & Phillip Shaver	Bernard Weiner
John Cacioppo	Fritz Heider	Mark Zanna
William Cunningham		

____________________ **1.** Was the first to describe the crucial dimension along which we make attributions; developed balance theory.

____________________ **2.** Did research on infant–caregiver attachment patterns as predictors of adult romantic relationships.

____________________ **3.** With Hatfield, did research describing two types of romantic love: passionate and companionate.

____________________ **4.** Originator of the theory of cognitive dissonance.

____________________ **5.** Devised the "line-judging" procedure in pioneering investigations of conformity.

____________________ **6.** In a series of "fake shock" experiments, studied the tendency to obey authority figures.

____________________ **7.** Developed the concept of groupthink.

____________________ **8.** Under the name of Walster, did early study on dating and physical attractiveness; with Berscheid, described types of romantic love.

____________________ **9.** Concluded that attribution has not only an internal–external dimension but a stable–unstable dimension.

____________________ **10.** Proposed an evolutionary view of attraction; did cross-cultural research on priorities in mate selection.

____________________ **11.** Studied the "self-fulfilling prophecy."

____________________ **12.** Helped to create the social neuroscience field.

____________________ **13.** Studied the neuroscientific basis of prejudice.

Answers: 1. Heider **2.** Hazen & Shaver **3.** Berscheid **4.** Festinger **5.** Asch **6.** Milgram **7.** Janis **8.** Hatfield **9.** Weiner **10.** Buss **11.** Zanna **12.** Cacioppo **13.** Cunningham.

Self-Quiz

1. Which of the following characteristics do we tend to attribute to physically attractive people?
a. low intelligence
b. friendliness
c. unpleasantness
d. coldness

2. Cognitive structures that guide our perceptions of people and events are termed:
a. attributions
b. stigmata
c. schemas
d. concepts

3. Inferences that we make about the causes of our own and others' behaviour are termed:
   a. attributions
   b. stigmata
   c. schemas
   d. concepts

4. Bruce performed very well on the examination, which he attributed to native ability and hard work. Which attributional bias does this illustrate?
   a. the fundamental attribution error
   b. the actor–observer bias
   c. the self-serving bias
   d. illusory correlation

5. According to this viewpoint, men emphasize physical attractiveness in mate selection, while women emphasize the ability to acquire resources. Which theory does this describe?
   a. evolutionary theory
   b. cognitive dissonance
   c. sexual propensity theory
   d. attribution theory

6. Which of the following could be an example of the fundamental attribution error?
   a. Ralph described himself as a failure.
   b. Ralph thought that the reason he failed was that he was sick that day.
   c. Jayne said Ralph failed because the test was unfair.
   d. Sue explained Ralph's failure in terms of his incompetence and laziness.

7. Which influence technique involves asking for a small request in order to increase the likelihood of the target complying with a larger request later?
   a. foot-in-the-door
   b. feigned scarcity
   c. reciprocity norm
   d. lowball

8. Which of the following is, in general, likely to reduce the persuasiveness of a message?
   a. The receiver's viewpoint is already fairly close to that of the message.
   b. The receiver has been forewarned about the message.
   c. A two-sided appeal is used.
   d. The source is physically attractive.

9. Subjects in Group A are paid $1 for engaging in a dull task. Subjects in Group B are paid $20 for the same task. Which theory would predict that Group A subjects would enjoy the task more?
   a. balance
   b. cognitive dissonance
   c. reinforcement theory
   d. observational learning

10. In making a decision, you rely on the opinion of experts and the behaviour of your best friends. According to the elaboration likelihood model, which route to persuasion have you used?
    a. central
    b. peripheral
    c. attributional
    d. 66

11. Which of the following is the best statement of conclusion concerning Milgram's classic study involving the learner, teacher, and ostensible shock?
    a. Under certain circumstances, people seem to enjoy the opportunity to be cruel to others.
    b. People have a strong tendency to obey an authority even if their actions may harm others.
    c. The more people there are who observe someone in need of help, the less likely anyone is to help.
    d. Aggression seems to be a more potent force in human nature than had previously been suspected.

12. Which of the following is most likely to function as a group?
a. shoppers at a mall
b. the audience in a theatre
c. the board of trustees of a college
d. passengers in an airplane

13. Someone witnesses a car accident. In which of the following cases is that individual most likely to stop and render assistance?
a. Only she saw the accident.
b. She and one other individual saw the accident.
c. She and 18 others saw the accident.
d. The other observers are pedestrians.

14. Suppose the original decisions of members of a group are represented by the following numbers in a group polarization study: 3, 3, 4, 4, 6. The range of numbers possible in the study is from 0 to 9. Which of the following possible shifts in decisions would demonstrate polarization?
a. 2, 3, 3, 4, 5
b. 7, 7, 6, 5, 5
c. 5, 4, 0, 2, 3
d. 9, 9, 7, 7, 5

15. According to Janis, what is the major cause of groupthink?
a. strong group cohesion
b. diffusion of responsibility
c. the tendency of group members to grandstand
d. group conflict

16. The research in which white interviewers interacted with black job candidates in a way that was less personal than how white job candidates were interviewed demonstrated:
a. the self-fulfilling prophecy
b. the fundamental attribution error
c. diffusion of responsibility
d. the reciprocity norm

17. The Stanford prison experiment demonstrated the influence of:
a. prejudice
b. implicit racism
c. attributional biases
d. social roles

18. Prejudice which is hidden or "kept underground" has been termed:
a. explicit
b. overt
c. implicit
d. direct

Answers: 1. b **2.** c **3.** a **4.** c **5.** a **6.** d **7.** a **8.** b **9.** b **10.** b **11.** b **12.** c **13.** a **14.** a **15.** a **16.** a **17.** d **18.** c.

InfoTrac Keywords

Attitudes
Attributions
Cognitive Dissonance
Discrimination
Groupthink
Self-serving Bias
Stereotype

Appendix B
STATISTICAL METHODS

Review of Key Ideas

1. Describe several ways to use frequency distributions and graphs to organize numerical data.

1-1. Identify the following methods that are commonly used to present numerical data.

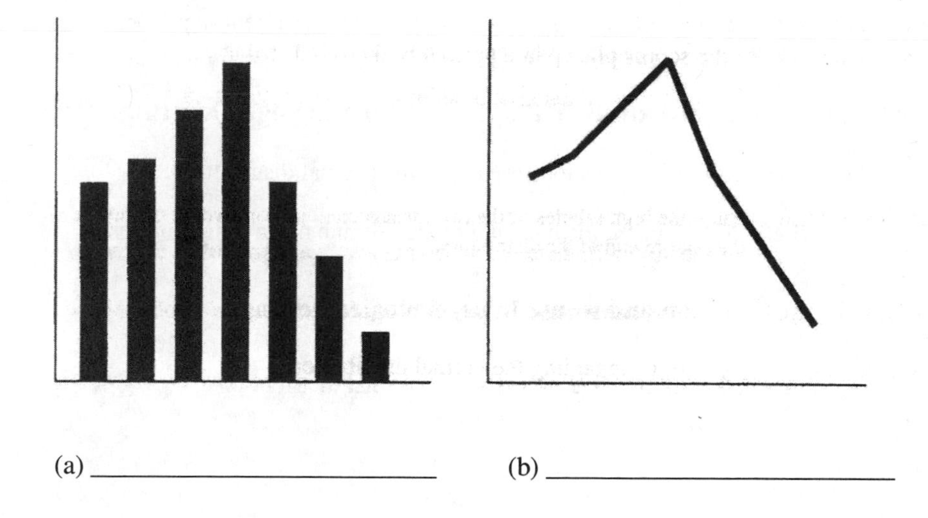

(a) ______________________ (b) ______________________

1-2. What data are usually plotted along the:

(a) horizontal axis?

(b) vertical axis?

Answers: 1-1. (a) histogram, (b) frequency polygon **1-2.** (a) the possible scores, (b) the frequency of each score.

2. Describe the measures of central tendency and variability discussed in the text.

2-1. Tell which measure of central tendency (the mean, median, or mode) would be most useful in the following situations.

(a) Which measure would be best for analyzing the salaries of all workers in a small, low-paying print shop that includes two high-salaried managers? Explain your answer.

(b) Which measure would tell us the most common shoe size for men?

(c) Which measure would be best for pairing players at a bowling match, using their individual past scores, so that equals play against equals?

(d) Where do most of the scores pile up in a positively skewed distribution?

Answers: 2-1. (a) the median, because the high salaries of the two management persons would distort the mean, (b) the mode, (c) the mean, (d) at the bottom end of the distribution.

3. Describe the normal distribution and its use in psychological testing.

3-1. Answer the following questions regarding the normal distribution.

(a) Where do the mean, median, and mode fall in a normal distribution?

(b) What is the unit of measurement in a normal distribution?

(c) Where are most of the scores located in a normal distribution?

(d) Approximately what percentage of scores falls above 2 standard deviations in a normal distribution?

(e) If your percentile ranking on the SAT was 84, what would your SAT score be? (See Figure B.7 in the text.)

Answers: 3-1. (a) at the centre, (b) the standard deviation, (c) around the mean (plus or minus 1 standard deviation), (d) 2.3%, (e) 600 (approximately).

4. Explain how the magnitude and direction of a correlation is reflected in scatter diagrams and how correlation is related to predictive power.

4-1. Answer the following questions about the magnitude and direction of a correlation, as reflected in scattergrams.

(a) Where do the data points fall in a scattergram that shows a perfect correlation?

(b) What happens to the data points in a scattergram when the magnitude of correlation decreases?

(c) What does a high negative correlation indicate?

4-2. Answer the following questions regarding the predictive power of correlations.

(a) How does one compute the coefficient of determination?

(b) What does the coefficient of determination tell us?

(c) What could we say if the sample study used in the text showed a correlation of -.50 between SAT scores and time watching television?

Answers: 4-1. (a) in a straight line (b) They scatter away from a straight line. (c) High scores on one variable (X) are accompanied by low scores on the other variable (Y). **4-2.** (a) by squaring the correlation coefficient, (b) It indicates the percentage of variation in one variable that can be predicted based on the other variable. (c) Knowledge of TV viewing allows one to predict 25% of the variation on SAT scores (.50 x .50 = .25).

5. Explain how the null hypothesis is used in hypothesis testing, and relate it to statistical significance.

5-1. Answer the following questions regarding the null hypothesis and statistical significance.

(a) In the sample study correlating SAT scores and television viewing, the findings supported the null hypothesis. What does this mean?

(b) What level of significance do most researchers demand as a minimum before rejecting the null hypothesis?

(c) What is the probability of making an error when a researcher rejects the null hypothesis at the .01 level of significance?

Answers: 5-1. (a) We cannot conclude that there is a significant negative correlation between SAT scores and television viewing. (b) the .05 level (c) 1 in 100.

Review of Key Terms

Coefficient of determination
Correlation coefficient
Descriptive statistics
Frequency distribution
Frequency polygon
Histogram
Inferential statistics
Mean
Median
Mode
Negatively skewed distribution
Normal distribution
Null hypothesis
Percentile score
Positively skewed distribution
Scatter diagram
Standard deviation
Statistics
Statistical significance
Variability

______________ **1.** The use of mathematics to organize, summarize, and interpret numerical data.

______________ **2.** An orderly arrangement of scores indicating the frequency of each score or group of scores.

______________ **3.** A bar graph that presents data from a frequency distribution.

______________ **4.** A line figure used to present data from a frequency distribution.

______________ **5.** Type of statistics used to organize and summarize data.

______________ **6.** The arithmetic average of a group of scores.

______________ **7.** The score that falls in the centre of a group of scores.

______________ **8.** The score that occurs most frequently in a group of scores.

______________ **9.** A distribution in which most scores pile up at the high end of the scale.

______________ **10.** A distribution in which most scores pile up at the low end of the scale.

______________ **11.** The extent to which the scores in a distribution tend to vary or depart from the mean.

______________ **12.** An index of the amount of variability in a set of data.

______________ **13.** A bell-shaped curve that represents the pattern in which many human characteristics are dispersed in the population.

______________ **14.** Figure representing the percentage of persons who score below (or above) any particular score.

______________ **15.** A numerical index of the degree of relationship between two variables.

______________ **16.** A graph in which paired X and Y scores for each subject are plotted as single points.

_______________ **17.** The percentage of variation in one variable that can be predicted based on another variable.

_______________ **18.** Statistics employed to interpret data and draw conclusions.

_______________ **19.** The hypothesis that there is no relationship between two variables.

_______________ **20.** Said to exist when the probability is very low that observed findings can be attributed to chance.

Answers: 1. statistics **2.** frequency distribution **3.** histogram **4.** frequency polygon **5.** descriptive statistics **6.** mean **7.** median **8.** mode **9.** negatively skewed distribution **10.** positively skewed distribution **11.** variability **12.** standard deviation **13.** normal distribution **14.** percentile score **15.** correlation coefficient **16.** scatter diagram **17.** coefficient of determination **18.** inferential statistics **19.** null hypothesis **20.** statistical significance.

Appendix C
INDUSTRIAL/ORGANIZATIONAL PSYCHOLOGY

Review of Key Ideas

1. Describe the subdivisions of I/O psychology

1-1. In a humorous commentary several years ago, psychologist Jerry Burger said he longed to hear, just once, someone in a theatre asking, "Is there a social psychologist in the house?" (Burger, 1986). Burger's comments reflected not only his wish that psychology be recognized outside the halls of academia but his desire for application. Industrial/organizational (I/O) psychology is an applied field, and it involves the application of psychological principles to the world of ________________.

1-2. I/O psychology stresses application, but it is also a research area that emphasizes the scientific method. Like clinical psychology, the other major applied area, I/O is committed to the ________________–practitioner model.

1-3. I/O was originally called industrial psychology, a term that now comprises one of the two major subdivisions of the field. Industrial psychology involves mainly (personnel/work environment) issues.

1-4. The second subdivision is the relatively newer emphasis on the cultural context of the work environment, the norms, values, and ways of interacting that relate to the company's goals. This is the subdivision termed ________________ psychology.

Answers: 1-1. work (the workplace, industry) **1-2.** scientist **1-3.** personnel **1-4.** organizational.

2. Discuss recruitment and selection of employees, as well as the issue of employment discrimination.

2-1. The bigger the pool of applicants, the more likely it will contain qualified individuals, and to obtain applicants, it is necessary to ________________ them. So, it is important not only to be able to assess applicants but to do those things that cause individuals to ________________ for the job in the first place.

2-2. Selection in the recruitment process goes both ways: while the employer is assessing the applicant, the applicant is also evaluating the employer. It is important to realize that recruitment is a (mutual/one-way) process in which both parties are examining the degree of fit.

2-3. Who is selected for a particular job? Researchers Schmitt and Chan (1998) have identified five major changes that affect hiring in many modern organizations. First, in an age of computers, the speed of technological ________________ requires a willingness and ability to continually (learn new/maintain old) job skills.

2-4. Second, there is a growing reliance on (skilled individuals/teams) to accomplish work.

2-5. Third, the advent of fax, e-mail, and cellphones has dramatically changed the way organization members ________________ with one another, with potential effects on bonding, morale, and commitment.

2-6. Fourth, most organizations are ________________ rather than local, which requires members to be able to work well with people from different cultures.

2-7. Fifth, the Canadian economy is continuing its shift from a *manufacturing* to a *service* orientation, a shift that requires understanding the customers and their needs. For this reason, there is also an increased emphasis on applicants' (technical/interpersonal) skills.

2-8. Not all modern companies emphasize the factors outlined above. In a rapidly changing work environment, however, the match tends to be between the person and the (organization/skill requirements) rather than the person and the job.

2-9. ________________ ________________ legislation in Canada, which prohibits discrimination in the workplace, as well as employment ________________ legislation, which promotes the entry and retention of people from designated groups, have had a dramatic impact on the field of industrial psychology.

Answers: 2-1. recruit, apply **2-2.** mutual **2-3.** change, learn new **2-4.** teams **2-5.** communicate **2-6.** global **2-7.** interpersonal **2-8.** organization **2-9.** human rights, equity.

3. Discuss the importance of employee training and the ingredients of effective training programs.

3-1. In the modern workplace, many routine tasks have become obsolete, computers have increased importance, and knowledge requirements are constantly changing. For these reasons, company programs for ________________ employees have taken on a special significance. Training programs are needed on a continual basis in (very few/virtually all) organizations.

3-2. Human Resources and Skills Development Canada (HRSDC) identified essential ________________ needed by Canadian workers, which include reading text, document use, numeracy, writing, oral communication, working with others, thinking skills, computer use, and continuous learning. HRSDC also provides occupational profiles and skill development and training programs.

3-3. The characteristics of good training programs are that companies (a) value training, which involves ________________ employees to participate; (b) have a clear idea of ________________ training is needed and ________________ should receive it; (c) match the ________________ of training with the type of training task (e.g., lectures may not be best for training widget assembly); and (d) ensure that the training actually works, that training ________________ back to the job.

Answers: 3-1. training, virtually all **3-2.** skills **3-3.** (a) encouraging (urging), (b) what, who (which employees), (c) method (type) (d) generalizes.

4. Summarize how performance appraisals can help organizations.

4-1. If companies are to thrive, they must make rational decisions about their employees. Companies must decide who is to be promoted, receive a pay increase, or be discharged. That is the task of performance appraisals: to help organizations make fair, accurate, and useful ________________ about employees.

4-2. Fair and accurate feedback may also be a key factor in motivation, and performance appraisals may help employees develop realistic self-________________.

4-3. A fair, accurate, and rational appraisal system may also help build satisfaction and ________________ in company employees.

4-4. Especially in today's litigious environment, decisions about differential pay raises, promotions, or discharge cannot occur without reason. Performance appraisals help provide a ________________ defensible basis for decisions.

Answers: 4-1. decisions (appraisals, assessments) **4-2.** assessments (appraisals) **4-3.** morale (cohesion) **4-4.** legally.

5. Explain the concept of organizational culture and the ASA cycle.

5-1. What has customs, values, and traditions? The answer is: just about any human group—and business organizations are no exception. Companies have traditions, rituals, ways of talking, informal or formalized rules for attire, and so on, which comprise the organization's ________________.

5-2. How are these company cultures established? First, the individual who ________________ the company may have a strong influence on the values, initial hirings, and vision of the organization.

5-3. Second, the culture evolves as it interacts with the external ________________. Some aspects of culture are adaptive in the marketplace, and some are not.

5-4. Third, the values and norms of an organization develop, in part, as a means of maintaining effective working ________________ among employees. Different people create different cultures.

5-5. Corporate culture is also communicated through memos, statements of official policy, and corporate philosophy. In other words, culture is communicated not only indirectly through informal contact but ________________ as well.

5-6. A basic tenet of social psychology (Chapter 16) is the similarity–attraction relationship, that people are attracted to others who are similar to them in personality and values. In this context, the ASA cycle is not surprising. Organizations are ________________ to applicants who fit the company culture, and they ________________ those people as employees. Those who don't fit the culture leave, the process of ________________.

Answers: 5-1. culture **5-2.** founded **5-3.** environment (world, marketplace) **5-4.** relationships **5-5.** directly **5-6.** attracted, select, attrition.

6. Explain why organizations increasingly depend on work teams.

6-1. Why has emphasis changed from the individual to work teams? First, there has been an enormous increase in ________________ on which business decisions are based, and a pooling of knowledge and skills seems to work better.

6-2. Second, the workforce of today is better ________________ than that of a century ago and more capable of the leadership roles called for in teams.

6-3. Third, teams are thought to be better able to ________________ to rapidly changing skills that may be required in the modern workplace. Some research has found, however, that decisions by teams (are always/may not be) superior to those made by individuals.

6-4. Like other social groups, teams vary in size, roles filled by members, and duration. In addition, teams (must/need not) meet face to face. That is, some teams may be "virtual" and communicate, for example, through e-mail.

Answers: 6-1. information **6-2.** educated **6-3.** adapt (adjust, change), may not be **6-4.** need not.

7. Describe the nature of the psychological contract between employers and employees and the ramifications of violating the contract.

7-1. In addition to the written contract that may accompany employment, there exists a ________________ contract that involves expectations on the part of employers and employees. For example, employees may believe that they have the obligation to work hard and be loyal and that, in exchange, the company has the ________________ to provide job security and promotion.

7-2. While both parties to the contract have beliefs about the obligations of the contract, the two sides (always/may not) share a common understanding about its terms.

7-3. There are differences in power between the two sides. The contract maker is the employer, and the contract taker is the ________________. The employee, generally with (less/greater) power, must either accept the terms or leave the relationship.

7-4. As with any contract, violation of the psychological contract weakens trust, and failure of one of the parties to meet its perceived obligations leads to a deterioration of the ________________ on which the work is based.

Answers: 7-1. psychological, obligation **7-2.** may not **7-3.** employee, less **7-4.** relationship.

8. Describe the three dimensions of work motivation.

8-1. Job performance depends on a number of factors, including the employee's ambition or work ________________ (related to achievement motivation, discussed in Chapter 10.)

8-2. Work motivation may be described in terms of three dimensions: *direction*, *intensity*, and *persistence*. Label each of the following.

(a) ________________________: *How much* effort is being shown?

(b) ________________________: *Toward which* activities is energy expended?

(b) ________________________: *How long* will the effort endure?

8-3. Each dimension relates both to the organization and the employee. Organizations want the maximum energy expended, the element of ________________, on company tasks, the factor of ________________, over a long period of time, the element of ________________. To accomplish these aims, employees want jobs that will hold their interest and inspire them.

8-4. Performance in I/O psychology may be thought of as the evaluation of behaviour related to some standard. Job performance is determined by three factors: ________________, including the intelligence or skill of the employee; ________________ constraints, the environment and equipment available; and ________________, the willingness to expend effort.

Answers: 8-1. motivation **8-2.** (a) intensity, (b) direction, (c) persistence **8-3.** intensity, direction, persistence **8-4.** ability, situational, motivation.

9. Summarize prominent themes in research on leadership.

9-1. Research on leadership involves an enormous number of factors, from which three themes seem to emerge: the ability to (1) influence, (2) establish relationships, and (3) make sound decisions. First, leaders must be able to persuade, to change attitudes, to provide an appropriate model, and, in general, to ________________ what others do.

9-2. Second, effective leaders have interpersonal skills and inspire the trust and loyalty that permit the development of favourable ________________ among subordinates, peers, and superiors.

9-3. Third, effective leaders develop strategies and solve problems. In other words, leaders must make successful ________________ that move the company toward its goals.

9-4. What makes a good leader? This is a difficult question to answer because so many factors are involved, but three themes emerge: the ability to ________________ others, to establish favourable ________________ and to make sound ________________.

Answers: 9-1. influence **9-2.** relationships **9-3.** decisions **9-4.** influence, relationships, decisions.

Reference: Burger, J. M. (1986). Is there a Ph. D. in the house? *APA Monitor, 17*, 4.

NOTES

NOTES

NOTES

NOTES

NOTES

NOTES

NOTES

NOTES

NOTES

NOTES